ELEMENTS OF CHRISTIAN PHILOSOPHY
Etienne Gilson

Elements of Christian Philosophy

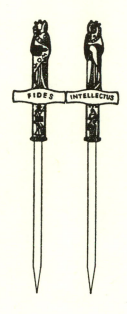

ETIENNE GILSON

GREENWOOD PRESS, PUBLISHERS
WESTPORT, CONNECTICUT

Library of Congress Cataloging in Publication Data

Gilson, Étienne Henry, 1884-
   Elements of Christian philosophy.

   Reprint of the ed. published by Doubleday, Garden
City, N. Y.
   Bibliography: p.
   Includes indexes.
   1. Thomas Aquinas, Saint, 1225?-1274--Theology.
I. Title.
[BX1749.G54 1979]   189'.4   78-10231
ISBN 0-313-20734-8

Reprinted in 1978 by Greenwood Press
A division of Congressional Information Service, Inc.
88 Post Road West, Westport, Connecticut 06881

Library of Congress Catalog Card Number 78-10231

ISBN 0-313-20734-8

Printed in the United States of America

10 9 8 7 6 5 4 3 2

Nihil obstat: Armand Maurer, C.S.B., *Censor Deputatus*

Imprimatur: ✠ James C. Cardinal McGuigan, D.D., *Archbishop of Toronto*

Date: 14 November 1959

Acknowledgments:

The author wishes to thank the following publishers for permission to use materials under their copyright: Doubleday & Company, Inc., for permission to quote from St. Thomas' *On the Truth of the Catholic Faith*, Book I, tr. A. C. Pegis, and Book II, tr. J. F. Anderson (Garden City, N.Y.: Doubleday & Company, Inc., 1955 and 1956); B. Herder Book Co., for permission to quote St. Thomas' *Compendium of Theology*, tr. C. Vollert, S.J. (St. Louis: B. Herder Book Co., 1947); Random House, Inc., for permission to quote many passages from *Basic Writings of Saint Thomas Aquinas* and *Introduction to Saint Thomas Aquinas*, tr. A. C. Pegis, (New York: Random House, Inc., 1944 and 1948).

FOREWORD

The words "Christian philosophy" do not belong to the language of St. Thomas Aquinas, but they are the name under which, in his Encyclical Letter *Aeterni Patris*, Pope Leo XIII designated the doctrine of the Common Doctor of the Church in 1879. Such as it is described in this epoch-making document, Christian philosophy is that way of philosophizing in which the Christian faith and the human intellect join forces in a common investigation of philosophical truth.

The study and the teaching of Christian philosophy are both beset with many difficulties. First of all, in the form it has been given by St. Thomas, it presupposes for its understanding an elementary knowledge of the philosophy of Aristotle. The study of the Philosopher takes time, and when the moment comes for the student to tackle the doctrine of Thomas himself he still needs to be trained in the art of uniting the light of faith and the light of the intellect. As often as not, he has been warned to be careful about keeping his faith out of philosophical research in order to preserve whole and entire its rational purity. It is then too late for any student to adopt a new approach to St. Thomas, and it is to be feared that the very nature of Thomism will remain thereafter unknown to him.

Another difficulty arises from the theological method followed by St. Thomas in those very works in which his own philosophical views are found in their purity, namely, the two *Summae* and the long series of his *Disputed Questions*. As a theologian, Thomas felt perfectly free to draw arguments from many and diverse philosophies and to confirm his conclusions by means of all sorts of reasons whose very multiplicity is liable to embarrass beginners.

This complex situation is the problem to which the present book seeks to bring, if not a solution, at least a working introduction. Its author's experience suggests that students often fail to find their way in the teaching of the Common Doctor for lack of a proper mastery of fundamental principles or elements. We call here "elements" those key notions and doctrinal positions that are not always explicitly stated in the discussion of each particular problem, but whose knowledge is required for a complete understanding of St. Thomas' answers. Such are:

5

first and foremost, the specific nature of the way in which the theologian uses philosophy according to the view of St. Thomas; second, the Thomistic notion of being, including the consequences it entails for the doctrine of the transcendentals; last, not least, the impact of this same notion on the many philosophical problems in whose data it is included —God, substance, efficient causality, creation, the structure of finite being, the nature and unity of man, the soul, the human intellect and its object. These and other key notions are so many basic doctrines that need to be correctly understood before the student attempts to face the colossal array of particular questions and answers, objections and replies, that make up the body of the Christian philosophy of St. Thomas Aquinas.

The detailed study of St. Thomas really has no end, but this fact is one of the charms of a life spent in the company of the Common Doctor of the Church. Something new is always there to be learned from him. The real danger is that the student may spend years pondering St. Thomas' doctrine without realizing that he has not yet even begun to grasp its meaning. This is bound to happen every time the student misses the only true gateway there is to the proper understanding of Thomism, namely, a certain metaphysical notion of being tied up with a certain notion of the Christian God. To describe these two notions, and to show them at work in a small number of capital problems, such has been our main concern in writing the present book. *Elements of Christian Philosophy* does not pretend to replace any other book. We would rather like to think that it will help to confer upon other interpretations of St. Thomas the fullness of their own religious meaning.

CONTENTS

7

Contents

ELEMENTS OF CHRISTIAN PHILOSOPHY

PART I. REVELATION AND THE CHRISTIAN TEACHER

Chapter 1. The teacher of Christian truth

The nature and significance of the work done by Saint Thomas Aquinas cannot be fully understood by those who approach it as if there had been nothing before it.[1] When he himself began to teach theology and, later on, philosophy (as he was to do in his commentaries on Aristotle), Thomas Aquinas was well aware of the general context in which his own work was necessarily going to be done.

Up to the last years of the twelfth century, when the Christian world unexpectedly discovered the existence of non-Christian interpretations of the universe, Christian theology had never had to concern itself with the fact that a non-Christian interpretation of the world as a whole, including man and his destiny, was still an open possibility. When Thomas Aquinas began to develop his own doctrine—that is to say, about 1253–54—Christianity had already discovered Greek philosophy. The discovery owed nothing to Thomas Aquinas himself. To be sure, his later commentaries on Aristotle were to be major contributions to a better interpretation of the teaching of the Philosopher; but anyone pretending that he was discovering the world of the Greek philosophers about 1250 would simply have been at least fifty years late. By that time, every Christian university teacher knew that a non-Christian explanation of the world was possible; he even knew what that explanation was, at least in its broad outline. But the question of the proper attitude to adopt toward it was very complex, and every teacher had to evolve his own answer.

To a man of the thirteenth century in western Europe, what did the term "philosopher" mean? Among other things, it meant a pagan. A philosopher was a man who, born before Christ, could not have been informed of the truth of Christian Revelation. Such was the situation of Plato and Aristotle. The Philosopher *par excellence* was a pagan. Others, born after Christ, were infidels. Such was the situation of Alfarabi, Avicenna, Gabirol, and Averroes. Whatever the case, it can be said that in general one of the connotations of "philosopher" was a "pagan" philosopher. Of course there is nothing absolute in the use of words, and exceptions can always be found. For instance, Boethius has sometimes been called a "philosopher" and counted as one. But this use of the word is exceptional, and countless cases can be quoted in which the *pagan* connotation of the word "philosopher" is certain.[2]

Here, however, we should be careful to observe that this was a question of usage, not of definition. In describing *philosophia*, no thirteenth-century theologian would have said that, in essence, philosophy was pagan. Had he been asked to define a philosopher, the same theologian would probably not have said that, unless he was a pagan, a man could not be a philosopher. The point I am emphasizing is that, as a matter of fact, when a theologian said "the philosophers" or "a philosopher," what he normally had in mind was a man who, not being a Christian, had dedicated his life to the study of philosophy.

The general truth of this remark is confirmed by the frequent antithetical use made by thirteenth-century theologians of the words *philosophi* and *sancti*. Albert the Great does not hesitate to quote two different series of definitions of the soul: those by the *sancti* and those by the *philosophi*. "A philosopher," in other words, was not a "saint"; that is, he was not a man sanctified by the grace of baptism. If a theologian thought it proper to resort to philosophy in his own theological work, as was the case with Thomas Aquinas, he was not normally called a philosopher, but rather a *philosophans theologus* (a philosophizing theologian) or, more simply still, a *philosophans* (a philosophizer). This was not a strict rule. But judging from their customary use of the two words, it does not seem to have entered the minds of thirteenth-century theologians that one and the same man could be, at one and the same time, both a "philosopher" and a "saint".[3]

One of the consequences of this all-embracing classification was that in its concrete reality philosophy appeared to many a theologian as an undifferentiated mass of doctrines containing the teachings of almost all those who, being unacquainted with Christian truth, or not accepting it, had tried to achieve a consistent view of the world and of man by means of reason alone. This philosophical conglomerate is well represented by the encyclopedia of Albert the Great, in which elements borrowed from all available sources are blended together and reduced to a sort of loose unity. If we knew them better than we do, such encyclopedias as the unpublished *Sapientale* of Thomas of York would give us a still more impressive view of what the word *philosophia* meant to the mind of a thirteenth-century theologian. Aristotle is there, especially in his Averroistic interpretation, but so are Avicenna, Gundissalinus, Gabirol, Cicero, Macrobius, Hermes Trismegistus: in short, the whole philosophical literature available at the time is represented in it.

Here special mention should be made of the influence exercised by the masters in arts in the first European universities. Having to teach the doctrine of Aristotle, they first had to ascertain the exact meaning of his writings. In so doing, they naturally had to discount Christian faith and theology, but they also had to separate the teaching of Aristotle from the foreign elements which his translators and interpreters had blended with it. It is a revealing fact that, in his *Commentary on the Sentences* of Peter Lombard, Thomas Aquinas still considered the *Liber de Causis* an authentic work of Aristotle. This was much more than a mere case of false attribution. In order to attribute the Plotinian *Liber de Causis* to Aristotle, one must have an extremely vague notion of the overall meaning of Aristotle's metaphysics.

During the years he spent in Italy, from 1259 to 1268, Thomas Aquinas found at his disposal new translations of the writings of Aristotle, or revisions of older translations, made by William of Moerbeke, and he availed himself of this opportunity to write commentaries on the nature of Aristotle's doctrine. It is difficult to characterize in a few words the new Aristotle seen by Thomas Aquinas. Some of the features at least are easily visible. Strictly speaking, it is not correct to say that Thomas baptized Aristotle. On the contrary, everywhere that Aristotle either contradicts the truth of Christianity (the eternity of the world) or simply falls short of it (creation *ex nihilo*), Thomas either frankly says so or at least does not attribute to Aristotle what he did not expressly assert. For instance, it is remarkable that, in commenting on the *Metaphysics* of Aristotle, in which the causality of the Prime Mover plays such an important part, Thomas Aquinas does not once use the word *creatio*. Neither does he attempt to prove the immortality of the soul in his *Commentary* on the *De Anima*. Aristotle had not presented the whole philosophical truth, and Thomas was well aware of the fact, but he did not try to make him say it.

On the other hand, Thomas Aquinas has clearly seen that, in the writings of Aristotle as we now have them, a certain number of points are incompletely determined, and he saw no reason why, in such cases, an interpretation of the doctrine attributed to the Philosopher should necessarily be preferred on the ground that it was the least easy of all to reconcile with the teaching of Christian faith. For instance, on the problem of the agent intellect, there was in Averroes a noticeable hardening of the position of Aristotle; but Thomas did not consider it useful to render Aristotelianism as more brutally opposed to Christian truth than it actually was in the authentic teaching of Aristotle himself. In short, it can be said that Thomas has removed from Aristotle all the obstacles to Christian faith that were not evidently there. At any rate, if he has baptized Aristotle, Thomas did not do so in his commentaries, but rather in his own theological writings. When he did so, baptism produced its normal effect: the *vetus homo* first had to die so that a new man could be born. The name of this new Christian had to be a Christian name: not Aristotle, but Thomas.

After thus removing the unnecessary obstacles, Thomas Aquinas found himself in a rather different position from that of the other theologians. There was nothing fundamentally wrong with this purified Aristotle; his only shortcoming was that, on certain points, he had simply failed to see certain truths, and this failure could be remedied by completing his doctrine. The real difficulty was that, in order to complete Aristotle, one had first to modify certain basic notions in philosophy and, thereby, to submit the philosophy of Aristotle to far-reaching modifications. Even purified of gross errors, Aristotelian doctrine still could not provide Thomas Aquinas with a ready-made philosophy; but he seems to have seen it as the very summit of philosophical speculation. Aristotle really was for Thomas the Philosopher *par excellence:* that is, a witness of the very best that the natural reason of man can do when it investigates truth without the help of divine revelation.

From this point of view, Aristotle appeared to Thomas Aquinas as having stated, not the whole truth accessible to human reason, but at least the whole philosophical truth. Thanks to the accomplishment of Aristotle, Thomas knew how far philosophy could proceed on the way to complete truth. By the same token, Thomas had gained a clear notion of what it meant to philosophize, and this knowledge deprived him of the simple answers to which, before him, theologians had often resorted. More precisely, Thomas could not content himself with adopting, in any particular case, the kind of philosophy that was easiest to reconcile with Christianity. For instance, he could not borrow his definition of the human soul from Aristotle and at the same time borrow from Plato his demonstrations of the immortality of the soul. What is most important to realize in approaching the works of Saint Thomas Aquinas is that precisely because he had now understood what a philosophical view of the world really meant, he could no longer content himself with philosophical eclecticism in developing his own theology. If his theology was to make use of philosophy, then it was up to him to provide his own philosophy. In other words, as a theologian Thomas needed a set of philosophical principles to which he could resort every time he had to do so in the course of his theological work. Described in general terms, these principles can be said to be "a reinterpretation of the fundamental notions of Aristotle's metaphysics in the light of Christian truth."[4] The three Thomistic notions of being, of substance, and of efficient cause can be defined in practically the same terms as in the doctrine of Aristotle; however, the ancient terms borrowed from Aristotle receive in Thomism an entirely new meaning.

This fact entailed two consequences affecting the theology that Thomas had undertaken to establish. First, he had to submit the philosophical eclecticism of his predecessors to a critical examination. Since, in discussing any particular theological problem, he was not content to employ the philosophy that promised to reconcile reason and revelation at the cheapest possible cost, he necessarily had to eliminate all the theological positions which, though acceptable in an eclectic system, were incompatible with his own conception of philosophy.

On the other hand, because *theology* is intimately related to religious life, a theologian could not simply suppress all that had been accomplished and taught before him in his own field. This made it necessary for Thomas to reinterpret the positions of his predecessors in the light of his own philosophical principles. Hence the curious—but inevitable —illusion of perspective that makes him appear as a man constantly misunderstanding the teaching of his predecessors. That this is an illusion can easily be detected from the fact that the result of his so-called misinterpretations is always the same: to make all his predecessors teach a doctrine that very much resembles what he himself was teaching. Thomas Aquinas has his own doctrinal language, but he is always willing to accept the language of someone else, provided he can make it say what he himself holds to be true. Such constancy in the orientation of his interpretative method cannot result from a series of accidental misinterpretations. What he makes Boethius say, or what he attributes to the author of the *Liber de Causis* (sometimes against positive historical evidence), simply expresses his desire to leave intact the already-accepted language of theology, and to preserve the substance of truth contained in ancient doctrines. It is to make this result possible that

Thomas ceaselessly pours new wine into old casks—after mending the casks.

The traditional syncretism upon which (or within which) Thomas had to do his critical work was made up of many different elements. The logic that it used was entirely Aristotelian. In metaphysics it appealed to the interpretation of Aristotle provided by Avicenna, minus its obvious errors from the point of view of Christian faith. It also made use of the *Liber de Causis*, of Gabirol's *Fons Vitae*, and of many other secondary sources in which the Platonic tradition was dominant. Such was particularly the case with Boethius. But the nucleus of this eclecticism was provided by what still survived at that time of the theology of Saint Augustine. There was a good reason for this. Augustine was by far the highest theological authority in the Latin Christian world. His *De Trinitate*, among many other writings, was a constant object of meditation for all theologians, and the many fragments of Augustine inserted by Peter Lombard in his *Sentences* were enough to insure the survival of his influence in the schools of the thirteenth century. Yet the philosophy used by Augustine in elaborating his theology had been that of Plotinus—or rather a revised version of it.[5] The personal philosophical thought of Augustine is to Plotinus as the personal philosophical thought of Thomas Aquinas is to Aristotle. The problem, then, was for Thomas Aquinas to maintain what he himself held to be true without playing havoc with theological positions that either were sound in themselves or at least had been commonly taught as safe for many centuries. In 1959, some 685 years have elapsed since the death of Thomas Aquinas, so that his authority appears to us as long-established. But we are likely to forget that when Thomas died in 1274, 844 years had elapsed since the death of Saint Augustine. If it was difficult for Thomas Aquinas to substitute new philosophical notions for those of the Philosopher *par excellence*, it was equally difficult for him to replace with new theological interpretations those bequeathed to him by the highest theological authority in the Latin world, a Father of the Church: Saint Augustine.

One thing at least is certain. However we may decide to interpret the work of Saint Thomas, it always remained in his own mind that of a teacher of Christian truth—that, and nothing else. Thomas is sometimes credited with having led a sort of double intellectual life: in philosophy, that of an Aristotelian; in theology, that of a teacher of the Christian dogma.[6] Neither in his life nor in his writings can we find the slightest trace of such a double personality. Born in 1225, Thomas was

six years old when, in 1231, he was made a monk. His parents entered
the six-year-old boy as an oblate in the Benedictine monastery of Monte
Cassino. Never was a father more fully justified in maintaining that he
knew what was best for his son. From then on Thomas always be-
longed to some religious order, first as a Benedictine, then as a Dominican. In a way he never ceased to behave and to feel like a Benedictine,
and his attitude to study is entirely dominated by this fact.

Since early Christian times there had been disputes on the extent to
which Christians (especially priests, and more especially monks) should
be allowed or encouraged to carry on advanced studies. Thomas
Aquinas never hesitated on this point. In his *Summa Theologiae* he
boldly asked the question in its most challenging form: not simply
whether monks should be allowed to study, but rather whether some
religious order should be established with the sole purpose of dedicating
itself to study.[7] And his answer to the question was yes.

It is worth while to consider the arguments advanced by Thomas in
support of his conclusion. Some of them are based on the demands of
the active life: a preacher has to learn something if he really wants to
preach. His other arguments are based on the necessities of the contemplative life. To limit ourselves to this second category, let us first remark that the kind of study Thomas has in mind is what he himself
calls *studia litterarum;* that is to say, the traditional education of the
liberal arts. Before reaching this question, while describing the nature
of the contemplative life, Thomas Aquinas had assigned as its primary
object the scrutiny of divine truth, because such contemplation was the
goal of the whole human life. In a secondary way, and as an approach to
this loftiest of all the objects of contemplation, Thomas had attributed
to the contemplative life the consideration of the effects of God,
through Whose knowledge we are, so to speak, led by the hand to the
knowledge of their Author. Obviously, this inclusion of the study of
creatures among the legitimate ends of the contemplative life entailed
the recognition of scientific and philosophical learning as legitimate
objects of monastic study.

This is a position from which Thomas Aquinas never departed. He
always maintained that scientific and philosophical study was permitted
to monks. He even explicitly maintained that a religious order, if it was
dedicated to study in virtue of its very foundation, could legitimately
include science and philosophy in its program—provided only that these
studies were undertaken in view of the contemplation of God as their
proper end. Thomas is perfectly clear on this point: "Even the contem-

plation of the divine effects secondarily belongs to the contemplative life, inasmuch precisely as, by it, man is led to the knowledge of God."[8]

This should suffice to define the nature of the writings of Saint Thomas Aquinas. They often resort to the consideration or (as he himself does not hesitate to call it) the contemplation of the world of natural things. For him, however, science, logic, and philosophy never serve any other end than to permit a more perfect contemplation of God. To the oft-disputed question, "Is there any philosophy in the works of Saint Thomas Aquinas?" the simplest answer is, "Yes, there is, but it is always there with a view to facilitating man's knowledge of God."

The fact itself is beyond discussion. The next question is: would a philosopher call "philosophy" this study of nature and this pursuit of philosophical speculation conceived as an approach to the contemplative knowledge of God? The answer to this question naturally depends on the philosopher himself and on his own idea of what philosophy is. The Thomistic view of philosophy would not appeal to the supporters of scientism or logical positivism, but neither would the view of philosophy proper to these schools be in agreement with the philosophical aspirations of all our contemporaries. Many philosophers who have nothing in common with Thomas Aquinas would definitely refuse to accept such a narrowing of the field of philosophy. At any rate, the Greek philosophers—to consider the only philosophers whom Thomas Aquinas knew—were of the opinion that to know God was the supreme aim of all true lovers of wisdom.

I would like to pause here a moment, because this is a point that apparently has escaped the attention of many among the critics of Thomas Aquinas (some of them Catholics) who are genuinely surprised to see a Christian, a theologian and a monk, exhibit an intense interest in the works of a pagan like Aristotle. But, precisely as a Christian monk, Thomas Aquinas was deeply impressed by the fact that many centuries before him the pagan Aristotle had already pursued the same objective that he himself was still establishing as his own. We would not hesitate on this point if only we had a little more imagination. It is quite possible that, in order to convince some of our contemporaries that Thomas Aquinas was a true philosopher, it is cleverer tactics to present him as interested in nothing besides philosophy; however, from his own point of view, the greatest philosophers had themselves been chiefly interested in God.

Let us re-read the surprising statement made on this point by Thomas Aquinas. To him the true name of Wisdom was Jesus Christ. Christ is therefore Truth. Now what does Christ Himself say about this? Here is the answer of Thomas Aquinas:

> *According to His own statement, divine Wisdom testifies that He has assumed flesh and come into the world to make the truth known: "For this was I born, and for this came I into the world; that I should give testimony to the truth" (John 18:37). The Philosopher himself establishes that first philosophy is the science of truth, not of any truth, but of that truth which is the origin of all truth, namely, which belongs to the first principle whereby all things are. The truth belonging to such a principle is, clearly, the source of all truth; for things have the same disposition in truth as in being.*[9]

Far from imagining that one should find any conflict between the ends of philosophical inquiry and those of theological inquiry, Thomas thinks that their ultimate object is one and the same. If the knowledge of God is "the highest peak at which human investigation can arrive,"[10] there is essential agreement between the teaching of the doctor of Christian truth and that of the philosopher. At the level of natural knowledge, the philosopher too is a theologian.

What, then, is the difference between them? Thomas himself asked the question in the same passage of the *Summa* in which he maintained that a religious order could be established for the purpose of supporting study. He asked it under the form of the following objection:

> *What a Christian monk professes should be different from what is professed by pagans. Now, among the pagans, there were some professors of philosophy. And even now some seculars are called professors of certain sciences. Consequently monks have no business to study Letters.*

To this objection Thomas Aquinas answered that, even when they study the same subjects, philosophers and monks do not study them with the same end in view:

> *The philosophers used to profess Letters as part and parcel of secular education. But it chiefly belongs to monks to dedicate themselves to the study of the writings which concern the doctrine that is according to godliness (Tit. 2:1). As to the other branches of*

*learning, their study does not befit monks, whose whole life should
be spent in serving God, except to the extent that such doctrines are
made subservient to sacred doctrine.*[11]

We are here being assured, by Thomas Aquinas himself, that all his
study and writing, including of course his commentaries on Aristotle,
exhibited this difference from the study and writing of the "philosophers": for him, the study of Sacred Scripture was their true end. In
this, Thomas can be said to have kept faith with his religious vocation:
Aut de Deo, aut cum Deo; when he was not talking about God, he
was with God. Nor is this fanciful historical invention. At the beginning of his *Summa Contra Gentiles,* Thomas Aquinas made his own
the words of Saint Hilary of Poitiers: "I am aware that I owe this to God
as the chief duty of my life, that my every word and sense may speak
of Him."[12]

Very few people today realize the place that the teaching of religious
truth occupied in the personal life of such a man as Saint Thomas
Aquinas. Not only its teaching, but even its study, was to him the
highest form of the Christian apostolate. And since his personal views
on this point are likely to cause some surprise, it will not be amiss to
summarize his answer to this question whether a man who is skillful in
teaching others is bound in conscience to give up the study of theology
in order to dedicate himself to the salvation of souls.

With his usual good sense, Thomas begins by saying that the answer
to the question should be a conditional one. There are cases and circumstances. Something that is better when considered absolutely is not
better in all cases. Absolutely speaking, a pearl is of more value than a
loaf of bread, but one can easily imagine circumstances under which
a loaf of bread would be better than a pearl.

Nevertheless, considering the problem in itself, one must say that, in
all types of constructive work, the task of the architect is nobler than
that of the workmen. Although he does nothing with his own hands,
the architect contributes more to the erection of a building than he
would if he were a stone carver or a carpenter. The same remark applies
to the work of "edification," which, as appears from the very word,
also consists in building or erecting a kind of spiritual edifice. Co-
operating in this task there are, first, manual laborers, so to speak; namely,
those who dispense the sacraments and take care of individual souls in
all sorts of particular ways. But there are also architects; namely, the
bishops, called *episcopi* (that is to say, *superintendents*), because they

supervise the work done by their priests. Then there are the professors of theology (*theologiae doctores*), who are the chief artisans, investigating and teaching the best way for others to procure the salvation of souls. Absolutely speaking, then, it is better to teach sacred doctrine; and if done with good intention this work is more meritorious than to busy oneself with the individual salvation of this or that man. The same argument demonstrates that to teach religious truth to those who can profit by it in order to help others as well as themselves is better than to teach it to simple people who can put it to good use for themselves alone. Of course there are special cases in which both bishops and professors of theology should interrupt their proper function in order to work for the salvation of some individual soul. Of its nature, however, the higher of the two offices is that of the man who is in charge of teaching sacred doctrine: the theologian.

Such language on the part of Saint Thomas Aquinas does not lead us to think of his philosophical activity as being particularly anxious to protect itself against possible theological influences. In the light of his own explicit statements, his religious faith and his monastic profession (especially under the well-defined form of the Dominican monastic life) have been the highest "formal" elements in the structure of his personality. That even his way of philosophizing was directly affected by this fact should be considered a kind of *a priori* certainty. Since it is not, however, the only thing to do at this point is to try to present a truth whose evidence is such that it leaves very little room for demonstration.

Chapter 2. Sacred doctrine

The first question raised by Saint Thomas Aquinas in the *Summa Theologiae* is about the nature and domain of sacred doctrine (*sacra doctrina*). By these words Thomas means any body of instruction (doctrine) made holy by its divine origin (sacred); in short, any body of instruction whose teacher is God. Sacred Scripture pre-eminently deserves this title, because it contains the very word of God. Still, as will be seen, the title extends to all that which, under any form, derives its truth from the divine revelation or co-operates with it in view of its divinely appointed end.[1]

It is typical of the position of Thomas Aquinas that his first question about sacred doctrine should be that of its necessity. Was it necessary that God should teach men? Was it necessary that He should impart to men, by way of revelation, the body of instruction we call "sacred doctrine"? The very question implies the possibility of a doubt, and the reason for such doubt precisely is that there already exists a body of instruction covering the whole field of human knowledge; namely, philosophy or, as Thomas himself prefers to call it, the "philosophical disciplines," that is to say, the body of the disciplines, or sciences, that constitute philosophy. His second objection, in the first article of the *Summa*, states the case for philosophy in terms so perfectly clear that even today there is nothing more to say in its favor:

> *Knowledge can be concerned only with being, for nothing can be known, save the true, which is convertible with being. But everything that is, is considered in the philosophical disciplines—even God Himself; so that there is a part of philosophy called theology, or the divine science, as is clear from Aristotle (Metaph., V, 1, 1026 a 19). Therefore, besides the philosophical disciplines, there is no need of any further doctrine.*[2]

Against this all-sufficiency of philosophy, Thomas Aquinas naturally maintains that, besides the philosophical sciences, a further doctrine is required; namely, Scripture, of which Saint Paul has said: *All scripture, inspired of God, is profitable to teach, to reprove, to correct, to instruct in justice* (*2 Tim. 3:16*). From this very moment Thomas clearly marks the characteristic difference that sets this doctrine apart from all the others. The teaching of Scripture, the doctrine of Scripture, is "inspired of God." As such, it "is not a part of the philosophical sciences discovered by human reason." This initial distinction dominates the problem of the relationship of philosophy and theology; in fact, it dominates the whole teaching of the *Summa Theologiae* in the sense that everything in it must be either contained in Scripture or in some way related to the teaching of Scripture, itself a doctrine inspired of God.[3]

It is typical of the nature of faith that its very necessity is here being established on the authority of Scripture, itself an object of faith. Still, after saying that the existence of such a divinely inspired teaching was something "useful," Thomas proceeds to show that, in a certain sense, this usefulness is a "necessity." The reason "it was necessary for man's salvation that there should be a knowledge revealed by God, besides the philosophical sciences investigated by human reason," is that God has freely decided to associate man with His own beatitude. This is what is meant by saying that the ultimate end of man is the beatific vision; that is, eternal life with God. Now there was for God absolutely no necessity to make this decision; but, in fact, God has made it, with the consequence that now "man is directed to God as to an end that surpasses the grasp of his reason." And this also is something we learn from divine revelation and believe as true: *the eye hath not seen, O God, besides Thee, what things Thou hast prepared for them that wait for Thee* (*Isai. 64:4*). From this truth the necessity of revelation clearly follows.

If man has been directed by God to an end that surpasses the grasp of his reason, then man finds himself in this situation: that, left to himself and unaided by God, he is unable to reach his own end. For indeed a man cannot direct his thoughts and actions to an end unless he first has knowledge of that end. "Hence it was necessary for the salvation of man that certain truths which exceed human reason should be made known to him by divine revelation."

Supposing the will of God to save man, this was indeed a necessity, but Thomas extends this necessity beyond the order of the truths about God that escape the grasp of human reason. He goes as far as saying that "even as regards those truths about God which human reason can investigate, it was necessary that man be taught by a divine revelation."[4]

The reason for this further necessity is the same as that which accounts for the first one; namely, that no man can possibly be saved unless he knows his ultimate end, God. The salvation of man, which is God, depends upon the knowledge man has of God not only through revelation but also through reason. In other words, all that which contributes to man's knowledge of God, Who is man's salvation, contributes to man's salvation. To understand the position of Thomas Aquinas on this point correctly, it is important to keep in mind the concrete nature of the problem. The question is not about the relationship of revelation to philosophy in general. Thomas is not asking himself whether, absolutely speaking, philosophical inquiry is able to provide man with a knowledge of the truths about God that human reason can investigate. His problem rather is: in fact, if God left men to themselves, how many among them would succeed in acquiring such knowledge? His considered answer is that "the truth about God, such as reason can know it, would be known only by a few, and that after a long time, and with the admixture of many errors." Obviously, the result would be that very few men could be saved; moreover, if we are to understand that even these few could not know the philosophical truth about God without the admixture of many errors, then we may well wonder whether, practically speaking, salvation is possible at all.[5]

To repeat, for this is important, the question is not about the theoretical possibility of such knowledge by a human understanding unaided by revelation. Such a possibility is granted. One could even raise the question as to how many men the word "few" represented in the mind of Thomas Aquinas. What would their proportion be in comparison with the whole of the human race? All this, however, is irrelevant to the actual question asked by him. His only point is this: "In order that the salvation of men might be brought about more fittingly and more surely, it was necessary that they be taught divine truths by divine revelation. It was therefore necessary that, besides the philosophical disciplines investigated by reason, there should be a sacred doctrine by way of revelation."[6]

This conclusion disposes of the much-disputed question whether it is possible to believe, by supernatural faith, truths revealed by God which of themselves are accessible to natural knowledge. This is not only possible, it is necessary. A whole article of the *Summa Theologiae* has for its object to prove that "it is necessary to believe that which can be proved by natural reason" concerning God. In proof of this, the *Sed Contra* simply affirms as an indisputable fact that "it is necessary to believe that God is one and incorporeal, things that are proved, on the strength of natural reason, by philosophers." The arguments of Thomas Aquinas in support of his conclusions in no way deny the distinction introduced between metaphysics and sacred doctrine from the point of view of their formal objects. The practical problem of salvation dominates the whole discussion. His arguments are well known. Through faith, men reach the saving truth about God more quickly than through natural reason; a very large number of men would be deprived of such truth if they had to purchase it at the price of philosophical study; finally (and this concerns all men), faith is more certain than reason, especially in matters of divinity. A sign of this is the errors and the contradictions of the philosophers in their effort to achieve some knowledge of God by means of the unaided natural reason.[7]

There are some interpreters of Saint Thomas who think that this conclusion does not apply to such an elementary knowledge as the very existence of God, but this is not the case. Thomas Aquinas entertained no illusions as to the achievements of pagan philosophers in these matters. He did not think that the providence of God, His omnipotence and His exclusive right to be worshiped, had been discovered by the natural reason in ancient times.[8] Therefore, such truths are rightly included among the articles of faith (*unum, patrem omnipotentem*). As to the very existence of God, it is true that, of itself, it is no article of faith (since it is naturally knowable). In a passage which we shall have to examine in another context, Thomas explicitly says that this truth and similar ones "are not articles of faith, but are preambles to the articles; for faith presupposes nature and perfection the perfectible." But this conclusion calls for two precisions.[9]

First, the existence of God has not to be believed by those who understand the demonstrations. But how many men do actually understand them? For those who do not, whatever their number, there is a strict obligation to believe these preambles.[10]

A second precision, whose importance will disclose itself progressively, is that even when the natural reason can establish a certain truth about God, it never grasps it in its fullness as applying to the God of the Christian faith. Thomas Aquinas has several times quoted the words of Saint Paul (*Heb. 11:6*): *But without faith it is impossible to please God. For he that cometh to God must believe that he is: and is a rewarder to them that seek him.*" The question is to know whether the God of Whom we must believe that He is, in approaching Him as the rewarder of those that seek Him, is identically the same Whose existence can be demonstrated in five different ways.

There are serious reasons to doubt it. As has been seen, the existence of God is included among the *credibilia*, not as a *credibile simpliciter* (an object of belief that can be believed only), but as preambulary to all the *credibilia*. But the God in Whose existence we believe is more than the Prime Mover of Aristotle or than the Necessary Being of Avicenna. These philosophical gods are not really preambles to faith for the simple reason that, in the minds of the pagan philosophers who first proved their existence, they were unrelated to it. Speaking of the articles of faith, Thomas Aquinas observes that they play in theology the same part as do the first principles of natural reason in philosophy and in the various sciences. Now there is an order among these principles. Some of them are contained in others and, in fine, they all are reducible to the principle of contradiction. "And, likewise, all the articles are implicitly contained in some prime believables, to wit, the belief that God is and that His providence cares for the salvation of men, according to *Heb. 11:6: he that cometh to God must believe that he is: and is a rewarder to them that seek him.*" To which Thomas presently adds:

> *For in the divine being* (esse) *is included all that which we believe eternally to exist in God, and in which our beatitude consists; and in our faith in His providence is included all that which is ordered by God in time in view of man's salvation, that is, the way to beatitude.*[11]

Obviously, all the articles of faith are not implicitly contained in the rationally demonstrated conclusion that there is a Prime Immovable Mover. There is ample room for belief beyond the God Whose existence we know.

There is then a part of philosophy called "theology, or the divine science," and it investigates the truth about God inasmuch as it can be known by natural reason,[12] but this does not prevent sacred doctrine from considering the same truths in another light. Just as an astronomer and a physicist can investigate the same phenomenon, such as an eclipse, the one (the physicist) by direct observation, the other (the astronomer) by mathematical demonstration, so too:

> *. . . there is no reason why the things which are treated by the philosophical disciplines, so far as they can be known by the light of*

natural reason, may not also be treated by another science so far as they are known by the light of the divine revelation. Hence the theology included in sacred doctrine differs in genus from that theology which is part of philosophy.[13]

And, let us not forget, this is true in those instances when theology and philosophy are treating *the same things*.

The difficulties accumulated by certain commentators of Saint Thomas arise from their failure to distinguish between the formal order which determines the generic difference of the two disciplines (metaphysics, or natural theology, and sacred doctrine) and the concrete order of the general economy of salvation which ultimately dominates the theological speculation of Thomas Aquinas. His doctrine has been turned upside down. Whatever he says in order to safeguard the rights of theology has been interpreted as safeguarding the rights of philosophy. Now to this Thomas himself would have no objection at all; only, it is not what chiefly interested him.

The better to see his own point, let us consider the consequences he has deduced from the proposition so often quoted by those who strive to establish the complete independence of philosophy and who want to do so on the basis of authentically Thomistic principles. Thomas certainly maintains that the same truth cannot be both believed and known by natural reason by the same person and at the same time: *non est possibile quod idem ab eodem sit scitum et creditum.*[14] Of course something can be believed by one man and known by another one, and this is why God has revealed even truths accessible to human reason. The same man can also know something of a certain object (for instance, the existence of God) and believe something else about the same object (for instance, the Trinity). But one should particularly remember that the rule applies only when it is a question of knowing one and the same object. For it to be the same object of apprehension, it is not enough that it properly bears the same name; it has to be the same object apprehended with the same determinations. And so it is that, as a philosopher, a man cannot believe the existence of a Prime Mover after he has demonstrated its existence; but the same man can know the existence of the Prime Mover and, as a Christian, believe by supernatural faith in the existence of the Christian God.[15]

This entails a first and general conclusion. If a certain truth is, of itself and absolutely speaking, an object of faith (as exceeding the grasp of reason), then it cannot possibly become an object of knowledge.

Such truths constitute what Thomas calls the body of truth proposed in common to all men as something to be believed (*id quod communiter omnibus hominibus proponitur ut credendum*), and are an object of faith purely and simply (*et ista simpliciter fidei subsunt*). In short, they constitute the order of the "commonly not known" (*communiter non scitum*). This position[16] admits of no restriction. It calls for this remark, however, that while some of our own contemporaries use it chiefly in order to prove that philosophical knowledge should be kept pure of religious belief, the main concern of Thomas Aquinas is the other way around. Not the purity of *scientia*, but rather that of *fides* is what he chiefly aims to preserve. The reasons adduced by the theologians in favor of the truths of faith do not intend to demonstrate their truth; they merely are "persuasive arguments" tending to show that what is proposed for belief is not of itself "impossible"; that is, rationally absurd. In other cases there will be in theology straight rational demonstration, but the premises will be some truth known by faith, so that, in the last analysis, the conclusion will still be believed, not known.[17]

This fact dominates the interpretation of the answer of Thomas Aquinas to the question whether sacred doctrine is a science.[18] There was nothing new in calling sacred doctrine a science. In fact, Thomas has borrowed the word from Saint Augustine,[19] but has given it a new meaning. In the language of Augustine, *scientia* signified a mode of knowing, and therefore a doctrine, both certain and true. In the language of Thomas Aquinas (and this is the mark of the century on his doctrine) *scientia* fully preserved this Augustinian meaning, but it added another one: the Aristotelian meaning of the word as pointing out a body of conclusions deduced from principles. No doubt, to give theology the form of such a science could not be done without first solving a few difficulties.

In order to establish that sacred doctrine is a science, Thomas resorts to a general distinction between two kinds of sciences. Some sciences directly "proceed from principles known by the natural light of the intellect, such as arithmetic and geometry and the like"; others "proceed from principles known by the light of a higher science",[20] as are, for instance, optics, which borrows its principles from geometry, and music, which borrows its own from arithmetic. The difference is that, in the first case, the principles of a science are self-evident; in the second case, the principles of the science in question are reducible to those of a higher one. Now, precisely, this is the case of sacred doctrine. It proceeds from principles "made known in the light of a higher science, namely, the science of God and of the blessed. Hence, just as music accepts on authority the principles taught by the arithmetician, so sacred science accepts the principles revealed by God."[21]

Here Thomas Aquinas is effecting a transposition. The notion of "science" applies to sacred doctrine only in an analogical way. For indeed it is true that a body of knowledge is a science because it proceeds from certain principles from which it holds both certitude and unity; and it is also true that certain sciences borrow their principles, not directly from the natural light of the intellect, but from higher sciences which, themselves, immediately proceed from such principles. Since it proceeds from principles of its own, sacred doctrine truly is a science, with this difference however that, in the case of optics and of music, the principles of the higher sciences from whose conclusions they themselves proceed are known by the natural light of the intellect, whereas, in organizing itself as a science, sacred doctrine proceeds, following the natural light of the intellect, from principles revealed by God. In other words, the intellect of the theologian proceeds from principles transcending the order of natural reason. This accounts for the statement previously made by Thomas Aquinas, that the natural theology of the philosophers and the theology that is part of sacred doctrine do not belong in the same genus. There is a radical transcendency of theology over the merely natural sciences, including even metaphysics, because, grounded as it is on the word of God, it enjoys the unique privilege of proceeding from principles made known, by revelation, in the light of the science that God has of Himself and of all other beings.[22]

It is essential to understand the nature of this exclusive privilege enjoyed by the theology that is part of sacred doctrine. It is indeed a science, but in a sense distinctly its own. Among the other sciences, even the highest ones are submitted to strict limitations owing to the nature of their formal objects, but this is because their own principles are made known by the light of the knowledge that man has of things. On the contrary, because it proceeds from principles made known by the knowledge that God Himself has of everything, actual or possible, the theology that is part of sacred doctrine transcends all conceivable limitations. Most of the controversies concerning the nature and object of theology in the teaching of Saint Thomas Aquinas arise from a repeated overlooking of this point.

The third article of the *Summa* has for its proper object to make this truth as clear as possible. It asks whether sacred doctrine is one science. The question is directly related to the very possibility of such a science as the theology that is part of sacred doctrine; and here again, for the third time, looking at what Aristotle calls a science, Thomas Aquinas attempts to situate the theology he himself has in mind in relation to the type of knowledge considered scientific by both scientists and philosophers. Now, in order to be a science, a body of knowledge has to be *one*. Being and unity stand or fall together; so much so that, as will be shown, to be and to be one are one and the same thing. In the case of natural theology and of the other sciences, the condition is easily fulfilled. Any body of knowledge owes its unity to that of its object. The object itself has to be taken, not in its materiality, but from the point of view of "the formality under which it is an object." This begins with the powers of knowing themselves. For instance, because color is the formal object of sight, all colored objects are included in the object of sight. A man, a tree, an animal, a stone are different beings, materially speaking, but inasmuch as all of them are colored objects, they make up one single object of knowledge known by one distinct mode of knowing, sight.

The comparison fits the case of the theology that is part of sacred science. It borrows its principles from the science of God made known to us by revelation. Now Scripture deals with all sorts of subjects. First, because it is a history, it "treats of individual facts, such as the deeds of Abraham, Isaac, and Jacob, and the like."[23] Then it speaks of practically everything under the sun: man, animals, plants, minerals, the universe in all its parts as well as human life under all its aspects. What is there that has not been mentioned in Scripture, either as a matter of historical record or as included in the work of God? Sacred doctrine cannot be one science, because its object has no unity. But if it is not *one*, it *is* not at all. To this difficulty, the answer naturally lies in the unity of the formal object of the theology that is part of sacred doctrine. This formality consists in its "being divinely revealed." Consequently, whatever is revealed by God falls under the formal object of one and the same science. It is the science that considers all the objects having in common the formality of having been divinely revealed.[24]

The direct intention of this answer is to remove the difficulty arising from the diversity of the objects included in Holy Scripture. But something else is in question beyond their diversity. Several different points were making it difficult to attribute to one single science all the teachings included in Scripture. One of them has already been mentioned: Scripture often deals with particular historical facts, such as the deeds

of Abraham, Isaac, and Jacob; but there is no science of the particular;
only the universal is an object of science. In order to overcome this
very serious difficulty—in fact, a difficulty insuperable in a truly Aristotelian perspective—Thomas Aquinas resorts to his own notion of the
formal object of theology; namely, the "being divinely revealed." First
he boldly affirms that particular facts are not what sacred doctrine is
principally concerned with. Rather, they play in Scripture the part of
examples to be followed in our lives. Thomas must have felt that this
first answer was somewhat inadequate, for in the account of the work
of the creation and redemption of man, a great many particular facts
are adduced to more important purposes than mere moral edification.
On the contrary, the second part of his reply is very much to the point:
these individual facts are introduced "to establish the authority of those
men through whom the divine revelation, on which this sacred scripture
or doctrine is based, has come down to us."[25] Since they contribute
to establishing the authority of the inspired writers, all these particular
facts are directly relevant to the formal object of theology, that whose
knowledge has come to us through divine revelation.

Another difficulty can be more easily disposed of. Aristotle says that
a science is one if it "treats only of one class of subjects."[26] Now
sacred doctrine treats of the Creator as well as of His creatures, although God and His works cannot be considered as forming one class
of objects. To this the easy answer is that there is such a thing as a
unity of order:

> *Sacred doctrine does not treat of God and creatures equally, but of
> God primarily and of creatures only so far as they are referable to
> God as their beginning or end. Hence the unity of this science is
> not impaired.*[27]

The last objection is the most serious one and it is directly relevant
to our problem. Not only are the objects considered by the theologian
varied, but some of them are likewise considered by the philosopher.
For instance, sacred doctrine treats of angels, but philosophers also treat
of angels under the name of separate substances. Sacred doctrine treats
of material bodies in dealing with the work of creation, but the same
bodies fall under the consideration of the astronomer, the physicist, the
biologist, and the other scientists whose sciences are entirely distinct
from theology. Even morality, so important a problem for theologians,
is discussed by philosophers under the name of ethics. If sacred doctrine

includes disciplines that belong to distinct philosophical sciences, it cannot be one science.

The answer of Thomas Aquinas to this difficulty is so complete, it says so much in so few words, that it first must be reported in full:

> *Nothing prevents inferior powers or habits from being diversified by objects which yet agree with one another in coming together under a higher power or habit; because the higher power or habit regards its own object under a more universal formality. Thus the object of the* common sense *is the sensible, including, therefore, whatever is visible or audible. Hence the* common sense, *although one power, extends to all the objects of the five senses. Similarly, objects which are the subject-matter of different philosophical sciences can yet be treated by this single sacred doctrine under one aspect, namely, in so far as they can be included in revelation. So that in this way sacred doctrine bears, as it were, the stamp of the divine science, which is one and simple, yet extends to everything.*[28]

Comparisons should not be pressed unduly, but this one deserves careful attention. If it means anything at all, it entails consequences so far-reaching that few among the disciples of Thomas Aquinas dare to follow them up to their ultimate implications. What is the relation of the *sensus communis* to the objects of the five external senses?[29]

What Thomas Aquinas calls the "common sense" (*sensus communis*) has little to do with the good practical sense in everyday affairs which these words now signify, but it coincides with one of the early English meanings excellently described in the Oxford Dictionary: "an internal sense which was regarded as the common bond and centre of the five senses." Applied to our own problem, this would lead us to conceive the theology that is part of sacred doctrine as playing the role of a common bond and center of the philosophical disciplines or of the various sciences studying some of its objects.

It is easy to see what could interest Thomas Aquinas in this comparison. Such as he himself understood it, the "common sense" is "one common power" that judges the acts of the various external senses: *potentia judicativa de actibus sensuum . . . una et communis*. Moreover, the common sense is the fontal root of all the senses: *fontalem radicem omnium sensuum, qui est sensus communis*. A third characteristic of the "common sense," and one that Thomas Aquinas stresses at length, is its aptitude to perceive the objects of different external senses simultaneously and, consequently, to compare them and to appreciate their differences. It is noteworthy, in fine, that the "common sense" is more noble than the particular and external senses because, receiving the actions of the particular senses in an immaterial way, it is both their common root and their common term.[30]

In applying these remarks to the relationship of sacred doctrine to the philosophical disciplines, one first notices that, if the comparison fits to any degree and in any way, the proper function of theology is not to perform the operations of the various sciences any more than the "common sense" perceives the perceptions, or "immutations," of the external senses themselves. All the sense perceptions terminate in the "common sense" as all the radii of a circle terminate at its center: the "common sense" is the center, it is not one of the radii. This image suggests the notion of a sacred doctrine placed, as it were, at the very center of all the philosophical disciplines, perceiving their own perceptions of philosophical truth, including their differences or even their oppositions, but dominating them because it is able to judge of these differences and to unite them in its own unity as countless diverging radii unite in the center as in their common origin and term.

These images suggest to the imagination the picture of a theology which, without being engaged in the proper business of any particular philosophical science, but rather keeping at a distance, remains nevertheless informed of everything they do. All their particular reports ultimately come to theology as to a sort of clearinghouse where they are compared, discerned, judged, and, at the same time, ordered and united. About in the same way as the "common sense" knows that sound is not color, but that one and the same object is both sonorous and colored, so also theology gathers together the varied information it receives from logic, physics, biology, and metaphysics; it pieces this information together and from its transcendent point of vantage it sees all this fragmentary knowledge as so many parts of a higher unity.

It is true, no comparison can be perfect. The philosophical disciplines do not really spring up from theology as from their common root. Nor do their respective reports ultimately reach it as if to inform sacred doctrine were their natural end. Of itself, philosophy, including natural theology, belongs in the natural order. It is unable to direct itself toward the supernatural order of revealed truth; in fact, it does not suspect its existence or even its likelihood. On the contrary, sacred doctrine is fully aware of the presence of natural theology as well as of that of all the other philosophical disciplines. It sees them as unconsciously directed to a transcendent end of which, left to themselves, they know nothing. Seeing philosophy in the light of the divine revelation, sacred science descries in it possibilities of which natural theology itself is unaware. In short, what a theologian considers in the works of the philosophers truly is philosophical in its essence and nature; what the theologian sees in Plato or in Aristotle truly is philosophy, but his view of it is always that of a theologian. Sacred doctrine envisages philosophy such as it can be seen, in a higher light, as a possible help in the great work of man's salvation.

To forget for a single moment this fundamental position of Saint Thomas Aquinas is to run the risk of misinterpreting his true attitude toward philosophy. It also is to put the very existence of sacred doctrine in jeopardy. As has been said, in order to be, sacred doctrine must be one. Any extraneous element introduced into it must be integrated with it or otherwise sacred doctrine will become a haphazard accumulation of heterogeneous information; and the only way for theology to achieve this end is by considering everything in the light of its own formal object. This sacred theology necessarily does every time it considers one of the revealed truths that exceed the human reason. By definition, such truths cannot possibly become known to man except by divine revelation. That is why Thomas Aquinas calls this kind of truth the "revealed" *par excellence:* it is the kind of knowledge that cannot be known unless it be revealed to man by God.

On the other hand, we have already noted that, as a matter of fact, God has chosen to reveal to man even certain truths that, of themselves, do not exceed the natural light of reason. Since it is naturally knowable, say by philosophy or any one of the sciences of nature, a truth of this kind does not belong in the class of the essentially "revealed" (*revelatum*); still, since it has actually been revealed, it is a possible object of revelation. In Thomas Aquinas' own language, it belongs in the class of the divinely revealable truth: *divinitus revelabilia.* Such also is the ultimate reason why this class of truths about God can enter the structure of sacred doctrine without endangering its unity: it is included in the formal object of theology as being actually revealed by God.[31]

But what is the theologian going to do with natural theology, physics, biology, and the other sciences? Exactly the same thing, because every subject about which something has been revealed by God is thereby included in the class of the "revealable." In a sacred doctrine that considers the universe as created by God, the class of the *revelabilia* is an all-embracing one. In describing the work of the six days, Scripture leaves nothing out, so that there is nothing that sciences and philosophy can say which is not related to some object of a possible revelation. The easiest way to understand this point is to ask: what is there that is not included in the science God has of His own work? Obviously, nothing. Now sacred doctrine considers everything under the formality of "being divinely revealed." Hence the conclusion of the third article of the *Summa:* sacred doctrine can treat objects which are the subject matter of philosophical sciences, not indeed as objects of these sciences, but as includable in revelation (*revelabilia*). In this way, sacred doctrine is in the mind as a stamp of the divine science (*velut quaedam impressio divinae scientiae*), which is the one and simple science of everything.[32]

One may well wonder if a higher notion of theology was ever formed by any theologian, or even if one can think of a higher one. At any rate, there is no point in reading the *Summa Theologiae* in any other spirit unless, of course, one is prepared to misinterpret it from beginning to end. All the other questions concerning the nature of sacred doctrine derive their answers from the same fundamental notion. For instance, some ask whether sacred doctrine is a practical science. No, because it is not chiefly concerned with what man can do, as is the case with moral science, but rather with God, Who is the maker of man. Consequently, sacred doctrine is not a practical science but rather a speculative one. Still, being *magis speculativa*, sacred science does not exclude practical knowledge. Other sciences are either speculative or practical, but a science that is in the mind of man as a stamp of the divine science cannot suffer such limitation; sacred doctrine includes the speculative and the practical, "as God, by one and the same science, knows both Himself and His works." Nothing shows better than this answer how, because of its transcendent origin, sacred theology refuses to enter the categories that fit the philosophical sciences and the sciences of nature. It is "more speculative than practical," but its competence knows no limits, and this always for the same reason: "Sacred doctrine, being one, extends to things which belong to the different philosophical sciences (practical as well as speculative) because it considers in each the same formal aspect, namely, so far as they can be known through the divine light."[33]

The import of this conclusion is clearly marked by Thomas Aquinas at the very beginning of his answer to the question asked in the fifth article of the *Summa:* "Whether sacred doctrine is nobler than other sciences?" We already know it is. For, since it is speculative in part and practical in part, it belongs in a higher order than the sciences that have to be either wholly speculative or wholly practical. In Thomas' own words, "it transcends all other sciences, speculative and practical" (*omnes alias [scientias] transcendit tam speculativas quam practicas*).[34] All its prerogatives derive from this source. Considered as a speculative science, sacred doctrine surpasses all the others by its greater certitude and by the higher dignity of its subject matter: by its greater certitude because the other sciences derive their certitude from the natural light of the human reason, which is liable to error, whereas sacred doctrine derives its certitude from the light of the divine science, which cannot err; by the dignity of its matter, since the other sciences treat only of objects that do not exceed reason, whereas sacred science treats chiefly of those objects that exceed reason. Considered as a practical science, it is also the highest of all, because the nobility of such sciences is in proportion to that of their ends. Now theology is ordained to the noblest of all conceivable ends, man's eternal beatitude.

There is something deceptive in the very simplicity with which Thomas Aquinas formulates this all-important conclusion. Many understand it as meaning that sacred doctrine is nobler than the other sciences, without clearly realizing that, properly speaking, no comparison is possible between them. Sacred doctrine stands alone; it does not belong in the same class as the other sciences. The confusion that obtains on the relationship of philosophy to theology has no other cause than this usually overlooked fact.

One of the most frequently quoted passages of the *Summa* is the answer to the second objection in the fifth article of the first question. The objection states that theology cannot be nobler than the other sciences because it so often draws upon the philosophical sciences, and the science that draws upon another one is usually inferior to it. To this the answer is, once more, that what is true of the other sciences is not true of theology and, once more, for the same reason. Sacred science does not really draw upon the philosophical sciences in the sense that it borrows its principles from them. It owes them nothing of what it knows and teaches. Sacred doctrine borrows from these sciences merely their method of exposition and, generally speaking, whatever can help to facilitate the understanding of its teaching. And rightly so, since the teaching of sacred doctrine is above reason; our intellect is more easily persuaded to assent to sacred doctrine if it approaches its teaching by means of what is naturally known to us in the other sciences. Moreover, higher sciences sometimes draw upon lower ones which they make subservient to their own ends; for instance, when political science makes use of military science. Hence the notorious conclusion of Thomas Aquinas: sacred science "does not draw upon the other sciences as upon its superiors, but uses them as its inferiors and handmaidens"; or still more bluntly: "Other sciences are called the handmaidens of this one: Wisdom sent *her maids to invite to the tower (Prov. 9:3).*"[35]

A perfectly correct remark often made about this formula is that it does not purport to be a definition of philosophy and of the philosophical sciences; it merely defines what they are for sacred science when this noblest of all sciences deems it advisable to use them in view of its own end. What is not correct is the inference that, left to themselves, philosophy and the philosophical sciences are in a better condition than when they answer the invitation extended to them by Wisdom. Here, however, we are reaching a point where demonstration is powerless to convince precisely because one of its premises is faith in the truth of the divine revelation. A philosopher who does not believe in the truth of the word of God has no reason to admit that philosophical wisdom can benefit from engaging in the service of sacred Wisdom. This simply means that he does not want to be a theologian. But for him who makes profession of being a Christian and who believes in the truth of the word of God, the situation is entirely different. There is something naïve, not to say ludicrous, in fearing to hurt the dignity of any science, be it the highest of all, which is natural theology, by making it subservient to sacred doctrine. Thomas Aquinas was placing upon metaphysics and all the other sciences a much higher price than their defenders. He did not love philosophy less, he loved sacred doctrine more, and he considered the latter so exalted that for any science to be ranked as inferior to it was far from being a dishonor. Rather, just as there is for man no greater honor than to serve God, so there is for philosophy and science no greater honor than to serve as the handmaid of theology. But we have forgotten the highest meaning of the word "wisdom." In fact, we have allowed the very notion of theology to become lost, and metaphysics, instead of succeeding to its royal title, became lost along with it.

To the reader of Thomas Aquinas, however, the eminent dignity of sacred doctrine should remain an undisputed fact, or otherwise there is no point in reading him. To the question asked by the sixth article: "Whether this doctrine is wisdom?" Thomas answers that "this doctrine is wisdom above all human wisdoms, not merely in any one order, but absolutely."[36] Nor should this be considered an idle title. As the Wisdom of wisdoms, and transcending them all much more radically than even metaphysics transcends the other sciences, sacred doctrine has authority to order and to judge. This authority comes to it from the fact that it is about the highest cause of the universe, that is, God, essentially and absolutely. It is therefore sacred doctrine that holds the ultimate answer to any question examined by any science, because its object is God known in all possible ways. Thomas Aquinas says so in a formula whose meaning should not escape the attention of those who wish to define the relation of philosophy to theology in his doctrine. Sacred theology does not merely add itself to natural theology, it includes natural theology; sacred doctrine "treats of God not only so far as He can be known through creatures, just as philosophers knew Him—*that which is known of God is manifest in them (Rom. 1:19)*—but also so far as He is known to Himself alone and revealed to others. Hence sacred doctrine is especially called a wisdom."[37] In short, that which is known of God to the philosopher *qua* philosopher is also known to the theologian *qua* theologian.

All these considerations confirm the already-stated conclusion that sacred doctrine exercises a sort of judicial function with respect to the other sciences. It does not interfere with their proper work, which consists in establishing conclusions in the light of their own principles. Sacred doctrine finds itself in a peculiar situation with respect to other sciences, and this, as always, because of the transcendency of its own source. In the other sciences, a lower one receives its principles from some higher one. Not so with sacred doctrine. Natural theology, which is part of philosophy, does not receive its principles from sacred theology. It receives them from the natural light of reason working on the data of sense experience. Still, because sacred doctrine derives its principles from the science that God has of Himself and of all things, it judges the principles of the other sciences. In Thomas Aquinas' own words: "It is not its business to prove the principles of the other sciences, but only to judge them."[38] On the strength of this authority, sacred doctrine condemns as false whatsoever contradicts revealed truth in the other sciences. The absolute character of its authority is best seen from the fact that the very "principles" of the other sciences fall under its jurisdiction, and since Thomas Aquinas makes no exception, we must include among them even the principle of metaphysical knowledge itself; namely, being.

Having reached this point, we need hardly ask this further question: Whether God is the subject matter of this science? He is. The principles of sacred doctrine are the articles of faith, and faith is about God. Moreover, just as everything is an object of sight inasmuch as it is colored, so also everything is an object of theological knowledge inasmuch as it is referred to God. "In sacred doctrine all things are treated under the aspect of God, either because they are God Himself, or because they refer to God as to their beginning and end."[39] Properly understood, this conclusion discloses the ultimate reason why there is practically no limit to what can be included in the object of theology. Its unity is not that of a whole including its parts, or of a genus including its species, or of a substance including its accidents. The unity of sacred doctrine is one of order. It treats of all things "so far as they are ordered to God as to their principle or as to their end."[40]

The perspective adopted by Thomas Aquinas on this problem keeps it free of most of the difficulties that usually confuse its discussion. Such difficulties arise only from the surreptitious introduction of some element foreign to the truly Thomistic data of the problem. The object of sacred doctrine is clearly defined; it is God; its cause is the science of God Himself; its formal light is that of the divine revelation; its principles are the articles of faith from which the theologian can proceed to prove something else, provided, of course, that his interlocutor subscribes to the truth of these articles. So far, there is no problem.

There still is no problem when sacred doctrine resorts to the methods and notions of philosophy in order to make more clear the meaning of its own teaching. In such cases—and this is the rule in what we call "scholastic" theology—the theologian makes use of human reason, not in order to prove the truth of faith, but merely as a method of exposition. Starting from some article of faith, the theologian argues in order to manifest consequences implied in it and which, therefore, necessarily follow from it. Thus to resort to human reason in expounding the teaching of faith does not do violence to its nature. On the contrary, "since grace does not destroy nature, but perfects it, natural reason should minister to faith as the natural inclination of the will ministers to charity."[41]

The real difficulties arise when the opponents of sacred doctrine believe nothing of divine revelation and nevertheless deny an article of faith or some of its necessary implications. In such cases, the theologian knows with certainty that the opponent is wrong, because he is contradicting divine revelation, whose teaching is infallible. On the other hand, the theologian cannot argue from the truth of faith against a philosopher whose arguments are drawn from reason. The only thing that the theologian can then do is to oppose what is bound to be a defective use of reason by a better use of reason. In other words, sure as he is of the truth of sacred doctrine, the theologian nevertheless must then argue as if he were a philosopher.

Almost all the difficulties we meet in interpreting the doctrine of Thomas Aquinas arise from positions he upheld while fulfilling this part of his theological program. To use the method of the philosophers in view of an essentially theological end unavoidably creates ambiguous situations. First, the theologian cannot pretend to demonstrate any theological truth on the strength of the unaided natural reason. Consequently, if he invokes philosophical arguments in favor of the teaching of faith, there always will remain a gap between what he says and what faith itself actually teaches. Theology, then, is a transposition into the language of reason of a truth that exceeds reason. Second, when the theologian has to cope with arguments borrowed from the doctrine of some famous philosopher—for instance, Aristotle—he may have to choose between two possible attitudes, either to show that, in fact, the said philosopher has not upheld the views contrary to faith attributed to him, or else resolutely to refute such views as philosophically erroneous. To do the first involves the theologian in endless arguments on problems in history of philosophy: Thomas Aquinas spent a great deal of time discussing such problems: what did Aristotle really teach on the eternity of the world, on the divine providence, on the nature of the human soul, etc.? In such cases, his usual attitude was to argue on the ground of philosophical authority. And rightly so, for since the teaching of revelation is then being opposed on the strength of the authority of some philosopher, it is fitting that a theologian should redress this wrong interpretation of the philosopher's doctrine, this unjustified appeal to his authority. But if the theologian thinks that a famous philosopher, however great his authority, has been wrong, then the only thing for him to do is to refute such a philosophical error by establishing the contrary philosophical truth. This too Thomas has often done, thereby introducing into the very texture of his theology genuine philosophical argumentations. The *Summa Contra Gentiles* is full of them, but they also abound in the *Summa Theologiae*, so much so that some of his very opponents, such as Siger of Brabant, have not hesitated to borrow from the theological works of Thomas Aquinas whole sections which, by simply suppressing their scriptural authorities, they easily have transformed into philosophical speculation.

Most of the time, however, Thomas Aquinas preferred to follow a subtler way; namely, neither to invoke philosophical authority nor to refute it, but rather to improve the doctrines of the philosophers in order to bring them as near as possible to the teaching of the true faith. By adopting this attitude, Thomas Aquinas was preparing no end of trouble for his future historians, but he was not thinking of them. The dominating historical fact one should always bear in mind is that, in the thirteenth century, for reasons foreign to our own inquiry, philosophy and the doctrine of Aristotle were supposed to be practically one and the same thing. As a theologian, Thomas Aquinas considered it his duty to open the minds of men to the possibility of the truth of faith by showing that philosophy not only did not contradict it, but rather favored it. This was to him a natural attitude to adopt. He was certain of the truth of faith much more infallibly than of the truth of philosophy; but he also felt sure that truth could not possibly contradict truth, and since philosophy was pretending to say the truth, to help philosophy to say it was tantamount to helping it to be philosophy. And since, to most of his contemporaries, philosophy spelled Aristotle, Thomas Aquinas would naturally strive, whenever possible, to place philosophical truth under the patronage of Aristotle. This was not so hard to do, at least in the many cases when different philosophers, upholding different philosophies, themselves invoked the authority of the Philosopher *par excellence*, Aristotle. But Thomas Aquinas did not even need this encouragement. He has made Aristotle say the maximum of truth it was possible to attribute to him on the strength of any one of the expressions he had used. How often Thomas clearly realized that he was making Aristotle say things he never said, this remains for the most attentive of his historians a matter of supposition.

But Aristotle was not the only authority to be submitted to this treatment. Plato, Boethius, Avicenna, Averroes himself have been made to say by Thomas what they should have said in order to be both philosophically right and theologically irreproachable. The most original part of the contribution made by Thomas Aquinas to philosophy has its origin in this rational reinterpretation of the philosophies of the past in the light of theological truth. Philosophically speaking, the way a philosopher arrives at truth is irrelevant to it; a philosophical statement should always be judged on its philosophical merit; but to say that a certain doctrine belongs to Aristotle is to make a historical statement which, as such, should be judged on its historical merits. Because his own perspective was not a primarily historical one, Thomas Aquinas has left his historians at grips with many an insoluble problem. But this is of little importance. After all, the main object of a historical study of Thomism is to ascertain the true meaning of its teaching. Interesting as it is, the origin of the doctrine, besides being ultimately hidden in the secret of personal psychology, is but indirectly relevant to its meaning.

If this general view of sacred doctrine is justified, the nature of the doctrine contained in the *Summa Theologiae* should be clear. Since its aim is to introduce its readers, especially beginners, to the teaching of theology, everything in it is theological. This does not mean that the *Summa* contains no philosophy; on the contrary, it is full of philosophy. Since the philosophy that is in the *Summa* is there in view of a theological end, and since it figures in it as integrated with that which is the proper work of the theologian, it finds itself included within the formal object of theology and becomes theological in its own right.

For the same reason, the order of exposition has to be theological. Now the object of theology is God. Everything in it must therefore start from the notion of God or be related to it. Thomas Aquinas never varied on this point: philosophers proceed from things to God; theologians proceed from our knowledge of God to our interpretation of the nature of things. Naturally, if the theologian needs to establish some point in a philosophical way, as will be the case with the existence of God, it will be necessary for him to proceed, in this particular case, according to the exigencies of the philosophical method. Even then, however, he will not separate himself from theology, since Saint Paul himself has said that men can succeed in establishing the existence of God by starting with the consideration of His creatures. Above all, the theologian will place at the beginning of his theology a problem that would normally appear at the end of philosophy.[42] As a preamble to theology proper, the problem of the existence of God becomes a question of knowing what the philosophers have known of this truth, then of judging it, of interpreting it, and, if necessary, of perfecting it in the light of a higher truth.

PART II. GOD

Chapter 3. The existence of God

The subject matter of sacred doctrine is God. Like any other science, theology presupposes the existence of its object. Not that it would remain objectless if it were left to itself: the patriarchs, the just of all times have never needed anything more than God, the word of God, and their faith in revelation in order to master the knowledge of saving truth. But since we are intending to order theology after the pattern of a science, we can admit that the question: is there a God? should come before the question: what is God? And since the theologian resorts to philosophy in order to make theological truth more easily accessible to human understanding, it is natural that his first question should be about the existence of God.

On this problem, however, a theologian cannot do much more than apply to the philosophers for philosophical information. The existence of God is a philosophical problem; several different philosophers have given several different demonstrations of this naturally knowable truth. The position of a theologian on this point unavoidably consists in collecting philosophical evidence, in sifting it, in weighing it and ordering it in view of his own theological purposes. Nothing forbids the theologian to invent one or several proofs of his own, but he also can content himself with accepting and reinterpreting old ones. After all, if the existence of God is a philosophically demonstrable conclusion, there must have been some philosophers able to demonstrate it. The natural attitude of a theologian on this point should therefore be, at least in the beginning, that of a listener who gathers philosophical information before interpreting it.

In our own presentation of the doctrine of Thomas Aquinas on this question, we shall follow the order of the *Summa Theologiae*, distinguishing as clearly as possible the doctrine itself from our own interpretation of it. General considerations on the meaning of the proofs of the existence of God in the theology of Thomas Aquinas will be introduced at the end of the exposition and under the sole responsibility of their historian.

I. THE EXISTENCE OF GOD IS NOT SELF-EVIDENT

Some think that the existence of God does not need to be demonstrated because the knowledge of this truth is inborn in the human mind. And, indeed, if every man is born with the innate knowledge that there is a God, this truth cannot possibly be demonstrated. How could one prove to us a proposition that we already know to be true? Now it has been maintained that every man has an inborn knowledge of the existence of God. For instance, according to Saint John Damascene, *The knowledge of God is naturally implanted in all.*[1] If this is true, Thomas Aquinas is right in saying that, according to this position, "the existence of God is self-evident."

Had Thomas Aquinas been of the opinion that a theologian should favor all the philosophical positions that confirm the teaching of revelation with the minimum of intellectual effort, he would have accepted this position rather than go to the trouble of looking for complicated philosophical demonstrations. But the problem at stake is one of philosophical truth. Now, in fact, there are men who deny the existence of God. There are atheists: *The fool said in his heart: There is no God* (*Ps. 52:1*). If the knowledge of the existence of God were naturally implanted in all, this kind of folly would not be possible. Consequently, the existence of God is not self-evident in the sense that has just been defined.

This conclusion suffices to establish the consequence that the existence of God stands in need of being demonstrated. At this point, however, Thomas Aquinas gives a striking example of philosophical thoroughness. He shows his reader that no error is finally eliminated until one understands the reasons it has taken place. In the present case, the problem is to know why, if the knowledge of God is not naturally implanted in all, some people believe that it is.

A first answer is that, in fact, there are religions and, consequently, there is such a thing as religious education. From the earliest years of their lives, children are brought up to think that there is a God. In a child, custom becomes indistinguishable from nature, so that years later the grown man cannot remember a time when he did not know there was a God. Hence he forms the natural conviction that such knowledge is innate in the human mind. This remark is sometimes useful to remember,[2] and especially when it is quoted as an argument *against* the existence of God. It is sometimes said that education and custom sufficiently account for our conviction that there is a God. To this Thomas would reply that custom does indeed account for the fact that our notion of God seems to be innate in the human mind, and this precisely is the reason why the existence of God stands in need of being demonstrated; but if this notion is not innate, what is its origin?

This new question is of great importance. Its import can be expressed as follows. The philosophers who say there is no God seem to take it for granted that, in this problem, the burden of the proof rests entirely with those who uphold that there is a God, whereas, if there is no God, they themselves have to account for the extraordinary fact that there is a notion of God and a widespread belief in His existence. This time, education, custom, and tradition do not provide satisfactory explanations; on the contrary, what now has to be accounted for is the very existence of various beliefs in the existence of God to be found in human society. Whether there is a God or not, the fact remains that there is a notion of God and that this notion stands in need of being accounted for. To resort to mythology and to the mythical function of the human mind is not to answer the problem; it simply is to beg the question. For whatever cause may be assigned to our notion of God, it is a fact that this notion does exist, that its cause has been something in the human mind, and that, *especially if there is no God*, it remains to explain how the human mind has been able to cause it. In fact, the problem is so real that this is one of the two ways followed by Descartes in his demonstration of the existence of God. According to Descartes, that there is a God is the only conceivable explanation for the fact that a notion of God is present in the human mind.[3]

Thomas Aquinas has not overlooked the question. According to him, too, there is in the human understanding an objective cause for the widespread belief that, to use John Damascene's own words, the knowledge of God is naturally implanted in all. This reason is merely indicated at the beginning of the *Summa Theologiae*,[4] at a place where, because it presupposes conclusions that were to be established later on, it could not possibly be given a complete justification. For the same reason, this exhaustive explanation cannot be given here, but we can follow the example of Saint Thomas and give at least a sketch of what it is going to be.

Expressed in simple terms, the answer is that there is a God, Creator of heaven and earth, cause of its existence and ultimate end of all the beings it contains as well as of all their operations. This will be shown to be true. But if one supposes it to be true, one must accept the consequence that, whether they realize it or not, all beings are acting in view of God as in view of their ultimate end. The created beings that do not share in intellectual knowledge cannot possibly be aware of this truth. Intellectual beings are at least conscious of their desires and of the pleasure they experience in attaining the objects of their appetitions. This enjoyment of what they desire constitutes what, rightly or wrongly, they call happiness. In fact, since God is their last end, what men are pursuing in the enjoyment of creatures, under the name of happiness, is God. Their will is orientated toward God, only they do not know this. For this reason, it can be said of man that he does not know God exists, although it is true that man naturally desires happiness, that he knows he desires happiness, and that, in fine, the happiness he desires is God.

In order to make this clear, Thomas Aquinas uses a comparison:

> *Man naturally desires happiness, and what is naturally desired by man is naturally known by him. This, however, is not to know absolutely that God exists, just as to know that someone is approaching is not the same as to know that Peter is approaching, even though it is Peter who is approaching; for there are many who imagine that man's perfect good, which is happiness, consists in riches, others in pleasures, and others in something else.*[5]

When, in consequence of some reasoning, a man has proved that there is a God, he easily realizes that this God had always been the object of his desire. God was that which, under the name of happiness, he was pursuing as his ultimate end. When a man knows that God has always been the end of his desire, he cannot help feeling that he has always known God.

A second way of maintaining that the existence of God is self-evident is suggested by the famous argument of Saint Anselm in the second chapter of his *Proslogion*. Still, Thomas Aquinas does not name Anselm, nor can it be said that he is trying to refute him. Thomas is less interested in particular doctrines such as they have actually been maintained by philosophers than in pure philosophical positions. Several different doctrines can sometimes be reduced to one single pure position. For instance, we have just seen Thomas reducing the doctrine of the innateness of the knowledge that God exists to the doctrine according to which the existence of God is self-evident; we are now going to see him perform a similar reduction of the argument of Saint Anselm. However Anselm himself may have worded it, if his argument is valid, it amounts to saying that the existence of God is self-evident.

"A proposition is self-evident," he said, "because the predicate is involved in the essence of the subject. For instance, *Man is an animal*" is a self-evident proposition because "animal is contained in the essence of man." Can it likewise be said that *existence* is included in the essence of God? Reduced to its essentials by Thomas Aquinas, this is what the argument of Anselm signifies. For indeed, the name *God* signifies a being than which no greater can be conceived. When His name is understood, God exists in the mind that understands it. Now to exist both mentally and in reality is greater than to exist only in the mind; therefore, the being than which no greater can be conceived exists both mentally and in reality. Since this conclusion follows from the very analysis of the essence of God (*i.e.*, a being than which no greater can be conceived), the proposition *God exists* can be said to be self-evident.

Here again the temptation to follow the line of least resistance offers itself to the theologian, but Thomas Aquinas once more refuses to accept it. If the argument is not satisfactory from the point of view of philosophical reason, the fact that it concludes in favor of the existence of God is no sufficient justification for it. Still, while rejecting it, Thomas will be careful to show the reason responsible for the error.

A proposition can be self-evident in itself, but not to us, or it can be self-evident both in itself and to us. The proposition *God exists* belongs in the first class. It is evident in itself because, as shall be seen, there is absolutely no distinction between the essence of God and His existence. More exactly, God is His own existence. Consequently, if we knew the essence of God, to know His essence would be the same as to know His existence. This is to say that, in itself, the proposition *God exists* is self-evident, but it is not so to us because the essence of God is unknown to the human mind in its present condition. There is therefore only one way for us to make sure that there is a God; namely, to demonstrate the truth of the proposition *God exists*. This can be done by starting from the consideration of God's effects.[6]

It would be an error to think that the method advocated by Saint Anselm, or at least followed by him, was never attempted again after its criticism by Saint Thomas Aquinas. The second proof of the existence of God proposed by Descartes in his fifth *Metaphysical Meditation* is a reinterpretation of the argument of Saint Anselm. Thomas

Aquinas would have raised against it the same objections. It is all a question of philosophical method. The method advocated by Descartes derives its inspiration from mathematics. Accordingly, Descartes attributes to the objects of thought all the properties that necessarily belong to their ideas. In the present case, he considers that existence belongs to God as necessarily as it belongs to the triangle that the sum of its angles should be equal to two right angles. What is typical of the attitude of Thomas Aquinas is that, while agreeing to attribute to the notion of an object whatever necessarily follows from its definition, he absolutely refuses to include existence among the properties attributable to any object on the strength of its definition. This is essential to the doctrine of Thomas Aquinas. Actual existence can be either experienced or inferred from another actually given existence, it cannot be deduced from any definition. Thomas would answer to Descartes as follows. *If* God exists, then His existence belongs to His essence much more necessarily than the properties of the triangle belong to it in virtue of its definition. For if there is a God, He cannot not be, whereas, if there were no God, there would be nothing else. But the problem precisely is to know if there is a God, and the only way to answer it is to proceed by way of demonstration.

II. THE EXISTENCE OF GOD IS DEMONSTRABLE

It has been held that the existence of God is not a rationally demonstrable truth but that it must be held as true on faith; that is, as revealed by God to man.

On the contrary, it has been revealed by God to man that His existence can be demonstrated. Scripture even says, at least in a general way, how this demonstration can be achieved. In a text that was to be quoted time and again by theologians and philosophers, the Apostle has said that *the invisible things of him . . . are clearly seen, being understood by the things that are made (Rom. 1:20).* Now the first thing to be known about anything is whether it exists. Consequently, Saint Paul has told us in this passage that the existence of God can be clearly seen (that is, demonstrated) and that it can be seen from the consideration of the visible things of nature.

The same conclusion follows from a more general reason. God created man with all the gifts that he needed in order to attain his ultimate end. No added revelation was necessary for Adam to know that there was a God and that God was his ultimate end. Original sin obscured this knowledge and weakened in man the power of knowing. A revelation then became necessary to remind man of his ultimate end; but the human understanding never ceased, even without revelation, to be able to know that there was a God. Man has always been able to know enough of his God to feel himself obliged to render Him worship. Man has always been able to find himself obliged to respect and to serve a supreme being as well as to obey the elementary rules of morality whose knowledge has never been absent from his understanding. Even now the situation remains the same for all the men who either do not know that there has been a divine revelation or else, knowing of its existence, do not believe in it. In short, since man has always had obligations binding him to God, he must have always been able to know enough about Him in order to know these obligations.

Besides, such knowledge is at least possible. We cannot achieve a perfect knowledge of God. Only God knows Himself perfectly. We cannot even know the existence of God with the kind of evidence we would have if our knowledge of it could be deduced *a priori* from what we know of God's essence. As has already been said, the essence of God is unknown to us. There is therefore only one way left open to us if we wish to arrive at the conclusion that God exists. It consists in starting from the consideration of things and in inferring from their existence, such as it is given in sense experience, the existence of a Being that is not given in sense experience. In the doctrine of Saint Thomas, all the ways that lead the human reason to the knowledge of God will comply with these specifications.

The same remark can be expressed in more technical terms. This is what Thomas Aquinas himself does in the *Summa Theologiae* I, q.2, a.2, where he answers:

> *Demonstration can be made in two ways. One is through the cause, and is called* propter quid [because of which]; *this is to argue from what is prior absolutely. The other is through the effect, and is called a demonstration* quia [that]; *this is to argue from what is prior relatively only to us.*

Using this terminology, which is borrowed from logic, we shall say that all our ways to God are demonstrations *quia*. First of all, there is nothing *because of which* God should be as in virtue of a cause. God simply has no cause. If there is a God, all the rest is because of Him; as to Himself, He is absolutely. But His effects are given first to us in sense experience, and by starting from them and inquiring into their possible origin, we can ascertain that there is a God.

What is the nature of such a demonstration? In a demonstration *propter quid*, the reasoning starts from the cause and shows that the conclusion follows from it as its effect. In a demonstration *quia*, the notion of the effect comes first. Moreover, the conclusion of the demonstration is not the essence of anything, but its existence. In other words, starting from an effect whose existence is given in sense experience, we shall infer the *existence* of a cause about which, at the moment, nothing else is known except the fact that it exists and that it is the cause of this effect. As to what can be known concerning the *essence* of the cause (*i.e.*, that which the cause is) a further investigation will be required in order to establish it.

This remark enables the reader of Saint Thomas to understand correctly the method used in establishing the existence of God. In this kind of demonstration a regular pattern is followed; namely, X has a cause, this cause is what we call God, hence there is a God. Applying to it the terms usually applied to the description of syllogistic reasoning, Thomas Aquinas says that, in such cases, the *meaning of the name* of the thing whose existence is at stake is used as a middle term. In a demonstration through the cause (*propter quid*), the middle term would be the essence of the thing, but in demonstrations from the effects (*quia*), since what is at stake is an existence, the middle term can be only the meaning of the name whose existence is being affirmed. For instance, suppose the starting point of an argument is the existence of motion. The demonstration will consist in proving that motion has a cause, then in saying that the word "God" precisely means such a cause; whence it follows that God exists. As will be seen, Thomas Aquinas lays all the stress on the demonstration of the major; there is a prime cause of X; once this has been established, the rest hardly needs to be mentioned.

In the last analysis, this kind of demonstration assumes the form of a syllogism, but its main part consists in building up its own major; that is to say, in establishing the existence of a prime cause in a certain order of effects. In order to do so, the philosopher must bring into play all sorts of notions, or even of principles, whose use can be verified by means of syllogistic reasoning but which cannot always be syllogistically demonstrated. In the case of principles, they cannot be demonstrated at all. Moreover, the whole demonstration presupposes the presence to the mind of a certain notion of God; namely, that which Thomas himself calls "the meaning of the name." In other words, one cannot inquire into the existence of a thing without having some notion of what, if it exists, the thing is.

All this implies that every demonstration of the existence of God presupposes the presence of a certain notion of God which is itself not the conclusion of a demonstration. This precisely is the notion of God of which Saint Paul says that, through the mere sight of His creatures, God has manifested it unto them. There is a sort of spontaneous inference, wholly untechnical but entirely conscious of its own meaning, in virtue of which every man finds himself raised to the notion of a transcendent Being by the mere sight of nature in its awesome majesty. In a fragment from one of his lost works, Aristotle himself observes that men have derived their notion of God from two sources, their own souls and the orderly motion of the stars.[7] However this may be, the fact itself is beyond doubt, and human philosophies are belatedly discovering the notion of God. This notion had been present to the minds of men during we do not know how many millennia, under however confused and obscure a form, when for the first time Greek philosophers undertook to submit it, so to speak, to a critical examination.

One cannot overlook this background of spontaneous inference without missing the true meaning of the proofs, or ways, followed by Thomas Aquinas in his discussion of the problem. As a matter of fact, mankind does have a certain notion of God; for centuries after centuries men without any intellectual culture have obscurely but powerfully felt convinced that the name *God* points out an actually existing being; and even today, countless human beings are still reaching the same conviction and forming the same belief on the sole strength of their personal experience. Philosophy or no philosophy, this is what actually happens, and no one can approach the problem without taking these facts into account. Only, something entirely new happens when a philosopher transfers these spontaneous convictions to the ground of metaphysical knowledge. He then asks himself: what is the rational value of these natural beliefs? Is it possible to turn our natural notion of God into a rationally justified knowledge? Can the affirmation that there is a God assume the form and acquire the value of a scientifically demonstrated conclusion? One should not consider these questions as unimportant. It is certainly important to know whether or not the proposition *there is a God* can be numbered among those that are demonstrably true. Still, one should also know that what is called a proof of the existence of God is a technically accurate recognition, by means of a demonstrative process, of the truth of this proposition.

This is particularly evident in the case of a theology such as that of Saint Thomas Aquinas. No theologian can pretend that, in beginning his work, he still does not know that there is a God. On the contrary, there have been theologians to maintain that the existence of God is impossible of demonstration precisely because, having been revealed to us by God Himself, we must hold it as true on faith. Now, one cannot believe and know one and the same thing at one and the same time. Consequently, since we already believe that God exists, His existence cannot possibly be demonstrated.

On this point, two extreme positions must be avoided, the one according to which the existence of God is an article of faith and, in consequence, cannot be demonstrated, the other one according to which the existence of God is so easily accessible to human reason that it cannot possibly be the object of an act of faith.

The existence of God is not an article of faith. But what is an article of faith? The object of faith properly so called is the believable; that is, the saving truth that God has revealed to man because, of itself, it escapes the light of reason unaided by faith. Strictly speaking, the believable is that which cannot be held as true otherwise than on faith. For the sake of brevity, let us say that, by definition, the object of faith is *unseen*. More precisely, the object of faith is *the unseen concerning God*. Where there occurs something that is unseen in a way of its own, it is called an article of faith. On the contrary, where several objects of faith are all related to a single one and can be comprehended under it, only the latter is an article of faith. This remarkable notion assimilates the articles of faith to the principles in the order of intelligible knowledge. Taken together, a principle and its consequences constitute a sort of believable unit, a single complex object of belief. For instance, that God has suffered is something that can only be believed, but if we believe that God has suffered, to believe that he died and was buried does not create a new difficulty. On the contrary, if we believe that God died and was buried, to believe that on the third day he rose again is a new *unseen*. Far from being includable under the preceding one, it rather looks like its denial; for to believe that God can suffer and die is a difficulty, but to believe that, after His death, God rose again only makes the first difficulty still more difficult to understand. Thus, the unseen about God distributes itself under a certain number of headings that are called articles of faith. Since, of itself, the existence of God is philosophically demonstrable (as is seen from the fact that several philosophers have demonstrated it), it does not belong in the category of the *unseen* (the essentially invisible); consequently, it cannot be counted among the articles of faith. It cannot even be included under any article of faith. In Thomas Aquinas' own words, truths of this sort are so many "preambles" to the articles of faith.[8] A well-chosen expression indeed, since, unless one knows there is a God, how can he believe anything about Him?

The other extreme is represented by those who maintain that, since it can be known, the existence of God cannot possibly be believed. As has been said by some philosophers, a formal act of faith in the existence of God is impossible. The reason for this position is the well-known thesis of Thomas Aquinas, that just as it is impossible to see and not to see one and the same thing at one and the same time, so also it is impossible to know and to believe one and the same truth at one and the same time.

This, however, applies only to actually known, understood, and scientifically demonstrated truth. There is at least one case in which it does not apply; namely, when a man cannot understand a demonstration which, of itself, is accessible to human reason. For instance, there is no doubt that the existence of God is demonstrable, but if somebody cannot understand the demonstrations of this preamble to the articles of faith, which is the situation of each and every child, not to speak of quite a few adults, he can at least believe it. In other words, what can be known by some can also be believed by others. For the latter, the existence of God does not become an article of faith, something that it cannot possibly be, but it certainly is an object of faith.[9]

What precedes is clear. What follows is less clear and it can provide material for many disputed questions.

Starting from the part in it that is easier to grasp, let us say that a certain part of a certain object can be known while another part of it is only believed. For instance, the same man who knows by demonstration that God exists can only believe that the same God is one in three persons. This does not entail any real difficulty.

One must, however, ask a more subtle question. Is it impossible to know part of a certain truth and, at the same time, to believe another part of it? In the case of the existence of God, it certainly is impossible to know by demonstration that there is a Prime Immobile Mover and at the same time to hold on faith that this Prime Mover is, or exists. This would be a contradiction in terms. But God is much more than the Prime Mover of Aristotle. If there is a Prime Mover, we know that He is God, but whereas the proposition *the Prime Mover is God* is completely true, the proposition *God is the Prime Mover* is not an unqualified truth. It is true of God, but it is not the whole truth about Him. God has not revealed Himself as the Prime Mover, for, although He is truly the Prime Mover, He is still an infinity of other things, rationally knowable or not, that we all accept as true of Him in the same simple act whereby we hold Him on faith to be, and to be the very God He actually is. To believe in the existence of God is not to believe the existence of the Prime Mover, of the Prime Cause, of the Perfect Being, or of the Ultimate End. It is not even to believe in the existence of a single being that is all these perfections together; it is to believe in the existence of Him Who has spoken to us, a thing that the Prime Mover as such never did. The God Whose existence we demonstrate is but a part of the God Whose existence we hold to be true on the strength of our faith in His words. In this sense, the God of rational knowledge is, so to speak, included within the God of faith.

A last possibility can at least be submitted to the reflection of Christian philosophers. We naturally maintain, as was said above, that to know and to believe the same thing at one and the same time is impossible. But, strictly speaking, what does this mean? It means that, after demonstrating the existence of a Prime Mover, who is God, it has become impossible for us to believe the same truth. Now, on the one hand, faith is a type of knowledge inferior to understanding; as a mode of knowing, merely to believe is not as good as to understand. On the other hand, if we consider these two ways of knowing from the point of view of their certitude, faith is incomparably more certain than understanding. Faith does not see the truth of its object (the *unseen*), but the intellect is more unshakably certain of the truth it believes than it would be if it assented to it on the strength of a demonstration. The reason is that the ultimate ground for our intellectual assent to revealed truth is the supremely infallible knowledge that God has of all truth. In fact, as will be seen, God Himself is Truth. Even the intellectual evidence of the first principles in us is only a *human* type of certitude; it does not compare with the absolute and infinite infallibility of God.

An immediate consequence of this truth was soon perceived by certain commentators of Thomas Aquinas. It is that, according to this doctrine, a philosopher should be less absolutely certain of the existence of God after demonstrating it than he was at the time when he held this conclusion as true solely on faith. There is something paradoxical in this conclusion; fortunately, it does not follow from the principles laid down by Thomas Aquinas.

However certain a man may be of his rational conclusions, he cannot fail to realize that, in human knowledge, there often is room for some undetected error. On the contrary, there is no possibility of error in our assent to faith, because the object of assent in faith is something that God Himself tells us is true. Faith in revelation is therefore a guarantee of truth that belongs in an entirely different order from the certitude of reason. Rational knowledge cannot give it, nor can faith be either increased or diminished by acquiring rational certitude or losing it. We cannot, at one and the same time, know and believe that there is a Prime Mover, but we can know that there is a Prime Mover and continue to believe in the existence of a God Who has revealed to us that He *is* at the same time many other perfections.

In order to respect the authentic doctrine of Thomas Aquinas in this important matter, it seems safe to say that, with respect to the salvation of mankind in general, it is necessary to believe even that which can be proved by natural reason; otherwise, given that the number of real philosophers is very small and the chances of error very high, few men would know the saving truth.[10] This certainly is the teaching of Thomas Aquinas. What can be said touching the other part of the problem is not supported by explicit statements of the Angelic Doctor. It seems probable, however, that his commentator Bañes was right in upholding the view that, "because the *habitus* of faith and supernatural light make the intellect more certain about the proposition *God is* than the natural light can cause it to be by means of arguments, one should not deny that even we, who have demonstrations of it, are in a way assenting to it through faith" (*non est negandum quin per fidem quodammodo assentiamus huic, deus est, etiam illi qui habemus demonstrationes*). Otherwise, Bañes goes on to say, a rustic assenting to the truth of God's existence through faith alone would be safer in his assent than a theologian assenting to the same truth on the strength of rational demonstration only. Hence, Bañes says, we somehow assent to this truth through faith so far as certitude is concerned (*quantum ad certitudinem*).[11] Nor is this to believe and to know the same thing at the same time, because, although these two assents bear upon the same object materially, they do not bear upon the same formal object seen in the same formal light.[12]

This being said, the general position of the problem in the doctrine of Thomas Aquinas is clear. For reasons tied up with the problem of human salvation, God has deemed it fitting to reveal to all men His own existence. At the same time, since some philosophers have been able to discover this same truth by means of human reason alone, the existence of God must be rationally knowable. The demonstrations given by these philosophers will now be examined in the light of this same natural reason.

III. DEMONSTRATIONS OF THE EXISTENCE OF GOD

Saint Thomas Aquinas has given demonstrations of the existence of God in several of his works. Since it was his intention, in the *Summa Theologiae*, to introduce beginners to the study of theology, it has become customary to follow the approach to the problem adopted by Thomas in this work, and for the same reason. Each one of the five "ways" expounded in the *Summa* will first be examined in itself according to the order followed by Thomas.

This justified preference, however, should not cause us to attribute to the letter of the five ways a sort of sacred character.[13] Leaving aside other considerations, which will find their place at the end of this chapter, we must observe at once that Thomas Aquinas himself has set forth certain of his demonstrations on several different occasions, and never twice in identically the same terms. Even the number of the ways followed is not everywhere the same: four in the *Summa Contra Gentiles*, five in the *Summa Theologiae*, one in the *Compendium Theologiae*. Lastly, what serves as proof of the existence of God in one of Aquinas' works can very well become a proof of one of His attributes in another one. To quote only one striking instance, the admirable Disputed Question *De Potentia*, q.3, a.5, establishes that there can be nothing that is not created by God. Obviously, to prove such a conclusion is tantamount to proving that there is a God. Moreover, the three reasons alleged by Thomas Aquinas in favor of this conclusion rest upon the deepest among his own metaphysical doctrines. Still, what he is proving in this text is not that there is a God, but rather that the true notion of God as prime cause excludes the possibility that anything can exist without being created by Him.

There is therefore some danger in turning into demonstrations of the existence of God arguments that Thomas himself never used to this purpose. One has seen critics of Thomas undertake to prove that the remarkable passage of the treatise *On Being and Essence* where he establishes that there is a being whose essence is its very existence, fails to establish the existence of God; but Thomas himself never intended this development as a proof of God's existence. It is not exactly fair or useful to refute demonstrations which, according to all appearances, he himself would not have considered satisfactory.

The general rule that facilitates the discussion of such problems is simple. It is never to use as a proof of the existence of God, in expounding the doctrine of Saint Thomas himself, an argument that he himself has not expressly formulated in support of this conclusion. In making use of other passages of his works in order to prove the existence of God, or in elaborating arguments to the same effect which, though not really his, intend at least to keep faith with the authentic inspiration of his doctrine, the following remarks should be kept in mind.

A truly Thomistic proof of the existence of God always starts from some thing or situation empirically given in sense knowledge. Only from an actually given existence can one legitimately infer a non-empirically given existence. For instance, change is a fact given in sense experience; actual being likewise is a fact given in sense experience; but the act of being in virtue of which a being is, or exists, is an object of the intellect, not an object of sense perception. For these reasons, actually existing being opens a way to the conclusion that God exists; the abstract consideration of the act of being, on the contrary, does not.

Second, the middle term of such a demonstration is always the meaning of the name "God" (*quid significet nomen*), it is never the essence of God (*non autem quod quid est*). In order to start from the notion of the essence of God (supposing we had a proper notion of it), we should have to presuppose that there actually is such an essence, which is to suppose that there is a God. Truly Thomistic demonstrations of this conclusion make no such mistake. They all conclude on such a remark as "who is God," "and that is what we call God," or "and He is the one we call God." Wherever it occurs, this clause is a sure sign that one is dealing with a truly Thomistic approach to the problem of the existence of God.

A third remark follows from the preceding one. There is a sort of universally known notion of God, present in a confused way to practically all human minds. Its origins are manifold: a spontaneous inference suggested by the sight of the universe, religious traditions inherited from antiquity, early impressions received in childhood from the education given by parents, and the like. The conclusion of each one of the ways followed by Thomas Aquinas regularly is that the Prime Mover, the Prime Efficient Cause, etc., precisely are the mysterious being whose confused notion was already present to our mind. Without such a provisional notion of what we are looking for, our intellect could not possibly find it.

In the case of a Christian philosopher, the question does not even arise. Since he is a Christian, he must needs believe that there is a God; namely, the being Who is the object of Christian religious worship. This belief is not a philosophical proof, it is not even the inchoation of a demonstration; only, at the moment he sets out to inquire into the possibility of one, a Christian cannot possibly pretend to have no notion of the meaning of the word "God."

In the *Compendium Theologiae*, Thomas begins by announcing that three main truths must be known about the divinity: first, that the divine essence is one; second, the trinity of the divine persons; third, the effects wrought by God. After this he presently declares: "Concerning the oneness of God, we must first believe that God exists (*primo quidem credendum est Deum esse*) and this is clearly seen through reason (*quod ratione conspicuum est*)." There is no difficulty about this; on the contrary, if a man mistook his belief in God for a proof of God's existence, he would not look for demonstrations of it.

A similar remark applies to the method followed in the *Summa Theologiae*. Before explaining his five ways, Thomas borrows from Holy Scripture an incontrovertible passage in which God Himself affirms His own existence: *On the contrary, it is said in the person of God: I am Who am (Exod. 3:14)*. Far from trying to forget his faith in the word of God before establishing God's existence, Thomas Aquinas reaffirms it in the most forcible way. And no wonder, since the God in Whose words he believes is the very same being Whose existence his reason is about to demonstrate. Faith in quest of understanding is the common motto of all Christian theologians and of Christian philosophers as well.

A. The way of motion

In dealing with the Thomistic ways of proving the existence of God we shall successively reproduce the relevant texts of the *Summa* in English translation,[14] distinguish their essential elements from the accidental ones, and give the reasons for their permanent significance.

The first and more manifest way is the argument from motion. It is certain and evident to our senses that in the world some things are in motion. Now whatever is moved is moved by another, for nothing can be moved except it is in potentiality to that towards which it is moved, whereas a thing moves inasmuch as it is in act. For motion is nothing else than the reduction of something from potentiality to actuality. But nothing can be reduced from potentiality to actuality except by something in a state of actuality. Thus that which is actually hot, as fire, makes wood, which is potentially hot, to be actually hot, and thereby moves and changes it. Now it is not possible that the same thing should be at once in actuality and potentiality in the same respect, but only in different respects. For what is actually hot cannot simultaneously be potentially hot, but it is simultaneously potentially cold. It is therefore impossible that in the same respect and in the same way a thing should be both mover and moved, i.e., that it should move itself. Therefore, whatever is moved must be moved by another. If that by which it is moved be itself moved, then this also must be moved by another, and that by another again. But this cannot go on to infinity, because then there would be no first mover and, consequently, no other mover, seeing that subsequent movers move only inasmuch as they are moved by the first mover, as the staff moves only because it is moved by the hand. Therefore it is necessary to arrive at a first mover, moved by no other, and this everyone understands to be God.[15]

The argument presents the typical characteristic of a proof of the existence of God. It starts from sense experience, it builds up its major premise (*there is a First Mover*), it borrows its minor from the meaning of the name (*this is what everyone understands to be God*), and the conclusion is so obvious that it need not even be formulated (*therefore there is a God*). The whole process can be reduced to the following syllogism: there is a First Mover, the First Mover is what is called God, therefore there is a God.

a. The language of the proof

The first way is presented by Thomas Aquinas as more "manifest" because the fact of motion from which it starts is particularly evident to sense. Nevertheless, its language is disconcerting to modern readers because it is borrowed from a scientific view of the world that has ceased to be considered scientifically valid.

In one of the versions of the proof given by Thomas Aquinas[16] we see at once that its general setting is the Greek universe of Aristotle. In it, directions in space are physically real; there is a "high" and there is a "low." The world is made up of four elements, with the heaviest one, earth, at the center of things. All heavenly bodies are satellites circling around the earth, each of them moved by its own mover, and the demonstration consists in showing that the number of these separate Movers must needs be finite. Less strongly marked, even there, than it was in Maimonides, the presence of the Aristotelian cosmography in this formulation of the proof cannot be overlooked.[17]

Though kept in the background, in the long exposition of the proof found in the *Summa Contra Gentiles*, the survival of the same cosmography remains recognizable in it. Thomas Aquinas is following Aristotle and therefore he has in mind the same universe as that of Maimonides, with the sun revolving around the earth and heavenly bodies moved by separate Intelligences.[18]

This astronomical setting is hardly visible in the *Summa Theologiae*. For reasons of his own, Thomas has deliberately toned it down, but another aspect of Aristotle's physics comes in the forefront; namely, his "qualitative" explanation of physical phenomena. According to the Philosopher, the world is made up of elements, or of mixtures of elements blended in diverse proportions. These elements are four in number: fire, air, water, and earth. Again, each element is made up of two of the four following sense qualities: dry, moist, hot, and cold. For instance, fire is both hot and dry, water is cold and moist, etc. These are the qualities of which Thomas Aquinas says that, when a body has one of them only in potency, it cannot acquire the quality unless it receives it from another body that has it actually, or, in Thomas' own words, in act.

This whole astronomical and physico-chemical structure of the universe began to lose its scientific value as early as the sixteenth century. For some time, misguided interpreters of Thomas Aquinas persisted in tying his philosophical arguments, whose validity is independent of science, with the always revisable notions he had received from the astronomers, the physicists, and the biologists of antiquity.[19] The reason for such an attitude is easy to understand; it was prudence. But we today are so far removed from the universe of the Greeks that to start from the physical framework of such a universe in order to prove anything is to disqualify the whole argument at the very outset. Qualitative physics is out of date; science admits only of quantitative explanations. Heat and cold are not opposite elements, they are simply two different states of one and the same matter. The spheres have likewise ceased to exist and their "movers" do not enter the order of astronomical explanation. The earth no longer is at the center of the universe. Last, and not the least in the Aristotelian perspective of an eternal universe, there would today be no problem as to what is setting it in motion. According to the law of inertia, it is no more difficult to account for motion than to account for rest. That which is moving continues to move in virtue of the same property of matter by which it remains at rest unless acted upon by some external force. At the level of purely scientific explanation, which was that of Aristotle, given that bodies are already in motion, no prime mover is required in order to account for this motion.[20]

It is therefore to be expected that, inasmuch as it sets into play one of several outdated scientific notions, the way of motion will have to undergo a measure of adaptation. The first thing to do, however, is to consider it such as it is; the reinterpretation or reconstruction it may require will then be taken into consideration.

b. The meaning of the proof

The initial sense experience that provides a starting point for the first way is that "in the world some things are in motion." This way is called the more manifest because nothing catches the eye and holds it more effectively than the sight of some change taking place or of some object moving from place to place. No scientific notion of movement is here at stake. The only fact required at the origin of the demonstration is the sense evidence that, under whatever form, there is motion in the universe. Even if it is sometimes deceived as to what is in motion, sense evidence is, by and large, a safe judge of the fact that there is motion, and so long as motion is observable anywhere in the world, the proof retains its necessary starting point. To repeat, the scientific notion of movement is not here at stake. The existence of movement is what counts; what the proof is about is an explanation of the very fact that motion is, or exists. In short, it seeks to find the *cause*, to explain *why* there is motion in the world.

The answer to this question must be taken from the only fact at our disposal; namely, motion itself. But there is no such thing as motion itself in itself. Motion is the condition of some thing, or being, that is actually moving. The concrete reality of motion is the moving thing itself. In order to describe what it is "to be moving" or "to be in motion," one must resort to two metaphysical notions designated by the terms "act" and "potency." These notions are difficult to grasp because of their very simplicity; but, precisely, it helps a great deal in understanding them if one realizes at once the reason they are so simple and the special nature of their simplicity. Act and potency add absolutely nothing to being. Being is act in virtue of the very fact that it is being. All that which is, is *act* inasmuch as it *is*. As to potency, it still is being, and therefore it still is act, but it is act considered in a state of possibility with reference to a still more complete actuality that it is capable of receiving.

The origin of these notions is our very experience of motion. In considering any given motion or change and in attempting to describe it, the mind immediately realizes that the subject of motion ("that which is moving") must be something that exists. Since, as has just been said, "to be," "actually to be," and "to be act" are one and the same thing, it is evident that the subject of any motion is something that already is in act to the precise extent that it is. On the other hand, "to move" or "to change" is always to acquire something that is lacking, be it only the place to which one is moving, or a certain quality whose possession seems to be desirable. This is why "motion" or "change" is often designated in philosophy by the common term "becoming."[21] For anything to become is to come to be. At first a certain thing is, but it is not yet all that it can be; then it begins to undergo a process of change at whose term the thing will have become that which it has been aiming to be. This process is motion itself. For it to take place there must obviously be a being susceptible of becoming still more actual than it is—that is, of being more than it is—and this is what is called "to be in potency." Potency is incomplete actuality considered in its aptitude to achieve a more complete state of actuality.

This analysis does not explain how such a process takes place, but it enables us at least to ask the question: what can be the cause that a being progressively becomes that which it can be, but is not? Since it is not yet what it is about to become, the changing being cannot be the cause of its own change. To say that it is would be tantamount to maintaining that it is giving to itself something that it does not have. Consequently, every motion, or change, is caused by something that already is what the subject of motion is about to become. Resorting to the technical terms already defined, we shall say that nothing can be brought from potency to act except by something that is in act.

An immediate corollary of this conclusion is that nothing can move itself. When this impossible thing seems to be happening, what really takes place is that one part of a certain being is moving another one, as the forward leg of a walking man is pulling the rest of his body ahead. To use once more the same technical language, let us say that one and the same thing cannot be both in potency and in act in the same respect and at the same time. Nothing is more evident, since to be both in act and in potency in the same respect would amount to being and not being in the same respect and at the same time. Once the identity of actuality and of being has been grasped, this conclusion follows in virtue of the principle of contradiction.

It is thus certain that "whatever is moved must be moved by another." It here matters little whether the thing that is being moved is one part of a whole, a whole, or a collection of whole objects subjected together to the same motion under the action of a single cause. On the contrary, it is important to decide in what direction the observer will look for an explanation of the process. Looking for it in the past, the observer will say that the thing that is now being moved is moved by something else, which itself has been set in motion by another, and so on indefinitely. At this early stage in our inquiry, we do not yet know whether the world has always existed, or whether there has been a beginning to its duration. According to the teaching of revelation, it is certain that the world has not always existed. Every Christian holds this truth on faith. Now, if the world has had a beginning, there is no reason that one should look for another proof of the existence of God. Only a creator can confer existence upon something that was not. This, however, is a theological inference based upon the faith of Christians in the word of God; it is not a philosophical argument. In order to limit itself to what can be affirmed on the strength of rational knowledge alone, our argument must therefore assume that the world has always existed. This is not to affirm its eternity, it is to construe the argument as we would do if we were certain that the world has always existed. The point is noteworthy in that it shows how careful the Christian philosopher must be to follow the straight rules of philosophical inquiry. If he does so in this case, the Christian philosopher will find himself at grips with this problem: supposing that there has been in the past an infinity of movers and of things moved, how is it that there has always been, and still is, a universe of beings incompletely in act and perpetually busy transmitting their own actuality to others or receiving it from them?

Understood in this sense, the problem under discussion is indifferent
to time. It can be asked for any moment of an eternally enduring universe such as the one that has just been described. Confronted with a
physical world innocent of motion and change, an observer could still
ask other questions about it. For instance, he could inquire into the
cause of its existence. But what is now at stake is simply the fact that,
in this universe of ours, motion is taking place. On the other hand, we
said that to be moving and/or to be moved are two modes of being.
The meaning of the question before us is therefore this: how can we
give a rational account of the presence of one of these two modes of
being in any given moment of time?

Since whatever is moved is moved by another, the question bears
upon a plurality of things that are simultaneously moving and being
moved. Their number may be large or small, it even may vary according to cases, but we need not worry about this point since the number
of the causes involved in the process is irrelevant to the question. Whatever their number, all the causes that simultaneously concur, bringing
about a certain change at one and the same moment of time, are really
constituting one single cause. This is true if their number is finite. For
if it were not finite, given that all the causes it contains are both moving
and moved at one and the same time, there still would be no single
cause to account for this whole structure of things in motion. In other
words, there would be no cause of which it can be said, appropriately
and without qualification, that it is *the* cause of the motions at stake.
On the contrary, one would have to go on to infinity in a series of things
each of which is both mover and moved. There would then be no first
cause of motion, the subsequent movers themselves could not move, and
there would be no motion at all. Therefore, there is a first mover; that is
to say, a mover that is absolutely first. All the other movers are moved
by it, and it is moved by no other one.

Having reached this point (the existence of a first mover), we have
established the major of the demonstration and the rest of the syllogism
can now be formulated in two propositions: If there is such a first mover,
it is what everyone understands by the name "God"; consequently,
there is a God.

This clearly shows the nature of what Thomas Aquinas calls a "way
to God." First of all, he does not pretend to have invented it. On the
contrary, it is essential for him that, having been discovered by a pagan
philosopher who knew nothing of a possible Christian revelation, this
demonstration borrows nothing from faith. Thomas Aquinas says: as

Christians, we know there is a God, but we would know this even though there were no Christian revelation. In fact, Aristotle was no Christian, and he knew it.

Second, the careful redaction of the *Summa Theologiae* can be read in terms of Aristotle's own cosmography (*i.e.*, a series of intermediate movers moving each one of the planetary spheres and moving one another from top to bottom), but the proof is not necessarily tied up with it. The proof applies to any universe wherein there is some change perceptible to sense.

On one major point, however, a difficulty arises. Why is it necessary to consider the movers and the things moved as hierarchically ordered? If they are not so ordered, there is no reason why the series of causes must be considered as finite, and why we must stop at a Prime Immobile Mover. This difficulty requires careful examination.

c. Interpretation of the first way

The source of the difficulty is easy to discover. It arises from the fact that, in Aristotle himself, the demonstration of the existence of a Prime Mover is inseparable from his own cosmography: the earth is at the center of the universe; around it a series of concentric spheres are moved by their own movers; at the top of the whole structure there is a single immovable Mover, cause of motion for all the rest. This close association of the proof with a certain system of physics was what invited the Thomistic commentator Bañes to say that an attempt to demonstrate the existence of God by means of another philosophy than that of Aristotle, besides being an error in physics or in metaphysics, would be temerarious with respect to faith![22] Nevertheless, since the system of the world professed by Aristotle has become untenable, Thomas Aquinas himself would not maintain it against scientific opposition.

This does not mean that the philosophical truth that Thomas saw in it has since ceased to be true. As it stands, the first way is borrowed from Aristotle and, substantially, from the interpretation of Aristotle's philosophy taught by Averroes. Let us remember what Thomas Aquinas is doing. In the *Summa Theologiae*, speaking as a theologian, he is presenting philosophical arguments to the effect that there is such a being as the one we call God. Some philosophers have already undertaken to prove this conclusion, among them Aristotle. Thomas offers to beginners in theology a simplified, though still a strictly conclusive, version of the proof; but the conclusion reached is one that can be established by such an argument; namely, a prime cause of all the movement there is in the universe. What Thomas himself does with this conclusion will be seen in due time; but the conclusion itself is exactly what interests him in the demonstration he is reporting. At this point, the proof of the Prime Mover means to Thomas Aquinas what the Prime Mover meant in the doctrine of Aristotle; but it does not occupy the same place, nor does it play the same part in the philosophy of Aristotle and in the theology of Thomas Aquinas. Consider.

First, in the metaphysics of Aristotle, there is no other formal proof of the existence of God than that of the Prime Mover.[23] If, in the mind of Thomas Aquinas himself, to accept this first way as conclusive would have made it difficult for him to accept any other one, he surely would have hesitated to burden his theology with it.[24] At any rate, he would not have given it a place of honor, as he did in his *Summa Theologiae* when he called it *prima et manifestior via:* "the first and more manifest way is the argument from motion." It is therefore at least probable that, while adopting it, Thomas Aquinas was reserving his own right to give it the meaning it should have in order to justify, not at all the natural theology of Aristotle, but the consequences that it was going to yield in his own theology.

A second reason invites one to think that even while restating the arguments of Aristotle for the existence of a Prime Mover, Thomas Aquinas could not possibly attribute to it the strict meaning it had in the philosophy of Aristotle. In what capacity does the Aristotelian Prime Mover move the universe? He does so inasmuch as he is, for the other intellectual substances, an object of love. The Aristotelian god does not move by causing, as an efficient cause, the movement there is in the world; he simply allows himself to be loved. The formulation of the proof, as given in the *Summa Theologiae*, is compatible with this interpretation; at least, it does not exclude it. On the other hand, Thomas does not say in what capacity the Prime Mover moves all the rest, so that, in the last analysis, he neither accepts nor rejects the Aristotelian sense of the interpretation. He only establishes the existence of a Prime Mover without saying in what sense he himself understands the notion of a moving cause. Such is not always the case. For instance, in the *Compendium Theologiae* where, significantly enough, he contents himself with only one proof for the existence of God, Thomas selects the way taken from motion, but this time he interprets it as proving the existence of an efficient cause of motion. This at least is suggested by his use of such expressions as "the stronger move the weaker," "the lower are set in motion by the higher," and particularly by his statement that "everything that is moved by another is a sort of instrument of the first mover."[25] In both the *Summa Contra Gentiles* and the *Summa Theologiae*, however, Thomas Aquinas deals with the moving cause and the efficient cause separately. It seems, therefore, to be his intention to propose to the reader two distinct ways to prove the existence of a God, a first one by way of moving causality only, and a second one by way of efficient causality only.

Interpreted in this literal way, the first way becomes independent of any scientific hypothesis as to the structure of the universe. The starting point is the existence of change. Change is possible only in beings whose actuality is incomplete, and its result always is either to add to their actuality or to subtract something from it. Now causality entails a relationship between two beings. The oft-repeated statement that nothing can move itself is taken as self-evident. It simply means that the contrary proposition is self-contradictory and literally unthinkable. The actuality of a being is one with its being; the degree of its actuality exactly measures that of its being; consequently, to say that something can add to its own being, or diminish it, is tantamount to saying that it has, or is, something it has not or is not. To be sure, a certain part of a being can act upon another part of the same being, but the same part cannot be, at once, cause and effect of itself. Thus understood, the starting point of the first way is the given existence of beings in a continuous state of change, none of which can be to itself the cause of its own becoming.

From the point of view of the natural sciences, such as astronomy, physics, or biology, this fact raises no problem. The object of science is to describe this world of change, or motion, such as the scientist finds it and, as the saying goes, to discover its "laws." For this reason a scientist is well founded in saying that, precisely *qua* scientist, he has no obligation to ask the problem of the existence of God. But science is far from constituting the totality of the knowledge accessible to the mind of any man, even to the mind of a scientist. The problems that escape the grasp of the methods used by the mathematical and experimental sciences do not cease to exist merely because they are not susceptible of scientific solutions. This is particularly true of the present problem. For science is not competent to deal with the origin of the universe whose nature it investigates; science simply takes the existence of the world for granted. Nevertheless, the existence of a world of change is in itself a problem, and it is up to the metaphysician to formulate the problem, to discuss it, and to solve it.

B. The way of efficient causality

The general intention of Thomas Aquinas in the whole article under examination is to establish the possibility of rationally demonstrating the existence of God, and he does this by showing that, in fact, several great philosophers have succeeded in demonstrating it. The first way was borrowed from Aristotle, in whose universe the true name of the cause of change, of motion, and hence of all generations and corruptions, was the *moving cause*. More exactly, Aristotle himself used to call it "the origin of motion." In the doctrine of Thomas Aquinas there is no real distinction between the moving cause and the efficient cause;[26] but Thomas found himself confronted with two different interpretations of Aristotle's doctrine, that of Averroes, according to whom the cause of motion really is the "moving cause" (*causa movens*), and that of Avicenna, according to whom there is, over and above the moving cause, a truly "efficient cause" (*causa efficiens, causa agens*).[27] In the doctrine of Thomas Aquinas, the moving cause can be the efficient cause of motion, but it can also be its final cause. For this reason, the "first way" can be read in a twofold manner. It can be interpreted as meaning that all beings are movers in virtue of their love of higher beings; they themselves are kept in motion by their love of the First Mover, who, because he is perfection itself, has no reason to move at all. Because he is to himself the object of his own love, the First Mover does not have to move in order to attain his own end; he is immobile, whereas all other beings are both moving and moved out of love of his perfection. But the same proof can be read in the language of efficient causality. This is how most modern readers spontaneously understand it. But *in his own exposition of the five ways*, Thomas Aquinas himself has specified the first way by attributing it to the order of the moving cause, whereas he has specified the second way by attributing it to the order of the efficient cause. The latter is the way we are now about to enter.

The second way is from the nature of efficient cause. In the world of sensible things we find there is an order of efficient causes. There is no case known (neither is it, indeed, possible) in which a thing is found to be the efficient cause of itself, for so it would be prior to itself, which is impossible. Now in efficient causes it is not possible to go on to infinity, because in all efficient causes following in order, the first is the cause of the intermediate cause, and the intermediate is the cause of the ultimate cause whether the intermediate cause be several or one only. Now to take away the cause is to take away the effect. Therefore if there be no first cause among efficient causes, there will be no ultimate, nor any intermediate, cause. But if in efficient causes it is possible to go on to infinity, there will be no first efficient cause, neither will there be an ultimate effect, nor any intermediate efficient causes, all of which is plainly false. Therefore it is necessary to admit a first efficient cause, to which everyone gives the name of God.[28]

The first point to be noted is that efficient causes are here considered as facts given in sense experience. In other words, we *see* that there are efficient causes.[29] This sensible experience of efficient causality consists in this, that we see some beings, or qualities of beings, follow from other beings, or qualities of beings. When we see that the presence of A is attended by that of B, we immediately perceive A as the cause of B. We also see why A is the cause of B. Whatever the objects or beings in question, everything proceeds as though A is giving B something that A has and that B has not. The simple and classical example of two billiard balls manifestly shows what we are talking about. If ball A is moving and ball B at rest, when ball A hits ball B, ball B begins to move; we then say that ball A is the efficient cause of the motion of ball B because ball A has communicated to ball B part of its own motion. Fire burns because it causes some combustible object to become fire and to burn in its turn.

The assertion that we perceive efficient causation by sense raises objections in the minds of modern philosophers. They say that causality always is an object of inference, such as this: the existence of B attends the existence of A, *therefore* A is the efficient cause of B. But (they add) nothing is less certain. It is the less certain as, immediately after saying that the affirmation of a relationship of efficient causality is an inference, the same philosophers begin criticizing it and undertake to show that such inference is not conclusive. From the fact that B follows A, these philosophers say, we cannot infer that A is the efficient cause of B. In a sense, their objection is valid. For A is not the cause of

B *because* the existence of B attends that of A; rather, the existence of B attends that of A for the reason that A is the cause of B. In short, the relationship of efficient causality is empirically given in sense experience. The abstract notions of cause and effect, along with the intellectual certitude that every change or becoming follows from some efficient cause, themselves follow from the immediate experience of causality exactly in the same way that all our judgments about existence and about being follow from the sense experience of existence and of being. This is how it is. Moreover, this is how it should be in a doctrine whose theory of knowledge rests on the certitude that nothing is in the intellect that was not first given in sense. The second "way," therefore, is justified in looking for its empirical basis in the sense experience of efficient causality.

This experience is that of an order. The efficient cause imparts something of its own being to that of the effect. We see this happening every time the presence of a certain being is attended by that of another being similar to the first one. This is the reason that the cause comes first, if not in time, at least in order. The notion of order is thus contained in the very notion of causality. Efficient causality itself *is* an order. Such is the meaning of the sentence: "In the world of sensible things we find there is an order of efficient causes," a statement which, in the mind of Thomas Aquinas, amounts to saying, as he presently does, that there is no possible case "in which a thing is found to be the efficient cause of itself." That "because of" which something else is must needs be different from it (otherwise, being cause of itself, the same thing would have already to be, in order to cause itself, before it could exist as its own effect). Let us therefore lay it down as a universal rule that each and every effect has for its efficient cause a being other than itself.

The same problem appears in connection with efficient causes that has already been discussed in connection with moving causes. To assign to each particular kind of effect its own particular kind of cause is the scientist's job. The question asked by the metaphysician arises beyond the order of physics and concerns the cause of the existence and operations of efficient causes in general. In order not to turn a concrete problem into an abstract one, let us rather say that what is at stake is the existence of efficient causes in the universe.

It is entirely possible that, in formulating his own argumentation, Thomas Aquinas himself had in mind the universe of concentric spheres described by Ptolemy. In such a view, the efficient causality exercised at the level of one of the spheres is accounted for by the efficient causality of the immediately higher sphere; moreover, the number of the intermediate spheres cannot be infinite because, were it so, there would be no first efficient cause and, consequently, there would be no intermediate causes nor any ultimate effects. In short, there would be no efficient causality at all. Now this is not true. Sense experience attests that there is efficient causality in the world; consequently, there must be a first efficient cause, and the number of the intermediate spheres must be finite, as astronomy says that it is.

The text of the *Summa Theologiae* does not explicitly appeal to this cosmography.[30] On the contrary, Thomas Aquinas once more carefully avoids all unnecessary entanglements in the science of his time. He does not mention the astronomical spheres, nor does he say anything about their number. On the contrary, in a passage well calculated to make us understand what he really is about, Thomas specifies that it does not matter "whether the intermediate cause be several, or one only." And indeed, if the problem at stake is to account for the existence of causality in the world, all the efficient causes taken together, whatever their number, can be considered as a single one. So long as none of them is the first efficient cause, the presence of efficient causality in the world remains unexplained.[31]

Such is the true meaning of the proposition that it is not possible to go on to infinity among efficient causes. When asked at this high metaphysical level, the question includes two terms only: on the one hand, all the efficient causes that are themselves caused by other efficient causes, and whose causality demands an explanation; on the other hand, the uncaused efficient cause that is the cause of all the others.[32] Since there are efficient causes, there is a first efficient cause. Thomas Aquinas presently adds: "to which everyone gives the name of God." Thus, for the second time, we ourselves can complete the argument. There is a first efficient cause; to be the first efficient cause is included in the meaning of the name of God; consequently, there is a God.

This second way differs from the first in many respects. By carrying the problem from the order of motion to that of efficient causality, it enables the metaphysician to ask a truly metaphysical question; namely: how is it possible that some beings are causes of other beings? Avicenna had clearly seen that, however we understand it, the notion of efficient causality participates, at least analogically, in the notion of creation. To be an efficient cause is to be a cause of being.[33] Guided by the same philosophical intuition, Avicenna had also seen that, in the precise case of efficient causality, it is indeed necessary that there should be a prime cause. Since all the intermediate causes, whatever their number, count only as one, the question of a hierarchy of causes does not arise. Causal efficiency is a fact experienced by sense knowledge.[34] To inquire into its possibility inevitably leads to positing a prime uncaused cause, and if there is such a cause, it certainly is one with the being we call God.

c. The way of possibility and necessity

Moving causality and efficient causality are not the only modes of being that require a philosophical explanation. Turning to another one, we can raise in different terms the problem of the existence of God.

> *The third way is taken from possibility and necessity, and runs thus. We find in nature things that are possible to be and not to be, since they are found to be generated and to be corrupted, and consequently it is possible for them to be and not to be. But it is impossible for them always to exist, for that which can not-be at some time is not. Therefore, if everything can not-be, then at one time nothing was in existence. Now, if this were true, even now there would be nothing in existence, because that which does not exist begins to exist only through something already existing. Therefore, if at one time nothing was in existence, it would have been impossible for anything to have begun to exist, and thus even now nothing would be in existence—which is absurd. Therefore, not all beings are merely possible, but there must exist something the existence of which is necessary. But every necessary thing either has its necessity caused by another, or not. Now it is impossible to go on to infinity in necessary things which have their existence caused by another, as has been already proved in regard to efficient causes. Therefore, we cannot but admit the existence of some being having of itself its own necessity, and not receiving it from another, but rather causing in others their necessity. This all men speak of as God.[35]*

The beginning of this third way can help us to understand what Thomas Aquinas considers an empirical starting point given in sense experience. For him, to start from possibility and necessity, two supremely abstract notions, really means to start from the visible fact that certain things are born and others die. In still other terms, it is to start from the fact that, for certain beings, it is possible to be and not to be. As in the cases of motion and of efficient causality, sense experience here means the apprehension of empirically given facts along with the notions and judgments through which we immediately conceptualize them. Such was the case with the two previous "ways." Certain sense perceptions are interpreted by the intellect in terms of motion and change (the first way), or else they are interpreted in terms of efficient causality (the second way); the same facts, or similar ones, will now be interpreted in terms of possibility and necessity.

Historically speaking, this means that Thomas Aquinas is once more calling upon the philosopher Avicenna[36] as a witness to the fact that the existence of God can be rationally demonstrated. The key notion in this proof is that of possibility in the order of being.

Starting from the fact that things come to be and pass away, which implies that it is possible for them to be and not to be, one can prove that the notion of a universe in which all things, without a single exception, would be merely possible is inconceivable without contradiction.

If the existence of a certain thing is merely possible, its non-existence likewise is possible, and we still are arguing on the premise that the world has always existed. Now, within a finite time, however long, a mere possibility may well not materialize. On the contrary, if it did not materialize during an infinite duration of time, it would not be a possibility at all. On the strength of these principles, one can say that if it has been merely possible from all eternity, there must have come a moment when a thing ceased to exist. But this applies to all merely possible things, singly and collectively. There should therefore have come a time when, given that all things ceased to exist, there was nothing in existence; and since what no longer is cannot bring itself back to existence, there still should be nothing in existence. Now this consequence is absurd, for there are things about which we are asking the question of their first cause; moreover, we ourselves must be existing in order to be able to ask the question. Consequently, the supposition that all beings are merely possible is an absurd one.

If not all beings are merely possible, some being must be necessary. Now, since it is impossible for one and the same thing to be and not to be at one and the same time, everything is necessary so long as it is. It is necessary so long as its cause makes it to be. This is called "to be necessary by another." In discussing the notions of motion and of efficient causality, we pointed out that one cannot go to infinity in the series of causes. For if all actually existing beings held their necessity from some other being, what there is of necessity in the world could not be accounted for. We must therefore admit the existence of a being that is necessary by itself; that is to say, a being which, having of itself its own necessity, is to others the cause of such necessity as they have. Whereupon, turning for the third time to "the meaning of the name," Thomas Aquinas observes that this being that is necessary by itself is "what all men speak of as God." Consequently, there is a God.

This third way has identically the same nature and structure as the previous two. It differs from them only in that it brings into play modalities of being that are, so to speak, practically identical with being *qua* being. The sense experience from which it starts is here translated into metaphysical terms nearly as abstract, and therefore as indefinable, as being itself. With good reason, Avicenna had observed that "thing," "being," and "the necessary" (*necesse*) are the very first notions formed by the human mind as soon as, through sense knowledge, it establishes contact with material things. And, indeed, being is necessary to the extent that it is. This is the philosophical point, too often overlooked by its readers, that confers upon the proof its true meaning. The third way does not consist in establishing that a necessary being is required in order to account for the possibility of the beings subject to generation and corruption, but rather in order to account for what they have of necessity (*i.e.*, of being) while they last. It will suffice to read again the end of the demonstration in order to place this point beyond doubt. The proof intends to show that one cannot go on to infinity in "necessary things" which have "their necessity" caused by another. Again, in reaching the conclusion of the proof, Thomas affirms the existence of a first necessary being causing in others *their* necessity. This point should be kept in mind, not only in interpreting the third way to God, but also in view of the time when, describing the nature of the created universe, Thomas Aquinas will attribute to its being an astonishing necessity.

D. The way of the degrees of perfection

The fourth way is taken from the gradation to be found in things. Among beings there are some more and some less good, true, noble, and the like. But more and less are predicated of different things according as they resemble in their different ways something which is the maximum, as a thing is said to be hotter according as it more nearly resembles that which is hottest; so that there is something which is truest, something best, something noblest, and, conse-

quently, something which is most being; for those things that are greatest in truth are greatest in being, as it is written in the Metaphysics. *Now the maximum in any genus is the cause of all in that genus, as fire, which is the maximum of heat, is the cause of all hot things, as is said in the same book. Therefore, there must also be something which is to all beings the cause of their being, goodness, and every other perfection, and this we call God.*[37]

In view of the many different interpretations proposed of this fourth way, it seems advisable to lay it down, as a sort of guiding rule of interpretation, that its nature should be conceived as similar to that of the preceding ways unless some compelling reason appears to attribute to it another one.

Like the first three ways, this fourth one starts from sense experience; namely, "the gradation to be found in things." For the fourth time, we are here provided with an opportunity to observe that what Thomas uses as a starting point is not a brute sense perception but, rather, an observable fact immediately susceptible of abstract formulation. The meaning of the words "more" and "less" is immediately intelligible to all, and all can quote without hesitation observable realities to which these two qualifications correctly apply.

A second remark is that we should not allow ourselves to be misled by some of the examples that are here quoted by Thomas Aquinas; namely, "true, noble, and the like." These expressions do not signify the truth of true judgments or the nobility attributed to certain beings by what is now called "judgments of value." What is here at stake is the good inasmuch as to be good is to be, and the truth inasmuch as to be true is a certain way of being. The question then simply is: are there, in fact, things given in experience as more or less good, more or less true, more or less noble, and the like? We are still looking for a metaphysical explanation of physically given modes of being.[38]

This remark is required for a correct understanding of the fourth way. Its meaning has been doubly obscured by the unfortunate choice of examples borrowed from the Aristotelian doctrine of the physical elements. Having to illustrate the truth that, in each particular order "more" and "less" are always predicated with reference to an absolute, Thomas Aquinas notes that a thing is said to be "hotter" according as "it more nearly resembles that which is hottest"; namely, "fire," which, being "the maximum of heat," is the cause that all hot things are hot. Such propositions as *fire is one of the four elements*, or else, *fire is the maximum of heat,* are meaningless from the point of view of molecular physics. This example can the more easily be discarded since, in the mind of Thomas Aquinas, it was no more than an illustration of a metaphysical truth for which no adequate example can be found in the physical world. This metaphysical truth is that, in any one of the many ways of being, "more" and "less" are predicated according as things more or less resemble absolute being.

If this is true, a new way lies open for us to the knowledge of the existence of God. That which is absolute in its own right is by itself that which it is. On the contrary, the reason that things are more or less good, true, noble, and the like, is that they more or less participate in goodness, truth, nobility, and so on. Consequently, it is in virtue of something absolutely good that all more or less good things are good, just as it is in virtue of something absolutely true that all more or less true things are true. But it has first been said that to be true, to be good, and to be noble are simply different ways of being. All the things that are said to be more or less any one of these perfections are therefore said to be more or less, and since they all are more or less inasmuch as they more or less participate in being, there necessarily must be a supreme being that is the cause that each and every thing that is, is a being. In Thomas' own words, "there must be something which is to all beings the cause of their being, goodness, and every other perfection." The rest of the argument can be foreseen. Coming back for its minor to the meaning of the name, Thomas adds, "and this we call God"; then he leaves it to us to conclude: therefore, there is a God.

In a sense, this fourth way can be said to be the deepest one from the point of metaphysical knowledge. Several excellent interpreters seem to have thought that it was specifically different from the previous ones because, in spite of the text of Aristotle that it quotes, it derives its inspiration from the Platonic doctrine of participation. But this is an excellent occasion for us to rid ourselves of the preconceived opinion that Thomas Aquinas has committed himself to following any particular philosophy implicitly, be it even that of Aristotle. It would be equally wrong to conceive him as practicing a sort of eclecticism, picking out of any philosophy those parts of it that happened to fit his own purpose. Thomas Aquinas considers philosophical doctrines from within the perspective of faith in revealed truth. This enables him to watch two or three different philosophies, each following its own method and making use of first principles in its own way, but all progressing toward one and the same truth. He himself has collected the results of these various efforts, and he has reformulated them so as to confer upon them a philosophical unity; but what matters to him is not the particular origin of each of the five ways; it is the philosophical value of each; in short, its truth.

We are fortunate in having at our disposal a remarkable passage of the Disputed Question *De Potentia*, q.3, a.5, wherein Thomas Aquinas reveals the various origins of the elements that go to the making of the fourth way. The question raised is whether there can be anything that is not created by God. The answer, of course, is in the negative. There is one universal cause by which all the rest has been produced. This is the teaching of the Catholic faith, "but it can be demonstrated in a threefold way." First, by showing that, if something is shared in common by several different beings, it must be caused in each by one single cause. "And this seems to have been the reason of Plato, who required, prior to all plurality, the existence of a certain unity, and this not only in numbers, but in the natures of things as well." Second, by showing that what is said to be more or less something in a certain order is said to be so because it is more or less near the unique term that is supreme in that order. Whereupon, quoting the same passage of the *Metaphysics* as in the *Summa*, Thomas concludes that one must posit "one being, that is to say, the most perfect and truest being, which, as has been proved by the philosophers, is an absolutely immobile mover and is most perfect. Whence it follows that all the less perfect beings must needs receive from Him their existence. And this is the proof of Aristotle in his *Metaphysics*."[39] Third, because all that which is by something else is reducible to something that is by itself. If there were a self-subsisting heat, it would be the cause of all hot things. Since there are many beings that are by something else, there must also be a being that is pure act and simple. "It is therefore necessary that all the other beings, which are not their own being, should hold it from this unique being by mode of participation. This is the argument of Avicenna in the *Metaphysics*, bk. VIII, ch.7, and bk. IX, ch.4."[40]

Read in the light of this passage, which is not a proof of the existence of God but contains at least three possible ones, the fourth way appears as the point of convergence of three distinct metaphysical efforts uniting, under our very eyes, in a common conclusion. From the point of vantage from which he is watching these efforts, the Christian philosopher sees them, so to speak, as a single effort to reach the prime cause of all things, starting from their degrees of perfection; that is, from their degrees in being. At the moment when it thus begins to move as freely in the mind of its readers as it moved in that of its author, the doctrine of Thomas Aquinas begins to be truly understood.

E. The way of purposiveness

The last way proposed by the *Summa Theologiae* is the simplest of all in the language it uses.

> *The fifth way is taken from the governance of the world. We see that things which lack knowledge, such as natural bodies, act for an end, and this is evident from their acting always, or nearly always, in the same way, so as to obtain the best result. Hence it is plain that they achieve their end, not fortuitously, but designedly. Now whatever lacks knowledge cannot move towards an end, unless it be directed by some being endowed with knowledge and intelligence, as the arrow is directed by the archer. Therefore some intelligent being exists by whom all natural things are directed to their end, and this being we call God.*[41]

We have entitled this demonstration "the way of purposiveness" because the fact that things act and operate as though they are aiming to achieve a certain end is the moving force of the argument. However, one must observe that Thomas Aquinas would rather call this fifth way a proof by the governance of the world. The appeal made by the proof to final causes ultimately aims to establish that all such causes presuppose the existence of an ultimate one which is the cause of all the teleological relations observable in the world.

For the last time, let us observe that the appeal to sense evidence goes far beyond brute sense perception. The starting point of the fifth way is the prima facie evidence that natural beings operate following a certain order and, as it seems, in view of certain ends. As a matter of fact, this is an overwhelming evidence. For, although objections can be raised as to the perfection of this universal order, its existence is guaranteed by the very fact that there are human beings, that they find themselves in a world in which life is possible, and, in fine, that there are philosophers thinking under such circumstances as make it possible for them to question the degree of perfection in the universal order. In saying that natural bodies act always, "or nearly always," in the same

way, Thomas himself gives us to understand that incidental exceptions
due to chance do not lessen the validity of the starting point.

It should also be noted that to be acting practically always in view of
a certain end is a certain way of *being*. Things whose operations are
directed to an end *are* not in the same way as being whose activities
(were such a supposition at all conceivable) would be purposeless and
disconnected. From this point of view, the fifth way is in no sense
different from the preceding ones: one of the modalities of being,
empirically given in sense experience, has to be accounted for by a
certain cause. What is this cause?

The data of the problem are simple. We are in a world in which by
far the greatest number of events and of activities exhibit a regularity
that cannot be the result of chance. On the other hand, an immense
number of these events and operations originate with beings that are
not endowed with knowledge. Consequently, the cause of the regularity,
order, and purposiveness present in the world is not to be found within
these beings themselves. There must therefore be, outside and above
the domain of these beings, some being "endowed with knowledge and
intelligence" by which they are directed toward their ends, "as the
arrow is directed by the archer." The end of the proof follows the
same pattern as the preceding ones. First, Thomas borrows his minor
from the meaning of the word "God" ("and this being we call God");
next, he leaves it to his reader to draw the conclusion: therefore, there
is a God.

The same proof is found in the *Summa Contra Gentiles*, formulated
in slightly different terms and directly concluding to the existence of
"someone by whose providence the world is governed, and whom we
call God."[42] In this work, the proof is attributed to John Damascene,[43]
but Thomas also attributes it to Averroes, at least as "hinted at" by
him. Assuredly, Averroes can be quoted as having taught a providence,
but he conceived it as limited to the order of the necessary and eternal
beings. It was therefore very different from the all-embracing Christian
providence. But John Damascene was a Christian writer and a theologian, and this time Thomas probably desired to have a non-Christian
philosopher to quote. Hence the slightly surprising presence of the
Commentator as a witness to the demonstrability of a providence ruling
the world.

No other text of Saint Thomas concerning the existence of God compares in importance with the article of the *Summa Theologiae* we have
been examining. It discloses five different ways to God and reduces them

all to the unity of the same structure: an empirical starting point discovered in the observation of a certain mode of being found in nature, a proof of the fact that the cause of the said mode of being cannot be found within natural things themselves, the necessity of affirming the existence of a prime cause whose actual existence is the only conceivable cause of the existence, within nature, of the mode of being under discussion. Four of these ways establish that it is not possible to go on to infinity in the series of intermediate causes. The fifth does not do so, perhaps for the sake of brevity, more probably because, since the starting point of the demonstration is the presence of regularity, order, and purposiveness in non-knowing beings in general, the necessity of ultimately positing a single providence for the whole world is immediately evident.

F. **The meaning of the five ways**

The problem of the existence of God is among the last that a metaphysician has to raise. On the contrary, a theologian meets it at the very beginning of his inquiry. One can even maintain that, strictly speaking, to prove the existence of God is not a necessity for a theologian. God Himself has spoken. He has revealed His existence to man in a thousand ways, but never more explicitly than when, speaking to Moses, God said to him: *I am Who am (Exod. 3:14)*. Thomas Aquinas has been careful to recall this decisive passage of Scripture in his *Summa Theologiae*[44] immediately before proceeding to his own exposition of the five ways to prove that God exists. Even before knowing God's existence as a philosophical conclusion, we know it on the strength of our faith in the word of God. This accounts for the fact that, in his *Commentary on the Sentences* of Peter Lombard, Thomas did not think it necessary explicitly to ask the question *whether God exists?* On the contrary, in his later theological works, the *Summa Contra Gentiles*, the *Summa Theologiae*, and the *Compendium Theologiae*, Thomas has given one or more demonstrations of the truth that God exists. His reason for doing so is obvious. *Scholastic* theology cannot remain indifferent to the first questions likely to be asked by men seeking to understand what they believe. If it is possible to *know* there is a God, no scholastic theologian can remain indifferent to the problem of how such knowledge is to be achieved.

In asking the question, however, a theologian cannot overlook the fact that this is essentially a philosophical question. Philosophers formulated the problem, discussed its data, and gave it one of several answers centuries before the beginning of the Christian era, and did so without even having any knowledge of the revelation contained in the Old Testament. In the perspective adopted by Thomas Aquinas, the correct answer to the question, *Whether it can be demonstrated that God exists?* is yes, the existence of God can be demonstrated from His effects. As a matter of fact, it has been demonstrated in several different ways and by several different authors, Christian or not. Hence, in the *Summa Contra Gentiles* the expressions used by Thomas Aquinas to introduce the arguments in proof of the existence of God: "We shall therefore proceed to set forth the arguments by which both philosophers and Catholic teachers have proved that God exists."[45]

Taken literally, these words imply that Thomas Aquinas simply borrowed from others a certain number of proofs that he himself considered rationally valid. Accordingly, historians have tried to discover the sources from which Thomas Aquinas derived his demonstrations. One of these sources, at least, is a certitude. Aristotle has provided Thomas Aquinas with his proof of the existence of a Prime Immovable Mover. Avicenna, too, has been put to good use, as has Moses Maimonides, John Damascene, and perhaps other ones whom we do not know. The investigation of this problem is of great historical importance and it even can throw some light on the philosophical meaning of the five ways or of some of their elements.

In the use of such historical information, however, two important points should be kept in mind. First, Thomas Aquinas did not merely reproduce the proofs that he borrowed from philosophers. Even in the case of the long Aristotelian proof of the existence of the Prime Mover, such as it is found in the *Summa Contra Gentiles,* Thomas submitted the borrowed material to a thorough reinterpretation. Completely Aristotelian, this demonstration is nowhere to be found in Aristotle under the precise form it received from Thomas Aquinas. Second, precisely because Thomas Aquinas has drawn on several different philosophies for the formulation of his proofs, one should not attempt to consider them as five complementary moments of one single demonstration. Each proof is valid in itself with respect to its particular conclusion; and, from every one of these five conclusions, what the human reason is able to know of the nature of God is something that can be demonstrated.

At this point it becomes a question to know in what sense Thomas Aquinas made these demonstrations his own. To be sure, since he presented them as five demonstrations, he must have considered all five of them as validly conclusive. On the other hand, is it certain that each of the various philosophers from whom Thomas Aquinas borrowed one of his proofs would have subscribed to the other four proofs? This is no easy question to answer, and no one can be sure that he is answering it in the proper way. Nevertheless, it is necessary to ask it if we want to achieve a reasonable interpretation of the authentic position of Saint Thomas on the question. The very meaning of the use made of philosophy in his theology is at stake.

As a theologian, Thomas Aquinas does not need to prove the existence of God. If a proof is required, he can provide it, but, absolutely speaking, since theology is about God, it takes the existence of its subject for granted. In the commentary of Thomas Aquinas on the *Sentences* of Peter Lombard, there are no proofs of the existence of God explicitly presented as such.

Moreover, as a theologian, Thomas Aquinas knows that philosophers have, in fact, proved the existence of the being all name "God," but he does not expect philosophers to prove the existence of the very God Who is the subject of his own theology. This point has been forcibly stressed by Bañes: "All these arguments, taken together, do not immediately and explicitly prove that God exists (*Deum esse*), and much less that God is that most perfect being than which nothing more perfect can be conceived (for the proof of this point is being reserved for the following questions); but they most efficaciously prove that, in nature, there are found certain perfections and properties (prime mover, prime cause, necessary being, etc.) that can belong to no one else than to God; therefore, virtually and implicitly, these arguments prove the existence of God. For the first argument proves that there is in nature a prime immovable mover, and the other arguments efficaciously prove other properties, which can belong to God alone."[46]

A third point worthy of note is the sovereign indifference exhibited by Thomas Aquinas toward a classic difficulty then dividing the philosophers. We have already mentioned the problem. It was to know who is in charge of proving the existence of God, the physicist or the metaphysician (*i.e.*, the theologian)? According to Avicenna, the existence of the Prime Being is demonstrated in metaphysics. Starting from the operations of the Prime Being and arguing from the respective properties of possible being and necessary being, the metaphysician establishes the existence of the *Primus*. On the contrary, Averroes maintains that the existence of the Prime Cause can be proved only by the physicist. The import of the doctrine is a far-reaching one, for if

Averroes is right, there can be no other demonstration of the existence of God than the proof that there exists a Prime Mover. All the other so-called demonstrations are mere probabilities.[47]

From the point of view of philosophical knowledge properly so called, this was a decisive issue. The two contradictory positions cannot be upheld by the same philosopher at one and the same time. In fact, the philosopher Siger of Brabant was to uphold the position of Averroes, and his proofs of the existence of God were to be physical; the theologian John Duns Scotus was to follow the position of Avicenna, and his own proofs were to be metaphysical. Duns Scotus has explicitly given the reasons for his choice, exactly as Averroes went to the trouble of justifying his own. Thomas Aquinas goes his own way as though this is not a problem. One cannot even say that he has chosen both positions. First, he proves the existence of God as Prime Mover following the example of both Aristotle and Averroes. Later on he follows the way of Avicenna without so much as mentioning the fact that the argumentation is becoming more metaphysical than physical. True enough, Thomas cleverly makes all his arguments look Aristotelian and therefore physical; the fact remains, however, that he is maintaining as compossible, and even as mutually complementary, proofs of the existence of God inspired by philosophies that were not only different but in declared opposition on this point. All the facts fall into place, on the contrary, if we suppose that all this was a theological inquiry into the results obtained by the philosophers, conducted by a theologian in view of his own theological end.

A short discussion of the import of the first two ways of proving there is a God will throw some light on the meaning of the present question. The first way, Thomas says, and the more manifest, is the way of motion. The second way is taken from the nature of the efficient cause. It has been asked by excellent Thomists whether there is any difference between these two ways. And indeed the question may well be asked, for to prove that there is a prime immovable cause of motion, or change, does not seem very different from proving that there is a first efficient cause. All things come to be by way of motion; hence the first moving cause is also the first efficient cause, and *vice versa*.

This is true, but precisely it is true if we interpret the first way and the second way in the light of the doctrine of Saint Thomas Aquinas. From his point of view, the efficient cause and the moving cause are one and the same. More precisely, moving and causing are for him one and the same thing; so much so that, in his language, the expressions *causa movens, causa agens,* and *causa efficiens* are interchangeable. The moving cause is the efficient cause in those cases when the effect is motion; inversely, the efficient cause is a moving cause inasmuch as, in the order of natural causality, to move is for it the only way to exercise its causal efficacy. In short, from the point of view of Saint Thomas himself, there is no real difference between the first two ways. To prove the existence of a prime mover and to prove the existence of a prime efficient cause is to prove one and the same conclusion.[48]

It then becomes a question to know why Thomas Aquinas has proposed these two ways successively and as two distinct proofs. The answer is that, since Thomas himself was restating proofs already given, as to their essentials, by some philosophers and Christian teachers, he was here following these thinkers in their own approaches to the problem. To limit ourselves to the first two ways, it can be said that, even under the completed form Thomas Aquinas has given it in the *Summa Contra Gentiles,* the proof by the moving cause would be accepted by Averroes, but Averroes would accept no other proof. The distinction between the two orders of motion and of efficient causality is as foreign to his own doctrine as it is to that of Aristotle. Today every reader of Saint Thomas understands the *prima via* as if it dealt with the efficient cause of motion, whereas, in the mind of Aristotle himself, the Prime Mover moves as final cause. This spontaneous transposition has had for its effect to render the first way practically useless; it then becomes one with the proof by the efficient cause whenever the effect at stake is motion.

Similar remarks have already been made with respect to the third way. Either directly or indirectly through the intermediary of Moses Maimonides, the demonstration rests upon notions borrowed from Avicenna's metaphysics. But one must make a choice. If the correct proof of the existence of God is that of Aristotle as interpreted by Averroes, the proof inspired by Avicenna becomes vulnerable to criticism. Averroes has often criticized Avicenna, and we know very well that the fundamental notions of their philosophies are not the same; so much so that we cannot favor the philosophy of Averroes in order to justify the *prima via* and then favor the philosophy of Avicenna in order to justify the *tertia via.*[49]

The endless controversies about the fourth way,[50] as well as the differences of opinion as to its philosophical value, sufficiently indicate that its insertion in the general scheme of the metaphysics of Saint Thomas raises perplexing difficulties. To be sure, these difficulties are not insuperable; still, they are there. Despite the clever use made by Thomas of a principle of Aristotle, it is difficult not to concede that an influence foreign to the true spirit of the Philosopher is here at work. Aristotle did indeed say that "the maximum in any genus is the cause of all in that genus," but he never applied this principle to being itself. In an eternal and uncreated universe such as his, becoming, not being, is what needs to be accounted for.

No such problem arises in connection with the fifth way, which is taken from the purposiveness observable in the universe. In the *Summa Contra Gentiles,* as we have seen, Thomas himself presents it as an argument proposed by Saint John Damascene. It can, indeed, be found in his *De Fide Orthodoxa.* Still, as if he wished to make things more complicated for us, Thomas presently adds that Averroes hinted at the argument.[51] Let us not enter the maze of the discussions among his interpreters, who want to know whether, and up to what point, Aristotle and Averroes really taught a doctrine of the divine providence. There certainly is a sense in which they did, but the name of John Damascene is enough to remind us of the Christian sense in which this notion is being here understood by Thomas Aquinas. In this instance, as in the previous ones, a Christian notion is present behind arguments borrowed from even non-Christian philosophers.

It is a striking fact that, although not one of the five ways seems directly to lead to the God of Saint Thomas Aquinas, one feels behind each and every one of them the presence of his notion. It may not be easy or even possible to encompass all these demonstrations within the limits of one philosophy, but one cannot read them without feeling that they all are true, and not only possible but also compossible as well as mutually complementary when seen from the point of view of a higher type of knowledge. In more simple terms, any Christian reader of Thomas Aquinas immediately realizes that the Prime Mover is the same as the Prime Efficient Cause, which, in turn, is the one and unique Necessary Being and thereby the Supreme Being, cause of all other beings as well as their ultimate end. It may well be that not one of the various philosophies exploited by Thomas Aquinas is able to justify these conclusions in the sole light of its own principles, but they all become fully satisfactory in the light of a certain notion exclusively proper to Thomism; namely, the notion of being which, understood in the fullness of its Thomistic meaning, is one with the notion of God. And indeed the God of Saint Thomas is, at once, the Prime Mover, the Prime Efficient Cause, the only Necessary Being that is necessary by itself, the supreme Being *qua* Being, and the Universal Providence of all beings without exception. He is all this in virtue of the fact that He is the very being He is. There is no other doctrine than that of St. Thomas, philosophical or theological, Christian or otherwise, in which God deserves all these names, understood in the infinite fullness of their intelligible meaning.

If this be true, each one of the five ways, conclusive as it is in its own way within the particular doctrine from which it derives its inspiration, assumes its complete significance only when it is interpreted in terms of the doctrine of Saint Thomas himself. Precisely when, at a later stage in the *Summa Theologiae*, the Thomistic notion of the Christian God finally attains the fullness of its determination, each particular proof appears at once as intimately related to all the other ones. There still are five ways, each of them sufficient and complete in its own order, but their conclusions then seem to merge. They no longer lead the mind, the one to the god of Aristotle, another one to that of Plato or of Avicenna; they all immediately lead to the unique and true God of Christianity, Who is the God of Saint Thomas Aquinas.

This is to say that the five ways of Saint Thomas are not given their full meaning until we understand what they meant to the Angelic Doctor himself. Each one of them brings us nearer to a certain notion of God which it does not quite reach, but which it enables us to form at the price of a further philosophical effort; after it is formed, this notion of God works backward, so to speak, retroactively illuminating the meaning of the ways that have led us to it. This interpretation unavoidably raises difficulties to minds unacquainted with the Thomistic notion of theology or oblivious to its meaning. They forget that, even when he is handling philosophical problems, a theologian after the heart of Thomas Aquinas considers them as included under a higher formal object and sees them in a higher light.

This may be the proper time to remember the comparison made by Saint Thomas of sacred doctrine and the "common sense." Comparisons should not be carried too far. Theology is a science, not a sense. The five ways are not five different modes of sense knowledge, they are five rational demonstrations. Still, a certain analogy is rightly suggested by this very bold image. Because of its higher generality, theological knowledge perceives as related and as mutually complementary data that philosophical speculation knows as unrelated or even as heterogeneous. The *sensus communis* does not perceive sounds as colors, or tastes as odors; on the contrary, it perceives their differences, but, at the same time, it perceives these distinct qualities as united in certain substances. A soft, sweet-scented and pink leaf may be a rose petal; only the *sensus communis* can perceive these sense qualities as distinct, yet given together in one single object. Similarly, because he knows each proof of the existence of God under a higher formal character, the theologian perceives the five ways in their philosophical differences, but, at the same time, he sees them all as different determinations of one and the same object. A rose petal is not its color only, or its scent, or its softness, it is that which unites in itself all these qualities and many others. It can likewise be said that God is not the Prime Mover only, nor is He simply the Prime Cause or the Ultimate End; God is He Whose proper name includes the preceding ones, plus an infinity of other names, each of which has to be learned from the consideration of some particular aspect of reality experienced by man.

Chapter 4. Metaphysical approaches to the knowledge of God

To meditate is to apply one's own mind to the close and prolonged examination of a certain thought or train of thought. The notion seems to have been first formed in connection with the theological consideration of particularly lofty and recondite truths about the divinity. It was also applied to the mental contemplation of religious truths practiced as an essential requirement for the progress of the spiritual life. It is noteworthy that philosophy began to make use of the name at the very moment it decided to cut loose from theology. The *Metaphysical Meditations* of Descartes have been the first notable instance of a philosophical inquiry conceived after the pattern of a spiritual contemplation of the primary notions and truths conceived by the human mind.

The inquiry itself, however, was far from unknown to the scholastic theologians. So long as scholasticism survived as a scientific approach to theological truth, it necessarily preserved the contemplative habit familiar to minds accustomed to make God the constant object of their reflections. When scholasticism degenerated into a method of disputation, the stress was put on a certain acquired cleverness in the use of dialectical argument, which, although it was very useful in itself, invited its students to *start from* the first principles rather than to *dwell upon* them in view of deepening their interpretation. The time has now come for minds still interested in the acquisition of metaphysical wisdom to recapture the meaning of a fruitful method of philosophical investigation.

Once more, it is a fact that a theologian can help us toward a better understanding of some of the characteristics proper to metaphysical knowledge. Apart from the Thomistic proofs of the existence of God examined in the preceding chapter, many passages are found in his writings dealing with the possibility and nature of other approaches to the knowledge of God. Some are found in the *Summa Theologiae*, quite a few in the *Summa Contra Gentiles*, others in the *Disputed*

Questions, and even in the commentaries on Holy Scripture. The most famous among them appears in the early tract of the Saint, *On Being and Essence.* In short, they can be met in the most unexpected places. Some of them are better known than the rest because various interpreters of Thomas Aquinas have used them as supplementary proofs of the existence of God. Thomas Aquinas himself has done so with one or two of them. As has been noted, what is given as one of the "five ways" in the *Summa Theologiae* can be used in another work by the Master as a demonstration of the eternity of God, as a proof that there is nothing that has not been created by God; in short, in support of a variety of other conclusions.[1] Paradoxically enough, the most general way to characterize this class of passages is to say of all of them that it is difficult to know whether or not they intend to prove the existence of God. As will be seen, they all lead the mind to the conclusion that there is something that is prime in a certain order, and, in this respect at least, they very much resemble any one of the five ways; but, on second thought, it appears that their emphasis is less on the existence of the prime cause than on its nature. This point requires some elucidation.

One of the characteristics of the five ways, such as they were interpreted in the preceding chapter, is their apparent unconcern with the exact nature of their respective points of arrival. So long as the prime cause, to whose existence one of the five ways concludes, cannot possibly not be the being we call God, no further question is raised. That is, none is asked at that precise moment; but it is already clear that, sooner or later, the question will have to be asked. It cannot be a matter of indifference to know whether God's most proper name is the Prime Mover, or the Prime Efficient Cause, or, again, the Prime Being, the Necessary Being, or the Universal Providence of the world. Are all these names equally proper names of God? Do they all designate Him as that which He is first and foremost? A large part of the literature devoted to the five ways has had for its object to elicit from the ways answers to questions they were not intended to solve, still less to ask. Their only object was to prove the existence of a being which, if he does exist, can be none other than the one whom we call God. Since they all conclude equally in the affirmative, the five ways are strictly equivalent. This is precisely what allowed Thomas Aquinas to borrow his different proofs from different philosophies without, at the moment, going to the trouble of establishing their mutual compatibility.

It becomes imperative to do so, on the contrary, as soon as the problem of the nature of God is singled out for particular consideration. Ways to God that are equivalent as equally leading to the demonstrated knowledge of His existence cease to be equivalent when seen as so many ways leading to the knowledge of His nature. Some of them can take us nearer than others to the determination of the true essence of God, or, to use the traditional designation of the problem, to the knowledge of the "proper name of God." All the passages in which Thomas seems to be carrying on a sort of metaphysical meditation on the nature of God belong among these philosophical determinations of the divine essence. Had the existence of God not yet been demonstrated, most of them could be used as proofs of the conclusion that there is a being, known to all as God, whose actual existence is beyond doubt. Still, this is not what they are intended to prove by their author. Considerations of this sort have for their proper object to answer the question: What is God? From this point of view, the five ways are far from being equivalent.[2]

The method followed by Thomas Aquinas in the discussion of this problem deserves careful attention. As he himself understands it, the object of theology is to achieve a scientific understanding and formulation of the object of faith. This cannot be done without resorting to the resources provided by philosophy. But philosophy is not something to be created *ex nihilo* by the theologian; it exists, and the first thing to do, if one intends to use it as the handmaid of theology, is to investigate it from the twofold point of view of its method and its conclusions. This is the reason why, before defining a theological position, Thomas often proceeds to a general survey of the philosophical issues involved. Using the history of philosophy as a means to his own end, he seems to consider the successive efforts of various philosophers (or schools of philosophy) to answer a certain problem as a sort of collective philosophical undertaking whose conclusions are at the disposal of the theologian to criticize, to redress, to complete, and finally to incorporate within his own theological inquiry. This fundamental character of the theology of Saint Thomas is too often overlooked. Having always seen philosophical progress as cumulative, he often conceived his own function as that of a theological arbiter of philosophical doctrines. For this very reason, he often practiced a kind of theological criticism of the data provided by the history of philosophy. One can also call this a critical history of philosophy conducted in the light of the divine revelation.

The main object of this kind of investigation is to determine how far different philosophies, working in the natural light of reason alone, have advanced on the road to truth. This cannot be done by looking at them from the outside. On the contrary, the theologian who undertakes this task is committing himself to a complex effort of information, of metaphysical meditation, and of theological judgment. He has to recapitulate, so to speak, by accompanying it from within, the pilgrimage of the human mind in quest of the true notion of God.

I. MATERIALISTIC SCIENTISM

As Saint Thomas Aquinas understands it, the history of philosophy is in fact a philosophy of its own history. To him, the historical order of succession among doctrines has its cause in the very mode of the acquisition of human knowledge. That there has been progress in the conquest of truth is a fact. In Thomas' own words, "The ancient philosophers gradually, and as it were step by step, advanced in the knowledge of truth."[3] This is a lesson our theologian learned from Aristotle, who, placed almost at the origin of philosophical inquiry, already considered himself as benefiting by the accumulated efforts of his predecessors.

In his *Metaphysics*, Aristotle recalls that to know a thing is to recognize its first cause.[4] In other words, our understanding does not stop asking the question "why" about anything until it gets the answer after which there is nothing more to ask. Of course the level of the answer depends on the level on which the question has been asked. This is a fact that dominated the whole discussion of the problem. It has dominated it in the past, it still dominates it today. Most metaphysical disagreements are due, not to any flaws in the definition of ideas, or to any inconsistencies in argumentation, but rather to the different levels of reality on which different philosophers are asking their questions.

This diversity is itself an irreducible fact. Some metaphysicians either refuse to ask certain questions or else they refuse to ask them above a certain level beyond which it seems to them that all is incertitude. The motives that prompted the early philosophers to interpret reality as they did are still at work in our own day. According to Thomas Aquinas, there is an order in the acquisition of knowledge; hence, naturally, the first philosophers found it easier to stop their inquiry after the first step. Many of their successors still do. They stop at the consideration of what Thomas called the sensible accidents of bodies, because knowledge begins with sensations, and the objects of sensations are precisely sensible qualities, such as color, size, shape, weight, and motion and change of all types. The immediate evidence of sense knowledge, its universal accessibility, the ease with which one man's experience can be checked against that of another man—everything invites the philosopher to stay there and not to overstep this level before investigating its practically infinite possibilities.

Aristotle had already remarked, in fact, that to do so is tantamount to accounting for reality in terms of matter alone. And indeed, all these sensible qualities are material qualities, so that, following this view, the sole and universal cause is the material cause. Another way to say the same thing is to say that *matter* is the substance of all things. And indeed, to posit a substance is enough to account for its accidents; consequently, to consider anything as a material substance should make it possible, after due investigation, to account for all its accidents.

One well-known feature of the philosophy of Aristotle is that, at this level, he himself deemed it enough to explain the sensible appearance of bodies by elementary qualities and combinations of qualitatively constituted elements. This qualitative physics has been replaced, since the seventeenth century (Francis Bacon, René Descartes), by a physico-mathematical interpretation of phenomena according to which quantity has become the chief principle of explanation. The amazing practical fecundity of the physico-mathematical method has ensured its success, but even from the properly speculative point of view the kind of knowledge procured by this method has proved perfectly fitted to the nature and character of human understanding. The kind of knowledge in which sense data are given an intelligible meaning, as is the case with modern physics, provides the human mind with a set of tangibly or visibly verifiable conclusions. Only the scientist in whose mind a certain truth about nature is shining for the first time knows what it is truly to know. The joys of scientific discovery are not the noblest of joys, because the objects of scientific knowledge are not the noblest conceivable objects, but they surpass in intensity all the other joys of natural knowledge, because their object is the most perfectly proportioned of all to the natural aptitude of the human mind.

It is small wonder then if today, as in the early days of Presocratic speculation, so many excellent minds refuse to ask questions about reality beyond the level of matter. Still, such questions must be asked, because they unavoidably arise in all minds speculating about nature in a scientific way. Scientists well know that there probably will be no end to the progress of scientific investigation, but this is not the present point. Scientific investigation itself, considered in its existence and in its very possibility, is what is here at stake. Matter is a sufficient principle of explanation so long as its very intelligibility is taken for granted. But why should it be taken for granted? The very same movement that first prompted man to investigate the properties of material substances will unavoidably lead him to wonder about the conditions that made such an investigation possible. Everything is scientifically intelligible in science, except its very intelligibility.

The philosophical affinity between the early philosophies of those whom historians aptly call the Presocratic "physicists" and the attitude of modern scientism can be seen from their common indifference to the problems of efficient causality. "Indifference" is not to say enough; "hostility" would better describe their attitude, for if matter is supposed to account for everything else, matter itself cannot possibly be accounted for. To such philosophers, when questions cannot be answered, they must not be asked. Such a materialistic outlook thus leads us to ignore in reality all that which cannot be accounted for in terms of material substances and of material accidents, including the very existence of the material substance and its accidents. In this view of the world, Thomas says, one is practically obliged to deny that matter has a cause and totally to disregard problems of efficient causality.[5]

II. THE CAUSE OF SUBSTANTIAL MUTATIONS

An important advance was achieved when, in the course of time, some philosophers raised their investigation above the level of material causality. They realized that even material substances cannot be purely material. A substance is such because of a substantial form. Accordingly, these philosophers refused to account for physical transmutations only by means of accidental modifications of matter; they traced them to the presence of forms succeeding one another in matter. Naturally, they had to assign a cause for this perpetual exchange of forms in matter, and the cause had to be immaterial, as form itself is. Thus, Anaxagoras posited Intellect (*nous*) as the cause of these substantial transmutations, a notion which, moreover, made it possible to account for the very order according to which these changes in form seemed to take place. Others invoked other causes. For instance, Empedocles considered substantial changes as caused by Friendship and Discord; that is to say, by forces of attraction and repulsion. In our own day, a similar view of reality can be found in the somewhat adventurous, but often suggestive, meta-scientific theories that ascribe to some trans-physical energy the succession of natural forms in the world. While the dialectical materialism of Marxism might serve to illustrate materialistic scientism, the various forms of evolutionism (from Spencer to Bergson and Teilhard de Chardin) can be considered modern equivalents of the Presocratic doctrines of Anaxagoras and Empedocles.

Compared with materialism, such positions are considerable advances toward a complete explanation of reality. Whatever principle they may choose to invoke, they are bound to conceive it as a cause, and even as a universal cause of all the substantial transmutations that take place in the world. This is particularly clear in the case of such modern doctrines as those of "emergent evolution," of "creative evolution," and in the various forms of "vitalism" whose ultimate purpose is to account for physical change, including its apparent purposiveness, by means of one single universal cause.

Nevertheless, the limitation of even this second point of view is apparent. However impressive these universal views of natural change may be, they stop at the explanation of substantial becoming; that is to say, at the generation and corruption of substances, as well as the order according to which these changes take place. They leave out the ultimate problem of the cause of the very being of these substances. In the mind of Thomas Aquinas, a sure sign that a doctrine does not go beyond the problem of substantial change is that, in it, the existence of matter itself is not accounted for.

This is an important point to remember in evaluating certain modern interpretations of universal evolution that consider themselves either as easily reconcilable with Christian theology or even as being themselves Christian theologies scientifically formulated. All such views of the world presuppose a given reality whose mutations they explain, but for whose existence they do not account. These remarks do not mean that the cosmic hypotheses formulated by certain scientists at the end of their properly scientific speculation are of no value. Far from it! Such scientific extrapolations are often helpful in orientating experimental research. As to the metaphysician, or even the theologian, he should always be ready to listen to what contemporary science has to say concerning a universe the knowledge of which is the only valid starting point for his quest of God. It is literally true that the amazing progress achieved by science since the time of Copernicus and Galileo has provided philosophers with an incomparably better field of metaphysical reflection than the rather simplified universe of the Greeks. Still, so long as it moves within the limits of a *given* universe, philosophical reflection has not yet reached the level of metaphysical knowledge. The remark made on this point by Thomas Aquinas is of decisive importance. Science deals with beings as *such*-and-*such* beings; metaphysics deals with them as *beings*.

III. THE CAUSE OF BEING

With Plato, Aristotle, and their successors, philosophy crossed a threshold in its quest of the prime cause of reality. Beyond the cause of accidental mutations and beyond that of substantial mutations, these philosophers raised their consideration up to the cause of beings *qua* beings; that is, to the cause in virtue of which beings *are*. We have here an excellent opportunity to observe the Christian philosopher at work. Among all the doctrines he might choose to consider as useful for his own work, Thomas Aquinas retains only those that aim to discover the Prime Cause of being as such. Plato, Aristotle, and their successors deserve to be singled out for particular consideration, because the ultimate conclusion of their philosophies was that there exists a cause of the totality of being. Here, again, an advance can be observed in the discussion of this problem. We all know what being is, at least in an empirical way, and we all could attempt a sort of verbal pointing out of its notion; but to penetrate its depth has taken metaphysicians a long time: in fact, it has taken many centuries, and even today not all minds are equally prepared to grasp its ultimate meaning. The history of philosophy will help us in our philosophical effort by placing before us, under the concrete form of actually existing doctrines, the three decisive moments of this metaphysical quest of God.

A. Being and unity

The name of Plato figures in this meditation as a sign. It does not invite an archaeological study of the works of the father of Western philosophy, but rather it points out a direction for the reflection to follow. Within the wealth of philosophical themes accumulated in the writings of Plato, there is none more characteristic of his thought than the notion of "unity." To have identified its meaning and importance as a problem was for Plato to have bequeathed us much more than a simple definition. The part played by unity in human thought is an eternally puzzling one. Since it is implied in the very use of the mind, no man can think, know, or speak without acting as though this notion held for him no secret; even so, it is a most secret one. The difference between the metaphysician and other men does not consist in his having found the word in the riddle; only, he has had the intellectual courage to face the riddle.

The name of Plato evokes at once the doctrine of Ideas. The function of these archetypes is, above all, to account for a disconcerting character of the objects given in sense experience. They are multiple without being mere multiplicity. Language itself bears witness to this truth. Of their nature, names point out given individuals, but, at the same time, they are virtually capable of pointing out an unlimited number of other individuals more or less similar to the first one. The very structure of language thus raises the problem of the relationship of the one and the many. It shows that experienced reality is, in fact, a multiplicity graspable as a unity. Plato's answer to the problem was that many individuals participate in the unity of an archetype that is immaterial, immutable, and unique, and that also serves as their common Idea. Because they share in it, individuals can be designated by its name (all "men" participate in the Idea "Man"), but because they only share in it, without being it, individuals are imperfect imitations of their Idea. They are imperfect and therefore multiple imitations of its unity.[6]

Plato's greatness is best seen from the fact that, having proposed this answer to the problem, he was the first one to argue against it and to show it to be fraught with all sorts of difficulties. To "refute" the Platonic doctrine of Ideas is child's play. Any beginner in philosophy can do so; only, if he does, his chances of ever progressing in the study of philosophical wisdom are slender. For it remains that one fails to see how the Idea of Man can be participated in by men, since, in order to participate in it, an individual man must, at one and the same time, be possessed of the whole of human nature (in order fully to be man) and possess only part of it (in order to be *a* man). Plato himself has stressed the difficulty by showing that, were it so, what is one would have to be many, and what is many would have to be one. Still, in spite of his own objections to his own doctrine, Plato never gave it up, nor could he easily do so; nor indeed can we do so, because, in point of fact, reality is just that way.

The interminable, and unterminated, disputes concerning the problem of "universals" has no other meaning. To name a thing is to signify it as one of a class of similar things, all equally signifiable by the same name. What, then, is "generality"? If it is a thing, it has to be singular, in which case it cannot be participated in, but if it is merely a property of names, how is it that things themselves are namable? What is there, in their own ontological structure, that makes it possible to apply to things names that will fit some of them, although they may conceivably not fit others? We are not now concerned with the respective merits of the various answers given to the problem of universals. What matters here is the permanence of the problem itself. In the last analysis, even after choosing what looks like the best answer to it (let us say "moderate realism"), we still face a conclusion which, so far as we can see, is bound to be true, but whose ultimate meaning we do not clearly perceive. If the species "man," one in itself, is many as present in many individuals, what is it for "man" to be one? If it is to share in the same nature, notion, or definition, what is it for each individual to "share"? Excellent philosophers have said that for specific forms to share in the nature of one species is to resemble it and, thereby, to resemble one another. But, again, what is resemblance, or likeness, if it is not that which makes a plurality of objects to be one? When all is said and done, the mystery remains, hardly less opaque than in the beginning, because it is found at the very core of reality.

This is how it should be. Every time being *qua* being is at stake, we cannot scratch its surface without immediately reaching the level where the presence of mystery makes itself felt. It is so naturally inherent in the very possibility of knowledge, taken under its simplest forms, that we find it waiting for us in the mere apprehension of any single object. *An* object is *one* object; that is to say, it is an object that is *one*. This does not necessarily mean an object that is simple; it means that the primary condition for it to be an object is that it should be graspable as if it were simple, by an act of simple apprehension. For an object to be two objects would amount to being neither one. To be, at once, both a man and a tree, or two different men and two different trees, is to be neither a man nor a tree; it is to be nothing at all, except, of course, a monstrous or poetic fiction of the mind. This is the fundamental truth expressed by Leibniz in his well-known formula: it is one and the same thing to be one *being* and to be *one* being.[7]

Thomas Aquinas was right in his interpretation of Platonism, and what he could not verify in the dialogues of Plato he could at least observe in the later works of the Neoplatonists, themselves directly or indirectly inspired by Plotinus.

What is at stake in Neoplatonism is a question already raised by Plato but left by him without an answer. If for a thing to be is to be one, is not unity the very root or cause of being? The import of the question is evident. If we answer in the affirmative, the consequence will be that being is not the first principle either in reality or in knowledge. Prior to being and higher than it in importance, dignity, and efficacy, there will then be the One transcending being in perfection and generating it while maintaining its transcendence. Plotinus, Proclus, the unknown author of the *Liber de Causis* (a Neoplatonic work upon which Thomas Aquinas found it worth while to write an important commentary), all have carried the logic of the position to its ultimate implication, which is that being itself flows from a transcendent non-being, secret and ineffable, of which, if it is considered in itself, one can only say that it is the One.

Of course there are difficulties. If everything that is, is only inasmuch as it shares in unity, how is multiplicity possible? In such a view, being flows from a one-knows-not-what, of which nothing can be said except that it is a non-being. But if being begins only after the One and below it, how can being share in unity if, of itself, the One is not? These classic difficulties are not about words; they are about what the mind of man knows of its primary object. To meditate upon them is no waste of time. On the contrary, there is room for progress and there are degrees even within the apprehension of the first and self-evident principle of human knowledge. Metaphysics is essentially a reflection on the first principle. It takes years for each one of us to grasp it, just as Aristotle and Saint Thomas are agreed that it has taken many centuries for the cumulative reflection of mankind to realize its meaning.

Confronted with these difficulties, what should one do? The wisest course to follow is to wait and see. However we look at it, being is inconceivable without direct reference to unity. Whatever difficulties may be found in defining its nature, their relationship is beyond doubt. Then let us unhesitatingly affirm that, in some sense or other, being flows from the One, because, of its nature, unity precedes multiplicity. This may not be the ultimate answer to the question: What is God? but it is part of the answer. The prime cause of being must necessarily be one single cause. And indeed, when something is found to belong in common to a plurality of different objects, its common presence in them cannot be accounted for by that which, in these objects, is different. Now being is commonly found in everything that is, and since each and every thing has its own way of being, things cannot hold their being from themselves; they must hold it from a single cause: "And this seems to be the argument of Plato, who wanted all multiplicity to be preceded by a certain unity, not only in numbers, but in the nature of things as well."[8]

B. Being and perfection

The name of Aristotle brings to mind a world of changing substances whose generation and corruption perpetually succeed one another out of love for the pure actuality of Self-Thinking Thought. This is, in fact, the system of the world presupposed for the validity of the first of the five ways to prove God as a Prime Immovable Mover. Thomas Aquinas has resolutely preferred the world of Aristotle to that of Plato, and his choice was of decisive importance. Plato had been interested in discovering the highest principles of intelligibility; that is to say, the supreme notions in whose light the nature of reality could be understood by the human mind. How should we understand reality (*ousia*, entity) in order to render it intelligible? With Aristotle, the problem of being takes precedence over the problem of its intelligibility. Always dealing with substances, Aristotle was chiefly interested in explaining how they could be, operate, act upon other substances, and, inversely, be acted upon and caused by other actually existing beings. The philosophies of Plato and of Aristotle represent, in their complete generality, the two main attitudes the human mind can adopt with respect to reality.

To understand the reason for the choice made by Thomas Aquinas is, by the same token, to understand what interested him so much in the philosophy of Aristotle. The reason is simple. To a Christian, nothing really matters except God, and as Thomas Aquinas understood Him, God was the absolute perfection, not merely of truth or of intelligibility, but of Being. Since the world of his own theology necessarily had to be a system of relations, not between principles of intelligibility and their participants (Ideas and particulars), but between beings (God and creatures), Thomas would naturally feel attracted toward the Aristotelian universe; he therefore adopted it, but not without first submitting it to two radical modifications. First, in agreement with Avicenna, he interpreted the Aristotelian world of moving causes as a system of relations of efficient causes and of effects. This change effectively permitted him to substitute the God of Scripture for the Prime Mover of Aristotle. Second, it enabled Thomas to give its full force to the principle laid down by Aristotle that, wherever there are degrees of perfection in a certain genus, the most perfect in the genus is the cause of the less perfect. What Aristotle had had in mind was a hierarchy of substances or of qualities determined by their forms; in the mind of Thomas Aquinas, the Aristotelian degrees of perfection were to be conceived, at one and the same time, in terms of formal and of efficient causality.

A sure sign that Thomas Aquinas is thinking in terms of the Aristotelian approach to God (revised in a Thomistic sense) is the use he makes of an example borrowed from Aristotle. We have already met it in the exposition of the fourth way. To make clear that the supreme degree in any genus is the cause of all in that genus, Thomas quotes the remark of Aristotle that "fire, which is the maximum of heat, is the cause of all hot things."[9] What Thomas Aquinas here calls fire is the element fire which, being fire itself in its very essence, is necessarily absolute heat and the cause of all heat. Of course this qualitative physics has ceased to be valid, but the fact is without importance since, in any case, no physical example can adequately express a metaphysical truth. The point we are invited to understand is that, in whatever order of reality, the words "more" and "less" always point out degrees of perfection in being.

If we consider it more closely, this second consideration of being seems to merge with the first one. At the level of substantial being it asks the same question already asked concerning the one and the many. This is so true that, in the *Summa Theologiae*, Thomas Aquinas closely associates these two approaches to the knowledge of the Supreme Being: "Hence Plato said that unity must come before multitude and Aristotle said that whatever is greatest in being and greatest in truth is the cause of every being and every truth."[10] Confronted with a multiplicity of unequal goods, we wonder how perfection, which in itself is one and whole, can be participated in in various degrees by different beings. And the answer is that things are more or less perfect, more or less perfectly being, to the extent that they participate in absolutely perfect being. Now, "to participate in" is "to be caused" by, "for whatever is found in anything by participation must be caused in it by that to which it belongs essentially."[11] Thus, the plurality of partial beings given to us in experience irresistibly suggests to the mind that their cause is Being itself. In this way, God becomes for us, in our metaphysical consideration, the First Being by which are caused all the things whose various degrees of perfection are various degrees of participation in being.

It seems obvious that, instead of stressing the divergences between these first two metaphysical approaches to the nature of God, Thomas Aquinas intends to show them as two converging ways. God is one, origin of the many; God is also being, cause of all being, and since being is perfection, God is absolute perfection, cause of all the greater or lesser degrees of perfection to be observed in reality. Quite clearly, moreover, the second approach is a deeper one than the first, which follows the way of the one and the many. If being is what we are after, then the metaphysics of Aristotle will take us nearer to it than the metaphysics of Plato. Still, this is no reason why we should dismiss Plato and refuse to follow his road as far as it will take us. These positions are mutually exclusive only from the limited point of view of the metaphysician, but the theologian sees the goal toward which they are striving and which neither can fully reach because it lies beyond the limits of their common domain. Nor is the Aristotelian approach the deepest possible one, for what does the word "being" mean? A further discovery remains to be made *within* the very notion of being.

c. Being and existence

Thus far, the driving force behind our investigation has not been the desire to account for reality by means of a multiplicity of cause. On the contrary, since unity and being are convertible, we have not even attempted to get out of being. The same remark applies to the third approach to the nature of God that is offered to him by a third philosophical guide. After Plato and Aristotle, Thomas himself names Avicenna: after two pagans, a Moslem. And why not? Thomas Aquinas is not consulting these men about the truth of the divine revelation. His only intention is to learn from them what philosophy has to say on the subject of natural theology, and he finds Avicenna on the same line of inquiry as Plato and Aristotle, only ahead of his great predecessors.

The complex nature of Avicenna's philosophy helps us to understand this situation. A remarkable philosopher, but also a Moslem, Avicenna had found himself confronted with a considerable body of Moslem theological speculation whose influence upon his own thought Averroes repeatedly denounced. Roughly speaking, one can call Avicenna's philosophy a Moslem philosophy. This character of his doctrine explains why, on some important points, the philosophy of Avicenna suited the needs of a Christian theologian better, for instance, than the doctrine of Averroes, so anxious to keep out of philosophy every notion of religious origin.

Avicenna was one of the first philosophers to realize the significance, for philosophy, of the notion of creation and to see that it entailed the recognition of a new type of causality. In the doctrine of Aristotle, the production of beings by other beings was attributed to the action of movements acting upon moved things. In this respect, the moving cause (*causa movens*) was the typical Aristotelian cause; it acted by imparting to matter various motions whose ultimate effect was the production of new beings. Avicenna clearly saw that, owing to the doctrine of creation, the theologians, in fact, accept a different notion of causality. Without denying causality by way of motion, they are bound to distinguish from it the kind of causality whose effect is, not merely motion, but the very being of the effect produced. They call this efficient causality. They therefore distinguish from the "moving cause," which produces a being by producing the motions required for its generation, the "efficient cause," whose effect is the very existence of the caused thing. Henceforth, the primary notion of "existence" will remain inseparable from the notion of "actual being."

How far Avicenna himself has pushed his own analysis of the notion of creative causality is a point for historians of philosophy to decide. At any rate, he pushed it far enough to oblige his successors to take the notion of "existence" into account. Thomas Aquinas himself has done so with such an attentive seriousness that, as will be seen, his own metaphysics ultimately rests upon it. Among the data of sense experience, the most strikingly evident information to be found about things is that they are. To say that they are and that they have actual being, or actual existence, is to say the same thing. But the plurality of particular existences raises the same problem as does a plurality of beings or a plurality of substances. The existence proper to each thing is only one particular existence; it does not exist in virtue of itself, and hence is not actual existence itself in itself. This is to say that each and every particular existent is a participation of one single self-existing being that is existence itself and nothing else. This notion will remain at the center of our inquiry. There is therefore no need for us to proceed now to a more complete elucidation of its meaning. Let us simply accept it, and this less for itself than for the notion of actual existence it implies. In this way, Thomas says:

. . . one must posit a being that is its very own being, and this is proved by showing that there is a prime being that is pure act, in which there is no composition. It is therefore necessary that all the other beings, which are not their own being, should exist in virtue of this one single being, so that they have being by mode of participation. This is the argument of Avicenna.[12]

With this notion, our understanding is reaching the ultimate limits of the domain so far open to metaphysical exploration. This is the reason why philosophers, though they usually agree that being is the first principle of human knowledge, so often disagree as to the nature of being. Is being existence? Or is existence, in being, the cause that being actually is? These and similar questions have been raised time and again, and one cannot say that, even among the Scholastics, they have received unanimously accepted answers. Nor is this to be wondered at. For we know there is a God, and if God is pure actual existence, our own notion of existence necessarily retains something of the blazing evidence of its object. Naturally known to all men, the notion of being resembles one of those lights whose blinding intensity makes it impossible to discern anything definite near it, in them, or beyond them.[13]

A new field of metaphysical prospection is here offering itself to our inquiry. Before being anything else, the objects of sense experience are so many existents. Their only possible common cause, *qua* existents, is therefore Existence. But what is Existence? Thomas says it is that which, being absolutely immovable and most perfect, is also absolutely simple; in short, a being that is to itself its own being. How can this be conceived?

Chapter 5. The essence of God

Concerning man's knowledge of the essence of God, nothing compares in clarity and in perfection of philosophical style with the first two articles of the questions on the treatise of Boethius *On the Trinity*.[1] In reporting their doctrine one sometimes wonders if it would not be better simply to reprint the text of Thomas himself, such as it is. The only justification there may be for proceeding differently is the desire to stress the essential points of an otherwise perfectly clear doctrine presented by its author in a perfect formulation.

I. WHETHER THE HUMAN MIND CAN ARRIVE AT THE KNOWLEDGE OF GOD?

In asking whether the human mind can achieve some knowledge of the essence, or nature, of God, it is appropriate that we first determine man's natural ability to know.

On this precise point Thomas had to take into account the doctrine of the divine illumination attributed to Saint Augustine. It is not for us to decide whether Augustine actually taught such a doctrine. Still less are we interested in gauging the degree of fidelity achieved by the "Augustinians" of the thirteenth century in reporting the position of their master on this point. Thomas Aquinas was not primarily interested in criticizing the position of Augustine, much less refuting it. On the contrary, he preferred to go out of his way to patch up any differences, real or otherwise, that seemed to arise between his own doctrine and that of Augustine. What Thomas undertook to examine was not a man or a school; it was a philosophical position. Precisely, Thomas Aquinas was opposing the thesis that, in order to know truth, the natural light of the intellect needs a further illumination by the divine light. Other doctrines than that of Augustine could be quoted in support of such a view. Every time a philosopher conceives intellectual knowledge as a more or less direct sight of intelligible Ideas, he has a tendency to make us see truth in the light of these Ideas rather than in that of our own intellect. Some difficulties then necessarily follow, particularly with respect to our knowledge of God. These Thomas wanted to avoid.

Knowledge is in us the result of an action exerted upon us by some object. In knowing an object we are, in some way or other, impressed by it. In this sense, knowledge is said to be a "passion" in the primary meaning of this word, which is a state resulting in us from some action exercised upon us by an object.

In the case of sense knowledge, this is the whole truth. As cognitive powers, the senses are essentially passive. Sight and hearing cannot feel or experience anything unless they receive impressions from some objects. On the contrary, intellectual knowledge seems to require a twofold power. First, a passive one similar to that of sense, for if nothing is acting upon it, the intellect has no object to know; next, an active power which enables the intellect to combine and distinguish its own concepts after it has formed them, and to do so in an active way, so to speak, at will. It even has to do something every time, under the impact of a sense perception; it has to abstract from it an intelligible notion. We undergo sense perceptions and we receive their images, but we form abstract notions or concepts. For this reason, the intellect itself divides into two distinct powers: it is active inasmuch as it produces the intelligible principles through which it forms the abstract notions by an act of its own (and therefore it is called the "agent intellect"); it is passive inasmuch as it receives in itself the intelligible principles or species of the abstract notions produced by its own active power (and therefore it is called the "possible intellect").

In the thirteenth century, the relationship between these two and distinct intellectual powers was a subject widely discussed in schools. Some theologians, following the Moslem philosopher Avicenna, maintained that only the possible intellect was a power of the human soul; according to them, the agent intellect was a separate intellectual substance; that is, a sort of angel. Accordingly, such philosophers and theologians maintained that our own knowledge of truth is caused in us, not by our own intellect, but by the light it receives from above and from the outside, caused in us by that separate substance, the agent intellect.

Thomas Aquinas always opposed this doctrine for two reasons, a philosophical one and a religious one. Speaking as a theologian well versed in the doctrines of the philosophers, particularly that of the Philosopher, Thomas Aquinas always maintained, in the teeth of evidence, that Aristotle considered each man as endowed with an agent intellect of his own. On this point, moreover, the teaching of Scripture visibly favors that of the Aristotelian philosophy. It is written in *Psalms 4:7: The light of Thy countenance, O Lord, is signed upon us.* Scripture says it is *signed upon* us, not that it *shines upon* us from outside. The light in which we know truth is in us, it is truly ours.

This conjunction of a twofold authority, human and divine, is impressive enough by itself, but reason supports the position of Aristotle as interpreted by Thomas Aquinas. There can be discussion concerning the true meaning of Aristotle's doctrine of the human intellect; there can be no discussion as to its true meaning in the mind of Thomas Aquinas himself. Whatever the personal opinion of Aristotle on the subject may have been, that of Thomas Aquinas himself still stands on its own ground. Its ultimate justification, from the point of view of reason, is that all natural beings are endowed with the principles and causality to accomplish their proper operations. This is a sort of primary evidence. For if a being is not endowed with the power required for the performing of a certain operation, this operation does not belong to that being. In the present case, if the intellectual light in which man knows is not that of an intellect truly his own, then intellectual knowledge cannot be said to be his own knowledge and the truth he knows is not his own truth. Now, intellectual knowledge is a fact, and it can be observed in every one of us. It is completely arbitrary to suppose that we do not possess the powers required for performing the operations we actually perform. In other words, since man is a being of nature, and intellection is a natural operation, there is no reason for us to imagine that this operation is being performed in man by somebody other than man. Hence the conclusion of Thomas Aquinas:

> *Since the other active natural powers, conjoined with the corresponding passive powers, suffice to account for natural operations, so too, since it has in itself a passive power and an active power, the soul is sufficiently endowed to perceive truth.*[2]

Each particular position, in the doctrine of Thomas Aquinas, should be understood in the framework of his general view of the world. In this case we are being invited to put man in the place where he belongs in a naturalistic view of nature. A theologian has no right, for whatever purpose, to attribute to man operations exceeding the powers of human nature. Man knows some truth; if he is not able to know this truth by powers that are truly his own, then let us simply say that true knowledge is not naturally accessible to man. This would be a sort of universalized skepticism. But if, on the contrary, we think that man is naturally able to achieve true knowledge, then let us say that he does so in the light of an intellect truly his own, so that he really is the cause of his own knowledge of truth.

This conclusion eliminates all doctrines according to which true knowledge requires a sort of supplement of light, superadded by God to the natural light He gave us in creating our intellects. But this position entails its own limitations. Our intellect is a finite being and its powers are finite powers. Sufficient as it is to produce its own effects, it does not suffice to produce any effect located beyond its limits. This means that the human soul is sufficient to achieve true knowledge in the order of natural truth, but it cannot achieve further knowledge without receiving some new power superadded to its natural one.

There are therefore two orders of true knowledge. First, there are the truths knowable in the light of the agent intellect, such as the principles naturally known to the human mind along with their necessary or possible consequences. These make up the whole body of natural knowledge, actual or possible. No additional intelligible light is required for this kind of knowledge; the naturally innate light of the intellect is sufficient to achieve it. There are, however, certain truths to which the understanding power of the intellect does not extend. These are the truths of faith, exceeding the intellect's reach. Such also are the future contingents and similar truths which, hanging on free or contingent causes, are not susceptible of rational prediction. The human mind cannot know these things unless it be enlightened by a new light superadded to its natural light.

It is a well-known fact that many theologians feel somewhat uneasy about this position, because it seems to grant to the human mind, in the field of natural knowledge at least, an excessive independence with respect to its Creator. Others, on the contrary, rejoice in such a position because it seems to insure the complete autonomy of the human mind with respect to God in both being and operation. But neither one of these opposite attitudes is justified in the perspective of genuine Thomism. On the contrary, both are wrong for one and the same reason; namely, that natural beings are all created natures. As natures, they must be equipped with all the natural powers required for the completeness of their essences; as created, they are and operate only in virtue of the divine operation in them. This point will be closely scrutinized later. For the present let it suffice to observe that, in order to be what it is, a created nature must needs be, at one and the same time, both a nature and a created being whose preservation hangs on the continuation of the same efficiency by which it has been created. Consequently, beyond the operation whereby He has instituted the natures of things, attributing to every one of them their proper forms and their own operating powers, God is still performing in things the works of His providence, directing and moving the powers of all things to their proper acts. In this sense, the whole creation is subject to the governance of God in the same way that his tools are subject to the free decisions of a worker.[3] However, since the creation and the conservation of natures simply make them to be and to remain natures, our general conclusion should be that the human mind depends upon the divine operation in its knowledge of truth, but that it needs no new illumination from God in order to know natural things. In such cases our mind needs only to be moved and directed by its creator. On the other hand, there are supernatural truths, and these our mind cannot know without an additional light such as that of the divine revelation.

The impact of this doctrine on the problem of man's knowledge of God is of supreme importance. For the natural knowledge of God cannot exceed what can be known of Him from the quiddities of material things that are the objects proportioned to our own cognitive powers. In Thomas' own words, "in this life, our intellect has a determinate relationship to the forms that are abstracted from sensations."[4] Such objects are finite. Consequently, no natural knowledge thus formed by the human mind can represent God; His immaterial essence cannot be attained by means of abstraction from material things. Generally speaking, there are no material data from which the knowledge of a purely immaterial object can possibly be abstracted. Moreover, since all objects naturally knowable to man are finite, no knowledge of them obtainable by means of abstraction from sense can possibly represent an infinite being, such as the essence of God. In other words, the twofold fact that human knowledge has to be abstracted from sense, and that it deals only with finite objects, makes it impossible for us to grasp the very essence of God, such as it is known by the blessed.

Since to know God *by His essence* is not naturally possible for man, the only knowledge of God still accessible to us is the kind of knowledge that is obtained when a certain form is known from its effects. Even in this case, two ways of knowing have to be distinguished, because there are two kinds of effects. Some belong in the same order as the causal power by which they are produced; they are its equals. By knowing effects of this sort, it is possible to know fully the powers and the quiddities of their causes. But there is another class of effects; namely, those that lack this equality with the power of their causes. By starting from such effects, the human mind can comprehend neither the power of their efficient cause nor, consequently, its essence. The only thing that can be known of such a cause, starting from such effects, is that it is. Now this precisely is what happens in the case of our knowledge of God. Since all the effects of God are unequal to their cause, the only thing we can know about Him is that He is. Neither His power nor His essence is naturally knowable to us.

This position has been an eminently traditional one. The surprise it causes today in the minds of some modern theologians is due mainly to the difficulty they find in grasping its true meaning.

One of the obstacles to be overcome is the illusion that, if the only thing we know of God is that He is, there is for us no way left to progress in the knowledge of the divinity. But it is not so. In the case of effects unequal to their causes, our knowledge of the cause improves according as the true relationship of the effect to the cause becomes better known.

This improvement occurs in three different ways. First, it occurs according as we know better the efficacy of the cause in producing its effects. In the case of God, to know Him as the creator of His effects certainly is to know Him much better than to see Him only as the moving or the final cause of the world. A second improvement takes place if we investigate God as the cause of higher and higher effects. For instance, to know God as the cause of intellectual substances is to know Him better than to see Him only as the cause of material substances. How far this can make us progress in our knowledge of God has been seen in the preceding chapter. If we know God only as the orderer of material beings, we know that He is a supreme mind; if we know He causes all substances as their Prime Mover, we know that God is a substance, the prime and supreme entity; but if we know God as the prime cause of all existents, then we know that He Himself is the prime and the supreme Existent. All this, however, does not tell us *what* God is; it still tells us only *that* He is. We now know of Him that He is the cause of existence; but the very nature of such a cause, this is what we do not know. The third way in which the human understanding can progress in its knowledge of God as a cause is the progressive elimination of our illusions on the true nature of such knowledge. It consists in knowing God as more and more removed from all that which appears in His effects. This is what Dionysius says in his

Divine Names: that God is known, as the cause of all things, by transcending them and by being removed from them.[5]

Such is the Thomistic form of the traditional doctrine of the "learned ignorance." It has nothing in common with the passive inertia of an understanding giving up all hope of grasping its object. On the contrary, knowing as it does both its own nature and that of its proper object, the negative theology of Thomas Aquinas is an energetic and eminently positive effort of the mind against the self-deception that it knows the essence of its highest object. Negative theology is a fight relentlessly carried on by the human intellect against the always recurring illusion that, despite all that is said to the contrary, man has a certain positive notion, limited though it may be, of *what* the essence of God really is. Everything in man's intellect rebels against such an attitude. It is not natural to man to busy himself about its objects in order to make sure that he does *not* know them. Even if it knows that it cannot trust images in conceiving immaterial objects, the intellect at least hopes that these images will direct its inquiry toward a deeper truth; we do not usually consider our mental representations as enemies to be defeated but rather as helpful co-workers in our quest of truth.

Not so here. In deep agreement with the most radically imageless mysticism there ever existed, that of Saint Bernard of Clairvaux, Thomas Aquinas invites us to transcend all representation and figurative description of God. If we can imagine what something is, then God is beyond it; if we can grasp the definition of a certain thing, then that thing is not yet God. Nor is it enough to have said this only once; the aim of the doctrine of Thomas Aquinas on this crucial point is to invite us to a sort of intellectual asceticism calculated to rid our intellects of the delusion that we know *what* God is. This requires such an effort on our part that the grace of God and the gifts of the Holy Ghost are here required to help our intellects in this, their highest undertaking. Not that we should expect from God the revelation of any new notion; the grace of God is required here, not to add anything to our knowledge, but rather to give us the strength to acquire nescience and to keep it after acquiring it, instead of continually relapsing into deceptive images of the infinite Being.[6]

The meaning of this doctrine is something everyone has to learn for himself. There is no point in endlessly repeating something that Thomas himself has so often repeated without in any way changing our natural attitude with respect to the problem of our knowledge of God. Nor will anything ever change it. When all is said and done, we shall continue to teach others what God is, what we do know (after all!) of the essence of God. Perhaps we shall ourselves find it hard to realize fully that the summit of the human knowledge of God is to know that we do not know. Then is for us the time to go back to Thomas Aquinas and to meditate at length upon the meaning of formulas he could not have written without first having given the problem the full attention it deserves. Here at least is one of them, the more deserving of our attention as it says absolutely everything Thomas wanted us to understand on this point:

> *They say that, on reaching the term of our knowledge, we know God as unknown, because our mind is found to have made its supreme progress in knowledge when it knows that the essence of God is above all that which it can apprehend in this life; and thus although* what *God is remains unknown, that He is, nevertheless, is known.*[7]

This is the spirit in which one should approach the impressive series of chapters devoted by the two *Summae* to the progressive determination of what a metaphysician must say concerning the nature of God. Such as they are, these chapters constitute the most perfect demonstration of negative theology ever given by any scholastic theologian; but what should be particularly noted is the eminently positive nature of this intellectual effort which, by progressively leading us to the conclusion that God is *not* like any being given in human experience, finally raises Him infinitely above anything that can be seen, imagined, or quidditatively conceived.

II. THE SIMPLICITY OF GOD

From what precedes it follows that for the human intellect to know what God is consists chiefly in progressively determining what God is not. This Thomas Aquinas calls "to use the way of remotion."

In a certain sense, this is already the way we use in determining the nature of the things whose essences are known to us. We first locate them in a genus, which makes us know them in a general way, as when, for instance, we say that man is an animal; then we add to the genus a difference in order to show that man is *not* like many other species of animals; namely, all those of the irrational animals. Here, however, the case is still different. In defining man, we can start from the notion of a certain genus; in defining God, there is no genus from whose notion we can start, since God does not include in His notion species sharing in the common nature of the divinity. Moreover, in defining man, we can add to the genus "animal" a positive difference, "rational." We have a positive notion of what reason and rational knowledge are. In the case of God, on the contrary, just as we cannot start from any genus, so we cannot determine it by adding any positive differences to it. The result of this situation is that we shall have to determine progressively an area within which, could we form it, a positive notion of God would be found; and the only way for us to determine this area consists in piling up negative differences, each of which will say one of the things that God is not. The final result will necessarily be a negative one and, therefore, an imperfect one, since it will not tell us what God is in Himself. At the same time, it will be a true knowledge of God, since it will make us know God "as distinct from all things." Thomas Aquinas will never vary on these two points: speaking of the divine substance, "we are unable to apprehend it by knowing *what it is;* yet we are able to have some knowledge of it by knowing *what it is not.*"[8]

In two places in the works of Thomas Aquinas, in the *Summa Contra Gentiles* and in the *Summa Theologiae,* we can follow, as it were, step by step, his own approach to the particular notion of being that lies at the core of his own metaphysical view of reality.

In the *Summa Contra Gentiles,* starting from the demonstration of the existence of God as the prime absolutely unmoved mover of the universe, he proceeds directly to a progressive determination of the notion of God. This method offered to him a twofold advantage. It set out from the Aristotelian notion of God, which the philosophers were likely to concede, while at the same time it joined immediately the Augustinian notion of God, which had so long been familiar to Christian theologians. For, indeed, to say that God is absolutely unmoved, or immobile, and to say that He is both immutability and eternity, is to say one and the same thing. Accordingly, following the way of progressive remotion, Thomas successively establishes that God has neither beginning nor end, that there is in God no passive potency, no matter, nothing violent, unnatural, or corporeal. Then, in the *Summa Contra Gentiles,* I, chapter 21, it is proved that God is His own Essence and, finally, in chapter 22, that in God actual being and essence are identical. This conclusion is of decisive importance for the determination of the Thomistic notion of being. It establishes that there is a being that is being itself, and nothing else, so that, knowing what God is, we are sure to know what pure being actually is. The way followed by Thomas Aquinas in the *Summa Contra Gentiles* consisted in successively eliminating all the conceivable types of composition.

Considered from the point of view of history, this development by way of remotion added nothing to the traditionally received notion of the Christian God; that is, at least, up to chapter 21. It would be easy to accumulate texts in which Saint Augustine had already established the equivalence of the notions of God, of being, of immutability, and of eternity. Moreover, Augustine had expressly used these philosophical notions in order to facilitate the interpretation of the passage of *Exodus* (*3:13–14*) in which, asked by Moses for His name, God Himself declared that His own name was HE IS. A short passage of the treatise *On Christian Doctrine* is enough to establish the identity of the notions of being and of immutability in his theology: "He supremely and primarily is who is wholly immutable, and who has been fully entitled to say: I AM WHO AM, and: thou wilt tell them, WHO IS has sent me unto you." As to the equivalence of immutability and essence, or entity, the decisive text is found in the *De Civitate Dei:*

> *For God undoubtedly is* substantia, *or, if it is better to name him in that way, God is that* essentia *which the Greeks used to call* ousia. *For just as* sapientia *comes from* sapere, *and as* scientia *comes from* scire, *so also* essentia *comes from* esse. *And indeed who is more than He Who said to His servant Moses: I AM WHO AM, and thou wilt say to the children of Israel: WHO IS has sent me unto you.*[9]

Thomas Aquinas himself could not have progressed any further following the way of essence; that is to say, supposing that the notions of being, essence, and entity are identical. But, precisely, he did enter a new way at the very moment he passed from chapter 21 to chapter 22. In the latter, Thomas Aquinas proceeded to one further reduction, by removing from God any distinction between essence and what he usually calls the *esse* of God. Of this *esse* we know very little at first, except that in God it is that to which entity or essence (*essentia*) or quiddity (*quiditas*) has to be reduced. In other words, we know of *esse* that it is that from which the essence of God is in no way distinct.

In translating *esse* into English, the use of the word "being" is almost unavoidable, but it is not wholly satisfactory because the normal English translation for *esse* is *to be*, while *being* is a perfect rendering of the Latin *ens*. Hence, even while using *being* as an equivalent of *esse*, one should keep in mind that, since Thomas Aquinas has already proved, in chapter 21, that God is in no way distinct from His essence, the *esse* now at stake cannot be once again the essence. In fact, it is not the name of a thing; in Thomas Aquinas' own words, it is "the name of an act." Again, if the essence of God were not His *esse*, God would not be His own essence; He would not be through Himself; He would be in virtue of His participation in the very *esse* that His own essence is not. This argument introduces a radical distinction between God, Whose essence is His own being, and other beings, which are only because their respective essences *have* each a being that they *are* not. Obviously the aim and scope of the whole dialectical development are to identify God with the very act without which entity itself (*essentia*) would not be. To say that God is simple means that He is the Pure Act of Being. This decisive chapter culminates naturally in the well-known conclusion:

> *This sublime truth Moses was taught by our Lord. When Moses asked our Lord: "If the children of Israel say to me: What is His name? What shall I say to them?" The Lord replied: "I AM WHO AM . . . thou shalt say to the children of Israel: HE WHO IS hath sent me to you" (Exod. 3:13–14). By this our Lord showed that His own proper name is HE WHO IS. Now names have been devised to signify the natures or essences of things. It remains, then, that the divine being* (esse) *is God's essence or nature.*[10]

The same conclusion is reached in the *Summa Theologiae* following a shorter and more abrupt metaphysical way. The conclusion of the second question of the *Summa* is that God exists; the conclusion of the third question is that God is absolutely simple because, in Him, essence and being (*esse*) are the same. Everything proceeds as though this preliminary conclusion is the gateway to Christian theology. And indeed its importance can hardly be exaggerated. Since, indeed, the subject matter of theology is God, each and every one of the conclusions established by the theologian must necessarily be affected by this initial notion of God.

The first step on the way to this conclusion is the proof that God is not a body. Strictly speaking, this is a truth known to the simple believer, since it is written in the *Gospel of Saint John* (4:24): *God is a spirit*. But, precisely, the object of theology is to facilitate for faith the understanding of what it believes and, on this point, by resorting to philosophical argument, the theologian can establish this truth in three ways.

He can do it, first, by proceeding from the first of the five ways to the existence of God, which has proved that "God is the First Mover, Himself unmoved." Now no body is able to move unless it is moved, as can be shown in the case of all the different kinds of motion. In fact, the conclusion that no material thing can be the cause of its own movement has been included in the very formulation of the "first way." Consequently, the "first mover, moved by no other," which everyone understands to be God, is not a body.

Second, the same conclusion can be reached starting from the third way, which has proved that God is the First Being. In proving this conclusion, Thomas Aquinas resorts to one of the deepest notions of his metaphysics; namely, the primacy of act over potency. Practically all scholastic theologies make use of the division of being into act and potency, but some of them understand it to mean that being is always either act or potency or a combination of both according to some proportion. The position of Thomas Aquinas is that, absolutely speaking, being is act. All that which is, is act inasmuch as it is. Even potency is being in some way, or otherwise, being nothing, it cannot be potency, but to the extent that it is not nothing, potency shares in the nature of being and therefore of actuality. This implies that, if there is a first being, such a being must be prior to all potentiality (otherwise, coming after potentiality, such being would not be first); consequently, the first being must of necessity be pure act, free of all potentiality. This conclusion excludes the possibility that God is a body, for bodies are continuous in space; as such they are divisible to infinity, and to be capable of being divided, actually or in thought, is to be in potency with respect to divisibility. It is therefore impossible for God to be a body.

The same conclusion can be reached in still another way, starting from the fourth way, which, on the basis of the gradation to be found in things, has established that God "is the most noble of beings." For if this is true, given bodies are not the noblest of beings, God cannot possibly be a body. That bodies are not the most noble of beings is obvious, for some of them are animate while others are inanimate. Now to be animate is nobler than to be inanimate, and since some bodies are not animate, animation depends upon something else, whose nature is not that of a body. We call this something else a soul, whose nature is other, and nobler, than that of the body it animates. Consequently, God cannot be a body.

This conclusion eliminates from the notion of God the material composition of parts in space, but, at the same time, it implicitly eliminates another one, the substantial composition of matter and form. To be a body is to be composed of matter determined by dimensive quantity, which is a form; but it has been proved that God is not a body; consequently, He is not composed of matter and form.[11] The import of this second conclusion is that, had we to choose between the notions of matter and form to signify God, we should place Him on the side of form and consider Him a wholly immaterial form. First, it has been seen that God is pure act; a form can be pure act, whereas matter always implies potentiality. Second, matter owes its goodness and perfection to form, and since God is the first good and the highest, there can be in Him nothing that only participates in goodness. Third, "every agent acts by its form" (because form stands on the side of act), and since it has been shown (by the second way) that God is the first efficient cause, "He is of His essence a form, and not composed of matter and form."[12]

This leaves us at grips with the purest of metaphysical notions. Let us suppose God is pure form: what kind of form could He possibly be?

In the objects of sense experience, form is that by which a thing is that which it is. For instance, in a man, there is a subsisting subject (*suppositum*)—namely, that which is man; and there is its form, essence, or nature—namely, his "humanity." Now all the things from which we derive our knowledge are, in fact, composite. They are composed of a subsisting subject (*suppositum*) and of the essence or nature that makes it to be a subject specifically determined by its form. Should this be applied to God, one would have to say that, just as a man is man owing to the nature or essence of humanity, so God is God owing to the essence or nature of His divinity.

In denying of God this further composition, the theologian enters the domain of a truth that is not representable to the human understanding. Since all the beings empirically known to us are composite, it is impossible for us to conceive something truly simple. If we have to speak of such a thing, we must resort to the only language at our disposal, which fits composite beings, not simple ones. This we do when, having to speak of God, we describe Him as a being that is God in virtue of His divine nature or essence, His Godhead. But then we have to correct our language because, in God, essence or nature is the same as God.

At this point the theology of Thomas Aquinas is moving along the lines once defined by Boethius and followed by many later theologians, for instance Gilbert of Poitiers. Boethius had forcibly distinguished in every substance between that which is (*id quod est*), or the subsisting subject, and that whereby it is that which it is (*quo est*); namely, the essence or nature of the thing. The justification for this distinction was that, in things composed of matter and form, the subsisting subject (*suppositum*) comprises elements that are not included in the natures or essences of such things. For instance, in a man, the subject includes a certain individuating matter, with the individuating accidents that make him to be this and that individual man, whereas nothing of all this is included in the nature or essence of man in general. In Thomas' own words: "this flesh, these bones, and the accidental qualities desig-nating this particular matter, are not included in *humanity;* and yet they are included in the reality that is *a man.* Hence, the reality that is a man has something in it that humanity does not have"—namely; its individuating determinations. To conclude, if God is a form, He should not be conceived as a being individuated by matter, but as a self-individuated being, as all pure forms necessarily are. Hence, if God is pure form, He *has* not His Godhead; He *is* His Godhead. In Him, *that which is* and *that which He is* are identical.

This conclusion is of course intimated by Scripture. The relation between God and the Godhead is of the same nature as that between a living being and life. But Scripture does not say that God *has* life; it says that God *is* life: *I am the way, and the truth and the life* (*John 14:6*). Thus, God *is* His very Godhead, His own life, and so with all that can be predicated of Him.[13]

We are now reaching, in the *Summa Theologiae*, the point that exactly corresponds to the passage from chapter 21 to chapter 22 in the first book of the *Summa Contra Gentiles*. "Passage" is perhaps a better word than "transition." For in passing from *Summa* I, q.3, a.4, to I, q.3, a.5, we are jumping from the metaphysical world of Boethius into that of Thomas Aquinas. And there is no warning. The new ques-tion is: "Whether essence and being (*esse*) are the same in God?" The question is intelligible in one sense at least; namely, that we under-stand the meaning of the word *esse* in the doctrine of Thomas Aquinas. One of the main difficulties of the doctrine is that the only case in which the word has the fullness of its meaning happens to be the case in which it properly applies to the being of God, or rather to the being that God *is*.

The conclusion reached in *Summa* I, q.3, a.3, represented the ultimate point of arrival of Christian theological speculation: a God Who is a pure immaterial being, a self-subsisting form, and, more precisely, the subsisting form whose whole essence is *to be the very Godhead*. What we now are asked to do, if we can, is to go beyond essence, nature, or form. It is correct to say that God is His Godhead, but this is not yet the whole truth. And we should be able to suspect what the whole truth actually is, for when Moses asked God for His name, the answer was not: I am my own Godhead; the answer was: *I am HE WHO IS.* The whole truth of the case, therefore, should be that "what subsists in God is His being."[14]

What does the word "being" mean in this context? Since we are invited by Thomas Aquinas to pass beyond the level of essence, the word necessarily means that which, in being, is not essence. Thomas Aquinas takes it for granted, in these words, that there is indeed such a thing. The decision is a revolutionary one in the history of metaphysics. Is there, in being, anything that lies beyond the reality of that, in it, which is? True enough, real being implies existence, but what is existence, after all, if not essence itself posited in actual reality by the efficacy of some cause? If it is a question of God, is not His existence the perfect actuality of an essence that is self-subsisting being itself? To posit God as the perfection of entity itself seems to many good minds a sufficient approximation of a being whose essence in any case exceeds our grasp. They see no point in adding to the affirmation of its reality that, over and above being supremely real, it exists.

Thomas Aquinas, however, establishes this decisive position in three ways. First, he sets out from the notion of God conceived as the first efficient cause, whose existence has been demonstrated by the second of the five ways. It runs as follows. If the essence of God is not His own act of being (*esse*), then His being must have a cause. This cause can be either an internal one or an external one. In order to be an internal one, this cause should be one or several of the essential principles of God Himself; but this cannot be, for to be caused by one's own internal principles is to be caused by oneself; in fact, it is not to be caused at all. On the other hand, the cause of God's being cannot possibly be an external one; there can be no cause of the First Cause. Consequently, God is His own *esse*, His own act of being.

A second reason in favor of this position is drawn from God's perfect actuality. God is pure act. But the ultimate notion is not that of act, it is that of being: "Being is the actuality of every form or nature." This important principle, which we shall have many occasions to scrutinize, is nothing less than that of the absolute primacy of being and of the notion of being. No essence or nature has any actuality whatever except in so far as it can be said to be. As Thomas himself puts it: "goodness and humanity are spoken of as actual only because they are spoken of as being";[15] or, to put it more bluntly, there is no halfway house between being a being and being nothing. Therefore, in a being whose essence is distinct from its act of being, the act of being is compared to essence as actuality to potentiality. But we set out from the principle that God is pure act, and since in Him there is no potentiality, there can be in Him no essence distinct from the act of being.

A third reason is taken from the general rule that beings are what they are either by themselves or by participation, and that which has something, but is not it by itself, is it only by participation. For instance, something that is not fire but is set on fire is fire by participation. So also "that which has being, but is not being, is a being by participation." This is what would happen to the notion of God if His essence were not conceived as identical with His being. For it has been shown that God is His own essence; if, therefore, He is not His own being (*esse*), He will not be a being by essence, but only by participation. As a participated being, He will hold His being from another one. In short, God will not be the first being, which is an absurdity.

Dialectically speaking, the justification of the conclusion is faultless: "God is His own being, and not only His own essence."[16] There must therefore be some reason why it has failed to win universal approval, and the reason is that all such dialectical demonstrations presuppose the notion of being proper to Saint Thomas Aquinas. If the ultimate meaning of the word "being" is the act of being, the *esse* or *actus essendi* in virtue of which alone things can be called "beings," then all the arguments of Thomas Aquinas are convincing and all lead to a necessary conclusion. To those who perceive that *to be* is, in every thing, the ultimate act that causes it to be a *being*, the demonstration becomes crystal-clear. One should rather say that there is nothing left to demonstrate. He whose true name is HE WHO IS necessarily is, so to speak, by essence, the very act of being itself in its absolute purity. God does not own it, He *is* it.

The problems raised by the interpretation of this remarkable doctrine will be considered separately. For the present, we first must consider some immediate consequences that Thomas Aquinas has associated with it in the *Summa Theologiae*, and especially two of them whose purely philosophical formulation is unexpected in a theological work: God is not contained in a genus; there are no accidents in God.

The properly philosophical character of the first of these two questions is seen from the fact that, instead of being borrowed from

Scripture, the argument "on the contrary" itself is a straight metaphysical proposition: "Genus is prior to what it contains. But nothing is prior to God either really or in meaning. Therefore God is not in any genus." Many arguments justify the conclusion, among which there is one borrowed from Aristotle or, rather, from the Aristotelian notion of being.

The use made of it by Thomas Aquinas is interesting both historically and philosophically. In the theology of Aristotle, God is the Prime Mover, a distinct individual substance that nobody could possibly mistake for a genus. In the theology of Thomas Aquinas, God is Being, which some might well mistake for a genus. Now, precisely, Aristotle was careful to establish that being is not a genus, and this for a simple reason; namely, that every genus has differences outside itself (otherwise they would not be its differences), whereas being has no such differences, since the only difference distinct from being would be non-being, which cannot be a difference. For instance, in the definition of man as "a rational animal," "rational" is a difference of the genus "animal" because rationally is other than animality (there are non-rational animals); but in such formulas as "being is good," "being is true," or even "being is material" (or "immaterial"), all the so-called differences are likewise beings. If they were not beings, they would be nothing, not even differences; if they are beings they cannot be differences of being. From this purely Aristotelian position, Thomas concludes in the *Summa* that God is not in a genus.[17] It is therefore possible to be a Thomist on this point without being more than an Aristotelian.

But it is likewise possible to be a Thomist who goes far beyond the mere position of Aristotle. In order to do so, one has only to resort to the new notion of being developed by Thomas Aquinas. God is being, but being is *esse* itself; that is, the very act of being. In God, Who is pure and absolute being, there is nothing other than this pure act whose name is I AM. Consequently, there is in God no essence distinct from the *esse* He is, and this makes it impossible to include God in a genus. In order to greet this first application of his own metaphysical notion of being by Thomas himself, let us watch him at work, and let us be careful not to miss the important consequences he hastens to deduce from the doctrine:

> . . . *all members of one genus share in the quiddity or essence of the genus which is predicated of them essentially, but they differ in*

their being [all animals equally share in the genus "animality," but two particular animals are two distinct beings]. *For the being of man and of horse is not the same; nor is the being of this man and that man. Thus, in every member of a genus, being (esse) and quiddity— i.e. essence—must differ. But in God they do not differ, as was shown in the preceding article. Therefore it is plain that God is not in a genus as if He were a species. From this also it is plain that He has no genus or difference, nor can there be any definition of Him; nor, save through His effects, a demonstration of Him; for a definition is from genus and difference, and the means of a demon- stration is a definition.*[18]

Nothing could show better the plurality of levels on which the thought of Thomas Aquinas can move. The impossibility of giving *a priori* demonstrations of the existence of God, a conclusion accepted as early as the second question of the *Summa*, is here finding its ultimate justification. At the same time, we are learning to distinguish between the purely Aristotelian level and the properly Thomistic level in the theology of Thomas Aquinas. Every time Aristotle can serve the pur- pose, Thomas makes use of his doctrine, for the simple reason that it was then the recognized philosophy in the schools. Besides, although sometimes insufficient, this philosophy was usually true. But if the point at stake demands it, Thomas Aquinas brings into play his own meta- physics, as we have just seen him do. Let us posit this as a general rule: the truly and properly Thomistic doctrinal positions are usually recog- nizable by the fact that they ultimately rest upon the notion of being conceived as *esse* or as that which has *esse*. For this is the properly Thomistic notion of being, which in philosophy is the first principle and in theology is the proper name of God.

It is a serious error to overlook systematically what is, in the doctrine of Thomas Aquinas, his deepest principle of explanation; but it would be another error to systematize his theology on the basis of his own notion of God and of being. He himself did not attempt it. One would rather think he intentionally avoided doing so, as if to say that a theo- logian should keep open as many ways to truth as possible. In the fol- lowing article, in which he proved that there are no accidents in God, Thomas could have settled the question at once by observing that He Who is beyond even essence cannot possibly receive accidents, but he preferred lesser arguments. First, substance is in potency to its accidents; but there is no potentiality in God; consequently, there are no accidents in God. Second, God is His own being, and this time, the ultimate argument seems to be brought into play; but no; instead of resorting directly to his own notion of being, Thomas invoked that of Boethius according to which, although "that which is" may well receive additions, *esse* itself cannot. Third, Thomas remarks that "what is essential is prior to what is accidental," and since it is essential to God to be absolute prime being, there can be nothing accidental in Him.[19] All this is perfectly correct and founded on principles to which Thomas himself subscribes. But one cannot help thinking that he prefers to use arguments whose grounds will be recognized as valid by other theologians rather than to set forth arguments, perhaps even stronger ones, but whose validity will probably not be universally recognized by his contemporaries. How wisely he was acting can be seen from the fact that many theologians after him found it possible to uphold almost all of his theological conclusions, minus, however, the very notions which, in his own mind, had given them the fullness of their theological meaning.

After proving that God is His own being (*esse*) Thomas had no need to add further proofs in order to establish that God is altogether simple and, moreover, that He does not enter into composition with other things. But he had other reasons for doing so. His obvious intention was to review the reasons already given, and even in his conclusion he still recalled the possibility of points of view that he himself had overcome: "And so, since God is absolute form [to speak the language of Boethius] or rather absolute being [*ipsum esse*, to speak Thomas' own langugage], He can in no way be composite."[20] As to his reason for separately establishing that God does not enter into the composition of other things, it is made clear by the text of the article. Thomas Aquinas simply wanted explicitly to refute the errors of those who had identified the Holy Ghost with the world-soul, who had made God the formal principle of all things (Amaury de Bène and the Amauricians), or who, more stupidly still, had taught that God was prime matter itself (David de Dinant). Once more, different reasons can be adduced against these errors, but the decisive one remains the same: to enter into the composition of a whole would mean that God is one being among many others: "now, it has been proved that God is absolutely the first being."[21]

With this notion of God, Thomas Aquinas has already reached the summit of his theology. To posit God as the pure and simple act of being is, by the same token, to posit Him as absolutely perfect. The reason is that being (*esse*) is the most perfect of all things. As has already been said, "nothing has actuality except so far as it is." There is no point in imagining essences endowed with various degrees of perfection; no essence has reality except so far as some act of being (*esse*) causes it to be an actually existing thing. Hence the justly famous passage in which Thomas boldly declares that:

> . . . *being* (esse) *is the actuality of all things, even of forms them-selves. Therefore it is not compared to other things as the receiver is to the received, but rather as the received is to the receiver. When therefore I speak of the being of a man, or of a horse, or of anything else, being itself* (ipsum esse) *is considered as formal and received, and not as that to which being belongs.*[22]

Which means that, in Thomas Aquinas' own language, *esse*, the act in virtue of which an actually existing thing actually is, should always be considered as the most perfect element in the thing. In the structure of any given being, *esse* is an act with respect to which all the rest, beginning with the form itself, is in potency. To say that God is the pure act of being, therefore, is to say that He is supremely act and the supreme perfection. But this conclusion immediately leads to this further one; namely, that the perfections of all things are in God. Leaving aside the proof from the notion of God conceived as prime efficient cause, let us concentrate again on the properly Thomistic argument. Referring his reader to the article in which it was proved that in God essence is the same as *esse*, Thomas recalls that:

> . . . *from what has already been proved, God is being itself, of itself subsistent* (ipsum esse per se subsistens). *Consequently, He must contain within Himself the whole perfection of being.*

As if to remove all possible misunderstandings, Thomas then adds:

> *Now all the perfections of all things pertain to the perfection of actual being* (omnium autem perfectiones pertinent ad perfectionem essendi); *for things are perfect precisely so far as they have actual being in some way. It follows therefore that the perfection of no thing is wanting to God.*[23]

Having thus said what he wanted to say, Thomas carefully covers his tracks by invoking the authority of Dionysius the Pseudo-Areopagite. It would not be difficult for us to retranslate the formulas of Dionysius into the authentic language of Thomas Aquinas; but even this slight effort would purposelessly confuse the issue. Thomas Aquinas preferred to proceed under the authority of Dionysius, whereas today we rather feel that Dionysius should proceed under the authority of Thomas Aquinas.

From the notion of God, as from a point of vantage, the possibility that other beings should exist can clearly be seen. Should they be created, such beings would be like God in a remote way, yet in a true way. God is not contained in any genus, whereas all created beings are contained in some genus and in some species. Their likeness to God is thus bound to be a very remote one. Still, God is Being, so that everything that in any way is, must resemble the First Cause. This kind of resemblance is what Thomas calls an "analogy," by which he means a resemblance that does not consist in belonging to the same genus, or to the same species, but simply in sharing in the most common of all formalities, which is being. This is the most common of all formalities because it is found in all that which is not nothing. God is being itself, or, as they say, by essence; other things are beings by participation only, but of them, as of God, it can be said that they are, and this is precisely a relation of analogy. All relations of similitude that ultimately rest upon the bare fact that, in some way or other, their two terms *are*, are relations of analogy. There is then a resemblance between Being and beings. It is written in *Genesis* (*1:26*): *Let ; ma.. : man to our image and likeness*. There is at least one sense in which this is true, and this first sense is presupposed by all the others: *to be* necessarily implies a certain likeness to HE WHO IS.

III. HE WHO IS

In order not to interrupt the continuity of the demonstration, the proof of the simplicity of God has been pursued up to its first and immediate consequence, the perfection of God. For if God is the pure actuality of being itself in itself, then He is both simple and perfect. What remains to be seen is the meaning of the word *esse*, which Thomas Aquinas uses, rather than the word *ens*, to designate the divine being.

According to the *Summa Contra Gentiles*, the source of the doctrine can be found in Scripture (*Exod. 3:13–14*), in the already-quoted passage in which, answering a question of Moses, God Himself says that His name is I AM WHO AM. Since names are intended to signify the natures or essences of things, the words of the Lord should mean that

His essence, or nature, is the simple and perfect act expressed by the verb I AM.

Scriptural scholars, trained in the methods of philology and of biblical exegesis, sometimes express their doubts as to the correctness of this interpretation. Did the sacred writer have this meaning in mind when he wrote these words? But to Thomas Aquinas himself this was not the question.[24] There exists a colossal literature devoted to the theological interpretation of Sacred Scripture, and no one pretends that the inspired authors of the Bible have expressly intended to say all that their future commentators were going to make them say. Thomas Aquinas was less ambitious. He simply believed that, since we think that the sacred writers were inspired of God, we should not apply to their writings the same rules of interpretation we apply to books that are the products of the human mind alone. Thomas had two answers to this difficulty. First, he considered it as not unbelievable that Moses and the other divinely inspired writers had been permitted by God to understand several different truths under one single set of words, so that each and every one of these different truths was the meaning of the inspired author. This possibility opens for the later interpreters of Scripture a wide field of justifiable interpretation. The only question is to know if the meaning attributed to Scripture by its interpreter is in itself true, because if it is, even though the author of the passage may not have understood it, this meaning was certainly understood by the Holy Ghost, Who is the principal author of Holy Writ. Hence this golden rule: "All truth which, respecting the terms of the letter, can be fitted to Holy Scripture, is its meaning (*Unde omnis veritas quae, salva litterae circumstantia, potest divinae scripturae aptari, est ejus sensus*)."[25]

The only question for us to answer is: how do we know that this meaning of Scripture is true in itself? Once more, the question cannot be answered without taking into account the patient effort of the philosophers, pagan, Moslem, Jewish, and Christian, to elaborate an always less and less imperfect notion of God.

The philosophical starting point of this line of inquiry seems to be the distinction introduced by Aristotle between the two fundamental questions that can be asked about any object: *if it is* and *what it is*. The answer to the first question can be provided either by sense experience, when the actual existence of the thing is being perceived by sight, touch, or some other sense power, or it can be provided by the reason when, starting from this experience of an actually existing object, we affirm the existence of another one posited as its cause. This is what was done, for instance, when the first way concluded that there is a first unmoved mover. The answer to the question: what is this thing? is provided by the observation, description, or definition of what is called the nature, or essence, of the thing. In one short sentence Aristotle had already noted the fact that the knowledge of what a thing is does not imply the knowledge of its existence. The essence of a thing is an object of definition; the existence of a thing is an object of demonstration. So "what human nature is and the fact that man exists are not the same thing."[26] To which, as though prompted by a secret premonition, Aristotle added there is only one instance in which the actual existence of a thing can be deduced from its definition, without recourse to any demonstration; namely, if existence were the essence of the thing. In Aristotle's own philosophy, however, this is impossible because, "since being is not a genus, it is not the essence of anything." In Thomas Aquinas' own doctrine, being is still not a genus, but there nevertheless is a being whose essence is actual existence; namely, God, Whose very essence is *to be*. But we are anticipating the later development of our problem.

The position of Aristotle entailed the consequence that, in order to pass from the order of essence to that of actual existence, one had to pass from the order of definition to that of demonstration. On the other hand, Aristotle had no doubt as to the fact that to demonstrate the truth of an essential definition was, by the same token, to demonstrate its reality, its being. In his own words:

> *Hence the being of anything as fact is matter for demonstration; and this is the actual procedure of the sciences, for the geometer assumes the meaning of the word triangle, but that it is possessed of some attributes, he proves. What is it then that we shall prove in defining essential nature? Triangle? In that case a man will know by definition what a thing's nature is without knowing it exists. But that is impossible.*[27]

There was no reason for Aristotle to go beyond the domain of logic to that of metaphysics. As he himself conceived it, the universe was both eternal and necessary, so that, in it, the demonstration of the truth of an essence amounted to that of its being. All demonstrations were by the cause, and the effect of a cause was a being. Not so with Avicenna, a Moslem philosopher well informed about the Judeo-Christian notion of creation and of the actual gap there is, in reality as well as in logic, between an essence and its existence. An essence itself is a possible present to the mind of God, and of itself it does not contain the reason for its actual existence. Unless God gives it actual existence by mode of creation, the essence will never exist. In order to understand the notion of God, one must think of Him as of a being in which this problem does not arise, and the only way to do so is to conceive God as having no essence, or, in Avicenna's own language, no quiddity.

This position of Avicenna's was familiar to Thomas Aquinas. On several occasions, especially in the first half of his short career, Thomas Aquinas used not only the conclusion of Avicenna but even the main argument whereby he had tried to justify it. One of the most perfect expositions of the argument is found in the treatise *On Being and Essence:*

> *Whatever does not belong to the notion of an essence or quiddity comes from without and enters into composition with the essence, for no essence is intelligible without its parts. Now, every essence or quiddity can be understood without anything being known of its existing. I can know what a man or a phoenix is and still be ignorant whether it exists in reality. From this it is clear that the act of existing is other than essence or quiddity, unless, perhaps, there is a being whose quiddity is its very act of existing* (esse). *And there can be only one such being, the First Being.*

In the following chapter Thomas says again that "there is a being, God, Whose essence is His very act of existing. That explains why we find some philosophers asserting that God does not have a quiddity, or essence, because His essence is not other than His act of existing." And, indeed, such exactly had been the conclusion of Avicenna: the First has no quiddity (*quidditatem non habet*).[28]

The way followed by the Moslem philosopher and the Christian theologian is the same. In both doctrines, the notion of a God without an essence, or whose essence is his very *esse*, is reached at the term of an induction which consists in removing all composition from the notion of God. The whole process, however, presupposes that there are beings, or substances, given in sense experience whose structure reveals itself to the metaphysician as a compound of essence and existence. If this is true, then the conclusion follows: after removing essence, only existence is left, and this is what God is. But how do we know that empirically given beings are compounded of essence and existence? The argument used by Avicenna, and several times invoked by Thomas Aquinas, is often quoted as a demonstration of the distinction between essence and existence in concrete substances, but it does not really prove it. The argument proves only that, in a created universe, existence must come to essences from the outside and, therefore, be superadded to them. Any metaphysics or theology that recognizes the notion of creation necessarily agrees on this point. All Christian theologies in particular expressly teach that no finite being is the cause of its own existence, but this does not imply that existence is created in the finite substance as a distinct "act of being" (*esse*) added by God to its essence and composing the substance with it. In order to demonstrate his conclusion, Avicenna must have first conceived the notion of *esse* as a distinct metaphysical element of reality, after which, seeing it received by the essence at the time of its creation, he considered it as an additional element received in an essence and joined with it. In Avicenna's own language, or at least in that of his Latin translators, created existence comes to essence as a sort of "accident." For reasons of his own, Thomas Aquinas did not like to call existence an accident of essence. Still, like Avicenna, he considered it as "other than" essence, so that as soon as existence had been conceived as a distinct metaphysical element, it was necessarily to be described as that which in a substance is both distinct from, and united with, essence. The way of remotion therefore leads to the notion of a God Whose essence is His very act of existing; but it does so only if it sets out from a world of concrete substances endowed with individual acts of existing. And this does not seem philosophically demonstrable from the notion of substance alone. It can be demonstrated that no essence is the cause of its own existence, from which it follows that whatever has an essence, and exists, must exist in virtue of an external cause; but no one has ever been able to demonstrate the conclusion that, in a caused substance, existence is a distinct element, other than essence, and its act.

If the same doctrine were already found in the *Metaphysics* of Avicenna we could content ourselves with saying that Thomas Aquinas simply borrowed from him the position under discussion. This would still leave open the question of its demonstrability, but a historical explanation of its origin at least would have been found. Here again, however, the answer is not yet wholly satisfactory. Unquestionably, the metaphysics of Avicenna was for Thomas Aquinas an important aid. Our theologian has expressly quoted Avicenna as the philosopher who, going on this point further than even Aristotle, pushed the analysis of the notion of being beyond the level of substance to that of actual existence. Moreover, Avicenna so forcibly distinguished existence from essence that he turned it into a sort of accident. But the conclusion of Avicenna does not follow from the same premises as that of Thomas Aquinas, nor has it the same meaning.

Thomas Aquinas has been rather overgenerous with Avicenna as with every one of his predecessors. The fault is not common and, in a sense, it was not a fault, but this generosity makes things difficult for his historians. The God of Avicenna is pure being, with no essence, but being is here conceived as a pure necessity of existence. For this reason, the true Avicennian proof of the existence of God starts from the being that is of itself possible in order to infer the existence of a being that is of itself necessary. Because His very being is necessity, the God of Avicenna cannot not allow beings to flow from Himself. In a sense, He produces them freely, because He creates them by His own will; in another sense, He cannot not produce them, because His will, being the First Himself as the necessary principle of all good and of the very order of all good, cannot not approve that order. From this point of view, the possibles of Avicenna are possibles from their own point of view alone; as destined to flow from God, they are bound to become necessary in virtue of His will, and this at the moment when the order of the world will call for their existence. At that moment, each possible is caused to exist by the will of the First, and to make it to be consists, for the First, in imparting to it the necessity which, of its proper nature, the possible is lacking. Necessity so clearly is the very name for existence that, in the doctrine of Avicenna, to be caused to exist is to be made to be necessary-by-another. This also accounts for the well-known fact that Avicenna considers actual existence, if not truly an accident, at least an addition to, and an appendage of, essence. It is its ultimate act in the sense that it comes to essence as its ultimate complement, not as the first act that makes it to be a being.

If we grant Avicenna this notion of being, the distinction of essence and existence becomes demonstrable within the limits of the notion. Possibility that is an attribute of essence itself *qua* essence and the fact that there are generations and corruptions conclusively prove that, in generated beings, essence must be given existence by some exterior cause, which ultimately is God. Let us add that Thomas Aquinas fully agrees with this kind of reasoning; in fact, it is substantially the "third way" to prove the existence of God. But Thomas Aquinas probes further and more deeply than Avicenna into the nature of finite being. To him, existence cannot be "added to" essence for the simple reason that, without existence, essence is nothing, so that it cannot receive anything. As will be seen later, essence owes to existence the very being without which existence could not even be received in it. The ultimate truth of the Thomistic notion of being is that existence is not in a being received under the form of a participated and temporary necessity, but rather under that of a participated act of being. In Avicenna's doctrine, the Necessary-by-itself causes the necessaries-by-another; in the doctrine of Thomas Aquinas, Being-by-itself causes beings-by-a-cause. This is the reason why, starting from the Avicennian analysis of finite being, one can conclude to the Avicennian distinction of essence and existence, and this is a method of which Thomas has made good use; but one cannot conclude to the Thomistic distinction of essence and existence because, under its properly Thomistic form, the distinction presupposes the notion of *esse* conceived, in concrete substances, as the highest intrinsic principle of their very being. It is of course always dangerous to maintain that something is *not* there; hence, subject to correction by some more penetrating historian, we tentatively submit that there is nothing like the Thomistic notion of an intrinsic act of being (*esse*) in the Avicennian notion of a possible essence that holds its necessity from another. What encourages us to maintain this interpretation of the doctrine as correct is that, in point of fact, Thomas Aquinas refuses to consider even finite beings as holding their necessity from another. Creation imparts to them their own necessity by the same act that imparts to them their own being.

To sum up what precedes, let us say that, *so far as we are able to see*, all the arguments one can use to establish the distinction between being and essence in Thomas Aquinas' doctrine presuppose the prior recognition of the notion of the "act of being" (*esse*). This cannot possibly be an intellectual intuition, because there is no such thing in Thomism. It can be only the extreme summit accessible to abstract knowledge. Actual existence is given in sense intuition. From the objects of sense intuition the intellect abstracts, among other notions, those of *being* (*ens, Seiendes, étant*), *thing* (*res, Ding, chose*), *matter* and *form* conceived as two distinct constituents of corporal substance. Moreover, conceiving apart that which the thing is and the fact that it actually is, we can form the two abstract notions of *essence* (question, *quid sit*) and of *existence* (question, *an sit*), but this is the point where most of the philosophers will stop while Thomas Aquinas insists on going on. Existence may mean either a state or an act. In the first sense, it means the state in which a thing is posited by the efficacy of an efficient or of a creative cause, and this is the meaning the word receives in practically all the Christian theologies outside Thomism, particularly those of Augustine, Boethius, Anselm, Scotus, and Suarez. In a second sense, existence (*esse, to be*) points out the interior act, included in the composition of substance, in virtue of which the essence is a "being," and this is the properly Thomistic meaning of the word.

The problem under discussion now is: how did Thomas Aquinas achieve the awareness of the very possibility of this notion? It certainly results from a supreme effort of abstraction, since, in order to form it, the intellect must conceive, apart from the condition of being an existent, the act owing to which the existent finds itself in this condition: *ipsum esse significatur ut quiddam abstractum.*[29] Now, obviously, to abstract this notion from that of substance and to distinguish it from the notion of essence was precisely to create it. How did Thomas come by this new notion? It is not a notion universally evident to all human minds. Far from it. The majority of philosophers will concede that it is a far cry from a possible thing to an actual thing. In Kant's own words, the notion of a hundred dollars may be the same for merely possible dollars and for actual dollars, but possible dollars and actual dollars are very different in reality. This will be conceded by all, but if an actually existing being has been produced by its cause, why should one attribute to it an "existence" distinct from the fact that it exists? This is the very point that Thomas is anxious to make us understand; but how can he make us see it if we don't? One cannot abstract from reality a notion whose object one fails to perceive. What has divided the Thomist school from the other schools of theology, ever since the thirteenth century, is a general reluctance to conceive the act of being (*esse*) as a distinct object of understanding. To tell the whole truth, even the so-called "Thomists" have been and still are divided on this point. No such disagreement would take place if the presence, in things themselves, of an act in virtue of which they can be called "beings" were a conclusion susceptible of demonstration.

This impasse is an invitation to us to give up the philosophical way—from creatures to God—and try the theological way—from God to creatures. Thomas Aquinas may well have first conceived the notion of an act of being (*esse*) in connection with God and then, starting from God, made use of it in his analysis of the metaphysical structure of composite substances.

At first sight, this is not very likely. All our notions of God are directly or indirectly borrowed from our notions of finite beings, and if we did not first discern the act of existing in the structure of God's creatures, how could we think of identifying it with the very essence of the divine being? Still, this is a good time to remember the curious remark made by Thomas himself at the end of the *Summa Contra Gentiles,* I, chapter 22, where, after establishing that God's essence is His very *esse,* the theologian adds that "this sublime truth Moses was taught by our Lord." Now, Moses could not learn this sublime truth from our Lord without at the same time learning from Him the notion of what it is to be a pure existential act. This invites us to admit that, according to Thomas himself, his notion of *esse* can be learned from the very words of God.

But in what sense can this be true? As has been seen, Thomas Aquinas considered an authentic meaning of Scripture every interpretation of it which, respecting the detail of its letter, was true. He also firmly believed that revelation instructs reason in many truths which, although they are revealed to it, can be grasped by it. Now, precisely, there is no known case of an interpretation of Scripture more closely fitting the letter of the revealed text than the present one, and it so happens that, in this instance, there is something arresting about the grammatical structure of the sentence. In the form in which Thomas was reading it in its Latin translation, the sentence was trying to say something that cannot be correctly said following the received laws of grammar. God said to Moses that His name was I AM, or HE IS. Even the natural theology of Avicenna had not gone as far as that. On the other hand, generation after generation of theologians had read these words of *Exodus* without realizing their tremendous metaphysical and theological possibilities. By a disconcerting conjunction—which, however, is an actual fact—the Thomistic commentary on *Exodus 3:13* achieves a perfect coincidence of the strictest literalism in adhering to the text of Scripture with the maximum of metaphysical depth in its speculative interpretation. In order to reach the new metaphysical notion of being, which identifies it with its very act, one has only to accept the words of Scripture at their face value. For if one does so, what other meaning can he give to the proper name of God, I AM? It is at least possible that the Thomistic notion of being was born at the moment when, for the first time, a metaphysician fully informed of the philosophical history of the notion happened to be, at the same time, a theologian fully conversant with Scripture. Should this be true, the origin of the notion would be tied up with theological reflection; the *esse* that God is would have been known, on the strength of His own word, before a participation of it was conceived as the act of a finite essence and, therefore, as joined to it. Here history is once more reaching one of its impassable limits: individual psychology. The result at least is clear: it is one and the same thing to conceive God as pure *Esse* and to conceive things, so far as they *are*, as including in their metaphysical structure a participated image of the pure Act of Being.

IV. REFLECTIONS ON THE NOTION OF BEING

The essentials of the doctrine can be summed up as follows. No composite being is a necessary being; the quiddity of a necessary being is its being; God is the being in which being and essence are the same.[30] The position is the more remarkable as, from within the historical perspective adopted by Thomas Aquinas himself, it appeared as the conclusion of the slow metaphysical progress achieved from the time of the Presocratic philosophers of Greece to his own day. This was in no sense a discovery of the notion of being, which, since it is the first principle, is as old as the human mind, but it was a discovery *within* the notion of being. The ultimate meaning of "being" is not to be in this or that way; it is *to be*. What did this mean in the mind of our theologian?

His own formulation of the conclusion is significant. Before Thomas Aquinas, Avicenna had bluntly said that the First has no quiddity: *Primus igitur non habet quidditatem.* Thomas himself seems to have avoided this uncompromising language. Not that he had any objection to the truth of what it says, for if essence is understood as something in any way different from God's act of being, then it must be conceded that God has no essence. But Thomas Aquinas does not want us, or himself, to lose contact with the quiddity of sensible things, our necessary starting point in investigating the nature of God. To know something is for us to know what it is. If God has no essence, He has no "whatness," so that to the question: What is God? the correct answer should be, nothing. Many mystics have not hesitated to say so, in the definite sense that God is no-thing, but they certainly were not doubting God's existence. To say that God has no essence would be to render Him completely unthinkable. More important still, it would be to betray the true meaning of the negative method in theology. A negation necessarily requires an affirmation; namely, the very affirmation it denies. To say that God has no essence really means that God is as a beyond-essence. This is best expressed by saying that God is the being whose essence is to be beyond essence or, in other words, God is the being whose essence it is to be.[31]

This personal approach to the problem is in keeping with the spirit of Thomism. Before embarking on a voyage, a man must first take leave of all the persons and things with which he will have to part. Then he finds himself aboard the ship, in the strangely limited universe that will be his for a few days. Still, nothing decisive happens until the last moment comes, when, finally casting off her moorings, the ship sets out on her voyage. Then the traveler literally is "at sea," so much so that, asked where he is, he cannot reply with the name of any definite place. But this is not entirely true. Once on the open sea, the sailor still can say how many thousand miles away from such-and-such land he is. To the question, where are we? he would not answer, no-where; he would rather say something like this: we are so many miles east, or west, of such-and-such a coast. Something similar happens to us when we attempt to speak of God. So long as we have a precise notion of what God is not, words still preserve a positive meaning of a sort. In imagination, we can strip a substance of its accidents, then think of its matter apart, or of its form apart, and so long as we keep in mind the notion of its essence, we still know what we are talking about; but to conceive it without its essence, this is impossible, for its whatness is part and parcel of every actual reality. So also with our notion of God. When we reach the question, what is God? the time has come for our intellect to cast off its moorings and to set sail on the infinite ocean of pure *esse*, or *act*, whereby that which is actually is. Then, of course, we no longer can say where we are, because there are no landmarks where there is no land. But we remember that there was land and it is with reference to it that we still can steer our course and attribute to our-selves a location of sorts. What is the very last thing a concrete sub-stance would have to give up in order to achieve utter simplicity? Its essence, of course. In our attempt to describe God by removing from Him what is proper to the being of creatures, we must give up essence in order to reach the open sea of pure actual existence, but we must also keep the notion of essence present to the mind so as not to leave it without any object. This we do when, to the question, where do we find God? we simply answer, beyond essence. By establishing himself in the definite negation of posited essence, the theologian realizes that he is placing God above that which is deepest in the only kind of reality he knows. At that moment, the theologian is not beyond being; on the contrary, he is, beyond essence, at the very core of being.

This is to point out, in a negative way, an object of thought more positive than all the definable ones. Were we to say that God is *this*, be it essence, our proposition would entail the consequence that God is not that. On the contrary, in saying that God is neither this nor that, we implicitly affirm that there is nothing that, in His own transcendent way, God is not. To affirm that God is only being is to deny of Him all that which, because it is a determination of being, is a negation of it.

The act of being that is affirmed of God is entirely different from the abstract notion of being we form in our mind when we conceive it in its universality. Understood in this latter way, being is the most general of our concepts. It is a universal; that is to say, a being of second intention with no other reality of its own than that of a known object in our intellect. Thomas Aquinas usually calls it "common being" (*ens commune*), an excellent appellation indeed,[32] because all that which has actual being is particular, so that common being, by definition, cannot exist. The very reverse is true of the act of being we have attributed to God. Since He is His own act of being, which can be said of no other being, God is distinct from all other beings. As Thomas himself so forcibly puts it, by His own act of being, God differs from every other being: *Esse divinum, quod est ejus substantia, non est esse commune, sed est esse distinctum a quolibet alio esse. Unde per ipsum suum esse Deus differt a quolibet alio ente.*[33] The meaning of the doctrine is clear. All other beings have an essence distinct from their own act of being; only God's essence is His own act of being (*esse*); His existential purity individuates God, so to speak, and sets Him apart from all the rest.

It is characteristic of the theology of Saint Thomas Aquinas that, in it, the problem of the infinity of God really does not arise. If it is innocent of all limitation, even that which all other things receive from their own essences, a being is unlimited by definition. The word "infinite" is a negative one; it simply removes from the notion of the divine being all limitation, exactly as the word "simple" removes from it all composition. In both cases, however, the reality pointed out by the negative appellation is a most positive one. Since the act that God is, is not received in anything that can determine, qualify, or limit it in any way, Thomas Aquinas rightly concludes that, for God, to be and to be infinite are the same thing.[34]

PART III. BEING

Chapter 6. God and the transcendentals

The word "transcendentals" does not belong to the usual terminology of Thomas Aquinas. It was coined at a later date (so far as we know) to signify the group of properties that belong to being as being; namely, *one*, *true*, *good*, etc. The notions themselves, however, were quite familiar to Thomas Aquinas and he found a place for them in the two main expositions of his theology, the *Summa Contra Gentiles* and the *Summa Theologiae*. Today they are inseparable from his notion of God.

I. THE PROBLEM OF THE DIVINE NAMES

At the present point of our inquiry, the problem of the divine names is not an entirely new one. From the very moment we use the word "God" we have begun to name Him. Furthermore, we have considered the questions raised by the very name that God has chosen as His own in *Exodus;* and to repeat what God has said of Himself—namely, that He is I AM or HE IS—certainly is to name Him. On these occasions, some comments were made concerning the negative or analogical nature of the names attributable to God, but the discussion of the problem was intentionally left incomplete on two grounds. First, as is often the case in theology, it is necessary to secure a certain notion of God before proceeding to a complete discussion of our own knowledge of God. The theologian is like the philosopher in this, that his knowledge of God expresses itself in a language borrowed from material substances; hence, after establishing God's existence, the theologian must proceed to a critique of his own language concerning God. Second, the conclusions of our inquiry have been limited to the assertion of only one absolutely valid name attributable to God: Being; but many more names will now be given to Him, and this very plurality is in itself a problem. The transcendentals—one, true, good, beautiful—are such names. It will therefore not be amiss, before applying these names to God, to determine the limits of their validity.

From what has preceded it is clear that God *is* in a unique way. If we wish to attribute an essence to Him, then we ought to add at once that, in this unique case, essence merely means *esse*, the very act of being. This is enough to make us sure that, strictly speaking, no name can be attributed to God and to other beings in the same sense. On the other hand, the names theologians give to God cannot be entirely meaningless, or otherwise all theological propositions about God would be equivalent as being equally vain and devoid of meaning. The question to know is, what has a meaning in such names and what is the nature of their signification?

The origin of the positive element in our language concerning God is the effect-to-cause relationship between created beings and their Creator. As will be more fully explained in its place, because beings are inasmuch as they are acts, they are causes inasmuch as they are beings, and for them to be causes consists in imparting to other beings some of their own actuality. For this reason, effects necessarily bear a certain likeness to their causes. In fact, the being of an effect is a participation in the being of the cause from which the effect has received it. This also is the justification for our attributing certain names to God. If God is the cause of all things, they must all resemble God in some measure and in some way. To call God the name of one of His effects will amount to attributing to Him that in which such effect participates.

An abundant literature has been devoted to the notion of analogy in the theology of Thomas Aquinas, and indeed there are several kinds of analogies; but inasmuch as he is a theologian, Thomas is interested in only one of them—namely, the relationship there is between the creatures of God and their cause. The Greek word *analogia* means *proportion: secundum analogiam, id est, proportionem.*[1]

If we take proportion in its most general meaning in the language of Saint Thomas, it signifies any relationship between one thing and another. If the word is taken in its more restricted meaning of commensurability in a given proportion, then, of course, the disproportion between man and God is infinite and a knowledge of God would be impossible for us. In its widest acceptation, however, the word signifies *quamcumque habitudinem unius ad alterum:* any relation of one thing to another. Of the two examples quoted by Thomas Aquinas in the same passage, the proportion (or analogy) of matter to form, and the proportion (or analogy) of effect to cause, the second is of direct interest to us. The relation of effect to cause is the basis of the relation between man as understanding God and God as understood by man.[2]

This is nothing exceptional in the doctrine of Saint Thomas in which all the relations between man and God are relations of effect to cause. The positive element in our knowledge of God has no other origin. If we say that God is life, for instance, we say something that is true of God, for if there were no life in God, the First Cause, there could be no life in any of His effects. How, under what form, and in what sense life can be said to be in God is another and different problem; the present point at stake is that there is at least one sense in which it is true that God is life. There is in God that which must be there to account for the fact that what we call life exists as its effect and, therefore, resembles it as effects resemble their causes. In other words, if "a creature receives from God that which makes it like Him,"[3] then that which the creature receives must necessarily pre-exist in God. This also accounts for the fact that the many names said of God are not synonyms.[4] Assuredly, they all signify the same reality, God, but each particular name said of God signifies Him as having in Himself the particular created perfection pointed out by the particular name. The reality signified by these many names is absolutely one, but the significations of the names are not one since each particular name signifies a particular created perfection.

These remarks permit us to determine what it is possible to say of God as well as what it is not possible to say of Him.

Among the names, some signify a perfection without defect. For example, whether they are said of God or of creatures, such words as "goodness," "wisdom," "being," and the like, express unqualified perfections. These words can be used to name God as well as other beings. Of course they are predicated of God in a more eminent way than of creatures, yet, in the last analysis, they are properly said of Him. God really is what such names signify; that is, life itself, goodness itself, and so on. Not so when a name points out perfections realized in a created thing, such as stone (which has being) or man (having both being and life). In such cases, the perfections in question are named as limited by the specific nature of a certain creature. Since God escapes all limitations, such names cannot be attributed to Him properly. When they are said of Him, as often happens in the Bible, they are so many metaphors. Consequently, the only names properly said of God are those that signify, not creatures, but the perfections found in creatures; and if we qualify such names so as to make them signify some perfection in the supereminent mode under which it is found in God, then they are not only applicable to God, they become applicable to God alone. Such are, for instance, "the highest good," "the first being," and the like.[5]

This gives its true meaning to the doctrine of our analogical knowledge of God. In a striking passage of the *Summa Theologiae*, Thomas Aquinas has expressly declared insufficient the position of Alain of Lille, a twelfth-century theologian, according to whom the names applied to God signify, not God Himself, but His relations to creatures. In this view, *God is good, God is Life,* etc., would simply mean that God is the cause of goodness in things, the cause of life, and the like. But if this were true, since God is the cause of all things, including even bodies, all the names of creatures could be attributed to Him as to their cause. And yet we do not say that God is a body. The true meaning of the doctrine is that the names of God are said of the very substance of God; that is, of that which God Himself is. Besides, this exactly is what we have in mind in naming God. God is not good or wise because he causes goodness or wisdom; rather, on the contrary, God causes goodness and wisdom because He himself is good and wise. This is the true meaning of the proposition *God is good;* namely, that He Himself has, or is, in a supereminent way the perfection we find in His creatures in a participated and limited way only.[6] In the parallel passage of the *De Potentia*, Thomas says that such names signify something existing in God (*aliquid existens in Deo*), and this precisely is the positive element contained in all true predications of God. Far from making negative theology impossible, this element paves the way to it, for it is precisely that which negative theology will have to deny. In Thomas' own words:

> *The meaning of a negation always is founded in an affirmation, as appears from the fact that every negative proposition is proved by an affirmative one; consequently, unless the human understanding knew something of God affirmatively, it could deny nothing of God; and such would be the case if nothing of what it says of God could be verified affirmatively.*[7]

This leads to the conclusion that, whatever its ultimate meaning, the "negative" method in theology necessarily consists in systematically denying true propositions. The theologian does not deny them on the premise that they are false, but rather as a means of reaching a higher truth through their very denial. Thus, if one stays at their level, one will think nothing that is not true, and one's effort to overcome them will at no moment require one to consider them untrue. They are true indeed at their own level. But there is a higher one, which is that of negative theology.

The progress now to be achieved in our knowledge of God will therefore consist in leaving a certain truth behind us. To formulate this step in technical terms, Thomas Aquinas resorts to the distinction, classic in logic, between univocal and equivocal predication. One term is predicated of another univocally when it is predicated of it as its genus, its difference, or its accident; but none of these predications applies to God. A general reason in favor of this conclusion is found in the nature of the relationship that obtains between other beings and God. Since, as has been seen, God is His own *esse,* God is through Himself everything He is, whereas all other beings are what they are by participation. Everything is predicated of God by priority and of other things by posteriority only. For instance, God is called being because He is being itself by itself, whereas any other being is called a being as having being by participation. What is predicated by participation is not univocal with what is predicated in itself. Hence, nothing can be predicated of God and other things univocally.[8]

This conclusion seems to imply that everything is predicated of God and other things equivocally, and, in a sense, this is true. No name borrowed from creatures can be predicated of God without acquiring a different meaning. In this sense, all names said of God and creatures are said equivocally. Here, however, Thomas introduces an important restriction. There are many pure equivocals. They do not belong in the same genus or species, and between them, moreover, no relationship exists. The classical example is that of the word "dog," which is predicated of a certain animal species, but also, entirely by chance, of Sirius, the "dog star." Now, precisely, the last reason we have alleged to prove that no name can be univocally predicated of God and things also shows that not all names are predicated of God and things in a purely equivocal way. The reason is that everything is said of God and things by priority and posteriority; but this is an order, so that even though the names we give to God are equivocal, they are not purely equivocal because they are not "equivocals by chance."[9] Such names are equivocal because they are predicated of that which is a certain perfection by priority as well as of that which is the same perfection by posteriority.

This conclusion brings us back to our starting point. The names said of God and of creatures are said of God as of that which has in itself the perfection to be their cause, and of creatures as of that which is an effect of God. And this is what we call relation, proportion, analogy. The ultimate reason that makes it necessary for us to resort to negative theology is that all the names we say of God signify perfections found by us in creatures and possessed by posteriority, while we must say them all of Him in Whom they all are by priority. Now since in God all these perfections are His very essence, which itself is His own *esse*, there is for us no way to conceive them such as they are in Him. This situation has often been described by Saint Thomas in terms of a technical distinction between the thing signified by the name (*res nominis*) and the meaning of the name (*ratio nominis*). The thing signified by the name is in God by mode of priority and in other things by mode of posteriority; but since all the divine names are borrowed from creatures, the meaning of the name applies by priority to things. This is the meaning of the rule that God is named from His effects.[10]

The proper object of negative theology, therefore, is to prevent us from staying on the level where the names of creatures are uncritically understood as properly applying to God. In other words, negative theology consists in refusing to think that, because goodness, life, and the like, really are in God, they are properly represented by our concepts of them. Every one of our concepts is the concept of a creature, and we have none other. In his commentary on the *Divine Names* of Dionysius, Thomas accepts without any reservation the most extreme conclusions of the Greek theologian. The essence of God is above sense knowledge, above intellectual knowledge, above all given existence and existents; accordingly, God is neither sensible, nor intelligible, nor one among the number of the existents.

The essence of God is unknown to creatures as exceeding the power not only of human reason but even of the angelic minds. No natural cognitive power can know Him, except by the gift of a divine grace. So long as we are in this life, to know God, as best we can, consists in three things. First and chiefly, it consists in removing all things from God (*primo quidem et principaliter in omnium ablatione*); that is, in refusing to attribute to God any one of the things we see in the order of creatures. Second, it consists in transcending these things and in attributing them to God by excess (*secundario vero per excessum*); for we do not take away from God the perfections of creatures, such as life, wisdom, and the like, because there is any defect in God; we rather remove from Him wisdom, life, and the like, because He exceeds all wisdom, all life, and so with all the other known perfections. Third, we know God by way of causality when we consider that whatever is found in creatures proceeds from God as from its cause. Thus our knowledge follows a way contrary to that of God, for God knows creatures by His own nature, whereas we know God from His creatures and, even so, we know Him best by knowing that we do not know what He is (*hoc ipsum est Deum cognoscere, quod nos scimus nos ignorare de Deo quid sit*):

> *Our mind knows God as being not only above all that which is beneath itself, but above all that is above itself as well as above all that it can comprehend. And knowing God in this way, finding itself in this state of cognition, the mind is illuminated by the very depth of the divine Wisdom, which it cannot scrutinize. For even this, that we understand God to be, not only above all that which is, but above all that which we can apprehend, comes to us from the depth of the divine Wisdom.*[11]

This rule applies to all the names of God, without exception. Even *esse*, "being," is the name of a creature. The only beings we know are creatures, the only way to be we know is that of creatures, and we cannot form any concept of what it is "to be" for the universal cause we call God. Why, then, is HE WHO IS the most perfect and proper of all divine names? The reasons are, first, because it does not signify a certain manner of being, but being itself, and since the essence of God is His very being, and since things are named according to their essences, no name can name God more properly than being; second, because the very universality of this name and its complete indetermination make it eminently applicable to God. Any other name means being plus a certain determination of it; but we know at least this, that however our intellect may determine what it understands about the essence of God, it will fail to grasp what God is in Himself. Hence, the less determinate the names, the less improperly they will apply to God; and since "being" is the least determinate of all, no other name is a more proper name of God.

In proving this point Thomas Aquinas makes a remark that should not pass unnoticed. It is that even the names of the transcendentals do not name God as properly as "being." "For all other names are either less universal, or, if convertible with it, add something above it at least in idea; hence, in a certain way, they inform and determine it."[12] This

is important to note in view of what will presently be said of the transcendentals. *Good, truth, one* are in no sense less universal than being,
since wherever there is being, these are there along with it. Still, they
say being *qua* good, or *qua* one, or *qua* true; they do not say being
qua being, which is precisely what God is best said to be.[13]

However careful one may be to stress the positive meaning of the
names attributed to God, one would betray the deepest intention of
Thomas Aquinas by not letting negative theology have the last word.
If anyone imagines that he has any proper knowledge of "that which
God is," or, in other words, of what one might call the "nature" of
God, he is deceiving himself. The declarations made by Thomas
Aquinas on this point are categorical.[14]

Starting from our natural knowledge of sensible things, we can know
that they have a cause. Hence, from the effects of God we can know
that He exists, and we also know of Him "what must necessarily belong to Him as the first cause of all things," but reason can know
whether God is, not *what God is.*[15] For the same reason, although we
know with certitude that the proposition *God is* is true, we can form
no notion of what it is for God actually *to be:*

> To be (esse) *can mean either one of two things. It may mean the*
> *act of being* (actum essendi), *or it may mean the composition of a*
> *proposition effected by the mind in joining a predicate to a subject.*
> *Taking* to be *in the first sense, we cannot know God's being* (non
> possumus scire esse Dei) *or His essence; but only in the second*
> *sense. We know that this proposition that we form about God when*
> *we say* God is, *is true; and this we know from His effects.*[16]

And again:

> *Neither a Catholic nor a pagan knows the very nature of God as it*
> *is in itself; but each one knows it according to some idea of causality,*
> *or excellence, or remotion.*[17]

Again, taking up the same distinction between the being of actual existence and the being signified in the proposition, Thomas declares that
ens and *esse* are each said in a twofold sense:

> *. . . for sometimes it signifies the entity of the thing, or its act of*
> *being* (essentiam rei, sive actum essendi), *sometimes it signifies the*
> *truth of the proposition, even in things that have no being* (esse),
> *as we say that blindness exists because it is true that a man is blind*

. . . In the first sense the being (esse) of God is the same as His substance, and just as His substance is unknown, so is His being. In the second sense, we know that God is because we conceive this proposition in our mind, from His effects.[18]

II. BEING AND UNITY

The word "one" has different meanings. Two of these must be distinguished from the very beginning. In its most common acceptation, "one" signifies the unity that is the principle of number. In this sense, "one" belongs in the genus of quantity and is a numerical determination adding a reality to being. To say that there is only one being of a certain species, or two, or three, is to add something to the notion of such a being, or beings.[19]

In a second sense, entirely different from the preceding one, "one" does not add anything to "being": "it is only the negation of division; for *one* means undivided being."[20] This primary notion can be more easily described than explained. If a being is simple, it is one and, by the same token, it is a being. If a being is composed of parts, so long as its parts are not united, it is not yet one and, by the same token, it is not yet a being. After its parts have joined in composing it, there arises, at one and the same time, a being and a unity; but if, at a later date, its component parts again divide, their compound loses both unity and being. "Being" and "one" stand and fall together. For everything there is no difference between preserving the unity and preserving the being of any given thing. In this sense, "the being of anything consists in its indivision," and this is the reason why it is said that "one" is convertible with "being": *unum et ens convertuntur.*[21]

The meaning of the doctrine is that "one" adds nothing to "being." It does not add to being any determination or limitation. Whatever is contained in the meaning and reality of "one" is already contained in the meaning and reality of "being." Still, since the two words have distinct meanings, there must be between these two notions and their objects at least a distinction in reason.[22] "Being" signifies being itself; "one" signifies being as undivided; and since being has to remain undivided in order to be, the two notions really point out two points of view on one and the same thing.

Thomas Aquinas has often restated this position: everywhere there is "one," there is also "being"; and, conversely, everywhere there is "being," "one" is present. This does not mean that the two notions are equivalent and can be indifferently exchanged. The reason they are always given together is that, in fact, the meaning of "one" always includes "being." "One" means "undivided being." This is implied in the remark made by Thomas Aquinas that the meaning of "one" is not only indivision but also the substance itself along with its indivision: *est enim unum idem quod ens indivisum.*[23] In still simpler terms, Thomas is saying that "one" includes "being" in its own meaning. Let us note his reason for saying so. If being were not included in the notion of unity, then the one could not even be the one, it would be nothing. The positive element included in the "one" is "being"; "one" means being as conceived in its unity; "one" posits being, it adds only the negation of its possible division: *Unum non addit supra ens rem aliquam, sed tantum negationem divisionis.* In short, *est enim unum ens indivisum:* "one" is undivided "being."[24]

In the mind of Thomas Aquinas himself, this point was important as marking one of the dividing lines between his own metaphysics and that of Avicenna, who, as distinguished from Aristotle and Averroes, considered "one" as adding something to "being." Today the authentic position of Thomas Aquinas needs to be recalled as a safeguard against certain attempts to turn his philosophy of being into a philosophy of the one. To be sure, since Thomism is a philosophy of being, and being is one, Thomism is also a philosophy of the one; but this is true only inasmuch as it is a philosophy of being. The convertibility of "one" and "being" is due to the fact that "one" really is another name for being. Thomas never says that the first principle is "one," or that the proper name of God is I AM THE ONE. His ways to the existence of God five times prove the existence of a prime being that is one; none of them proves the existence of The One. If it is true to say that one must choose between a philosophy of the one and a philosophy of being, Thomas Aquinas' philosophy undoubtedly stands on the side of being.

The true order of the notions in Thomistic doctrine is best seen from the answer to the objection that "one" is not opposed to "many" because, since "many" is defined with respect to "one," and *vice versa,* there seems to be a vicious circle in the definition. To this, Thomas denies there is a vicious circle precisely because the starting point of the definition is neither "one" nor "many," but "being":

> *What first falls into the intellect is being* (ens); *secondly comes the* negation of being. *From these two follows, in the third place, the notion of* division, *since, from the fact that something is con-*

*ceived to be a being, and not to be some other being, it is divided
from it in the intellect. Fourthly, the notion of "one" follows in the
intellect, inasmuch as this being is understood as undivided from itself. Fifthly, the notion of multitude follows, inasmuch as this being
is understood as divided from another one, and each one of them as
being one in itself. For however much certain things may be conceived as divided, there still is no notion of multitude unless each
one of the divided things is conceived as being one.*[25]

The convertibility of "being" and "one" should therefore not be
considered as entailing their equivalence. It is sometimes said that the
doctrine of Thomas Aquinas is a philosophy of unity, which is true,
but it is a philosophy of unity because it is a philosophy of being. Posit
"being" and you also posit "one," because "one" is nothing other than
being conceived in its indivision. If, on the other hand, you begin by
positing "one," you necessarily are positing "being," not because "being" is implied in "one," but rather because "one" itself is nothing else
than undivided "being." The primacy of being is absolute, unrestricted,
for the simple reason that whatever is different from being, is not.[26]

On the strength of these metaphysical positions it is easy to prove
that God is one. In the two *Summae*, Thomas Aquinas follows his usual
procedure, which is to open as many approaches as possible to each
particular conclusion; but his shortest way to it is obviously the one he
takes from the proper name of God. Here it is in its perfect simplicity:
"The proper being of each thing is only one. But God is His being, as
we have shown. There can therefore be only one God."[27] When it is
thus related to the fundamental notion of God as pure *esse*, itself
identical with that of His perfect simplicity, His unity necessarily follows:

*Moreover, a thing has being in the manner it possesses unity. Hence
each thing struggles as much as it can against any division of itself,
lest thereby it tend to non-being. But the divine nature has being
most powerfully. There is, therefore, in it the greatest unity, and
hence no plurality is in any way distinguished within it.*[28]

Similar remarks apply to the arguments mustered by the *Summa
Theologiae*, with this remarkable difference, however, that after giving
three different reasons for the oneness of God,[29] Thomas devotes a
special article to the demonstration of this further conclusion that God
is "supremely one." This time, of course, one argument is enough, and

it is that God is supremely one because He is supremely simple and supremely being. In Thomas' own words:

> Since "one" is "undivided being," if anything is supremely one it must be supremely being and supremely undivided. Now both of these belong to God. For He is supremely being (ens) inasmuch as His esse is not determined by any nature to which it is adjoined [no composition of essence and esse]; for He is esse itself, subsistent, absolutely undetermined. And He is supremely undivided inasmuch as He is divided neither actually nor potentially by any mode of division; for He is altogether simple, as was shown above. Hence it is manifest that God is "one" in the supreme degree.[30]

Thomas Aquinas never forgets the fundamental truth of his theology, but he is less interested in forcing it upon his readers than in leading them to truth by any way they may find easier to follow. An argument is good if it is true, and not every truth is ultimate. Still, it is important not to lose sight of ultimate truth, be it only in order fully to understand other truths, especially in such a time as ours when it seems that nothing will do except ultimate truth.

III. BEING AND THE TRUE

Aristotle did not include the true among the transcendental properties convertible with being. He even expressly refused to do so. At the end of Book VI of the *Metaphysics* he had asked the question whether the nature of the true was a subject to be discussed in metaphysics. The answer was no, because metaphysics is about being *qua* being, whereas the true is not in things but in the mind. Being is true by accident only, inasmuch as it is found in the conception of an intellect composing and dividing concepts. There is truth, or error, in the mind according as it conceives things as they are, or are not, in reality; so the consideration of these notions belongs to another science, such as logic, not to the science of being, metaphysics.[31]

The *Expositor* of Aristotle, Thomas Aquinas, was well aware of this position of the Philosopher. In his own commentary on the *Metaphysics*, Thomas faithfully analyzes the text of Aristotle, and he does so without adding to it any explanation, correction, or justification of his own: "True and false are in the mind, and not in things"; the composition and division of concepts, in which truth consists, *est tantum in intellectu, non in rebus;* again:

That which is being in the sense of the true consisting in such a composition is different from that which is a being properly so-called, for such beings are outside the soul and each one of them is either substance, or quality, or quantity, or some simple apprehension that the mind unites or divides.[32]

The case of the true is the same as that of accidental being, whose cause is indeterminate and, for this reason, escapes science. In short, because true and accidental being do not belong to being as being, they are by-passed by the metaphysician.

Not so in the doctrine of Thomas Aquinas himself. All the treatises containing a special chapter on the true as a transcendental keep faith with the authentic position of Thomas Aquinas, but they betray that of Aristotle. Those who attribute to Aristotle himself such a doctrine are once more speaking of the philosophy of Aristhomas, a *hircocervus,* without any other reality than that of a fiction of the mind.

There are two reasons for this. First, we have the word of God Himself to settle the question, since Our Lord says, *I am the Way, and the Truth, and the Life (John 14:6).* Next, precisely because God Himself is the truth, the relationship of being to truth is not entirely the same in the two doctrines. As can be expected, we shall see Thomas Aquinas follow Aristotle as far as is compatible with the requirements of his theology and there, having reached the parting of the ways, he will follow his own way.

In point of fact, the parting of the ways is announced by the very formulation of the question. As has been seen, in Aristotle there had been no question at all. Speaking of the being that signifies truth (in fact, the *est* of the *copula*), Aristotle had simply said of it that, in metaphysics, *est praetermittendum.*[33] The reason is, truth is in the mind, not in things. On the contrary, the first question asked by Thomas Aquinas on this point runs as follows: "Whether truth resides only in the intellect?"[34] A clear indication indeed that his own interest lies in the other direction. Thomas does not deny that truth resides chiefly in the intellect. Far from objecting to this position in Aristotle, Thomas quotes his very words and, by a very rare homage, quotes Aristotle in a *Sed contra:* "The Philosopher says, *The true and the false reside not in things, but in the intellect.*"[35] Still, the whole trend of this remarkable article[36] is to establish that, yes, truth does indeed reside in the intellect, but not *only* in the intellect; in a way, truth also resides in things.

The turning point is announced at the very beginning of the answer, where Thomas likens the truth to the good which, as will be seen, undoubtedly is a transcendental convertible with being. To be sure, the two cases are not identical, and the difference explains precisely why Aristotle himself had considered the good a transcendental to be included in metaphysics, while the true should be excluded from it. "*Good* names that towards which the appetite tends" and "*the true* names that towards which the intellect tends"; but good, the object of the desirer's appetite, *is in the thing itself*, whereas the true *is in the intellect* as knowing the thing such as it is. Obviously, this fundamental distinction does not make it easy to consider the true a transcendental; if it resides in the intellect, it cannot be a property of being *qua* being; it is a property of being *qua* known only. But this did not prevent Thomas from proceeding to his own conclusion. Good exists in the thing, but the appetite that desires it is also called good because its object is good; so, inversely, the true is in the mind, but the object of true knowledge is itself called true because it is an object of true cognition. In short, "the thing understood is said to be true in so far as it has some relation to the intellect."[37]

This remark would be accepted by any philosopher as a mere matter of language; and, in fact, we often speak of a thing as being "true to type," and nothing is more common than to say "this is a true X" or "this is not a true Y." But, precisely, such expressions invite us to take into account another kind of truth than that which is in the mind and not in the thing. It is accidental to a thing to be related to the mind as a known object, but if there are cases when the thing is related to an intellect as to the cause on which it depends for its existence, then its relation to mind is an essential one. For instance, it is accidental to the being of a house to be known by my own intellect, but it is essential to it to be known by the mind of its architect, because the knowledge the architect has of the house-to-be-built is the cause of its existence. Then the

> . . . *house is said to be true because it fulfills the likeness of the form in the architect's mind . . . In the same way, natural things are said to be true in so far as they express the likeness of the forms that are in the divine mind. For a stone is called true which possesses the nature proper to a stone, according to the preconception in the divine intellect.*

This does not oppose the doctrine of Thomas to that of Aristotle. Our theologian still thinks that "truth resides primarily in the intellect," but he adds to Aristotle that truth also resides "secondarily in things according as they are related to the intellect as their source." Nor is this secondary way of being true an unimportant one. With it, the very existence of things is at stake: "Hence, everything is said to be true absolutely, in so far as it is related to the intellect on which it depends."[38]

As an immediate consequence of this development, Thomas Aquinas posits the true and being as convertible terms, which means that, in our own metaphysical language, the true is one of the transcendentals. The justification of this conclusion is set forth by Thomas in terms of unsurpassable simplicity:

> *As* good *has the nature of what is desirable, so* the true *is related to knowledge. Now everything is knowable in as far as it has being. Therefore it is said in the* De Anima *that* the soul is in some manner all things, *through the senses and the intellect. And therefore, as good is convertible with being, so is the true. But as good adds to being the notion of the desirable, so the true adds a relation to the intellect.*[39]

Thomas Aquinas did not resign himself to accepting this conclusion. He had made it necessary, and no objection could force him to change his mind. After all, an opponent might say that, in the end, truth resides properly in the intellect, while being is properly to be found in things. But Thomas answers that the true resides in things *and* in the intellect. The true that is in things "is substantially convertible with being" that is directly and in itself, while "the true that is in the intellect is convertible with being as that which manifests is convertible with the manifested." In short, "truth and being differ only in idea," because being itself is both in the intellect and in beings.[40]

Verum et ens differunt ratione. Hence, as in the case of the one, there is between *true* and *being* a distinction of reason only. And let it be noted that, exactly as in the case of the one, this does not authorize the conclusion that, since being cannot be apprehended except under the aspect of the true, the true is prior to being. On the contrary, being can be apprehended without the notion of the true being also apprehended, whereas we cannot conceive the notion of the true without, at the same time, conceiving that of being. What has been said of the one holds of the true. Thomism is a philosophy of the true in the sense that it is a philosophy of being, and being is true, but the reverse is not correct; for while being can be apprehended apart from the true, the true cannot be apprehended apart from being. In fact, the true *is* being, or else it is nothing. "The true cannot be apprehended unless the notion of being is also apprehended; for being is included in the notion of the true."[41]

The intimate connection between the true and being appears from the fact that the true is logically prior to the good. We say "logically" because, since the transcendentals are convertible with being, there can be among them no order of real priority or posteriority. The reason for this is that "the true is more closely related to being, which is it-self prior to the good." And, indeed, truth is being present in the mind such as it is in itself; so "the true regards being itself absolutely and immediately," whereas the good names being as desirable to us because of its perfection. Moreover, "knowledge naturally precedes appetite; hence, since the true is related to knowledge, and the good to the ap-petite, the true must be prior to the good according to reason."[42] Any hesitation as to the transcendental status of the true should be removed by the clear answer to the second objection in the same article. The objection argues that since what is in things is prior to what is in the intellect, then the good, which is in things, should be logically prior to the true, which is in the intellect. To this Thomas answers that, since we are speaking of *logical* priority, the question is to know which is prior in the apprehension of the intellect, the good or the true? Here is the answer:

> The intellect first apprehends being itself; second, it apprehends that
> it understands being; and third, it apprehends that it desires being.
> Hence the notion of being is first, that of truth second, and the no-
> tion of good third, even though the good is in things.[43]

The meaning of Saint John now should appear in full, at least to the extent that the meaning of the names of God is accessible to natural reason. The same reduction of all the divine names to the pure act of being has to be achieved with respect to truth as with respect to unity. According to what precedes, things are true in themselves to the extent that they are conformable to an intellect, and the intellect itself is true according as it apprehends a thing such as it is. Now, in the unique case of God, it is not enough to say that His knowledge apprehends its object such as it is; His *esse* (the pure act of being that He is) is His very understanding: *esse suum . . . est ipsum suum intelligere*. More-

over, all other beings are true in themselves in so far as they are conformed to the knowledge God has of them, for God's act of understanding is the measure and cause of every other being, and He Himself
is His own act of being and of understanding. In this perfect coincidence of a being, of its knowledge, and of the object of its knowledge,
is found the identity of absolute being with its own truth. Because
God is *suum esse et intelligere* (which is God's *esse*), it must be said
of Him, not only that truth is *in* Him, but that He Himself *is* the
supreme and the prime truth.[44] Thus, with the theology of *esse*, the
conclusion of the *De Veritate* of Saint Anselm was finally receiving,
along with its proper limitation, its full justification. Each and every
thing has its own truth as it has its own being, but there is one truth
according to which all things are true. Things are true inasmuch as, in
themselves, they are conformed to their model in the divine intellect.[45]
Here as always, things are called true from a truth found in an intellect; in the last analysis, truth is said of things from the truth of the
intellect which God is, because His act of understanding and His act
of being are one and the same act.

IV. BEING AND THE GOOD

Neither the *Metaphysics* of Aristotle nor the commentary of Thomas
Aquinas has much to say on the good. On the contrary, the two
Summae abound in information on the subject. Dionysius certainly
played an important part in this restoration of a metaphysical notion
central in the philosophy of Plato, but which could not enter the structure of Thomism without undergoing a thorough reinterpretation.[46]

Quoting with approval a saying itself quoted by Aristotle, Thomas
describes the good as "that which all things desire." These well-known
words, however, *quod omnia appetunt*, are not a definition of the good,
they merely point out the sign by which its presence can be detected.
A thing is not good because it is universally desired, it is universally
desired because it is good.[47]

In itself, the good is being: "The good and being (*ens*) are the same
in reality; they differ from the point of view of reason only." In pointing out the ground for this distinction of reason, Thomas first recalls
the external sign that reveals the presence of goodness—namely, that it
is desired by all—but he presently goes beyond this empirical remark
and asks why something is desirable or actually being desired. His answer is that a thing is desirable inasmuch as it is perfect. Here, however,

Thomas makes this curious remark: *nam omnia appetunt suam perfectionem*. This appeal to psychological experience, rather infrequent in the metaphysical argumentation of Thomas, simply serves to point out the notion upon which the whole explanation ultimately rests; namely, perfection. For perfection is actuality itself, as opposed to mere potentiality. That which is only in potency still lacks perfection; it will acquire perfection by passing from potency to act or, as it is said, by actualizing its potentialities. Hence the well-known formula: *unumquodque est perfectum inquantum est actu*. But what is it to acquire actuality if it is not to acquire being? Consequently, a thing is good inasmuch as it is being: *intantum est aliquid bonum, inquantum est ens*. And indeed, since what is not being, or does not have being, is nothing, the act of being (*esse*) is the actuality of every thing. Hence goodness and being are really the same, but goodness is being conceived under the aspect of its desirableness, itself grounded in the very actuality of being.[48]

The convertibility of being and the good calls for the same remarks as that of being and the one. The metaphysics of Thomas Aquinas is a metaphysics of being (*i.e.*, of *Thomistic* being), not a metaphysics of the good. Of course, since the good is being itself under one of its aspects, there can be no real priority or posteriority between them. There is no "them," there is only being. Nevertheless, since the two notions are conceived as two distinct objects of thought, the question may be asked whether goodness is prior in idea to being. The answer is no, the notion of being is in the intellect prior to that of goodness. The reason is simple: everything is knowable inasmuch as it is. Consequently, "being is the proper object of the intellect, and is thus the first intelligible, as sound is the first audible"; and since "the first thing conceived by the intellect is being," being is prior to goodness in knowledge, as it is prior to everything.[49]

In this view, every being is good inasmuch as it is being. For to be is to have actuality, to have actuality is to have perfection, and to have perfection is to be desirable, which itself is to be good.[50]

In establishing this point of doctrine, Thomas Aquinas naturally drew on the Platonists, especially Dionysius. He could not do otherwise. Since Aristotle was of little help in matters of agathology, Plato had to be used as a substitute. In this respect, the *Liber de Causis* could help, especially because of its startling statement, so willingly quoted by Thomas Aquinas: *the first of created things is being* (*prima rerum creatarum est esse*). An elementary knowledge of Platonism suffices to suggest that here Thomas is making Platonism say something different from what it intended to say. Everywhere the influence of Plotinus really prevails; the first created thing is, indeed, being, but goodness is its cause, so that goodness is prior to being in reality. This point Thomas knows very well, having read it in Dionysius' treatise *The Divine Names*, in which, in assigning the rank of the various names of God, he gives the first place to goodness rather than to being.[51] The use Thomas makes of the *Liber de Causis* in this matter, therefore, is not the consequence of any unconscious misinterpretation of the doctrine; he merely sets it in the perspective under which it is seen to be true; namely, that of the final cause. Precisely because it is essentially desirable, goodness is a final cause. Not only this, but it is both prime and ultimate in the order of purposiveness. Even being is only because it is for the sake of something, which is its final cause, its end. In the order of causality, then, goodness comes first, and it is in this sense that Platonism receives from Thomas Aquinas all the credit to which it is entitled.

This interpretation was in keeping with the authentic spirit of Platonism, in which the causality of the good certainly transcended the order of entity or being. But Thomas could do full justice to Platonism without allowing it to jeopardize the absolute primacy of being. Without such a precaution, even the good could be nothing. Hence, in the Thomistic account of reality, although everything is there because of the good and for the sake of some good, the existence of everything first presupposes an efficient cause and a formal cause, for these causes are the actual and intrinsic constituents of being.[52]

Before passing to the theological applications of the doctrine, Thomas makes a last effort to integrate with his agathology some teachings of the Fathers of the Church that had become part and parcel of the school tradition.

One of them was part of the Augustinian heritage. Saint Augustine had written a treatise *On the Nature of the Good* (*De Natura Boni*), and, of course, Thomas Aquinas was not one to compose a Question *On Goodness in General* without first consulting his illustrious predecessor. Among the elements of the Augustinian doctrine retained by Thomas was an attempt to define the ontological constituents of goodness. These are three in number: *measure*, or *limit* (*modus*); *form* (*species*); and *order* (*ordo*).[53]

Thomas has integrated these notions with his own doctrine by relating them to his fundamental principle that the good is being as possessed of its actuality, or perfection, for its perfection is what makes it desirable; that is, good. For a thing to be perfect is to have the form that makes it to be that which it is, and the three determinations posited by Augustine all come from the form or are its prerequisites.

A prerequisite for the form is a certain mensuration and commensuration of its principles. For instance, a due proportion of matter to form, and a proportion of both to their efficient cause. These proportions (or commensurations) are measures and, since measures fix limits, they impart to the thing the measure (*modus*) that determines it. Furthermore, the form is that which places the thing in its own species. Now species are signified by their definitions and, according to Aristotle, *the definitions signifying species are like numbers*. Add anything to a number, or subtract anything from it, and it becomes another number; so, too, add anything to, or subtract anything from, a definition, and it becomes another definition and the species it defines becomes another species. Species is therefore an essential component of goodness. Finally, everything that has a form directs its operations toward that which will perfect it according to its form. To be is to act, to operate, and to tend toward an appropriate end. This is, precisely, order. It is therefore true that the essence of goodness consists in measure, form, and order.[54]

A second patristic element integrated with his agathology by Thomas Aquinas is a tripartite division of goodness given by Saint Ambrose in his *De Officiis:* the befitting (*honestum*), the useful (*utile*), and the pleasant (*delectabile*). Ambrose had understood his division as applying to human goodness in particular, but Thomas thinks that it should be extended to "goodness as such." And, indeed, whatever the good in question, if the appetite tends toward it as to a thing it needs in order to have something else (*i.e.*, as to a means), the good in question is included in the category of the *useful*. If the appetite tends to it as to something whose possession will bring it satisfaction and rest, it is called *pleasant* (*delectabile*). Incidentally, let us note that the definition of this particular kind of good will provide the correct answer to the problem of the beautiful, another transcendental, or another transcendental variety of the good. Lastly, if the appetite tends toward a thing desired for its own sake, its object is the *befitting*, or *honestum*, that which deserves to be loved, desired, and pursued for the sake of its own intrinsic perfection. Needless to say, goodness is not said of these three varieties univocally, as if all three participated in the nature of goodness equally and in the same way. Goodness is said by priority of the befitting, then, analogically, of the pleasant and, in the third place, of the useful.[55]

The six articles of this fifth question of the *Summa, On Goodness in General,* are a perfect example of a philosophical speculation elaborated by a theologian in view of his own theological work. Thomas Aquinas finds himself at grips with the task of defining the meaning of the name "good" as applicable to God. In order to do so, he needs a philosophical determination of the nature of goodness in general, and since he does not find it in the philosophy of Aristotle, he has to do what had already been done by some of his predecessors, particularly Albert the Great; that is, to elaborate an agathology. But he had to do it in his own way, on the basis of his own metaphysical notion of being, or otherwise his theology of the divine goodness would not fit his theology of divine being.

Having thus prepared his ground, the theologian is ready to ask the question: "Whether to be good belongs to God?" To answer this question is the object of a discussion of the *Summa* that is distinct from the preceding one; namely, question six, entitled *The Goodness of God.*

In accordance with his doctrine of the primacy of the good in the order of final causality, Thomas appeals to the desirableness of God for a starting point of his demonstration. Although he has not yet shown that God is the creator of all things, he nevertheless starts from the assumption that God has produced them all. Now every effect is like its cause, and the perfection of any effect is to resemble its cause as closely as possible; therefore, "every agent makes its like, and hence the agent itself is desirable and has the nature of the good." The universal cause is thus universally desirable and, being desired by all things, God is to all things their highest good. But this He is because He is first the efficient cause of all. As Dionysius says in *The Divine Names, God is called good as by Whom all things subsist.*[56]

Not only is God good, and the highest good because He is the supreme being, He is even essentially good. The expression has to be taken in its strongest conceivable meaning as signifying that, whereas all other beings are good only by participation (as effects of the prime cause), God is good by His very essence. And, indeed, His essence is His very being. As we have seen, it is the exclusive privilege of God to be He *cujus solius essentia est suum esse.* Consequently, being all that He is in virtue of His essence, God *is* His own goodness. All the names that are attributed to other things as pointing out some participated perfections, such as power, wisdom, and the like, are attributed to God as signifying His very essence, which is His very *esse*. Nor is God in view of any end; He Himself is to all things their common end, for He is their efficient cause, their desirable good, and their end.[57]

This conclusion leads to the genuinely Thomistic view of the world of creatures as made up of beings that owe to God everything they are, their goodness and their very being included, and which, at the same time, are good through their own goodness and exist through their own being. Always careful to multiply the ways of approach to truth, Thomas Aquinas never hesitates to state it in its fullness—that is, in its purity—when the time comes to formulate it. Unlike the prudent minds that never quite tell the truth because they find it dangerous to say it whole, Thomas Aquinas never says it by halves. In this case, his position is uncompromising on two accounts. Things owe to God everything they are, but they are in virtue of their own being, the very being they wholly owe to God:

> *All things are good inasmuch as they have being. But they are not called beings through the divine being, but through their own being* (non dicuntur omnia entia per esse divinum, sed per esse proprium); *therefore all things are* not *good by the divine goodness, but by their own goodness.*

The two apparently opposite sides of the same truth are here simultaneously affirmed with equal force, and since this phenomenon constitutes one of the essential features of Thomism, the point deserves careful consideration.

Thomas Aquinas always opposed the Platonic conception of a world of self-subsisting Ideas. On this point he unreservedly subscribed to the criticism directed against Plato by Aristotle: there are no such things as self-subsisting separate forms of natural beings. On the other hand, Aristotle agrees that there is a first being, which is being and good by essence, and from which all things derive the being and goodness they have. They participate in the first being and in the first goodness as effects participate in their causes, by resembling them. This clearly defines the position of Thomas Aquinas with respect to this aspect of Platonism. He knew, through the testimony of Aristotle, that some philosophers had spoken of a "one by itself and good and being by itself," so that all other beings were, and were one, by participation in these separate Forms of One and Being. The great progress achieved by Aristotle's metaphysics was to identify these forms with the very entity of the one self-subsisting Prime Mover and Cause of the universe.

Since this supreme being was, for the same reason, the supreme good, we can say that "everything can be called good and a being inasmuch as it participates in the first being by way of a certain assimilation."[58]

Truth, under all its aspects, is here given to us at once. *Being, one,* and *good* are really the same; they differ only from the point of view of the mind. God *is* unity and goodness, because His essence is to be HE IS; all other things are, are one, and are good as caused by God and as resembling Him in the manner that effects resemble their cause: this caused likeness is their very participation in God; in fine, each participated being has its own being and goodness (since it holds them from its cause) and, at the same time, each owes them to one and the same goodness and being.

After grasping the meaning of the doctrine, the reader of Thomas Aquinas realizes one of the possible meanings of the word he is reported to have applied to the *Summa Theologiae* at the end of his life: it looked to him like "straw." For his own theological wisdom was so closely one with his understanding, he probably could see the whole of its truth, as it were, at a glance, without going through the drudgery of the dialectical demonstration. We sometimes find the truth of his doctrine thus proposed for vision, rather than demonstration, in some passages of his works. For instance: "To be in act (*esse actu*) is for each being its good. But God is not only a being in act; He is His very act of being (*est ipsum suum esse*), as we have shown. God is, therefore, goodness itself, and not only good."[59] This is the full measure of the straight truth of the case, and Thomas Aquinas can say it in many more words, as indeed he does throughout the chapter of the *Summa Contra Gentiles* from which this quotation is taken and in which he restates in five different ways the identity of self-subsisting goodness and self-subsisting being in God. Still, when all is said and done, Thomas himself cannot say anything else or more. Besides, as he well knew, anyone can read it in Scripture: *One is good, God (Matt. 19:17).*

V. THE FORGOTTEN TRANSCENDENTAL: *Pulchrum*

Beauty does not occupy in the theology of Thomas Aquinas a place in any way comparable with that of unity and of goodness. Whole questions of the *Summa Theologiae* are devoted to proving that God is goodness itself and unity itself, but there is none devoted to proving that God is beauty itself. The treatment of this divine name (for God *is* beauty itself in itself) is relegated in the *Summa* to a simple answer to the first objection in Part I, q.5, a.4. But, precisely, this answer clearly shows that beauty has been neglected rather than forgotten, and it justifies the secondary place attributed to it in sacred doctrine.

The question raised in the objection was to know whether goodness has the aspect of a final cause. Significantly enough, the issue that will recall the existence of beauty is borrowed from *The Divine Names* of Dionysius: *Goodness is praised as beauty*. Obviously, the objection is for Thomas an occasion, provided by himself, to suggest what he would say about beauty if he deemed it necessary to his purpose to develop the point. For his interpretation of the objection is Thomistic through and through. It is that "beauty has the aspect of a *formal* cause," not of a *final* cause; hence, if in our estimation goodness is goodness because it is to be beautiful, we should consider it a formal cause rather than a final cause, and, of course, what is true of goodness in itself is also true of God.[60]

The answer to this objection establishes both that beauty truly is a convertible property of being and also that it is distinct from it from the point of view of reason. Beauty is goodness, which itself is being. The reason beauty and goodness in a thing are fundamentally identical is that a thing is both good and beautiful for the same reason; namely, its form. Only, to conceive a form as good is not to conceive the same form as beautiful. This Thomas will show by establishing that, in the last analysis, beauty is a certain good, but a good distinct from all the other classes of goods.

Let us go back to the definition of goodness: that which all things desire. As such, goodness is the form of a certain thing as the object of a desiring appetite. It is an end because desire is a movement of the soul toward an end. Now, to parallel the common saying about goodness (*id quod omnia appetunt*), Thomas has another one about the beautiful: *id quod visum placet*, that which pleases when seen. But sight is a cognitive power; consequently, if this be the case, beauty relates to form as known, whereas goodness relates to form as desired. This, of course, needs to be understood correctly. The words "when seen" refer not only to sight itself but also to every kind of perception or apprehension by either sense or intellect, provided real knowledge is involved. Moreover, the remarks made concerning the common description of goodness apply to this description of beauty. What is beautiful is not the pleasure we take in apprehending certain forms; rather, it is that which, in these forms, makes them objects of a pleasurable apprehension; and this, of course, will oblige us to look for beauty in the very structure of the knowing power as well as of the known thing.

Since it is an object of knowledge, beauty requires a certain proportion between the knowing power and the known object. Furthermore, it requires a certain proportion among the constituent elements of the known object, and even a proportion among the constituent elements of the knowing subject. These are not new notions introduced in view of solving the problem of beauty. Substantial goodness has already been described as requiring, by its very essence, measure, species or form, and order. Every cognitive power is a complex structure of elements, and so is the known object; and even the relationship of knowing power to known object is a proportion. Beauty consists in the due proportion of the thing, and this due proportion pleases the knowing power because this power itself, being a proportion, delights in duly proportioned things: *Unde pulchrum in debita proportione consistit, quia sensus delectatur in rebus debite proportionatis, sicut in sibi similibus; nam et sensus proportio quaedam est, et omnis virtus cognoscitiva.*[61]

This is to say that beauty is the cognition of a substantial similitude between two duly proportionate beings, and since similitude always concerns form, the beautiful properly relates to the formal cause. At the same time, it shows the peculiar nature of the pleasure experienced in the apprehension of beauty. As always, this pleasure accompanies an act, only this time the act it accompanies is one of apprehension, of cognition. The best formulation of this truth proposed by Thomas is found in a passage in which, asking whether only the good is cause of love, he poses as an objection to his view the remark of Dionysius that "the beautiful and the good are desirable and lovable to all." To this the answer is:

> The beautiful is the same as the good, from which it differs in reason only. For since the good is that which all desire, it is of the nature of the good that appetite finds in it its rest. But it belongs to the notion of the beautiful that apprehension finds its rest in its sight, or cognition. Hence the senses particularly related to the beautiful are those whose apprehensions are particularly cognitive. These are sight and hearing, which serve reason; for we speak of beautiful sights or of beautiful sounds, but we do not use the word "beauty" in speaking of the objects of the other senses. One does not speak of beautiful odors or of beautiful tastes. Thus it appears that the beauti-

ful adds, over and above the good, a certain relation to the power of knowing; so that we call good that which simply pleases the appetite, but, we call beautiful that whose very apprehension pleases.[62]

Once more, let us first admire the fact that, on such an important philosophical problem as the nature of a transcendental, we should be receiving information, so to speak by chance, in an answer to a third objection in an essentially theological work. But, above all, we must realize that in this answer Thomas is giving the reason why the beautiful has received no special treatment in either one of the two *Summae.* The beautiful is a variety of the good. It is the particular kind of good to be experienced, by a knowing power, in the very act of knowing an object eminently fit to be known. The beautiful is to knowledge what the good is to the desire of the will. The pleasure experienced in knowing the beautiful does not constitute beauty itself, but it betrays its presence. It testifies to the excellence of the commensuration there is between a certain power of knowing and a certain known object.

Our preceding remark concerning the incidental nature of some of our information on the philosophy of Saint Thomas is further confirmed by the fact that the basic text concerning the objective constitutents of the beautiful is included in the long answer to the question, whether the essential attributes are appropriated to the Persons in a fitting manner by the Holy Doctors. Among these appropriations, Thomas first considers the three attributes appropriated to the three Persons by Hilary: *Eternity is in the Father, the species is in the Image; and use is in the Gift.* Now the two notions of *species* and of *beauty* communicate by the notion of form. Hence, for Thomas Aquinas, an occasion to show in what sense "species or beauty has a likeness to the property of the Son."

In what does the beauty of a beautiful thing consist?

Beauty includes three conditions: integrity *or* perfection, *since those things which are impaired are by that very fact ugly; due* proportion *or* harmony; *and lastly,* brightness *or* clarity, *whence things are called beautiful which have a bright color.*

In writing this oft-commented passage, Thomas was remembering a passage in *The Divine Names* of Dionysius, *On the good and how it is attributed to God.* In it, Dionysius had called God "the cause of consonance and clarity" in all things. In his explanation of these words, Thomas had simply said that, indeed, we call a thing beautiful because it has a satisfactory proportion in size, a fine presence, and a fair complexion. Similarly, anything is called beautiful because it has a brilliancy of its own, spiritual or corporeal, and is constituted according to due proportion. God is the cause of clarity in things because He makes them participate in His own light; and He is cause of consonance in things on two counts: by ordering all things to Himself as to their end, and by ordering them with respect to one another. Hence everything is beautiful as having a form (through which it has *esse*), and this form is a sort of participation of the divine clarity. Ultimately, "everything is beautiful according to its own form; whence it appears that the being (*esse*) of all things is derived from the divine beauty."[63]

Many commentaries on these words, and especially on the passage of the *Summa Theologiae*, have been proposed by theologians, philosophers, writers, and artists. Unfortunately, if it is a question of understanding Thomas Aquinas as he himself understood his own words, certainty ceases as soon as we reach the end of his own commentary. It seems at least certain that, in his own mind, these constituent elements of the beautiful were directly and immediately related to the intrinsic attributes of fully constituted beings. Integrity is one of them, since perfection is actuality in being and an imperfect object is only in an imperfect way. Proportion or harmony is likewise counted among the essential constituents of the goodness of things: measure, species, and order. There remains only the mysterious *claritas*, by which, however, Thomas Aquinas does not seem to mean any mystery. Bright colors are beautiful because light itself is beautiful. Since this is given to us as a fact, the wise thing to do is to accept it as such.

We have been using many words and many names in speaking of God, but we have said only one thing. God is beauty because He is good, God is good because He is being, and since the essence in God is the very act of being (*esse*), there is nothing to set any limit either on goodness or on being. Therefore, God is perfect and infinite by the very fact that He is God. For Him, to be God simply is *to be*. And this is the only thing we have been saying thus far, that there is a proper name of God, and that name is: HE IS.

Chapter 7. Being and creation

The five ways to God all start from the actual existence of empirically given finite beings, or from the properties of such beings. They all likewise conclude that there is a prime cause of such beings, or of such properties of such beings. This prime cause is what men call "God." After we reach this conclusion, however, another metaphysical problem arises. It is this. If there is a God or a Supreme Being, why is this Supreme Being a cause? In other words, why should the Supreme Being have caused other beings to be?

The meaning of the question can be determined by considering the five ways successively. For instance, the existence of God can be established on the basis of the fact that there is change in the world; but after granting the conclusion, one cannot help wondering why the Prime Immovable Being should be a Mover. Likewise, if there are finite efficient causes, there must of necessity be a Prime Uncaused Being; but given such an Uncaused Being, how can one explain that He produced other causes? The same remark still more evidently applies to the third way, which, starting from the fact that there are in nature things that can be and not-be, concludes to the existence of a Necessary Being. Here, again, granting the point of departure of the proof, its dialectical validity, and the truth of its conclusion, one still cannot help wondering: if there truly is a Necessary Being, why should there be beings that are merely possible? The existence of the world of finite beings presupposes the existence of its cause, but the existence of the cause does not account for the fact that there are, indeed, finite beings. And the reason for this difficulty is at hand. It is that to infer necessity from contingency certainly is possible; what seems to be much more difficult, if not downright impossible, is to deduce contingency from necessity. In short, if there is no God, how could there be a world? But, if there is a God, why should there be a world?

This is not a problem proper to the doctrine of Thomas Aquinas. It is the problem that Leibniz was to define very properly as that of the radical origin of things (*De rerum originatione radicali*). To borrow from the same philosopher another formula, the problem is to answer the question: why should there be something rather than nothing? Now, if there is a Prime, Absolute, and Necessary Being, the question does not arise with respect to such a being. That which is necessary cannot not be; for the same reason, such a being cannot not be what it is; in fine, since it is integrally determined in virtue of its very necessity, there is in it nothing that cannot be accounted for: such a being is perfectly intelligible. This system of metaphysical relations is well expressed in the famous saying of Avicenna that *being, thing,* and *necessary* are the first notions that enter the intellect when it first meets empirically given objects.

This is why it has taken philosophical reflection so many centuries to push its investigation up to within striking distance of the problem of the very existence of reality. In this respect, the state of mind of the scientist very much resembles that of plain common sense: if something is there, many questions can be asked about its nature or its properties; it is even possible to wonder because of what antecedent conditions this and that being happens to be; but it does not spontaneously occur to common sense to wonder why, generally speaking, nothingness does not universally prevail; that is, why there is something rather than nothing. Aristotle is an excellent exponent of this attitude of mind in that he takes it for granted that, since there always is a movement before any given movement, this world of moving things must be eternal. How substances are being produced, either mediately or immediately, by the Prime Mover, is indeed a legitimate philosophical question; but the Prime Mover, the specific forms and prime matter have eternally been there, just as the Prime Mover has eternally been causing individuals to be produced by a ceaseless eduction of forms from an always present matter. Similar remarks apply to the metaphysics of Avicenna. As has been seen, Thomas Aquinas has praised him for pushing philosophical inquiry to the recognition of the problem of the very existence of being.[1] But even Avicenna's explanation of the origin of the world presupposes, along with the eternal existence of prime matter, that of a Prime Cause from whose self-knowledge the existence and order of things follow with strict necessity. By understanding His own essence, the Prime Being also knows what things must follow His own necessity and in what order they must follow from it, "and this very order flows, becomes and exists from the fact that the Prime Being understands it."[2]

Being

The revealed notion of creation, understood by believers and theologians alike as the absolute production of being from no other pre-existing condition than the free will of its creator, was pregnant with metaphysical possibilities still unknown to the boldest among the metaphysicians. Thomas Aquinas found in his own notion of God a way to develop these possibilities. Such as he himself conceived Him, God was more than the Prime Immovable Mover of Aristotle and even more than the Prime Necessary Being of Avicenna. As has already been said, though it is necessary to repeat it because this notion of God is truly the fundamental truth of Christian philosophy, the God of Thomas Aquinas is, beyond all essential determination, the pure and absolute "to be." This notion of God entails as its exact philosophical counterpart a corresponding notion of all that which is, without being the pure act of being; that is, of all that which, because it is only a certain being, is not God. In the hope of making as clear as possible the nature of the personal contribution of Thomas Aquinas to the solution of the problem of the radical origin of things, we shall run the risk of summarizing it in terms of a more modern philosophy and say that there is no metaphysics in which the relationship of the world to its Cause is conceived as being more thoroughly contingent than it is in the doctrine of Saint Thomas. At the same time, as shall be seen, this total contingency in the order of actual existence is total intelligibility.

Since the difficulty we face is to realize the meaning of the Thomistic notion of God, we propose to proceed from the problems related to the so-called "motives" of creation to the nature of the very act of giving being.

The starting point of our inquiry must remain the same; namely, the truth stated in the *Summa Theologiae* that "essence and being are the same in God." God can be said to be the "being-that-has-nothing-added-to-it" and which is such because its essence precludes the possibility of any addition. Since it can receive no addition, such a being cannot suffer any determination; it is therefore infinite and pure act by definition. Now the difference between knowing and non-knowing beings consists in this, that the nature of a non-knowing being is restricted to that which it actually is, whereas the nature of a knowing being can acquire, beyond its own form, the forms of other beings. It acquires them by knowing them. Hence the saying of the Philosopher that *the soul is in a sense all things*. But the soul owes this privilege to its immateriality, since the more immaterial a thing, the more cognitive it is. Since therefore God is the infinite and pure act of being, He is also the most completely free from any determination caused by matter; and thus, being in the highest degree of immateriality, He also is in the highest degree of perfection as to knowledge and intelligibility. Naturally, this result entails the consequence that God perfectly knows, not only Himself, but things other than Himself. God knows other things inasmuch as, in order perfectly to know Himself, He must know all things to which His own power extends; that is to say, all possible things.[3]

This seems to confront us with no other choice than the conclusion derived by Avicenna from his own notion of God: the First is, He knows both Himself and all the possibles, and, as He knows them, the possibles come to be, following in reality the same order they have in the divine mind. Not so in the doctrine of Thomas Aquinas, for what we call the divine intellect and the act of this divine intellect are identically God's own essence, which is God's pure act of being. In God, to understand is the same as to be. Now, since the pure act of being is infinite being, it is self-sufficient and no other being follows from it with any kind of necessity. This amounts to saying that, in such a doctrine, although God eternally knows Himself as imitable by an infinite number of possible finite creatures, there is in Him no necessity to cause any one of these possible beings to become actualities. The contingency of the universe is much more radical in the doctrine of Thomas Aquinas than in that of Avicenna.

Taken alone, knowledge is not able to cause anything. In the doctrine of Thomas Aquinas as well as in that of Avicenna, the knowledge of God is the cause of things only inasmuch as the will of God is joined to it; but Thomas Aquinas does not conceive the will of God as compelled to consent to the calculations of the divine understanding. In the first place, the results of these calculations are infinite in number, and there is no single set of possibles submitted for approval to the divine will to the exclusion of the others. Above all, what is true of God's intellect is also true of God's will. The will of God is identical with His essence, which itself is identical with His act of being. In Thomas' own words, "there must be will in God, since there is intellect in Him. And as His knowing is His own being, so is His willing." As such, the will of God is necessitated to will God Himself, because "He wills the being of His own goodness necessarily." As to other things, God wills them only in so far as they are related to His own goodness as to their end. But no other thing is necessary to God's own perfection. Hence, for God to will other things than Himself is not necessary. True enough, if God wills a thing, He cannot not will it, because God's will is immutable, but there is nothing, besides God Himself, that the will of God is necessitated to will.[4]

These rules facilitate the answer to some questions that philosophers have asked concerning the radical origin of things. One of them is: why did God create the world? Taken in its most indeterminate sense, the question is susceptible of an answer. The things of nature exhibit a natural tendency not only to acquire and to enjoy their own good, but also to communicate it to others as far as possible. Since we cannot think of God otherwise than by analogy with the beings given in experience, we naturally conceive Him as necessarily willing His own perfection and, secondarily, as willing things other than Himself because He wills to communicate to them, by mode of likeness, His own perfection. Still, strictly speaking, no *cause* can be assigned to the divine will.

The same position had already been maintained by Saint Augustine, and nothing better exemplifies the progress-in-continuity that is typical of the history of Christian philosophy than a comparison between the different ways the two Doctors have justified this same conclusion. According to Augustine, the problem is simple. It is only a question of knowing whether there can be a cause greater than the will of God. If not, then the will of God has no cause, for an efficient cause is greater than its effect. The passage of Saint Augustine is remarkable in this, that it directly asks the question in terms of efficient causality: *omnis causa efficiens est*. Now an efficient cause is greater than its effect, and since there can be nothing greater than the will of God, we must not seek for a cause of it.[5]

The position of Thomas Aquinas could not be more firm than that of Augustine. "In no wise has the will of God a cause." The difference between the two doctrines lies in the justification of the thesis common to both. Since a will is an appetite regulated by the intellect, the will follows from the intellect. Consequently, the cause that accounts for the knowing of the intellect also accounts for the willing of the will. Now, in God, to know is really the same as to be; to will, therefore, must also be in God the same as to be. Why do we speak of a will in God or of an intellect in God? Simply because these different words signify different ways of understanding one and the same reality conceived from several different points of view. When we say that God is, or is a being, we signify Him in Himself, without implying any relation to another thing; but when we say that God knows, or that God wills, we signify Him as exercising various operations specified by their respective objects. Still, leaving aside our well-founded mode of signifying God, all these names ultimately refer to the simple act of being, which God is.[6]

This gives its Thomistic meaning to the statement, common to Augustine and to Thomas Aquinas, that the will of God has no cause. The meaning itself is tied up with the notion, fundamental in the theology of Thomas Aquinas, that God is absolutely simple, to the point of absorbing in His pure act of being all the realities signified by our various predications concerning His essence. There is therefore for us a necessity to correct every one of our statements about God by adding to them this important restriction, that the multiplication of their terms in reality expresses an absolute unity. For instance, in the case of human knowledge, principles are the causes of conclusions in the sense that the knowledge of principles is, in our understanding, the cause of the knowledge of conclusions. Now, in a sense, this is likewise true of God. It is true of God that He understands principles to be the causes of conclusions, but since His act of being (and therefore His intellect) is perfectly simple, the knowledge God has of conclusions is not caused in Him by His knowledge of the principles; in God, the knowledge of principles and that of conclusions are one and the same thing. In fact, they are His own intellect, itself His very act of being.

The same remark applies to the divine will. God wills that effects be because of their causes and He intends all things to exist in view of their own ends. This accounts for the presence of purposiveness everywhere in the world of nature. But we should not imagine God after the pattern of a man who, by a succession of acts, first wills an end and then wills the means required in view of that end. If we wish to compare God to a man, we should rather imagine Him like a man who, in one single act, wills both an end and the means to that end. Only, in God, even the willing of the end is not the cause of His willing of the appropriate means; by one single act, God wills the end along with the means ordered to the end. Hence the conclusion stated by Thomas Aquinas in a set of perfect formulas:

> *As God by one act understands all things in His essence, so by one act He wills all things in His goodness. Hence, as in God to understand the cause is not the cause of His understanding the effect (for He understands the effect in the cause), so, in Him, to will an end is not the cause of His willing the means; yet He wills the ordering of the means to the end. Therefore He wills this to be as means to that, but He does not will this because of that.*[7]

And indeed there can be no cause of that which is the cause of all the rest.

Another problem, or rather pseudo-problem, has been asked and made famous by Leibniz: why did God create this world rather than any other equally possible one? Let us acknowledge the fact that this was no pseudo-problem in the philosophy of Leibniz. On the contrary, this was for him the fundamental question in what he himself was accustomed to call "theodicy." Proceeding on the strength of his famous "principle of sufficient reason," according to which there must always be a reason why things are as they are rather than otherwise, Leibniz wanted to "justify" God for having created this very universe of ours rather than another one. The only explanation he could find for such a choice was that, since a perfect God was bound to make a perfect choice, this universe was the best possible universe; that is to say, the universe in which the greatest quantity of good was achieved with the strictest simplicity of means.

To speak of "theodicy" in Thomism is to use a meaningless expression. There is no such thing as a Thomistic "justification" of God for having created this universe rather than another one. Being as such is good. Since God is the pure act of being, He is goodness itself in its perfection. Consequently, all that which God may happen to do, or to make, is likewise good, so that this universe must needs be a good universe. Moreoever, it is equally certain that, having freely chosen to create a universe made up of the very beings that this one contains, this universe is the best one it was possible to compose with such beings. Still, had God decided to create a different universe, that other universe would have been good too. It even would have been the best possible universe obtainable with the kind of beings entering its constitution. God cannot possibly do anything in a better way than that in which He does it. Such are His wisdom and His goodness that the works He chooses to make always are perfectly made. At the same time, one should remember that, since God is infinite, no finite being is such that better finite beings could not be conceived by an infinitely wise and good First Cause. On the contrary, there always is a possible universe better than any conceivable finite universe. Just as, in the case of numbers, there is no absolutely greatest number (since, given any number, the number $+ 1$ always remains possible), so also, however good any finite universe may be, there still would be room for a better one, and so on indefinitely.

There is therefore no such thing as an absolutely best possible universe. Whatever God does is both appropriate and right; His choice is perfect in any case, but He certainly could have created another and better universe because He "always can make something else better than each thing made by Him." Again, "God could make other things, or add to the present creation; and then there would be another and a better universe."[8] The doctrine of Thomas Aquinas on this point has been unintentionally summed up by a certain Dr. Boteler in *The Compleat Angler* of Izaak Walton. Speaking of strawberries, Dr. Boteler aptly says of them: "Doubtless God could have made a better berry; but doubtless He never did."

In order to make this point more clear, one has once more to go back to the fundamental notion of a God Whose proper name is HE IS. All the great theologians, before and after Thomas Aquinas, have realized that the ultimate cause for the existence of the world must be sought in the meaning of this most proper of all the divine names. For instance, one can say with Augustine that I AM means: *I am immutable, I do not change, I am eternal.* Starting from this notion of God, we could certainly account for the fact that Eternity has created a world of things enduring in time, or that Immutability has created a world of change; still, we do not see any particular reason why Eternity or Immutability should impart *being* to anything.

Or let us consider another great theology, that of John Duns Scotus. In it, the highest and most perfect concept of God accessible to the human understanding is that of Infinite Being. This is a very high notion of God indeed, but why should the fullness of entity, even conceived as infinite, become a giver of actual existence? Of course, Duns Scotus has an answer to this question, and it is a beautiful one: God is love. Because God loves His own perfection, He wants to have, so to speak, co-lovers of it; hence His will to create. If this lofty notion of the origin of the world were more generally recognized, dialectical materialism would have very few followers.

These answers to the problem are not only deep and lofty, they are true; and both are to be found included in the answer of Thomas Aquinas. The only point we are emphasizing is: are such notions of God directly and immediately conducive to the notion of a Creator? And our own answer to this question is: perhaps, yes, but much less so than the notion of God advocated by Thomas Aquinas.

The central place occupied by the notion of God conceived as *Ipsum Esse* in the theology of Saint Thomas is particularly visible in the remarkable Disputed Question *De Potentia*, q.2, a.1: "Whether there is in

God a generative power?" The question should be read in a spirit of complete objectivity, be it only because it so perfectly exemplifies the work of Saint Thomas at its best, when the theologian freely plays the whole field of intellectual interpretation, applying the same notions and the same methods of explanation to all objects, regardless of their natural or supernatural origin. And why not? If the notion of being, understood as that which has *esse*, is true, it must apply validly to all that which is: material things, human beings, spiritual substances, God.[9] Hence the global answer given by Thomas Aquinas to his own question. Starting from the principle that every being is act, and that every act is naturally self-diffusive, our theologian includes the two main forms of the divine activity under one and the same principle of explanation. He does so as if, even at the moment of passing from the order of nature to the supernatural order, no doubt can arise as to the continued applicability of the philosophical concepts to the second part of the operation.

The answer runs as follows:

It is of the nature of all act that it communicates itself as far as possible. Hence every agent acts inasmuch as it is in act. Now, for an agent to act is nothing else than to communicate, to the extent that this is possible, that whereby the agent is in act. But the divine nature is supremely and most purely act. Hence the divine nature also communicates itself as much as possible. First, it communicates itself to creatures by mode of resemblance only, and this everyone can see, for every creature is a being in virtue of its resemblance to divine nature. But the Catholic faith posits another mode of communication of the divine nature, that in which it communicates itself, so to speak, by a natural communication. In this second case, just as he to whom humanity is communicated is man, so also He to Whom the deity is communicated is, not merely similar to God, but truly God.

Thus, without resorting to any other concepts than that of act, borrowed from Aristotle's philosophy and submitted to a thoroughgoing philosophical reinterpretation, Thomas Aquinas can include in one single framework the internal processions of the Christian God and the operations of God *ad extra* to which the universe owes its existence.

Because He is Being, the Christian God is supremely act. For this reason, He is the origin of the Word. This is a procession of the intellect, by mode of likeness, and it is called a generation.[10] The other procession is one of the will and of love; so it is not a procession by way of likeness, "but rather by way of impulse and of movement toward something":[11] it is the procession of the Holy Ghost. Thus even the theology of the Trinity is rooted in the notion of a God Whose essence tends to communicate itself because it is the pure act of being.[12] But the notion of creation has no other origin. As an act of self-communication by the production of beings similar to their Cause, creation also verifies the principle that "everything acts inasmuch as it is in act." Even for the eminently actual God of Saint Thomas there is no necessity to create; but no other notion of God can more immediately and directly account for His creative activity than that which identifies His essence with the pure act of being.

The same can be said of the very nature of the creative act. No other notion of God, either philosophical or theological, provides a more immediate and a fuller interpretation of creation conceived as the divine giving of actual existence to finite beings. This is a privileged occasion for us to observe the exact meaning of an expression often used by Saint Thomas: *convenit, conveniens est*. It can be translated, according to cases, by such words as: it is "suitable," "fitting," "becoming," or "appropriate." In the language of Saint Thomas Aquinas, however, such expressions assume a forceful meaning when they point out a relationship of harmony between two beings, between two acts, or between a certain being and certain type of operation. It is eminently fitting that a Pure Act should act. As will presently be seen, it is also suitable that the proper operation of the Pure Act of being should consist in creating beings.

The reason for this short theological excursus should now be apparent, but it will prove rewarding to indulge in a second one, because the only point of view from which the true meaning of Thomism really appears is that of an all-embracing perspective which shows the "revealed" and the "revealable" seeking understanding in the light of the same principles.

It is commonly admitted that any question involving the dogma of the Trinity belongs in the order of essentially "revealed" truth and that philosophy as such has nothing to say about it. This is commonly admitted because it is true. There is no method whereby the dogma of the Trinity can be turned into a philosophical proposition. Nevertheless, since the science of the theologian is in him as an impression of the science that God Himself has of everything, there should be some advantage in approaching every problem from the point of view of theology. In fact, there is at least one theological question that the student of Thomas Aquinas cannot afford not to ask in connection with the notion of creation. The question is: whether to create is proper to any divine Person? In reading this question, most of us probably think that the answer is, yes, because we read in the Nicene Creed, speaking of the Son, that by Him *all things were made;* but we also remember reading there—this time speaking of the Father—that He is *the creator of all things visible and invisible.* At least two Persons are thus involved in the work of creation, and this is enough to establish that creation is the common work of more than one Person. What interests us, however, is the way in which Thomas himself justifies this conclusion:

> *To create is, properly speaking, to produce the being* (esse) *of things. And as every agent produces its like, the principle of the action can be considered from the effect of the action; for it is fire that generates fire. To create, therefore, belongs to God according to His being* (esse). *But God's being* (esse) *is His essence, which is common to the three Persons. Hence to create is not proper to any one Person, but is common to the whole Trinity.*[18]

It is necessary to believe that there is one God in three Persons and that this God is the Creator of all things visible and invisible. Salvation does not require any further theological and philosophical speculation concerning the how of the work of creation. On the other hand, the proper work of the theologian is to seek some understanding of his faith, and he does so by resorting to the principles of metaphysical knowledge. In the present case, since it is a question of determining the prime cause of certain effects, the theologian will proceed on the twofold assumption that every agent produces its like and, consequently, that the nature of the agent can be inferred from that of its effect. What is the effect to be accounted for? The very being of created things. It is therefore legitimate to infer that the *esse* of creatures has for its cause the very *esse* of God. Just as fire generates fire, so also Being produces beings; or, rather, the *Ipsum Esse,* or HE IS, we call God produces the *esse* in virtue of which each existent is called a being. Hence, following his personal meditation on the mystery of the divine Trinity, and religiously keeping in mind the very words of the liturgical prayer: *non in unius singularitate personae, sed in unius Trinitate substantiae,* and again: *et in personis proprietas, et in essentia unitas,* the theologian begins to enter the realm of mystery. We can rightly speak of the *substance* of God, and of the *essence* of God, and for those who are not theologians there is no necessity to speculate about the ultimate meaning of such words; it is enough to understand that, as applied to God, *substance, essence,* and the like, directly point out the one, single, and indivisible being of God conceived in its very unity. But the theologian is in quest of as much "understanding of faith" as he can gather by means of natural reason. So he begins to meditate, and, while doing so, he first remembers that in God there is no real distinction between substance and essence; then he further remembers that there is in God no real distinction between essence and that which, in finite beings, we call their act of being (*esse*). A conclusion then necessarily follows: in order to account for the very being (*esse*) of creatures, and given that "the principle of the action can be considered from the effect of the action," one must attribute the production of the finite acts of being to the very Act of Being which, in God, is what we call substance or essence. To be sure, a detailed study of this theological problem would show that every one of the three divine Persons shares in the work of creation; this is even the reason why Thomas says that to create is "common to the whole Trinity." Still, this conclusion ultimately means that to create properly belongs to the very being of God, and since the *esse* of God is identical with His *essentia,* which is common to the three Persons (*in essentia unitas*), it is because to create is the proper act of God's very *esse* that it is common to the whole Trinity.

From this capital conclusion many others follow which, as commonly accepted by all theologians as is the first one, derive from it, in the theology of Saint Thomas, the fullness of their meaning.

This is not an invitation to deduce from the Thomistic notion of God a more or less long series of consequences. Rather than consequences, the notions we are about to examine are corollaries immediately related to the notion of God conceived as the Pure Act of Being. As so often is the case in metaphysics, this is a matter of meditation much more than of deduction.

Perhaps the most immediate among these corollaries is that to create is an action proper to God. Because only God is the pure act of being, only God can give being. But a corollary of this corollary is that no finite being is able to cause the act of being of any other finite being. To say the same thing in more modern terms, no finite efficient cause is able to cause the very existence of its effects. An efficient cause can educe certain forms from a pre-existing matter, but the existence of matter and forms given in the potentiality of matter are both presupposed for the very possibility of efficient causality in the order of finite beings. This proposition has given rise to protracted controversies, not only between Thomists and their adversaries, but even among Thomists themselves.[14]

The reason for these controversies is the ambiguity of the word *esse*. If it is understood, as is often the case, as signifying the same thing as *ens* (that which has *esse*), then it must be conceded that finite efficient causes actually produce *esse* every time they are producing some effect. For an effect must be either something or nothing. If nothing, then there is no effect; if something, then that which is being produced must needs be; if it has being, it has actual existence; consequently, every efficient cause gives existence in every one of its operations.

Taken in this sense, the proposition would not be denied by Thomas Aquinas, but he would observe that the proper meaning of the verb "to be" is to have actual being. Now, if one maintains that a finite cause can cause another being, not merely to be in this and in that way, but absolutely to be, or to exist, then he is in fact attributing to a finite being the causal efficacy proper to God. If to create is the proper action of God, then nothing else can create; that is, nothing else can add to the quantity of actual existence produced by God on the day of creation. No finite being, then, can produce another act of being.[15]

One further corollary of the same notion of God concerns the nature of the very act of creation. As has just been suggested, to create is to produce effects in the very act by which they are. In other words, it is to cause in them that in virtue of which they can be said to be, or to be beings. The received expression, "to create *ex nihilo*," means precisely this. In Thomas' own words, "nothingness (*nihil*) is the same as non-being." To be produced from nothingness, therefore, means to be produced completely, totally, integrally, starting from strictly nothing else than the creative efficacy of God.[16]

It is small wonder that no philosophers have been able to think of such a mode of production before the time of the Christian revelation. All causal relations known in sense experience presuppose the existence of a given matter to which a form is imparted by some efficient cause. This is so true that a creative act cannot even be imagined. If we attempt to represent it to our own minds, we inevitably begin by imagining nothingness itself as something "out of which" the created being is made. This is to say that we spontaneously tend to think of the act of creating as if it were one more case of "becoming." But it is not so. The nature of the difficulty makes itself felt in the very absence of fitting words to formulate this mode of production proper to God. To us, anything that happens, any "event," is conceived as a change. But creation is not a change, because to create is not to make something from something else;[17] nor is it properly, although we sometimes use the expression, the "gift of being," because every gift presupposes the presence of something to receive it, and nothingness can receive nothing. The best we can do in order to express such an extraordinary mode of production is to say that creation is the production of being, taken in its totality, by Him Whose very essence is to be. We should not be surprised that we lack the proper words to describe the proper act of the Prime Cause, for which we also lack a satisfactory name. For, indeed, we call God *ens*, while He is not an *ens*—that is, a *habens esse*—but, rather, *Ipsum Esse*.

The exact nature of that which is being created follows from what precedes with the same necessity. The only things that can properly be created are those of which it has previously been said that they are capable of having an act of being of their own. These are substances. With perfect consistency Thomas observes that, since to be created is to be caused to be, to be created belongs to whatever it is proper to have an act of being; that is, to be a *habens esse*, a being. Now it has been seen that *esse* properly belongs to substances; that is, to that whose essence is such that it is capable of having an act of being of its own. Only substances, then, can be created. As to their forms, or their matter, or their accidents, which have no *esse* of their own, they are said to be "concreated" along with the substance which, properly speaking, is alone created.[18]

This remark leads to a subtler one. As has just been said, only the substance is a proper object of creation. This does not mean that there is in it anything that is not created; it means that the elements of the substance are included in the creation of the substance itself. They are created, not for themselves, but as parts of the substance. And, of course, the substance and its parts are all created at once. Still, if one could distinguish, within the substance itself, a point of impact that can be said to fall first under the creative act of God, one would say that this point is the very act of being of the substance; namely, its *esse*. Borrowing from the *Liber de Causis* a formula to which he imparts an entirely new meaning, Thomas Aquinas likes to repeat: "The first of created things is being."[19] By these words Thomas himself means to say that being itself presupposes no other effect of God, whereas, since all the other effects of God presuppose being (otherwise they would be nothing), the very act whereby things are, or exist, must be considered in each one of them as the first effect of God. This is but another way, but a particularly striking one, of saying that this very act —namely, *esse*—lies at the root of all the characteristics or determinations that are in any sense constitutive of any given finite being.

This conclusion entails the further corollary that, since it is the prime and immediate effect of creation, the existential act (*esse*) is found at the very core of being. In other words, given any particular being, its metaphysical analysis ultimately reaches, as that which is innermost in it, this very *esse* which is, at one and the same time, the point of impact of the creative efficacy of God, the inner principle in virtue of which the thing is a being, and the existential energy owing to which everything else in the thing can enter its structure and contribute to its complete individuation.

The kind of metaphysical glow that usually attends the statements of Saint Thomas when the relationship of *esse* to being and to God is at stake can be perceived in those often-quoted passages in which the supremacy of the act of being is forcibly stated. For instance:

> *To be* (esse) *is that which is most intimate in everything; it is that which is most deeply set in all things, because it is formal with respect to all that which there is in a thing.*[20]

In writing such words as *quod est magis intimum cuilibet et quod profundius omnibus inest*, Thomas obviously intends to use the strongest possible expressions in favor of the fundamental notion he is trying to establish. He could not very well more forcefully say the same thing, but he could say it differently. For instance: "God is, in all things, the proper cause of the universal being itself which is innermost in all things" (*ipsius esse universalis quod, inter omnia, est magis intimum rebus*).[21]

From this vantage point the true nature of the Christian universe of Saint Thomas Aquinas is easily seen. One has only to bring together these two propositions: the act of being is the proper effect of God, and: the act of being is innermost in every being. The conclusion then follows at once and it is found in the very same passage: "God operates in all things." It will not be amiss to read the whole passage once more and, this time, in its entirety, so as to note the consequence flowing from the principle:

And since the form of a thing is within the thing, and all the more so according as it is considered a higher and more universal thing; and because in all things God Himself is properly the cause of universal being, which is innermost in all things: it follows that God works intimately in all things.

There is always some peril in restating the doctrine of Saint Thomas in terms that he himself did not use. On the other hand, it is sometimes advisable to do so in order to render perceptible to modern ears essential truths that seem to have been easier to understand in the thirteenth century than they are today. To many of our contemporaries the notion of a supernatural order has become meaningless; only the notion of nature makes sense to their minds. But even among Christians it seems to have become rather common to speak as if there were some contradiction in attributing to nature anything like a religious character. Not so in the universe of Saint Thomas Aquinas. In it, the necessary distinction of the natural and the supernatural is most scrupulously observed, but Thomas was too fully aware of the genuinely religious inspiration of the greatest among the Greek natural theologies not to stress the religious implications of his own metaphysical positions. Even nature *qua* nature owes its whole being to God, and since everything acts and operates inasmuch as it is act, it can be said that no thing is, or operates, except in so far as God is present to it by His own being and operation.

The whole doctrine is expounded in the *Summa Theologiae*, I, q.8, a.1, which deals with the question: "Whether God is *in* all things?" Thomas Aquinas answers it in the affirmative, because "a thing is wherever it operates; but God operates in all things . . . Therefore God is in all things." In justifying this conclusion, Thomas makes clear that God is not present in things as if He were part of their being or essence; nor does He belong to the substance of anything as if He were one of its accidents. God is present to all things as an agent is present to that upon which it acts.

From the very beginning of the answer, the great importance of the notion of efficient causality in the doctrine of Thomas Aquinas makes itself felt. Some philosophers and theologians (even Christians) have objected to it because it seems to keep God out of His creatures and to limit His presence in them to the extrinsic relation of an efficient cause to its effects. But this objection overlooks what is essential in the doctrine; namely, that the first effect produced by God in His creatures is their very being. As has just been seen, "since God is being (*esse*) itself by His own essence, created being must be His proper effect." Now, God does not cause finite being only at the moment of its creation,

> . . . *but so long as, because it continues to be, the creature has to be preserved in being; as light is caused in the air by the sun so long as the air remains illuminated. Therefore as long as a thing has being, so long must God be present to it, according to its mode of being. But being* (esse) *is innermost in each thing and most fundamentally present within all things, since it is formal in respect of everything found in a thing, as was shown above. Hence it must be that God is in all things, and innermostly.*[22]

All the statements made by a great philosopher and theologian are important, and each one of them is necessary at the place where it is made; but not all of them are of equal importance. In every doctrine, there are key positions whose meaning guides and qualifies our understanding of all the rest. There is no more important and more central notion than this one in the doctrine of Thomas Aquinas. It is not enough to recognize its inevitability in the light of the Thomistic notion of God. Time and meditation are required if one wants to realize the fullness of its import. The theologians of the Middle Ages used to distinguish three different ways in which God is said to be "everywhere": by essence, by presence properly so called, and by power. Thomas Aquinas accepted this threefold distinction in the very terms it had been bequeathed to him. For it is true that God is present to all things by mode of power, since all things are subject to the power of God; and God is present to all things by mode of presence properly so called, since all things are present to Him; but, above all, God "is in all things by His essence, inasmuch as He is present to all as the cause of their being." The reason that this presence of God to things as their cause can be called a presence by essence is that, as has been shown above, God is creator of the world by His very essence and not separately through any divine Person. Thus, for God to be the cause of what is innermost in finite beings and to be present to them by essence are one and the same thing. Because that which in other beings is called their essence, or their substance, is in God His very act of being, Thomas boldly says that it is by His very "substance" that God is to all things the cause of their being. In Thomas' own words, God is in all things by His essence *quia substantia sua adest omnibus ut causa essendi.*[23]

This entails no confusion of the world of nature with the world of grace. Nature itself *qua* nature is here at stake. Had God decided to create this universe of ours, along with man such as man now is or such as he was first created, without adding to nature the gifts required for the fulfillment of its future supernatural destiny, it would still be true that God is immediately present to the universe by His very substance, or essence, as the cause of its very being. Some of God's creatures are aware of this truth. Human beings, for instance, are endowed with an intellect and, consequently, can know God. Among them there are some who enjoy the privilege of knowing God and of loving Him actually or habitually. This prerogative belongs to such men by grace. It can therefore be said that grace is the special mode of God's presence whereby, as a gift gratuitously superadded to nature, God makes Himself present to the substance of man as an object of knowledge and of love. But the universal presence of God in things is nothing superadded to their natures. Rather, it is that which constitutes their natures as natures by causing them to be; that is, to be "beings."

This is the conclusion of which we were saying, and of which we feel an urge to repeat, that it is not enough to understand it as the outcome of a compelling dialectical process. It takes time for such an all-embracing view of the world to persuade the intellect of its truth and to obtain from it more than an assent exacted by the force of logical necessity. To say that God is present in things by His very essence certainly is a metaphysical proposition. More precisely, it belongs within the order of natural theology, which is the crowning part of metaphysics. But it is also a theological proposition in the Christian sense of revealed theology, which is the theology that envisages the world in the light of the divine revelation. Lastly, this same proposition also belongs in the order of religious knowledge and of the spiritual life, for there is nothing that is not religious in a world to whose being the essence of God (which is *to be*) is immediately present. For him who realizes the meaning of such words, human life can (and should) become radically transformed; a whole spirituality can feed on the meditated awareness of a truth that places man, along with the whole world, in the constant presence of God, or rather of a truth that turns man into a God-inhabited being living in a God-inhabited world.

But Saint Thomas Aquinas never used unnecessarily loud words. The whole of this threefold truth is contained in a very simple sentence, which says that God is said to be in a thing "after the manner of an efficient cause, and thus He is in all things created by Him."

The philosophical and theological significance of the doctrine is best seen from the historical destiny it was to have. For history is a sort of laboratory, or proving ground, in which principles reveal their true meaning by unfolding their consequences. The Thomistic notion of God and of His immediate presence to all creatures entails the consequence that God is immediately co-operating with all the operations performed by all finite beings. This does not mean that creatures themselves do not exercise operations of their own. The reverse is true. Just as the immediate presence of God to creatures does not deprive them of their own being but, on the contrary, causes it to be, so also His immediate co-operation with their operations does not deprive them of their own efficacy but, on the contrary, causes creatures to be able to act as well as to be. In fact, the co-operation of God with the operations of creatures is but another name for His presence by essence to the whole of creation. To understand this truth as meaning that God substitutes His own being and efficacy for those of His creatures is to misunderstand it entirely. The presence of God to things causes their existence and their operations.[24]

To quote one single historical verification of this conclusion, let us mention the position of the highly un-Thomistic Dominican, Durand of Saint-Pourçain (*Durandus de Sancto Porciano*). As it was his intention to reject the doctrine of the immediate co-operation of God with creatures (*concursus divinus*), he very intelligently began by rejecting the thesis that "*esse* (to be) is more intimate than that whereby it is determined." But to deny that the act of being is more intimate to a substance than the very essence by which its *esse* is determined was clearly to strike at the very root of Thomism. Of course, it was also to ruin the doctrine of the divine co-operation.

This doctrinal correlation is pretty constant in the history of medieval theology. It illustrates the central place occupied in Thomism by the notion of *esse*. But what is even more remarkable about the method followed by Thomas Aquinas is that the deeper his philosophy became, the more closely we see him adhering to the very letter of Scripture. God *teacheth man knowledge* (*Ps. 93:10*); therefore, God moves the human intellect. *For it is God who worketh in you, both to will and to accomplish* (*Phil. 2:13*); therefore, God moves the will. *Lord, thou hast wrought all our works for us* (*Isai. 26:12*); therefore, all the operations of nature are first attributable to God. Let the fact be noted to the dismay of those masters of philological exegesis who think that the meaning of the sacred text is wholly contained in the grammars and dictionaries consulted by them in the light of their own personal understanding. One may well wonder on which side examination is really free, that of exclusively philological exegesis or that of the speculative theology of Thomas Aquinas. But perhaps the true problem is another one. In observing Thomas at work, one is irresistibly reminded of the description of Christian philosophy given in *Aeterni Patris* by Pope Leo XIII:

> *Those therefore who to the study of philosophy unite obedience to the Christian faith are philosophizing in the best possible way; for the splendor of the divine truths, received into the mind, helps the understanding, and not only detracts in no wise from its dignity, but adds greatly to its nobility, keenness and stability.*[25]

Chapter 8. Being and causality

The history of the notion of cause is one of the most neglected among the many chapters in the history of philosophy. At first Thomas Aquinas seems to have accepted it as he had received it from Greek philosophy, particularly from Aristotle. Nevertheless, he was aware that all philosophers had not used the term in the same sense. To begin with, he knew that, in the mind of Latin theologians, the Latin word *causa* had not exactly the same meaning as the word *aitia* in the language of the Greek Christian theologians. But he himself considered that there was at least one meaning that the notion of cause could not not have. For, unless the word means nothing, it signifies that which is necessarily followed by something else: *causa est ad quam de necessitate sequitur aliud*. Two characteristics determine the meaning of this notion: there must be consecution, and necessity in consecution.[1]

Common experience supports this notion of causality. There are things without which some other things would not exist and from whose actual operation some other things necessarily follow. We are saying some "other" things, for if something follows from a cause, it should be something other than the cause itself; the cause, Thomas says, is that from which the being of something else follows: *cum causa sit, ad quam sequitur esse alterius*. A detailed history of the notion of causality would probably show that its variations have followed the variations of the philosophical notion of being. Such is being, such too is causality.

Of all the philosophical notions affected by the influence of Christianity, that of efficient cause should be placed after the notion of being but near it. Modern scholastics are unanimous in passing severe judgment on the "father of modern skepticism," David Hume, whose criticism of the notion of causality they hold responsible for the coming of Kant and of modern idealism after him. Their criticism is well founded, but they themselves sometimes fail to realize that there is something mysterious about the notion of efficient causality, and that the mystery it contains is due in part to its Christian origin. This is so true that many great theologians have had misgivings about the notion. If a cause is, for another thing, the origin of its very being, is it not its creator? In one way or other, Christian theologians have done their best to prevent secondary causes from becoming creative causes. This is why Saint Augustine and, after him, Saint Bonaventure have adopted the notion of "seminal form" (*ratio seminalis*). By admitting that at the time of creation God gave being to all the future effects now latent in their causes, Augustine and Bonaventure were hoping to account for the causality present in the world without detracting from the exclusive power God has of creating.[2] In the seventeenth century, the much-abused occasionalism of Malebranche, a scientist, a philosopher, a theologian, and a priest of the Oratory of Jesus, was another way to solve the same problem: efficacy in the order of being is difficult to distinguish from creation, for what is it to create if not to produce being? Now only God can create; consequently, no secondary cause can be more than an occasion for the divine efficacy to exercise efficient causality. To refute Malebranche is a good thing, but no one can really refute him who does not first realize the true nature of the difficulty.

The doctrine of Thomas Aquinas himself supposes that the difficulty had been seen and so completely settled that there was no need to mention it. Reduced to its simplest terms, the problem was as follows. The true philosophy is that of Aristotle, who distinguishes four kinds of causes (moving, formal, material, and final), of which none is called the "efficient cause." Now, one cannot speak of causality in metaphysics without resorting to the notion of efficient causality. How can we justify this notion, and where can we find a place for it in the etiology of Aristotle?

The enumeration of the four kinds of Aristotelian causes did not include the efficient cause, but it did include what we call the moving cause. In fact, even this expression has no literal equivalent in the terminology of Aristotle. What we call the "moving cause" Aristotle himself simply designated as "that from which movement begins." This kind of causality was the only one Aristotle really needed in order to account for physical change as it was observable in nature. The universe of Aristotle consisted of substances, some of them eternal, the others ceaselessly coming to be and passing away. The proper object of physics, in the philosophy of Aristotle, was the nature of "becoming." The eternal substances themselves required no explanation; they were beings whose whole nature is to be being *qua* being, act, necessity. On the contrary, the existence of the things that are coming to be and passing away did have to be accounted for. This Aristotle did by conceiving every process of generation continued more or less felicitously according to the degree of docility of matter. But, even so, a new form, similar to its cause, would be educed from the potentiality of matter, and a new being would achieve actual existence. In the universe of Aristotle, therefore, the production of being was essentially the work of motion. The name given by Aristotle to the Prime Cause of the universe was the Prime Mover. And Aristotle was right in making the choice of this name, since, in his doctrine, it was as the origin of universal motion that God was the origin of universal being.

If this view of physical causality ever caused any difficulty in the mind of Thomas Aquinas, he has never mentioned it. The truth probably is that he accepted it while, as he was wont to do, giving it a new and deeper meaning entirely his own. Still, it is hard to believe that Thomas Aquinas could everywhere equate "moving cause" with "efficient cause" without realizing that doubts could be raised about the lawfulness of the operation. Two witnesses, with both of whom he was well acquainted, were at hand to warn him of the difficulty.

In his *Metaphysics*, Avicenna expressly distinguished two notions of productive causality: first, that of moving cause, proper to the philosophers, particularly to Aristotle, and which rightfully identified moving power with causal power; next, the notion of a creating cause, which is familiar to theologians, who resort to it in describing the mode of causation by which the First gives existence to the world of possibles offered by His intellect to His power and His will. There was a good reason why Avicenna should have to distinguish this second notion from the first. As a philosopher, he had stressed the fact that God was not only a Prime Mover, as He is in the doctrine of Aristotle and in reality, but first and foremost the prime cause of actual existence for all that which is, or exists. In short, the God of Avicenna was a truly efficient cause, a true *causa agens*, precisely because, in His own way, He was a producer of actual being.[3]

There is nothing surprising in this. Avicenna was a sincerely religious man.[4] He was a Moslem and, precisely as such, he shared with Christians their belief in the truth of the Old Testament. The influence of his religious beliefs on his philosophical positions is often evident; so much so that his metaphysics sometimes appears as a halfway house between the philosophy of Aristotle and that of the scholastic theologians. His influence on the evolution of Christian theology in the thirteenth and fourteenth centuries is clearly perceptible in the two outstanding instances of Thomas Aquinas and John Duns Scotus. True enough, there were in his doctrine elements that could not be accepted by Christian theologians. Above all, the Christian universe is the work of a supreme freedom, whereas the world of Avicenna flows from a supreme necessity. Despite what Avicenna himself says about it, his God is not free in the Christian sense of the word, and this difference has its root in the divergence between the initial meaning of *esse*, conceived by Avicenna as the absolute necessity of being (*necesse esse*), and *esse* in the theology of Saint Thomas, which first means the act that God claimed He was when He said to Moses that His name was I AM. Nevertheless, there were many points on which Avicenna's philosophical interpretation of the teaching of the Old Testament opened new possibilities for the reflection of Christian theologians. Besides, Moses Maimonides, the great Jewish theologian, had already read Avicenna and borrowed from him much of his interpretation of Aristotle. Coming after Maimonides, Thomas Aquinas did the same thing. To a large extent, the Aristotelian elements included in Thomas' early *Commentary on the Sentences* seem to have come to him through their reinterpretation by Avicenna. Thomas was aware then, certainly, of the nature of the problem raised by the identification of the two notions of moving cause and of efficient cause.[5] No one could read Avicenna and ignore it.

There is another reason why Thomas Aquinas could not have followed Avicenna on this point without noticing that, in so doing, he was introducing into the etiology of Aristotle a new notion of causality. Avicenna had died in 1037. Another Moslem philosopher, Averroes, who was born in 1126 in Cordova, in Spain, and who died in 1198, on the very eve of the thirteenth century, was extremely well known to Thomas Aquinas by his writings. Now, our theologian could not possibly have been unaware that one of the main reproaches directed at Avicenna by Averroes was precisely that he had allowed his religious beliefs to corrupt the truth of philosophy; that is, of course, of the philosophy of Aristotle. The notion of causality is one of the points on which Averroes has accused Avicenna of having spoken less as a philosopher than as a believer. In short, Averroes would have subscribed to no such notion as that of a "Moslem philosophy," nor is it surprising that among today's opponents of the notion of "Christian philosophy" some attach so much importance to the Latin Averroistic movement of the thirteenth century.

The nature of the problem, then, must have been known to Thomas Aquinas. But he had no need of the Moslem theologians to realize the significance of the biblical notion of creation from nothing as compared with the philosophical notion of efficient causality. The Latin translation of *Genesis* begins by affirming that, in the beginning, God created heaven and earth (*Gen. 1:1*). Now, as early as Saint Augustine, it became customary to use the verbs *creare* and *facere* indifferently. To Augustine, for instance, to create was really to make, so much so that many centuries later Thomas Aquinas was to reproach Augustine for having used the word *creare* equivocally, as meaning not "to make something from nothing" but simply "to improve something," "as when we say that a bishop is created." In fact, Augustine constantly used the word *facere* in order to signify what we now call *creare*, and this led him to speak of an *efficient* causality or, rather, to identify the two notions of causality and efficiency: all cause is efficient, Augustine says.[6] Hence, the notion of efficiency is here not only finding its way into that of causality, it is really absorbing it.

The aim of these historical remarks is to explain why, when Thomas Aquinas had to interpret the fourfold Aristotelian division of causes (moving, formal, material, and final), it does not seem to have occurred to him that the moving cause of Aristotle could be anything else than the efficient cause of the Christian theologians, especially of Augustine. At any rate, it could not be anything else to Thomas Aquinas. In his own language, there is no essential distinction between efficient cause (*causa efficiens*), acting cause (*causa agens*), and moving cause (*causa movens*); rather, all these denominations can be included under the name of "efficient cause"; that is, of any cause which, be it by making, by acting, or by moving, ultimately causes something to be.[7]

The personal contribution of Saint Thomas Aquinas, at least as far as we know in the present condition of Thomistic studies, seems to be that he found a justification for the notion of efficient causality understood as a production of being, although not as a production of actual *esse*, since no cause can produce existence properly so called save only God.

As has been seen in the preceding chapter, every being acts inasmuch as it is act (*i.e.*, inasmuch as it *is*). In acting, it produces an effect similar to itself; and since, in the case of God, the cause is the pure act of being, its effect must be some being. In creating beings, God has produced finite acts which, like Himself, are able to produce other beings. Naturally, created beings cannot create, since they themselves presuppose the creative act of God as cause of their own being as well as of their operations. Moreover, the operation of a finite being presupposes the existence of the very matter upon which it exercises its own efficacy. Still, since it is the effect of an efficient cause, created being must be able to produce something by its operation, and this something is necessarily a being.

This is what Thomas Aquinas himself says in a remarkable passage of his *De Potentia:*

> *All the created causes communicate in one effect, which is being* (esse), *although every one of them has its proper effect, and this distinguishes it from the others. For instance, heat causes the hot to be, and the builder causes the house to be. Thus, these causes agree in that they all similarly cause being, but they differ in that fire causes fire and the builder causes a house. There must therefore be a cause higher than all the causes, a cause because of which they themselves cause being, and of which being is the proper effect. This cause is God.*[8]

The analogy of the created universe to God results from the resemblance there exists between effects and their causes. Moreover, this same resemblance is the aspect of the cause that is communicated to its effect, so that an intimate unity obtains among the notions of causality, resemblance, and participation. In a world of beings caused by the Pure Act of Being, each and every manifestation of causal activity consists, for the cause, in communicating something of its own being to the effect: *causa importat influxum quemdam in esse causati.*[9]

The possibility of this communication is due to the natural communicability of the form which, specifically the same in both cause and effect, can nevertheless become numerically different owing to its individuation by different matters. Form, Thomas Aquinas says, is the similitude of the acting being.[10] Such is the reason that this kind of relation is called "transitive causality." Ever since David Hume subjected it to his penetrating analysis, it has been considered a scarcely intelligible notion. And indeed, from the very moment metaphysics had rejected the notion of being conceived as "that which has an act of being," it became impossible to conceive efficient causality as a transmission of part of its being by the cause to its effect. Efficiency is not creation, but creation is the prototype of causal efficiency, and if they are to be conceived as contributing to the very being of their effects, finite beings are efficient causes only inasmuch as, in acting, they imitate the first efficient act, cause of all other beings as well as of their causal fecundity. The true notion of efficient cause stands and falls with the Thomistic notion of God.

From such a point of view, the whole existential aspect of reality becomes susceptible of intelligible interpretation. The inner consistency of the doctrine is strikingly visible. A God Whose name is I AM, and to Whose infinite actuality it is most suitable that He should create, causes actual existence by a free decision of His will. This decision is free because God, being self-sufficient and removed from all things by the very purity of His actuality, is related only in a contingent way to whatever He may wish to actualize. However, this contingency is the very reverse of arbitrariness. Because God is *Ipsum Esse* (the very act of being), He is likewise good. To all being, goodness is an object of love. Hence, God loves Himself as He knows Himself; that is, infinitely. By the very same act of self-love God also loves all the possible participations in His own being, which is tantamount to saying that all His possible effects are lovable to His will inasmuch as, were they to be caused by Him, they would participate in His own being and perfection. But such possible participations are entirely unnecessary to God. This lack of ontological necessity is the reason God is free to create them or not. If He does so, creation is not a production of nature (as are the inner processions of the Trinity); it is an act of the divine will. On the other hand, if God freely chooses to create, since to do so is, for HE IS, to cause something else to be, it can be said that creation is the proper action of God—*creatio est propria Dei actio*—and this is but another way of saying that the finite act of being is the proper effect of God: *esse est ejus proprius effectus*. In fine, in every being, to be is the prime act; it is even the act of all the other acts entering the metaphysical structure of such being; consequently, it belongs to every being, inasmuch as it is act, to desire to communicate its own perfection and to do so by causing effects similar to itself. And this is the very meaning of efficient causality. A universe of beings imitating God in that they are and are causes, such is the universe of Thomas Aquinas. In it, the actuality of being is an ontological generosity: *omne ens actu natum est agere aliquid actu existens;* that is to say: "It is natural, for all being in act, to produce some actually existing being."[11]

In describing finite being as that which has *esse*, particular stress has been laid upon *esse*, which is the very act that turns a possible into a being. The reason for thus insisting upon the notion of *esse* is that it has so often been overlooked, or even rejected, by students of Saint Thomas

Aquinas. Essence is not the highest perfection in the order of being. Having asserted this truth in unequivocal terms, we must add that, although it comes next after the act of being, essence is an element of finite being of absolute necessity and very high nobility. Each essence is the possibility of an actual being endowed with its own finite degree of perfection. Even finite being is act and perfection. The world then is made possible by the very essences of the things which their own *esse* makes to be true beings; so that everything is called a being because of its *esse*, while it is called a thing on account of essence or quiddity.[12]

The mysterious character of the relationship of essence to actual existence has already been noted. So long as one keeps within the notion of the pure Act of Being, there is no essence to be distinguished from it. On the contrary, as soon as one begins to think of *a* being, it becomes necessary to conceive it as a participation in the pure Act of Being. In order to participate in it, the first condition is, *not* to be it. Now, not to be it is to be either nothing or something else. This possible something else is precisely that which can receive a particular act of being. The mode of participation that defines the being at stake is its essence, and the definition of the essence is called its quiddity. This is what we have stated by saying that every essence expresses a restriction of the Act of Being. As compared with this infinite act, essence is a very modest finite degree of perfection. But if it is like nothing as compared with God, it is a glorious thing as compared with nothingness. Essence is, for all that which is not God, the necessary condition of not being nothing.

This relationship of essence to being introduces another notion almost equally mysterious: that of the degrees of intelligibility. An essence is intelligible to us precisely because, in itself, it is a finite quantity of being and susceptible of being grasped by a quidditative concept and expressed by a definition. The higher the essence, the nearer it is to the Pure Act of Being and the less intelligible it becomes to us because, exceeding the kind of essences we are able to know (the essences of material things), it escapes our human mode of knowing. This we realize from personal experience. Our intellect is at home in the study of physical substances: physics, chemistry, biology, as well as in their abstract mathematical formulation. It already feels less at home in metaphysical problems, among which imagination is a nuisance instead of a help. In its attempts to reach the highest intelligible objects, particularly the first principle, our understanding is blinded by an excess of intelligibility. The difficulty proper to metaphysical meditation is not due to any obscurity on the part of the subject; on the contrary, it arises from more light than the human eye can see without suffering from it.

Aristotle had already taught this truth, although, as was natural, he himself understood it in terms of his own notion of being. The Philosopher seems to have conceived (or perhaps imagined) each specific essence (stone, plant, animal, etc.) as a certain quantity of being. Saint Thomas has often quoted the passage in which Aristotle says that "a definition is a sort of number"; just as:

> . . . *when one of the parts of which a number consists has been taken from or added to the number, it is no longer the same number, but a different one, even if it is the very smallest part that has been taken away or added, so the definition and the essence will no longer remain when anything has been taken away or added.*[13]

Translated into the language of Thomas Aquinas, this would mean that each essence represents the quantity of actual being (*esse*) participated in by a specifically defined substance. Obviously, this quantitative language ill fits the immateriality of its object, but Thomas Aquinas must have had something like this in mind when he repeated that, according to Aristotle, essences are like numbers. For a number is essentially a quantity; nevertheless, inasmuch as it is the very number it is, each and every number has qualities of its own. For instance, a number is either even or odd, and the addition or subtraction of one single unit is enough to make it pass from one of these categories into another one. In short, a simple variation in quantity brings about a specifically different being.

This is to say that quality and quantity are inseparable in reality. There is a quality of quantity, and if we agree to *imagine* essences as various quantities of actual being, the ontological density of each essence will determine a qualitative specification proper to it. There is less being in a material form, limited to be itself only because of its matter, than in an intellectual substance capable of becoming any other given being. Intellect, Aristotle says, is in its own way everything. Now, according to Thomas Aquinas, *quality* is a *mode* of the substance, and the very word "mode" (*modus*) signifies measure (*mensura*). Hence, the first mode of quality to be found in a substance is that which makes it to be the specifically distinct kind of substance it is. In this view, each specifically defined essence owes its quiddity to the measure of its participation in the infinite actuality of the divine being.

Numbers are greater and smaller than other numbers; they make up an order and a hierarchy of larger and smaller quantities in which every particular number has its own place determined by purely quantitative relations of *plus* and *minus*. In a universe in which essences are like numbers, beings must necessarily constitute a hierarchy, and since being and the good are convertible, a hierarchy of "quantities" of being is, by the same token, a hierarchy of degrees in goodness; that is, a hierarchy of perfection. Here Thomas joins the fundamental conception of the universe developed by Dionysius, in which the creative power of God flows down in a continuous stream of creatures, imparting to each of them, from the highest angelic hierarchy down to the humblest of minerals, such light and being as it is able to receive according to its kind. This hierarchical structure of the Dionysian universe survives in the created world of Thomas Aquinas, but its substance becomes deeply different.

In the universe of Dionysius the origin of beings was a communication of unity, goodness, and light. Dionysius was very far from ignoring the supreme importance of the notion of being; on the contrary, in the same spirit as the *Liber de Causis*, he considered being as the first creature of God. In his own personal language, Dionysius would say that actual being is found *prior to* all the other participations (*ante alias ipsius participationes*) and excels them all in nobility. Only, in Dionysius' doctrine, the being of creatures emanates from the transcendent non-being (*i.e.*, hyper-being) of God, whereas, in the very commentary of the doctrine given by Thomas Aquinas, it is as the being above all beings that God is, for them, the cause of their own being. The God of Dionysius is above being in the line of goodness; the God of Saint Thomas is above beings in the line of being.[14]

Let us therefore confine ourselves to the created universe of Saint Thomas himself. Their starting point is the same; namely, the verse of Scripture that both were fond of quoting: *Every best gift and every perfect gift is from above, coming down from the Father of lights, with whom there is no change nor shadow of alteration* (Jas. 1:17). In the universe of Saint Thomas, these gifts come down in the form of so many creatures, each of which receives from the power of God its own perfection along with its own being. The measure (*modus*) of their respective acts of being, according to their respective essences, also measures their respective degrees of perfection: *ex diverso modo essendi constituuntur diversi gradus entium*. Here again Thomas is using *modus* in its Augustinian sense of measure, not in its loose sense of "manner."[15]

The "diverse modes of being" are the specifications imposed upon the various acts of being by the various essences that receive them. And no wonder, since everything is related to goodness in exactly the same way as it is related to being.

This notion of a universe structured according to the degrees of perfection in its components has an immediate bearing upon the Thomistic conception of physical causality. Since everything acts inasmuch as it is act—that is, inasmuch as it *is*—a hierarchy of beings necessarily is a hierarchy of causes. Beings exercise efficient causality to the extent that they are and according to the place that their own degree of perfection assigns to them on the universal scale of beings. In the comparatively simple universe of Greek science, this metaphysical view of the world was substantiated by astronomy and by physics. At the summit, the Prime Mover; below and under him, the successive spheres with their heavenly bodies, each lower sphere being moved by its own desire of the higher one. The same cause accounts for the motions of the sublunary bodies; that is, for all the changes that provide the subject matter for the sciences of physics and biology. To be sure, God orders all things by Himself, but when it comes to carrying out His dispositions, God moves and causes inferior beings through the higher ones.[16]

The modern reader of Saint Thomas feels tempted to interpret such remarks as simply meaning that every higher being can act upon every lower one. The sense of the doctrine is a deeper one. This universe of ours is a hierarchical structure of superiors and inferiors in which efficient causality proceeds by gradation, in the precise sense that the higher beings not only can, but must, act upon lower ones. For indeed things are unequal because some are more perfect than others. Now, for a thing to be more perfect simply is *to be* in a higher degree than a less perfect one. And since to be in act is the same as to be perfect and to be, the more a thing is, the more in act and the more perfect it is. On the other hand, it is of the nature of that which is act that it should act, and it can act only upon other beings less perfect than itself, that is, upon beings in potency with respect to the very perfection which, because it itself has it, it can impart to them. The central point of this doctrine is that, in virtue of the very nature of being, the very inequality created by God in beings *demands* that the more perfect ones should act upon the less perfect ones. Both physics and ethics hinge upon this literally "cardinal" truth, for indeed just as, in the world of nature, causality is for the higher beings a sort of duty, so also, in human affairs, inferiors are bound to obey their superiors because it is of the very nature of higher beings to act upon lower ones. This social and political relationship of authority and of obedience therefore is rooted in the law of nature and, since nature is the creature of God, it is primarily rooted in the divine law: *et ideo sicut ex ipso ordine naturali divinitus instituto, inferiora in rebus naturalibus necesse habent subjici motioni superiorum, ita etiam in rebus humanis ex ordine juris naturalis et divini tenentur inferiores suis superioribus obedire.*[17]

A complete Thomistic view of the created world, including the law of its structure and the ontological root of its causal exchanges, is contained in the preceding lines. No deeper metaphysical view of the universe has ever been offered, but, at the same time, one could not think of a more distinctly theological one since its universal law can be described as a "natural imitation of God." All beings are imitating God by the mere fact that they are, but they naturally perfect their resemblance to Him by exercising their causal efficiency. God is Being, or rather *Esse*, and they are beings; God is a Creator of beings, and they are efficient causes that transmit existence to other beings and, in this sense at least, cause them to be. Hence, the remarkable saying of Dionysius in his *Divine Hierarchy* that there is nothing more divine than to become a co-worker with God, according to the words of the Apostle (*I Cor. 3:9*): *For we are God's coadjutors.* Nor is this simply what the world of Saint Thomas is, it also is what it aims to be. All things are tending to achieve the divine resemblance, which is their ultimate end, from the mere fact that they are acting and operating.[18] Thomas Aquinas calls this the natural assimilation of things to God: *naturaliter assimilari Deo.*[19] One can hardly imagine a universe whose physical substance and structure are more deeply permeated with a sacral and religious meaning. On the other hand, it would be just as difficult to think of a world in which the religious significance of beings is more intimately tied up with their physical substance—with the very core of their being. To be, to be a certain nature, and to operate according to the specific determination of such a nature, all this is, identically, to resemble God and to co-operate with God.

Having reached this deep level of the doctrine, one begins to realize the full meaning of the famous controversy carried on by Thomas Aquinas on the possibility of an eternal world. The ultimate reason for the answer is more profound than might be supposed from the mere formula of the question. Caught as he then was between philosophers who judged the world eternal and theologians who maintained that it could not have been created otherwise than in time, Thomas Aquinas had to disagree with both sides; and it is very important to understand why he had to disagree with the theologians.

The question was not: has the world been created in time? Under this precise form the problem had been settled by Revelation. It is written: *In the beginning God created heaven and earth.* There was therefore a beginning. For every Christian, the question of the fact itself is thereby settled. What is noteworthy from the point of view of the philosophers is that, not being informed by the Word of God that the world had a beginning, they naturally concluded that the world had no beginning. According to Thomas Aquinas himself, judging from the nature, structure, and operations of natural beings, there is no necessary reason to think that this universe did have a beginning. In short, Thomas was of the opinion that, had not God revealed to us that the world was not created from all eternity, the notion would hardly have occurred to the mind of a philosopher. This is why, even after refuting at length the arguments by which the philosophers pretended to demonstrate the eternity of the world, Thomas Aquinas showed that the arguments by which some theologians sought to prove that the world was not eternal, although probable, and useful against the contrary error, had no rational necessity.[20]

Thomas could not go further in this direction. For if, in fact, the world has been created from nothing, its nature cannot possibly involve a necessary existence. On the other hand, now that the world does exist, its nature is known to us, and we can safely predict that, speaking of the future, it is here to stay.

This was a surprising statement to many thirteenth-century theologians. Of course they all knew that the created universe was destined to subsist everlastingly in the future, under a glorified form, by the grace of the divine will; but they emphatically did not think that, after its creation, the world could subsist without a special assistance extended to it by God. In a theology like that of Saint Bonaventure, for instance, it was understood that, since it has been created from nothing, the world harbors in itself a sort of inner tendency to revert to its primordial nothingness. Borrowing a word from the Latin translation of John Damascene's treatise *On the Orthodox Faith,* they called this flaw in the structure of created being its *vertibilitas;* let us say, its "caducity." However we may translate the word, there is no such tendency to revert to nothingness in the world of Saint Thomas Aquinas. The Creator of this world is HE WHO IS; the very first effect caused by the Creator in producing this world is its very being (*esse*). How, and why, should that whose first property is to be contain an inborn aptitude to lose its existence? In the first place, it is no more in the power of any being to lose its existence, after receiving it, than it was in its power to come into being before the time of its creation. Then, although it cannot subsist for one moment for any other reason than because it is being conserved by God, we should not imagine the world as having no self-subsistence of its own. On the contrary, since the proper effect of creation is the very being of creatures, it would be absurd to maintain that creatures have not, as properly belonging to them, that which is the first effect of the creative efficacy of God. The question is not to know if creatures could subsist without the preserving action of God, but, rather, if the effect of this action is not to impart to creatures a being and a subsistence of their own.

The correct answer to the question, therefore, is that God causes the world to exist by imparting to it an actual existence of its own. Unless it receives it from God, the created universe can have no being at all, but since, in fact, God gives it actual being, each and every created being owns the very act (*esse*) in virtue of which it is said to be. Consequently, in so far as its own ontological structure is concerned, the created universe is sure to subsist indefinitely.

The objection that God could annihilate the world, if it pleased Him to do so, asserts nothing that is not true, but it is irrelevant to the problem. Even supposing that God did create the world in order to destroy it—a senseless supposition, since nothingness cannot be a final cause—this still would not entail the consequence that there is, within finite acts of being, a natural aptitude to cease to be. The consequence of their native contingency only is that, if it pleased their Creator to do so, He could destroy His creatures, which is a proposition that cannot be denied; but the proposition at stake is that there is supposed to be, in creatures, a natural tendency to lose their existence, and this is what Thomas Aquinas has forcefully denied. On the contrary, he maintains that "the nature of creatures shows that none of them is annihilated."[21] For they are either immaterial or material. If they are immaterial, they are forms, and there is in them no potency with respect to non-being. If they are material things, then their matter at least is eternal and their forms will always remain in the potentiality of matter, from which they can again be educed. Hence the remarkable statement made by Thomas that all the creatures of God are due to exist eternally, at least as to their matter, because creatures will never be annihilated, at least as to their matter, even though they may be corruptible: *omnes creaturae Dei secundum aliquid in aeternum perseverant, ad minus secundum materiam, quia creaturae nunquam in nihilum redigentur, etiamsi sint corruptibiles.*[22]

One of the best vantage points from which to survey this doctrinal position is the Disputed Question *De Potentia*, q.5, a.3, in which Thomas Aquinas bluntly asks the question: "Can God annihilate His own creation?" The answer is in the affirmative, and the reasons for this decision are multiple. First, since no creature *is* its own existence, there is no contradiction in conceiving it as not existing; now God can do all that which does not involve contradiction; so God certainly can deprive His creature of an existence that does not belong to it necessarily. Moreover, God can freely take back what God has freely given. If it is only a question of possibility, no doubt God can destroy His own creation.

In laying down this conclusion, however, Thomas reveals to us the existence of a doctrinal opposition between Averroes and Avicenna and his own position on the question. In his *Metaphysics*, Avicenna upheld the view that every being, outside of God, has in itself the possibility either to be or not to be. This agreed perfectly with his own notion of being conceived as a possible essence to which existence is added as an accident. As has been said, Avicennian essences are existentially neutral. Obviously, if essences are indifferent with respect to actual existence, the very nature of created being includes, of itself, an equal possibility to be and not to be. The only necessity to exist that can be found in such a nature must come to it from without. It comes to it from the only necessary being there is; namely, God. Such is the meaning of the well-known Avicennian formula that created beings can never be necessary through themselves, but only, while they are, in virtue of a cause that makes it necessary for them then to exist. A finite being is necessary while it lasts, but it is a *necese esse per aliud* only.[23]

The contrary view was upheld by Averroes in his *Metaphysics* as well as in his treatise *On the Substance of the Globe* (*De Substantia Orbis*). According to him, there are in the world at least certain creatures whose natures harbor in themselves no possibility not to be. These are the eternal substances, such as the heavenly bodies and their Movers. The deep opposition between the world of Averroes and that of Avicenna is clearly seen from the reason Averroes alleges in favor of this position. There are eternal beings, and eternal beings are necessary beings. Now, no being that is not eternal of its own nature can be made to be eternal by any external cause. True enough, it can be caused to exist eternally, but since its perpetuity would not be rooted in its own nature, it still would not be an eternal being. That which truly is eternal is so of itself; it is indestructible because it is the very kind of being it is. In this controversy Thomas Aquinas takes sides with Averroes against Avicenna. According to Thomas Aquinas, the only corruptible beings are those in which there is an inner possibility not to be. Even these cannot be "annihilated," because their component elements are indestructible, but they can be corrupted, because the temporary union of these elements can be dissolved, in which case the elements subsist but their compound itself ceases to be. This is to say that "the only things in which there is a possibility not to be are those in which there is a matter subjected to contrariety."[24] And indeed, since being comes to matter through its form, the separation of matter from its form in any material being is the end of that being. In this sense, all beings composed of matter and form are constantly threatened with the possibility of their decomposition. Such, however, is not the case with prime matter itself, or with the self-subsisting immaterial forms. These are eternal in themselves and of their own nature. They are purely and simply so.

It is remarkable to see Thomas Aquinas take sides with Averroes, the Aristotelian upholder of an eternally existing universe, against Avicenna, the upholder of a universe whose existence is accidental to it because it is eternally being created by God. The reason for this attitude of Thomas Aquinas is that, unlike Avicennian being, Thomistic being is the very reverse of an existentially neutral essence. On the contrary, in the universe of Thomas Aquinas, since forms are the proper receivers of actual existence, pure forms are so naturally apt to exercise the act of being that, having received it, they cannot possibly tend to lose it. As to the compounds of matter and form, it has already been observed that though their dissociation is always possible, even after their dissolution their matter remains under some other form, while the form itself, just as it has been educed from the potency of matter at the beginning of the process of generation, so it also returns to the potency of matter at the term of the process of their corruption. Hence the conclusion: "It therefore remains that in the whole created nature, there is no potency on whose account it is possible that something can tend toward nothingness."[25]

One should dwell upon this point with tenacity. If marveling is the beginning of philosophy, here is an amazing spectacle indeed, and one well calculated to initiate a chain of metaphysical reflections on the true nature of the Thomistic universe. On the one hand, Thomas wants the created universe of Avicenna. Rather, Thomas wants a still more radically created universe than that of Avicenna, one which perfectly fits the requirements of a Christian philosophy. Consequently, if Christian philosophy consisted in giving to the requirements of Christian faith the quickest possible satisfaction, Thomas should agree with Avicenna that no created being can be said to be in virtue of any inner necessity of its own. In fact, the reason quoted by Thomas Aquinas for attributing to matter an eternal existence in the future is the very same argument used by Averroes to uphold the eternal existence of the world in the past. This goes a long way toward explaining why, on close inspection, Thomas himself could not find in the world created by God, such as this world now is, any necessary reason to suppose that it had not always existed. There is no existential flaw in the solid ontological structure of the created universe. It is made by God as solid as if it had eternally subsisted in virtue of its own necessity.

The long-range import of this doctrine is that the created world of Thomas Aquinas is identically the intrinsically necessary world of science. There are not two worlds, the one for science, the other for theology. If the world of science is the real one, then it must needs be the very world that God has created.

A remarkable chapter of the *Summa Contra Gentiles* helps us to grasp the thought of Thomas on this all-important point. In it he was weighing the position of some contemporary theologians who, following the metaphysics of Avicenna, denied that there could be any "absolute necessity" in created being. The word "absolute" here dominates the problem. These theologians would not deny that there is some necessity in the world, but they would maintain that, since the origin of all things is a free decision of God, the necessity to be found in created being must needs be a conditional one. If beings are caused by God both to be and to be necessary, then they are necessary indeed. Even then, however, they might not have been created, so that there can be in them no absolute necessity.[26]

To this Thomas once more replies that the intrinsic necessity of a being has nothing to do with its cause. If we may imagine a modern example in order to clear up the meaning of the doctrine, let us pretend that some superhuman engineer succeeded in turning out a machine so conceived and executed that it could not cease to exist, unless of course its inventor deliberately set about destroying it; would not the existence of such a machine be necessary in itself? Should it be objected that, no, it is not necessary, since the engineer who made it could have not made it, the ready reply would be that if this imaginary machine had not been constructed, its existence would not be necessary indeed; nothingness cannot enjoy any necessity; still, since it has in fact been constructed, and made in such a way that of itself it is fit to endure eternally, this man-made object is indeed, in its own order, a necessary being. Compounds of matter and form are not of this kind; on the contrary, because of the presence of matter in their structure, such compounds are liable to disintegrate and therefore to cease to be. In the Greek conception of the world, even the heavenly bodies were considered as necessary in themselves because the potentiality of their matter was so perfectly actuated by their form that their disintegration was inconceivable. At any rate, some beings are pure forms, and for such as these, the notion of decomposition is senseless; since there is in them no conceivable reason that they should ever cease to exist, they are necessary in themselves. In Thomas' own words, their existence is an absolute necessity.

The created universe described by Saint Thomas is, at one and the same time, both integrally religious and integrally natural. Far from being paradoxical, this situation follows with necessity; for if nature owes to God both that it is and that it acts, God, in turn, owes it to Himself to create a world of nature resembling its divine cause and, therefore, endowed with all the attributes of true being. These attributes are actual existence and efficient causality within the limits defined by its quiddity. The more divine in its origin the world of nature is, the more natural it is bound to be in itself. No wonder, then, that the Greek philosophers, judging of it from the sole inspection of its structure, judged the world to be eternal.

It is not eternal, but only faith knows this with certitude. At any rate, reason assures us that, even though the created world did have a beginning, its nature is such that it will never come to an end. Hearing this conclusion, a large number of theologians have been known to protest. First, they have wondered on behalf of philosophy if it is possible for the same world to be freely created by God and nevertheless to include in its being an element of necessity. Next, as theologians, they have wondered if this necessary world that so perfectly fitted the requirements of a pagan philosophy like that of Aristotle could be reconciled with a Christian view of the world.

But Thomas Aquinas had no such misgivings. For it is said in Holy

Scripture that, in the beginning, God created heaven and earth; but it is also written that *the earth standeth for ever (Eccles. 1:4)*, and again: *I have learned that all the works which God hath made continue for ever (Eccles. 3:14)*. Once more, the literal meaning of Scripture points out the deepest philosophical truth.

PART IV. MAN

Chapter 9. The human soul

Of all the works of God, none is more important to know than man. Anthropology cannot be deduced from metaphysics. Like all other creatures, man is an essence actuated by an act of being, but it is particularly true of him that nature cannot properly be understood apart from such an act. In the case of man, not only his nature, but his very destiny, is at stake.

The theologians have always attributed to man a particularly exalted rank among the creatures of God. A rational being called by grace to share in the beatitude of the divine life, the "man" of the Christian Faith confronted philosophy with an almost insoluble problem. On the one hand, a theologian had to conceive man as endowed with a personal immortal soul, so as to insure the possibility of his future beatitude. On the other hand, the Christian belief in the resurrection made it necessary for the same theologians to attribute to human nature as a whole, and not only to the human soul, a substantial unity of its own.

It was not easy to find a solution that met these two requirements: a soul free enough from its body to be able to survive it, a body so intimately associated with the soul that it could share in its immortality. The first part of the problem could be dealt with if one decided to follow Plato; that is, to conceive the soul as a spiritual substance making use of a body, yet in itself so self-sufficient that, at the death of its body, it could survive and live a life of its own that was even better than its present one. In this view, however, since man was identified with his soul, there was no reason to conceive him as a composite of soul and body endowed with a substantial unity of its own. Such a man could enjoy the divine beatitude as a pure soul, so that there was no point in promising him that his body would be resurrected at the end of time. On the other hand, Aristotle provided a good explanation of the substantial unity of man. If the soul is the form of a body that has life in potency, each and every individual man is a substance made up of the union of a matter and a form, as solidly knit together as these are in any other physical substance observable in sense experience. Only, in this view, man becomes a material substance similar to the others. He is perishable and, at the moment of death, his form must return to the potentiality of matter while the matter of his body continues to exist, in potency to another form. It seems as though one has to choose between the immortality of the soul and the substantial unity of man.

Some Fathers of the Church had clearly seen the difficulty. Augustine, for instance, while accepting the definition of man as a soul using a body, corrected it in other passages where he stressed the fact that, more exactly, man was the unity of both body and soul.[1] In his treatise *On the Nature of Man*, Nemesius had warned Christian theologians against the Aristotelian definition of the soul as the form of its body. This, Nemesius had said, puts the immortality of the soul in jeopardy.[2] In the thirteenth century, after a long inquiry and not without hesitations, Albert the Great followed Avicenna in admitting that the soul can be defined from two different points of view. First, it can be defined in itself, in which case it must be conceived as a spiritual substance; then, in relation to its body, in which case it must be conceived as a form. Consequently, if we consider the soul in itself, it is a substance and we can agree with Plato; if we consider it in its relation to its body, it is a form and we can agree with Aristotle.[3]

This compromise could not last for long. Avicenna had given it an appearance of consistency by saying that the soul is indeed both a substance and a form: in itself, a substance; with respect to its body, a form. Even Thomas Aquinas sometimes used the same language. On the strength of at least one passage it can be maintained that, on this point, Thomas Aquinas followed Albert and Avicenna in their interpretation of Aristotle. Once more, however, this would be only a partial truth. Even when Thomas Aquinas seems to subscribe to what was after all but a compromise, he was going his own way; not including within one single formula two contradictory notions of man and his soul, but transcending them both and creating a third one. Thomas was able to transform the data of the problem and to submit a new solution of it on the basis of his own conception of the act of being.

The key to a correct understanding of Thomas' own position is his notion of the kinds of beings he himself called "spiritual substances." In opening the Disputed Questions devoted by Thomas Aquinas to the study of these beings (*De Spiritualibus Creaturis*), one naturally expects to find there an exposition of his "angelology," and sure enough it is there, but there is also something else. In the doctrine of Thomas

Aquinas, angels are separate substances; that is, they are pure spirits completely free of bodies. Human souls are not separate substances, because they are forms of bodies; nevertheless, they are spiritual substances.[4] Sometimes, using a still more precise language, Thomas calls human souls "intellectual substances," and rightly so, since, as will presently be seen, their intellectuality is the chief mark of their spirituality.

As early as his *Commentary on the Sentences*, Thomas Aquinas extended to human souls his general interpretation of the nature of created substances. Having exclusively reserved for God the absolute simplicity of essence—because, in God, essence is existence—Thomas Aquinas had to attribute to the human soul some sort of composition. As is well known, most of his contemporaries among the theologians had met the difficulty by attributing to all spiritual substances—angels as well as souls—a composition of matter and form. In their doctrine, the notion of matter did not necessarily imply that of corporeity. In the case of angels and souls, these theologians understood by the word "matter" the very potentiality of being or, in Augustine's own terms, its mutability.[5] Thomas Aquinas rejected this notion of a spiritual matter as foreign to the thought of Aristotle and strongly reflecting the Neoplatonism of Ibn Gabirol. Besides, he did not need it. Thomas Aquinas could find in his own metaphysics another principle to substitute for matter in the composition of spiritual substances, and thus to separate them radically, in their very immateriality, from the perfect and absolutely simple Act of Being.

Thomas Aquinas often called this composition one of act and potency. Moreover, his use of this abbreviated expression has contributed not a little to spreading the illusion that act and potency are two constituents of finite beings. In a sense they are, but when he uses such expressions what Thomas Aquinas really means to say is that all substances, including the purely spiritual ones (for instance, angels), are composed of at least two constituent elements, of which one is to the other in the relation of potency to act. More crudely, in all that which is, barring God alone, there is a composition of something that is potency with something that is act. No doubt that which is act stands on the side of form, because in human experience form is the best-known case of act; for the same reason, potency stands on the side of matter, in this sense at least: that in a compound it plays a part similar to that of matter with respect to form. Still, act need not necessarily be a form, nor is it necessary that potency be matter. And since we are here returning to a notion we have already defined, let it be said that a soul is a substance because it is composed of its essence, which is that of a spiritual form, and of its act of being (*esse*). In such an intellectual substance, the essence is to its *esse* in the relation of potency to act. To conclude, we are here confronted with a being made up of two elements, an actual element and a potential one. This mode of composition is typical of finite substances; and since it applies to the soul, the human soul is a substance in its own right.

Inasmuch as it does not include in its structure any materiality, the human soul is a simple form; that is, a simple quiddity, a simple nature. From this point of view, there is no essential difference between a human soul and an angel. *Angelus vel anima*—an angel or a soul—Thomas says, can be said to be simple in its nature because, in both cases, the quiddity is not composed of distinct elements such as matter and form; nevertheless, Thomas adds, there is in them a composition of quiddity, or essence, and actual existence: *sed tamen advenit ibi compositio horum duorum, scilicet, quidditatis et esse.*[6]

This position Thomas Aquinas held to the end of his career. Nevertheless, his interpreters sometimes betray a curious tendency to minimize its importance. One reason for this fact, no doubt, is that there is nothing Aristotelian in the notion of a spiritual substance composed of potency and act; that is, of essence and existence. Now, Thomas Aquinas certainly did his best to persuade his readers that his own notion of the human soul was, on the whole, the same as that of Aristotle. Thomas repeatedly attempted to vindicate Aristotle's doctrine on the soul against the objections directed against it by Nemesius. Whatever may be the historical truth on this point, it seems as though Thomas himself sincerely believed that, according to the Philosopher, the human soul is a spiritual substance able to subsist apart from its body, not a simple form inseparable from it. What it is quite impossible to maintain is that, in the doctrine of Aristotle, the human soul is a substance composed of an essence and an act of being.

But why did Thomas Aquinas maintain that the human soul, besides being the form of the body, is a substance in its own right? This cannot be said of all forms. Not only the forms of minerals or of plants, but even the forms, or souls, of most living beings are so tied up with their matter that, when for any reason the composite disintegrates, the form ceases to be. These are the material forms, properly so called. How do we know that the human soul is not one of these?

This is the moment when the consideration of intellectual knowledge,

its cause and its nature, becomes of paramount importance. To all external appearances, there is no reason that the human soul should not be
considered a common material form; that is, a form whose existence
endures as long as does the composite of matter and form of which it is
a constitutive element. Man has a body, and his soul is the form of his
body; why should his destiny be different from that of the other living beings whose structure is the same?

This would be true if the human soul did not perform at least one
operation besides informing and animating the matter of its body. It
knows; it exercises intellectual knowledge. As such, it is truly an "intellectual substance." Now, to have intellectual knowledge is to be able
to become, and to be, other beings in an immaterial way. When we see
a stone, the sight of it does not turn us into a stony substance. If sense
perception produced such an effect, we would not *know* the stone, we
would *be* it; we would be literally "petrified." This is still more true
of intellectual knowledge. For our intellect to know is to become the
known thing by assimilating only its form, not its matter, and this assimilation is made possible by the operation called intellectual abstraction. Obviously, to know material objects in an immaterial way is an
operation in which corporeal matter has no share. This is the fundamental fact upon which the whole development of metaphysical wisdom
ultimately rests; namely, that there is intellectual knowledge and that
the very possibility of such knowledge presupposes the existence of an
order of immaterial subjects, knowing powers, and operations. Intelligibility and knowledge are inseparable from immateriality.

How this can be done is another problem. We are here concerned
only with the fact that this takes place. Now the argument of Thomas
Aquinas is that only an immaterial substance can perform immaterial
operations and produce the kind of immaterial objects we call "concepts." The intellectual soul of man, then, must be an intellectual substance, a self-subsisting immaterial reality endowed with its own essence
and its own act of being. Such is not the case with material forms; that
is, those forms whose only function is to actuate a certain matter. The
form of a material substance is the act of a certain quantity of matter
which it turns into a body; it is nothing more; for this reason, the act
of being of such a form belongs to the whole substance, although it
comes to matter from the form. In the case of man, on the contrary,
to be (*esse*) is, first and foremost, the act of the intellectual soul, and
it is through the actuality of this intellectual substance that it becomes
the act of the body. This is what Thomas Aquinas intends to express in

saying that the human soul is a *forma absoluta non dependens a materia;* that is, a pure form, not mixed with matter, which owes this privilege to its natural immateriality, itself an effect of its resemblance and proximity to God in the universal hierarchy of beings. For this reason, the human soul has an act of being of its own, which is not true of the other forms of corporeal beings: *habet esse per se quod non habent aliae formae corporales.* Now to say this is exactly the same as to say that, because the human soul is a substance in its own right, there is in it a composition of what the human soul is and of its own act of being.[7]

This statement dates from the beginning of Thomas' theological career. His *Commentary on the Sentences* of Peter Lombard is an early work, but similar statements are easy to find in later writings; and no wonder, since this point is tied up with the very notion of being, which is the first principle in philosophy. The reason so few interpreters of the doctrine seem to take an interest in it is that nothing could be less Aristotelian than such a notion of intellectual substance; and since Thomas Aquinas is supposed to have borrowed his philosophy from Aristotle, they feel justified in disregarding the composition of essence and existence *in the substance of the human soul* as an element foreign to the nature of Thomism. And, indeed, in the philosophy of Aristotle, a form must be a material form, corruptible as the material substance itself is, or else it must be a separate substance, such as angels are in the theology of Thomas Aquinas himself. There is no room in Aristotelianism for an intellectual form that is, at one and the same time, the form of a body and a spiritual substance in its own right. Now, this is exactly what the human soul is in the doctrine of Thomas Aquinas. Only, Thomas did not content himself with accepting two seemingly contradictory positions; he transcended them both. The question was: is the soul an intellectual substance, or is it the form of a body? The answer of Thomas Aquinas was: the human soul is the form of a body *because* it is the precise kind of substance it is.

If this is true, and Thomas repeatedly says that it is, the soul of man is not the form of its body in spite of being a substance; on the contrary, it is *qua* substance that it is form. What does this mean?

There is composition of matter and form in all material substances. In all such substances, actual existence comes to matter through the form. This means that there is only one act of being for the whole compound; that is, for the whole substance, including its matter and form, its quantity and its qualities. In the case of man, the same principle applies, with this difference, however, that the being which then communicates itself to matter is no longer that of a simple form; it is rather that of a spiritual substance whose essence itself is actuated by an act of being of its own. In Thomas' own terms, it is the act of being proper to the form that is, by the same token, the act of being of the whole compounded substance; namely, man. The soul, Thomas says, has the being of a substance, and nevertheless it shares its being with the body; more precisely, it receives the body in the communion of its own act of being: *anima habet esse subsistens . . . et tamen ad hujus esse communionem recipit corpus.*[8] Were it not so, the whole being of man would not be one and the unity of man would not be a substantial unity. But this is not the case. On the contrary, there is only one single act of being, that of the soul, for the whole individual human substance, including the form, the matter, and all the individuating accidents. Thomism, then, is a doctrine in which the substantiality of the soul is the very foundation of the substantiality of man.

We are now at the very center of the anthropology of Thomas Aquinas. His whole interpretation of the nature of man rests upon the possibility that an intellectual substance can be united to a body as its form. This point is enforced by Thomas Aquinas with incredible metaphysical energy in the chapter of the *Summa Contra Gentiles* that is dedicated to the study of the question.

In the first place, Thomas makes it clear that, in the problem under discussion, the causality attributed to the act of being with respect to the substance is not efficient causality, but formal causality. As has been said, only God can cause being after the manner of an efficient cause. Besides, no efficient cause can hold its being in common with its own effect: since the effect owes its being to that of its efficient cause, the being of the cause must needs be other than that of its effect. Let it be understood, then, that the soul gives its being to the body by mode of formal causality, not of efficient causality.

We must add, however, that, within the metaphysical structure of finite beings, it is literally true that the soul shares with its body the very act of being that it itself receives from God. As an ontological block, man is made truly one by the unity of its single existential act:

> *For indeed, it is not unfitting that the act of being* (esse) *in which the composite subsists should be the same as the act of being in which the form itself subsists, since the composite exists only through the form, and neither one exists apart from the other.*

In thus sharing in the very being of the soul, the body does not become soul; it finds itself elevated, as its receiver and subject, to the act of being that the soul itself has as its principle and cause. The whole universe, as Thomas conceived it, is such a hierarchy of higher and lower forms in which the lower ones are, so to speak, raised above their own level by the perfection of the higher ones. One of the effects of this law is to confer upon a discontinuity in the degrees of being a sort of continuity of order; in agreement with the principle of Dionysius that the highest degree of the lower order always is contiguous with the lowest degree of the immediately higher one. The frequently quoted remark of Thomas himself, that the intellectual soul is like a sort of horizon, or border line, between incorporeal and corporeal substances, is here finding its full meaning. And why? Because, Thomas says, the human soul is an incorporeal substance which, at the same time, is the form of a body.[9]

We must refrain from pursuing any further the consequences of a notion which, since it is central in the doctrine, can lead to practically any other part of it. There is one point, however, on which it is impossible not to dwell in connection with this notion of the human soul, precisely because, rather than being one of its consequences, it is identical with it. It is the immortality of the human soul.

Few questions have raised more problems in the minds of the commentators of Saint Thomas Aquinas because, having neglected one of the essential data of the problem, they have placed themselves in a position in which it becomes impossible for them to understand its solution. Having eliminated the notion of being, which is the cornerstone of the doctrine, they cannot help getting lost in most of its parts.

In the writings of Thomas Aquinas himself, there is really no distinct problem of the immortality of the human soul. Assuredly, there always comes a moment when the question has to be expressly asked, but when it comes, the problem has already received its answer. This is visible in the *Summa Contra Gentiles*, Book II. After first demonstrating that, among the intellectual substances, there is something in act and something in potency (chapter 53), and then that to be composed of act and potency is not necessarily the same as to be composed of matter and form (chapter 54), Thomas proceeds straightway to prove that "intellectual substances" are incorruptible (chapter 55). For if "intellectual substances" are incorruptible, since the human soul is an intellectual substance, it is incorruptible. Only an illusion of perspective can make us imagine that there is any difference between the case of the separate intellectual substances, or angels, and that of the non-separate intellectual substances, human souls.

The principle from which Thomas Aquinas deduced the incorruptibility of the intellectual substances in general is their immateriality. Of its own nature, corporeal matter is divisible, because it has quantity and is extended in space, having *partes extra partes*. The decomposition or disintegration of the human body is therefore possible; in fact, it always takes place sooner or later, and this event is called death. In the case of a being composed of soul and body, such as man is, the disintegration of the body entails that of the being. Man dies when his body dies, but the death of man is not that of his soul. As an intellectual substance, the human soul is the proper receiver of an act of being. Having its own act of being, it itself is a being properly so called (*habens esse*). This act of being belongs immediately to the soul; that is, not through any intermediary, but *primo et per se*. Now that which belongs to something by itself, and as the proper perfection of its nature, belongs to it necessarily, always and as a property inseparable from it. This conclusion follows necessarily and it cannot be deduced in simpler words than those of Thomas Aquinas himself:

> *It has been shown above that every intellectual substance is incorruptible; now the soul of man is an intellectual substance, as has been shown; hence the human soul is incorruptible.*[10]

Thomas Aquinas accumulated many other arguments in favor of this all-important conclusion. Most of them stress the incorporeal nature of understanding and of its act, and rightly so. For if it is agreed that the soul exercises such an incorporeal operation, its existence as an incorporeal nature is thereby established and its immortality is possible; but its immortality is more than possible, it is certain, if this immaterial substance is actuated by an act of being of its own.

The reason the proofs of the immortality of the soul seem difficult to understand is that all are tied up with the mysterious element hidden in the notion of *esse*. Some object that if the soul is composed of essence and of an act of being, as indeed is the case, then it is not simple and there is no reason why this composite should not be exposed to disintegration in the same way as the composite of body and soul. But this objection overlooks the fact that what is at stake is the immortality of the soul itself. In the case of man, soul and body enter the constitution of his essence, so much so that, as is often said, man is neither his soul nor his body but the unity of both. This is the reason that when the human body ceases to be actuated by its soul it disintegrates and man himself likewise ceases to be. But the act of being does not enter the composition of the essence of the soul as if its function were to make it to be a soul; its effect is not to make it to be a soul, it is to cause the essence of the soul to be a being. Hence a soul is a composite inasmuch as it is a substance, because, unless it had its own *esse*, it would not be a being; but within this substance, the essence itself is simple, because, being immaterial and having no parts, it cannot disintegrate. An ever-recurring illusion causes us to imagine that, in being, essence is compounded with another essence, which is that of the act of being (*esse*); but that which causes a thing to be does not cause it to be that which it is. It does not complicate its essence, and if that which the act of being causes to be happens to be simple, then, of itself, the being at stake is safe against the very possibility of decomposition.

By far the worst obstacle to an understanding of the doctrine, however, remains the impossibility of imagining the act of being. And, because it is not imaginable, many infer that it is not intelligible. One does not need to go out of the school of Saint Thomas himself to find philosophers and theologians who are convinced that the doctrine of the Master becomes vastly improved if we eliminate from it this cumbersome and somewhat queer notion.

Historical experience shows that such is not the case, and the problem of the immortality of the soul provides an excellent proving ground in this respect. For instance, let us consider the doctrine of the great Franciscan theologian, John Duns Scotus. He never wasted any time refuting the Thomistic notion of *esse*. Scotus simply had no use for it. In fact, he could not find in it any meaning. To him, entity (*essentia*) was reality itself. If no cause has made it actually to exist, then it was only a possible; but after it had been made to exist by some efficient cause, no act of being could add anything more to it. In Scotus' own words: "That an entity could be posited outside its cause without, by the same token, having the being whereby it is an entity: this, to me, is a contradiction."[11] In short, a thing cannot be made to be twice, even by adding to it a so-called act of being.

There would be no point in arguing the case. This is a problem in the interpretation of the first principle. A Thomist feels inclined to think that Scotus is blind, but a Scotist wonders if Thomas is not seeing double. Many differences between the two theologians follow from this first one,[12] but the only one we are now concerned with is its impact on the problem of the immortality of the human soul.

Since there is no act of being in the doctrine of Duns Scotus, what is going to happen to the immortality of the soul? Simply this: it will cease to be demonstrable and will become a matter of faith. As Christians, Scotus says, we believe that there will be for us a future life; we therefore implicitly believe that the soul is immortal; we believe it, but we cannot prove it. And, indeed, we say that the human soul is the form of its body, so that the substance "man" is the unity of matter and form. When this unity disintegrates on the death of the body, its elements also disintegrate. This is visible in the case of the body. Before death, it was the body of a man; after death, there is no man left of whom this piece of matter can be said to be the body. On the other hand, if the nature of the soul is to be the form of a body, it cannot continue to be after it has no body to inform. Hence, if the form of the body survives its body, the fact is hardly less miraculous than the subsistence of the eucharistic accidents after bread and wine have ceased to exist.

Duns Scotus himself does not go that far. He does not consider the survival of the soul as a natural impossibility. On the contrary, he thinks there are probable arguments in its favor, which are even more probable than those in favor of the contrary conclusion; let us say that the immortality of the soul is a high probability, but it is not a certitude. In the last analysis, the immortality of the human soul is absolutely certain on the strength of religious faith alone. In the doctrine of Duns Scotus, this first conclusion entails a second one: we cannot *know* that the human soul is a substance in its own right, directly created in itself and for itself by God. And, indeed, since the soul is not a complete substance endowed with an act of being of its own and able to subsist apart from the complete substance, "man," it does not require to be created in itself. Man, not the human soul, is the substance; man, not the soul, provides a distinct object for the creative power of God.

The decisive part played in this problem by the notion of *esse*, or act of being, is not a historical construction; it is a fact. In the *Summa Theologiae*, I, q.75, a.6, Thomas proves that, since the soul has an act of being of its own, it cannot be corrupted in consequence of the corruption of another substance, be it even man: "That which has *esse* through itself cannot be either generated or corrupted except through itself." For the same reason, such a soul cannot come to be by way of generation (because no creature can cause actual existence), it can only be *created* by God. Conversely, such a soul cannot cease to be by way of natural corruption. In order to lose its act of being, it must be annihilated by God, for only He Who gave the soul existence can take existence away from it. Naturally, as a Christian theologian, Duns Scotus subscribed to all these conclusions no less firmly than Thomas. According to him, too, the soul was a distinct substance, immediately created by God and able to subsist apart from its body. Only, since he could not admit that the soul had an act of being of its own, the immortality of the soul remained for him an object, not of knowledge, but of faith: *sed haec propositio credita est et non per rationem naturalem nota.*[13]

A re-examination of this conclusion is provided by the extraordinary case of Thomas de Vio, Cardinal Cajetan, Minister General of the Dominican Order, a quasi-official interpreter of the theology of Saint Thomas Aquinas, who, in the evening of a long life spent in the study of the Angelic Doctor, finally subscribed to the conclusion of Duns Scotus, and did so for the very same reason.

In order to interpret this incident correctly, it is necessary to locate the problem in its historical context, not in order to satisfy idle historical curiosity, but because only history can help us to realize the philosophical data of the problem concretely.

One of the main reasons Thomas Aquinas often failed to convince his contemporaries and successors was that, from the thirteenth to the sixteenth century, it was commonly agreed that the doctrine of Aristotle and philosophical truth were practically the same thing. Even today, historians are still discussing the meaning of the doctrine of Aristotle on the nature of the soul and of man. Hence, we should not feel too surprised to see masters of the thirteenth and fourteenth centuries agreeing that Aristotle was right but disagreeing about what he had said. By and large, however, today there is some measure of agreement on the three following points: 1. Aristotle has said that there are, in man, cognitive operations that only an intellectual substance can perform. 2. An intellectual substance is a separate substance and, as such, it is naturally incorruptible. 3. Natural forms are not separate substances and therefore perish when the composite of matter and form disintegrates.

From these three points Averroes (the Commentator) had inferred that, according to Aristotle, the intellectual operations observable in man are caused in him by a separate intellectual substance that is present in him only by its operations. As separate, this intellectual substance is, by the same token, incorruptible and immortal; but its own immortality does not entail our personal immortality. We ourselves have a soul, which is personal to each of us and is the form of our body; but for this very reason it perishes along with the body. To sum up, that which causes intellectual knowledge in us is separate and immortal, but it is separate and immortal for the very reason that it is *not* the form of our body; it is not our soul.

The personal attitude of Thomas Aquinas on this point is very puzzling. First, of the doctrine of Aristotle he retained the notion that intellectual substances are incorruptible in virtue of their very nature. Next, he added to the doctrine of Aristotle the demonstration that the human soul is such an intellectual substance, and this was his personal contribution to the discussion of the problem. Third, Thomas undertook to prove that, according to Aristotle himself, this very same intellectual substance we call our soul was, at the same time, the substantial form of our body, so that a man is the substantial unity of both. The title of the *Summa Contra Gentiles*, Book II, chapter 70, runs as follows: "That *according to the words of Aristotle* the intellect must be said to be united to the body as its form." Why did not Thomas Aquinas content himself with setting forth his own doctrine, which is true, without maintaining that this true doctrine was also the doctrine of Aristotle, which, to say the least, was a highly debatable point?

The simplest explanation is that Thomas Aquinas sincerely believed it to be true. The contrary cannot be demonstrated. Still, there are enormous difficulties to overcome before subscribing to this conclusion. For the human soul to be an individual intellectual substance able to subsist apart from its body, the very first condition in the doctrine of Aristotle is that it should not be the form of a body, which it is in the doctrine of Thomas Aquinas. Conversely, the first condition for the substantiality of the soul in the doctrine of Saint Thomas is that it should have an act of being (*esse*) of its own, which, in the doctrine of Aristotle, it has not. Are we to believe that Thomas Aquinas himself failed to realize the significance of two points that mere historians of philosophy can see at once? Thomas Aquinas scrutinized the text of Aristotle more carefully than most of us; it would be rather hazardous to charge him with such a gross misinterpretation of a doctrine he knew so well.

Another explanation consists in saying that, himself a philosopher and a theologian, Thomas Aquinas was more interested in speculative truth than in historical accuracy. There is a great deal of truth in this explanation. As a theologian, Thomas was not interested solely in saying the truth; he wanted it to be accepted by all, and at a time when the philosophical authority of Aristotle reigned supreme there was little hope for anyone to be approved of if he was openly at variance with the Philosopher. Now, precisely, Averroes had presented his own doctrine as a faithful rendering of that of Aristotle.[14] In order to prevent Averroes from exploiting the authority of the Philosopher to the benefit of his own errors, Thomas Aquinas may have considered it a wise move to place his own notion of man under the patronage of Aristotle. That he had something like this in mind seems confirmed by his very words: "Now, since Averroes seeks to confirm his doctrine especially by appealing to the words and proof of Aristotle, it remains for us to show that, in the Philosopher's judgment, we must say that the intellect, as to its substance, is united to the body as its form."[15] *Since Averroes . . .* This looks very much like a deliberate counterattack. Averroes says that Aristotle is with him; why should not I show that he is with me?

We shall never know. But whatever its motives, this was a most unfortunate move whose historical consequences have been and still are disastrous.[16] First, by adopting this attitude, Thomas Aquinas has practically justified those among his adversaries who have identified his own anthropology with that of Aristotle. It has consequently become a classical move, on the part of his opponents, to show that since, in fact, the doctrine of Thomas Aquinas on the soul did not agree with that of Aristotle, it was bound to be false. Then the very disciples of Thomas Aquinas have allowed themselves to be misled for the same reason. In order to justify the Master, they have undertaken to prove that, on the contrary, his doctrine was identical with that of the Philosopher on this point. A rather weak move indeed, since Thomas Aquinas could have agreed with Aristotle and nevertheless been wrong. And a dangerous move as well, since if, in order to be true, the doctrine of Thomas Aquinas had to agree with that of Aristotle on the nature of the soul, it is much to be feared that the doctrine of Thomas Aquinas is false.[17]

Hence the possibility of a third attitude. A Thomist can still refuse to maintain that Aristotle proved the immortality of the soul, and at the same time maintain that it was possible to succeed where Aristotle had failed. In short, one can undertake to prove, on the strength of the true principles of Aristotle, a conclusion that he himself failed to establish. This has given rise to a curious variety of "Thomism," in which Thomas Aquinas attempts to prove the immortality of the soul without resorting to the principles of his own philosophy, and on the sole strength of the principles of Aristotle, who had not even thought of proving it.

The thing has been done and the result has been what it had to be. On December 19, 1513, the Seventh Session of the Lateran Council met under the presidency of Pope Leo X.[18] During the session, the Pope reiterated the condemnations issued in the fourteenth century against those who taught that the human soul was mortal. He also insisted that, "since the true cannot contradict the true," it ought to be possible to demonstrate the immortality of the soul taught by the Catholic faith. All the theologians attending the Council finally assented to the pontifical constitution, with only two exceptions. One of them was Nicolas Lippomani, Bishop of Bergamo, whose reasons for dissenting are not known to us. The second, according to Mansi, was "Reverend Father Thomas, Minister General of the Order of the Preachers," who "said that he did not approve of the second part of the Bull prescribing that philosophers should persuade their auditors of the truth of the faith."[19]

The name of the Minister General was Thomas de Vio, better known by the name of Cajetan. Needless to say, as a Christian and a theologian, Cajetan never doubted the immortality of the soul. He would not even deny that highly probable arguments could be quoted in favor of this conclusion. But Cajetan could not see how a professor of theology could feel obliged to provide his pupils with philosophical demonstrations of what he himself did not consider demonstrable.

This was a sensible attitude indeed. Only, the point of view of the Pope was that, if a man did not feel able to demonstrate philosophical conclusions which in themselves are demonstrable, he had no business to teach philosophy. As to Thomas Aquinas, he certainly was against pseudo-demonstrations. It is a truly Thomistic attitude to refuse to present as demonstrable a conclusion of faith that cannot be philosophically demonstrated. Thomas himself had refused, *contra murmurantes*, to present as demonstrable the creation of the world in time. It may seem therefore that Cajetan was simply doing what Thomas Aquinas had already done. But the situation was different. Thomas had considered indemonstrable the creation of the world in time, because the answer to the problem ultimately rested with the free decision of an all-powerful God. Now we know with certainty that, such being the case, no demonstration is possible; for since the will of God has no cause, how can anything be demonstrated about it? But the immortality of the soul depends upon the nature of the soul, whose notion is a purely philosophical one. In this case, the disagreement is about a problem whose answer, deeply hidden though it may be, should not be impossible to find, since it is hidden only in nature, not in the free will of God.

It was emphatically not Thomistic to say that there are no philosophical demonstrations of the immortality of the soul. In point of fact, twice in his own writings, and even three times if the Commentary on the *Summa Theologiae* is included, Cajetan himself had offered demonstrations of the immortality of the soul, but he had done so in a curious way. In his own *De Anima*, as well as in his Commentary on the *Summa*, Cajetan seems to have undertaken to prove the immortality of the soul on the strength of two truly Aristotelian propositions: the soul exercises acts in which the body has no part; and, the soul has at least one power (its intellect) whose existence is independent of the body. Now, these propositions permit the conclusion that there are, in man, operations immaterial in nature, but they do not justify the further conclusion that the cause of these operations is an intellectual substance endowed with an act of being of its own and, therefore, able to survive the death of its body. Obviously, on the strength of the principles of Aristotle alone, Cajetan could not prove what Aristotle himself had not been able to demonstrate. It is small wonder that Cajetan failed to convince, be it only himself, that he had found a real demonstration of the soul's immortality.

The facts are known. Years later, in his *Commentary on the Epistles of Saint Paul*, speaking of the mystery of predestination, Cajetan was to write that he could not see how it could be reconciled with free choice. "I do not *know* this," Cajetan says, "just as I do not know the mystery of the Trinity, as I do not know that the soul is immortal, as I do not know that the Word was made flesh, and the like, all things which, nevertheless, I believe." So, at the end of his life, the immortality of the soul, which he had hoped to demonstrate by the principles of Aristotle alone, and without resorting to those of Saint Thomas Aquinas, had become for Cajetan a pure object of faith, exactly like the mystery of the Trinity.

A similar remark is found in the Commentary of Cajetan on *Ecclesiastes* (*3:21*), where it is written: *Who knoweth if the spirit of the children of Adam ascend upward, and if the spirit of the beasts descend downward?* Here, Cajetan observes, the Sacred Writer is only raising a question:

Still, he is telling the truth in disclaiming all scientific knowledge of the immortality of the soul. For no philosopher has ever demonstrated that the soul of man is immortal, nor does there seem to be any demonstration of it; we rather hold it on faith, and as more probable than its contrary from the point of view of reason.[20]

There is no doubt concerning the final position of Cajetan on this point. As other Dominicans then said of him: "Thomas Cajetan has deviated [from Thomas Aquinas] to Harvey of Nedellec and to Scotus."[21] There is much less honorable company and we are not reproaching Cajetan with anything. The only business of a historian is to describe what has happened, as far as possible, just as it did happen. If doctrinal history can serve philosophical truth, it is by setting into relief the consecutions of ideas understood in their purity. In the present case, history teaches that, in the authentic doctrine of Thomas Aquinas, there is a necessary connection between the notion of "the act of being" (*esse*) and the demonstrability of the immortality of the soul.[22] But the notion of the human soul conceived as an intellectual substance is the very core of the Thomistic notion of man. Once more, the philosophical positions proper to Thomas Aquinas and integrated by him with his theology appear to be dominated by the key notion of the *actus essendi*. As will presently be seen, a similar relationship obtains between the Thomistic notion of being and the Thomistic notion of truth.

Chapter 10. Man and knowledge

A man sees a moving colored spot and says: *a dog*. The man and the dog are concrete individual beings, they are even bodies; that is, visible and tangible things whose actual existence can be verified by sense perception and, in case of doubt, can be checked by a comparison of the sense perceptions of several perceiving subjects. But the very word spoken by any one of these observers is also a concrete, particular, and material thing whose existence can be checked by a similar test. As a thing, a word exhibits all the characteristics common to material objects. As the nominalists of the Middle Ages used to say, a word is a *flatus vocis,* a vocal utterance. As such, it is a sound produced by the vibration of the vocal cords as air coming from the lungs is forced through them; such a biological and physical phenomenon can be observed, recorded, and measured.

The meaning of the word, on the contrary, is entirely different from both the speaker and his words. The word is not necessarily tied up with the thing it signifies. What is called "dog" in English is called *canis* in Latin and *chien* in French. In this sense, the meaning of a word is conventional. As is commonly said, words are the sensible signs, or marks, of the ideas a speaker has in mind when using them. Now, this "meaning," or "signification," is not a word, it is not the voice of the speaker, nor is it in any sense of the term a thing. It has no materiality; so much so, that it cannot even be an object of sense perception. For we can hear a spoken word, but we do not "hear" its meaning, we "understand" it. To understand the meaning of a word is to "know." The thus understood meaning of a word is a knowledge. The problems related to the nature of knowledge and to the relations that obtain between it and its objects are fundamental in philosophy. In a sense, since everything is given to us in and through knowledge, such problems are literally fundamental.

This is truly an occasion on which to remember the saying of Aristotle, that wonder is the beginning of philosophy. To wonder is not as easy as it seems to be when we are invited to express surprise at operations we perform quite naturally and which children themselves perform successfully as soon as they can begin to speak. Still, the paradoxical character of language should be clearly realized at the beginning of any philosophical reflection on the nature of human knowledge.

In common philosophical language, the objects of knowledge *considered as known* are called "notions," "concepts," even "ideas." A first remark to be made about them is that, taken *qua* objects of cognition, they are immaterial. As has been said, everything in language is material except its meaning. It has also been noted that, precisely because it is immaterial, the meaning of language introduces philosophical reflection to a non-physical order. This order is the very order of metaphysical reality.

The immaterial nature of knowledge can be established by simple inspection. We can see and hear men uttering the kind of sounds we call words, but the meaning of the words is not an object of sense perception. However, there is a positive proof of the immateriality of knowledge. It is that, as was noted by John Locke, all actually existing material objects are particular, whereas the meaning of most of the words we use in common language is general or, to use the terminology of the logicians, universal. There are in nature no such things as universal trees, animals, or men. A tree is always a particular tree, and so also are animals and men. But such, too, is the case with words. When Locke carelessly, although excusably, speaks of "general words" or of "general terms" he is obviously referring to words or terms whose meaning is some universal notion, not a particular object such as those pointed out by proper names. Names, or terms, are always singular, and they cannot be anything else because they are material noises, or sounds.

John Locke was admirably gifted for the analytical description of the human understanding. In Kant's apt description, Locke wrote its "physiology." Like Kant himself, however, he had a great gift for bracketing mysteries when he met them. In the present case, we find ourselves confronted with a most astounding phenomenon. A living animal, man, surrounded by individual material objects, is spontaneously impelled to utter sounds whose function is to signify notions, or concepts, each of which stands for a plurality of possible individuals. Naturally enough, Locke was duly impressed with the quasi-miraculous nature of the phenomenon; but on second thought he observed that, after all, it was necessary that this should be so, or otherwise the ideas hidden within the breasts of men could not have been made to appear:

The comfort and advantage of society not being to be had without communication of thoughts, it was necessary that mind should find out some external sensible signs, whereby those invisible ideas which his thoughts are made up of might be known to others.

And this certainly was necessary; that is, if it was necessary that there should be men living in society. But the problem is: granting that this is necessary, how is it possible? The great merit of Thomas Aquinas, on this point, was that he inquired into the conditions under which the fundamental fact of human language becomes possible. These conditions can be found nowhere else than in the structure of the knowing subject. There is only one subject able to turn sense perceptions of particular objects into signs of general notions; namely, man. And, once more, this evidence did not escape the attention of John Locke: perception puts the difference between animals and inferior beings, Locke says; to which he adds: "Brutes abstract not," for "the having of general ideas is that which puts a perfect distinction between man and brutes."[1] Nothing could better define the fact which, far from taking for granted, Thomas Aquinas had undertaken to investigate. His own approach to the problem was not, as Locke's was to be, through an essay on human understanding, but rather through an essay on the nature of man.

In studying the human soul, we found Thomas Aquinas caught, so to speak, between theologians who put the substantial unity of man in jeopardy by reducing man to his own soul and, on the other hand, Aristotelians who were putting the immortality of the soul in jeopardy by conceiving it as the form of the human body. His own answer to the challenge was that the soul was both a substance and a form, but, unlike his predecessors, he maintained that the human soul was a spiritual substance that was also a form, and that it was a form because of the very kind of spiritual substance that it was. The human soul does not simply experience a natural inclination toward its body, or a mere desire to animate it; the soul needs to have a body and to animate it, not primarily for the good of the body, but for its own good, because, unless it animated a body, the soul itself could not exist as a spiritual substance. This is the point we now have to understand.

The easiest approach to the problem is by way of the soul's name. "Soul" (*anima*) points out an intellectual substance, but it does not designate a distinct species of being. When theologians describe the origin of the universe, they speak of the creation of heaven and earth, of plants and of animals. Then they speak of the creation of man, but no special day was reserved by Scripture for the creation of the human soul, as something distinct from man. This is what Thomas Aquinas expresses, in his own technical language, in saying that, although it is a substance, the human soul is not a "species." Man (*homo*) is a species. The reason for this is that man is not only a substance, which even the human soul is, but a *complete* substance. The definition of man (the substantial composite of a body and a soul) completely describes any individual belonging in the species "man," save only its individuating accidents; but the definition of "soul" is not that of a completely determined substance. Many souls are not substances; namely, those of plants and of irrational animals. The soul of man is indeed a substance, but for this very reason we call it a "human soul." To be complete, the definition of the human soul includes the definition of man.

In order to clear up this point, let us try to conceive the human body and the human soul apart from man. In the case of the body, it clearly is impossible to do so. The dead body of what once was Caesar is not a man any more. In addressing it, Mark Antony does not say "Caesar"; he says "thou bleeding piece of earth" (*Julius Caesar*, III, i, 55). And, indeed, the corpse of Caesar may well be "the ruins of the noblest man that ever lived in the tide of times," but the ruins of a castle are not a castle, and the ruins of a man are not a man.

The same can be said of the human soul. Assuredly, since it is a substance, it survives the death of its own body, so that from this point of view the case of the soul is very different from that of the body. Still, although it is a substance, the human soul separated from its body is not a complete substance because, in order to be "human," it needs to be united with the body of a man. At the end of the play, when the ghost of Julius Caesar enters his tent, Brutus asks it: "Art thou any thing? Art thou some God, some angel, or some devil?" (*Julius Caesar*, IV, iii, 77.) The one question Brutus does not ask is: "Art thou a soul?" And, indeed, how could there be a soul where there is no body for it to animate? There is no human soul where there is no man.

Such, precisely, is the condition of the intellectual substance we call "soul" in the doctrine of Saint Thomas. The real substance, fully constituted in its own species, is neither the human body nor the human soul; it is *man*. The fullness of human nature requires that it be a substantial composite of a body and a soul, along with all the powers that are its instruments inasmuch as it is a knowing and acting substance. Now the same cannot be said of the soul. Unless it has or has had a body, a soul can neither know nor will. Even while it is surviving its body, which it does because it is a substance, the soul still does not constitute an individual belonging in what one might call the species "soul." As has been said, there is no such species. Thomas expresses this fact by saying that the human soul, while separated from its body, is in the condition of an "incomplete substance." It is complete *qua* substance, being composed of its essence and its act of being; but it is incomplete from the point of view of the definition of its species, because, without its body, it cannot perform the operations of a being that belongs in the species "man."

It is therefore impossible to define man as a certain species, or variety, of soul. The commonly received definition of man, as a "rational animal," correctly describes his nature. As an animal, man has an organic body; as rational, he shares in the nature of intellectual substances. Because of his body, man is specifically distinct from the separate and angelic substances; because of his reasoning power, man is specifically distinct from the brutes. Neither an angel nor a brute, man is to be found, on the universal scale of beings, somewhere between mere animals and angels. Now, what distinguishes brutes from plants is that they are capable of sense perception, and what distinguishes angels from men is that they are pure intelligences, able to know without resorting to sense perception. Man then must be endowed with a knowing power superior to sense and inferior to intellect. This mode of knowledge proper to man is "reason." Hence the common definition of man as a "rational animal."[2]

This conclusion was established by Thomas Aquinas in simple terms, but with unsurpassable clarity, in the passage of the *Summa Theologiae* in which, having concluded that the human soul is not man, but the form of man, he asks the question: Is man an angel? And his answer is: No, man is not an angel because, of its nature, the human soul is apt to be united with a body. Nor does this aptitude consist in a mere possibility. By its very essence, the human soul is unable to know without the collaboration of the body to which it is united. The soul, Thomas says, "in a certain way requires a body for its operation."[3] And indeed, unless it had sense organs and sense perceptions from which to abstract concepts, the human soul could not form any actual cognition. This explains what otherwise would sound as a violently paradoxical assertion; namely, that in man, the intellectual principle is united to the body as its form. It has to be united to the body as its form precisely because, were it not so, the soul could not exercise its intellectual operations.

In order to understand Thomas Aquinas on this point, one must observe that, when he says that the "intellective principle" is the form of the body, our theologian means that the human "soul," which is the principle of its own intellectual operations, is united to the body as its form. Why does Thomas go as far as saying that the "intellect" itself is the form of the body? Because, generally speaking, that by which a form primarily acts (its operative power) is the form of the thing to which the operation is attributed.[4] In the present case, the primary operative power of man is that in virtue of which he is called a "rational animal," and since reasoning is a certain discursive use of the intellective power, this intellective and reasoning power can be called the very form of man. To say "the human soul," "the intellective soul," or "the intellective principle" in man is, therefore, to say the same thing.

Over and above this direct argument, there is an indirect one. If one denies that the intellective principle can be the form of a body, he will have to explain why the knowledge acquired by the *intellect* of a man can rightly be said to belong to that man. If the intellect whereby I know is not the form of my body, how can the knowledge acquired by that form be said to be mine? The only correct answer to the question is that my intellectual knowledge requires, as its antecedent condition, my own sense perception of material being, from which, by way of abstraction, my intellect extracts the content of its concepts. In Thomas' own words:

> It is one and the same man who is conscious both that he understands and that he senses. But one cannot sense without a body, and therefore the body must be some part of the man. It follows, therefore, that the intellect by which Socrates understands is a part of Socrates, so that it is in some way united to the body of Socrates.

Thus, the intellective substance we call the human soul is, by its very essence, the form of a body.[5] Were it not so, the intellective power could not form any intellectual cognition, nor could man form any intellectual knowledge truly his own.

This conclusion invites us once more to turn our attention to the fundamental truth that the unity of each and every finite being ultimately rests with its own *esse*, its own act of being. Critics often wonder how an intellectual substance, such as the human soul, can at one and the same time exercise operations in which the body does not participate (*i.e.*, intellectual abstraction) and, nevertheless, constitute with the body a substantial unity. This is to forget that there can be only one single substance in which there is only one single act of being. Man is not composed of several *substances,* such as his soul, his body, and his intellectual power. The whole substantiality of man comes to him from his soul, which itself is related to its own act of being as potency to act. Let us recall the key truth upon which the whole anthropology of Thomas Aquinas rests:

> *The soul communicates that being* (esse) *in which it subsists to the corporeal matter out of which, and the intellectual soul, there results one being, so that* the being of the whole composite is also the being of the soul. *This is not the case with other non-subsistent forms. For this reason the human soul retains its own being after the dissolution of the body; whereas it is not so with other forms.*[6]

At the same time that it makes his personality possible, the oneness of his existential act ensures man's substantial unity and enables him really to possess his intellectual cognitions. Lastly, this point enables us to understand more fully the already-noted fact that the proper definition of man is not an *intellectual* animal but, rather, a *rational* animal. And, indeed, the only conceivable reason that some spiritual substances, such as souls, are form of bodies is that they need bodies in order to achieve their intelligible perfection. Were it not so, souls would be united to bodies to no purpose.[7] Now, an intellectual substance that begs its knowledge from material objects is not a separate intellect, as are angels; it has no direct intuition of intelligible truth; the only intelligible objects our intellect is able to apprehend are those that it has first to form by abstracting them from sense perceptions and to which it further applies itself under the discursive form of the intellective power: *reason.*

From these considerations, the nature, the operations, and the objects of human knowledge follow with necessity, and they are found to be, at the end of the deduction, exactly such as they are in reality.

In a first moment, the intellect (in its capacity as agent intellect) abstracts from sense knowledge the intelligible form which (in its capacity as possible intellect) it receives in itself and apprehends. It thus acquires an abstractive cognition. Were we angels, instead of men, we would intuitively apprehend intelligible essences by means of innate intelligible species, without having to animate a body, to receive sensations, and to abstract from them general concepts. Moreover, were we angels, we would not need to infer consequences from principles by a discursive process of reasoning; the whole series of its consequences would be intuitively seen and known as included within the principle, a little in the same way as, when we ourselves have finally mastered a certain body of knowledge, we seem to grasp it, as it were, with a single glance, in its entirety. But because we are men, we must resort to discourse. From our abstract concepts we cannot deduce consequences without associating and dissociating them by mode of judgments, then without constructing the chains of judgments we call reasoning, then concluding and finally returning by analysis to the notions from which reasoning took its start. The intellect first forms the principles as soon as it is in contact with material objects given in sense experience. The same intellect, functioning as reason, goes from principles to consequences, always in the light of the principles. In doing so, it performs the intellectual function specifically proper to man. In short, reason is the name of intellect inasmuch as it is a properly human intellect, united to a body and borrowing from sense knowledge the very substance of its cognitions.[8]

This ontological status of the human soul determines the nature of its proper objects of cognition. Animal souls, which are forms immersed in matter, feed on the sensible species such as they are received by their sense powers. At the other extremity of the hierarchy of knowing creatures, angels, or separate intelligences, know by intelligible species that they receive directly from God along with their own intellectual nature. In this again man is to be found betwixt and between. Being the form of a body, the human intellect feeds on concepts that it abstracts from bodies and from which, in turn, it deduces consequences by mode of reasoning. The proper object of the human intellect is neither the data of sense perception nor some pure intelligible apprehended by intuition; it is the intelligible essence whose concept it abstracts from the data of sense experience. The *essences* of things, as definable by their *quiddities*, are the objects that our human intellect is eminently fit to know.

This notion of "proper object" is very important. By "the proper object of a power" Thomas understands the object under whose notion the power in question grasps everything else. For instance, we say that sight perceives things, shapes, sizes, distances, and countless other sorts of objects. And this is true, but it remains that sight perceives only colors. The colored spots perceived by the human eye are interpreted by man as representing trees, dogs, or men, but this interpretation is the result of a more or less long experience in which all the sense powers and the reasoning power of man co-operate. Sight itself sees nothing else than colors; the colored (*coloratum*) is the proper object of sight, which perceives other objects only inasmuch as, being colored, they share in the nature of its proper object.[9]

The same notion applies to the human intellect. The object proportioned to it is the nature of the sensible thing; that is, what has just been called its essence, or quiddity, as expressed by its definition. This fact entails a consequence that affects the practical use of man's cognitive powers in all domains. This consequence can be formulated as follows: intellectual knowledge naturally tends to assume the form of an apprehension of abstract essences, or "quiddities," tied together by the discursive operation of reasoning. In saying that the proper object of the intellect is that which the thing is (*proprium objectum intellectus est quod quid est*) Thomas has provided a simple and exhaustive explanation for the tendency, so obvious in the human mind, to turn all its objects into abstract essences. Since these essences themselves are reducible to their definitions, and therefore to mere quiddities, the complex structure of reality finds itself represented by a pattern of abstract notions. To conceive such notions, to define them, to combine them or to separate them by his judgments, such seems to be the habitual and normal form of the intellectual activity of man.[10]

The fact is clearly visible in the history of metaphysics, particularly in that of Scholasticism, not at all because of its philosophical content, but rather because it was first conceived as a doctrine to be taught in schools by masters trying to make it intelligible to students. Nothing is more fit to be taught than a set of abstract notions, all of them accurately defined and woven together by the rules of syllogistic reasoning. Essentially it consists of definitions and demonstrations, as if the ideal approach to metaphysical problems were through a sort of mathematics of concepts. This is how it should be, and anyone with some experience of teaching realizes that to teach without resorting to this kind of abstract simplification is, if not impossible in itself, at least extremely difficult in practical reality.

Reduced to its essentials, this method coincides with what is often called the "method of exposition" as distinct from, and sometimes contrary to, the "method of discovery" or of invention. And, indeed, after completing all the intellectual operations required for the solution of a problem, we feel the need to present a discussion of it under a clearer and more ordered form, free of the many hesitations, corrections, and unnecessary complications usually attending the first attempts to solve problems. But the chief difference lies in this, that we usually solve problems by proceeding upward from the data of sense experience until we reach the general notions, or principles, in whose light those data can be understood; on the other hand, following the method of exposition, we go down from the principles to the concrete data we want to understand. The traditional methods of teaching cannot be changed. Besides, they are well adapted to the end pursued by schools and universities, which is to transmit to students the general results of scientific and philosophical research. The point to be kept in mind while teaching is that to inform students of the already acquired results of other thinkers is not to show them how to acquire new ones. More important still, the teacher should always strive to convey to his students the wholesome feeling that his well-ordered presentation of abstract concepts, although it represents the perfect product of human reason at its best, leaves out many characteristics of concrete reality. Thomas Aquinas was well aware of the fact. He both thought and said that the proper object of the human intellect is the essence, nature, or quiddity of sensible things, but he never said that in sensible things there was nothing deeper than essences or quiddities. On the contrary, Thomas Aquinas repeatedly warned against the illusion that essence is the deepest layer in the metaphysical structure of even material being. Moreover, Thomas forcibly stressed the fact that the essences we conceive apart in our minds do not necessarily exist apart in reality. We naturally conceive things by mode of abstraction, but reality is not made up of abstract notions ordered according to some pattern as if they were so many fragments of a mental mosaic. The abstract apprehension and co-ordination of essences is an absolutely necessary moment in the intellectual activity of man, but it is not the supreme achievement of the human intellect; for the ultimate end of the intellect is to conceive reality such as it is, and reality simply is not a mosaic of essences.

It would be a fruitful subject of reflection to consider the dreadful consequences of what might be called "the spirit of abstraction." In speculative matters, it invites the substitution of the definition for the defined, which is a sure way to render definitions sterile. It also invites the illusion that one can increase knowledge by merely deducing consequences from already coined definitions, instead of frequently returning to the very things from which essences and definitions were first abstracted. In the practical order, the spirit of abstraction probably is the greatest single source of political and social disorders, of intolerance and of fanaticism. Nothing is more uncompromising than an essence, its quiddity and its definition.

The reason for this fact lies in a characteristic common to all abstract notions and remarkably described by Thomas Aquinas in the second chapter of his commentary on the *De Hebdomadibus* of Boethius; namely, that the characteristics of the abstract are exactly opposed to those of the concrete.[11] Now reality is concrete, and this is the reason that abstract descriptions of it are liable to deform it.

Abstractions are mutually exclusive, because "to abstract" is "to set apart." The definition of an abstract notion expresses its very essence such as it is in itself. This is to say that the definition of an abstract notion posits it as "other than" any other notion. In the words of Thomas Aquinas, of anything whatever considered abstractly, it is true to say that it contains nothing foreign to its essence: *non habet in se aliquid extraneum, quod scilicet sit praeter essentiam suam.* If I say "humanity" I mean just that, and I do not mean "whiteness," because humanity is solely that whereby some being is a man, just as in saying "whiteness" I point out only that whereby something is white. Now a thing formally is a man by that which belongs to the notion of humanity, just as a thing formally is white in virtue of that which belongs to the notion of whiteness. In other words, a man is not man *qua* white, nor is a man white *qua* man.

Now the very reverse is true in concrete reality. Humanity cannot be whiteness, but a man can be white. Precisely, a man is that which has humanity, and there is nothing to prevent that which has humanity from also having whiteness. Generally speaking, there is nothing to prevent any concrete being from having anything that is not contradictory to its essence. A man can have many other things besides whiteness, or blackness, and humanity. To substitute abstract definitions for realities, and then to attempt to reduce concrete realities to their abstract definitions, is one of the surest ways to initiate revolutions. Revolutionists are often abstractionists; fanatics usually are dominated by one single notion, and this notion usually is an abstract one. Let it suffice to mention these extensions of the problem and to say that human knowledge should not be reduced to the knowledge of its proper object, or otherwise we shall never grasp what is the core of truth because it is the core of reality.

What is it to know truth? It is intellectually to grasp the essences of things such as they are and to associate them in our own minds, by means of judgments, in the same way they are associated in reality. If a man is white, if I perceive him as a man that is white, and if I say, "This is a white man," there is adequation between reality and the content of my judgment. I then say that my judgment is true when it expresses being such as being actually is. Now, in analyzing the notion of being, we stressed the fact that, in any being (any *habens esse*), that which has the act of being (*esse*) is the essence. It has also been said that the essence, or quiddity, is that which makes a substance to be a thing (*res*); it is not what makes a thing to be a "being"; rather, what makes a thing to be a being is its *esse*, or act of being. The classical definition of truth as the adequation of intellect and thing (*adequatio intellectus et rei*) is correct as far as it goes, but it does not go the whole way, and it stands in need of being completed in the light of the Thomistic notion of being. The definition is correct to the extent that the object of intellectual knowledge is supposed to be the thing (*res*). In this case, there is adequation between the intellect and the *essence* of the thing, but if truth is supposed to consist in a perfect correspondence between the knowing intellect and a known *being*, then it no longer suffices for knowledge to reach the essence. The act of being itself has to be reached, in and through essence, because this act is what makes the essence itself to be a being.

Thomas Aquinas expressed this truth in no uncertain terms as early as his Commentary on the *Sentences* of Peter Lombard:

Since a thing includes both its quiddity and its act of being (esse), *truth is grounded in the* esse *of a thing more than in the quiddity itself* (veritas fundatur in esse rei magis quam in ipsa quidditate). *For the noun "being"* (ens) *is derived from* esse (to be), *so that the adequation in which truth consists is achieved by a sort of assimilation of the intellect to the being* (esse) *of the thing, through the very operation whereby it apprehends it such as it is.*[12]

In the mind of Thomas Aquinas, this conclusion joins another one, much better known, yet too often forgotten in its practical implications. In this same work Thomas has distinguished between two fundamental operations of the human intellect. A first one, which Aristotle used to call the simple intellection of concepts (*intelligentia indivisibilium*), consists in the simple apprehension of essences. The definition or quiddity of an essence can be composed of several terms, but this plurality of terms is apprehended as a unit by an indivisible act of intellection. The quiddity of man ("rational-animal"), includes two terms grasped by a simple act of apprehension. The second class of intellectual operations is called by Thomas Aquinas "composition and division"; to-day we call it judgment. It consists in affirming that certain concepts can correctly be predicated of certain other concepts. The judgment, *all men are mortal*, is a composite of two concepts, animal and mortal. On the contrary, in the judgment, *no animal is immortal*, the judging intellect dissociates the two concepts "animal" and "immortal." Now, according to Thomas Aquinas, these two operations attain reality such as it is in itself, but not with equal depth. The first operation, which is the simple apprehension of the quiddity, attains the thing in its essence; it grasps the that-which-is. The second operation, which is the composition or division of concepts—that is, the judgment—attains the thing in its very act of being: *prima operatio respicit quidditatem rei, secunda respicit esse ipsius.*[13]

This conclusion, so firmly asserted by Thomas Aquinas, has often been either overlooked or intentionally rejected by many among his successors. And no wonder, since it is tied up with the Thomistic notion of the composition of essence and the act of being in created substances. In doctrines in which reality is identified with essences, and being with reality (*ens* with *res*), the object of true knowledge, even taken under its perfect form, which is that of scientific knowledge, is nothing deeper than essential being. To compose and to separate essences in the mind in the same way as they are composed or separated in reality then becomes the ultimate goal of true knowledge. Just as the concrete combination of essences is the very stuff of which reality itself is made, so also our knowledge of reality (and philosophy itself) assumes the form of a combination of quidditative concepts.

The philosophy of Saint Thomas is animated by a different spirit. In it, man is an existent among other existents. An existent is something that has an *esse*—that is, an act of being of its own—and since the essences or quiddities of sensible objects are the proper objects of human understanding, the second operation of the intellect cannot attain being without, by the same token, attaining the act that lies in it beyond essence. The human intellect thus reaches, even in its most natural operations, a layer of being more deeply seated than essences. Let us not forget the ontological standing of a universe composed of creatures; that is, of beings that bear the mark of the pure *Ipsum Esse*. In such a world, every being has in itself its own act of being, distinct from all the others: *habet enim unaquaeque res in seipsa esse proprium ab omnibus aliis distinctum.*[14] There is no such *esse* without an essence, or quiddity, whose act it is, but *esse* itself is not a quiddity. We apprehend it only as given in essences to which, as to its proper receivers, it imparts actual existence. It is therefore correct to say that, in every true judgment, the truth it affirms ultimately rests, beyond the essence, upon actual being.

This aspect of Thomism assigns to it a distinct place among all the other philosophies, Christian or otherwise. It is emphatically not an abstract philosophy of possible being. God IS, creatures *are*, or otherwise they would not be beings; human knowledge cannot have for its ultimate object anything else than beings properly so called. Assuredly, there is a place for possible being in the philosophy of Thomas Aquinas. This place is as large in Thomism as it is in the philosophies of essence, but it is not the first place. In Thomism, possible being comes second, as potency comes after act. In short, the proper object of the human understanding, in the philosophy of Thomas Aquinas, is the same as that of the sciences of nature, astronomy, physics, chemistry, and biology. In epistemology, the knowing powers of man have to be conceived so as to account for the possibility of such knowledge. In metaphysics, the science of being *qua* being must be understood as the science of that-which-has-an-act-of-being.

The impact of this doctrine on our knowledge of God is at least as important. The whole negative theology of Thomas Aquinas is tied up with his notion of *esse* conceived as the act of being. It is often said that the proper name of God is "Being" (*ens*) and, of course, this is a perfectly acceptable statement. Still, it is not wholly accurate, because God is not a *habens esse*. God is *esse*, in the simplicity of its pure actuality. God Himself has said that His proper name is HE IS, or I AM, and this was the very best that could be said to such a being as man, who knows of no other objects than composites of an essence and an act of being. As compared with God, however, even *Qui est* retains a trace of composition between two terms which is foreign to the simplicity of the divine being. There is no *Qui* in God; only an *est*, and of this *est* itself, which our judgment rightly posits as actual, we have no quidditative concept. Where essence is a pure act of being, it transcends itself and ceases to be conceivable as any definable essence. Hence the consequences, well known to the students of Thomas Aquinas but frightening to many less hardy theologians, that follow concerning the imperfection of our knowledge of God.

We have already noted this point, but it is essential to a proper comprehension of Thomism to observe the constant recurrence of some of his main positions at the end of apparently unrelated developments.

In the present case, to submit the same conclusion to a renewed examination is all the more useful as, of its nature, it is bound to meet with stubborn resistance in many minds. Man is prompted by an intense desire to know God, and, in fact, man does know something of God, something that God really and truly is; hence, in man, a natural tendency to think that he knows God much better than he actually does. In the light of the preceding conclusions, however, we should not require any lengthy reflection to realize how imperfect our knowledge of God necessarily is. An infinite being cannot be "comprehended" by a finite being. A being situated at the summit of immateriality (as being pure act) cannot be properly conceived by an intellect whose knowledge begins with sense and cannot wholly abstract from imagination. We cannot think of God without vaguely imagining Him. How could we trust any such "representation" of an entirely unrepresentable being?

These remarks apply even to the meaning of the verb *est*, or *is*. For we cannot conceive the meaning of "to be" otherwise than as pointing out that which "to be" is in the case of the only beings given in experience. These are all material beings perceptible by the sense and representable by the imagination. We know with certainty that there are immaterial beings—angels, for instance—but we cannot conceive what kind of beings they are, and one does not feel too encouraged by the efforts of the painters in that direction. How much more impossible is it for us to conceive what it is for God to be!

It is no wonder that so many find it hard, and almost dangerous, to follow Thomas Aquinas up to the ultimate conclusions of his negative theology. He himself was fully aware of the difficulty. Being a man, as we are, Thomas had experienced for himself the frustrated feeling of one who finds himself invited to refuse to conceive the very object of his intellection. This thoroughly unnatural effort nevertheless is the highest one that is required of us on our journey from creatures to God. The name WHO IS points out an object absolute, separate from the rest by the very purity of its actuality, and not determinable by any further qualification. Hence, in proceeding toward God by way of negation, we successively deny of Him all the properties, corporeal or incorporeal, that are found in creatures; for, even though God really is the highest among such properties as goodness, science, wisdom, and the like, we do not know what they are in God. Only one notion, then, remains in our intellect; namely, that God *is*, and nothing more. But it is for us all but impossible to think of a being *that it is*, being completely ignorant of *what* it is. Having reached this point, therefore, our mind finds itself in a state of confusion. Still, this is not the end of the pilgrimage. This "is" that we rightly affirm of God, we cannot attribute to Him as it is in creatures. But the way in which "is" is proper to creatures is the only one we perceive, imagine, and conceive such as it is in itself. In short, the being of creatures is the only one we truly know. The last thing to do, then, is to deny of God the only mode of actual existence we can properly conceive, so that, in fine, our intellect finds itself (so to speak) in the darkness of ignorance: *et tunc remanet in quadam tenebra ignorantiae*. Still, in the condition of this present life, Dionysius says that this ignorance is what unites us in the best possible way, for this is the sort of obscurity wherein God is dwelling.[15]

There is a continuity of order from the elementary judgment of existence formulated in matters of practical life and the highest of judgments formed by the contemplative affirming in darkness the existence of HE WHO IS. All our other judgments then become concerned with actual existence for the very reason that they are all concerned with beings, each of which imitates its Prime Cause for the simple reason that it is. When, at the term of his meditations, Thomas finds himself in utter darkness, the act of being is the last light he has lost from view before entering the blackness of his learned ignorance; it is also the first light he will see again on returning to the world of beings and of things in which we now live. In this doctrine, God is the first, the last, and the most infinitely eminent of all the cases in which the truth of the judgment is founded more ultimately on the act of being of an object than on its essence, because, in this unique case, the essence of the object is the very Act of Being.

It is hardly possible to talk about human knowledge in our own day without bringing to mind many problems not even mentioned by Thomas Aquinas. In consequence, his noetic may well look out of date. It is a little as though we described the astronomical system of Ptolemy without mentioning the fact that since the time of his death discoveries have been made in that field by Copernicus, Newton, and Einstein.

There is something true in these remarks. To know what has been said in philosophy, especially in noetics, since the time of Thomas Aquinas, is for us an absolute necessity. To mention only one development that Thomas Aquinas could not possibly have foreseen, or at least that he did not foresee, the extension of the mathematical method to practically the whole field of physics and of biology constitutes a new fact that has to be taken into account by any modern philosopher. In the time of Thomas Aquinas, science was dominated by the category of quality; today it is dominated by the category of quantity. In the thirteenth century, almost everyone believed that to know was to classify; today, almost everyone feels convinced that to know is to measure. There is no question of renouncing a methodology that has made possible the rise of modern science, along with the countless technical applications that are so many confirmations of its truth.

In the field of philosophy properly so called, the problem is entirely different. The main event that has taken place in it since the end of the Middle Ages is not symbolized by the name of Descartes, but by that of Kant. Descartes and Kant have this in common: that, in our own day, all agree that their doctrines are epoch-making events in the history of modern thought, though few agree with them. The gist of Cartesianism was that nothing should be accepted as true that was not susceptible of evidence at least equal to that of mathematical conclusions; how many philosophers could one find today, among those who praise Descartes, who would consider mathematically valid his proofs of the existence of a thinking substance, of an infinitely powerful God, and even of a universe of extended matter wholly innocent of all qualitative elements? Similarly, the gist of Kant's critical idealism was that experience is, before anything else, a construction of reality by an understanding endowed with categories of its own; in it, the element of necessity proper to scientific knowledge does not come from the world, but from the mind. How many professors of philosophy could we find today who would accept as valid the table of categories set up by Kant? How many would simply affirm that there are such things as his pure *a priori* forms of the human understanding?

This situation deserves careful consideration. It means that Descartes and Kant are now being praised for contributions to philosophy whose real value lies beyond that of their own philosophical systems. The gist of these contributions is one and the same. It can be called "idealism." Now idealism itself is not any particular system of philosophy, but rather an attitude of mind that can express itself in many different ways. In itself, it can be described as the tendency to reduce, if not reality, at least human knowledge, to the elements contributed to it by the human mind.

From this point of view, idealism is, for philosophy, an always open possibility, and the constant presence of this possibility is what is now symbolized by the name of Kant, quite irrespective of the clockwork to which he reduced human knowledge in his *Critique of Pure Reason*.

This has been clearly expressed by Karl Jaspers at the beginning of his lectures on *Vernunft und Existenz (Reason and Reality)*. To begin with, Jaspers says, we think of ourselves as of beings included within a certain whole constituted by the external objects that surround us. To us, that which thus exists around us is what we call external reality. But we know that what thus surrounds us is itself surrounded by something else, which, in turn, is included within another beyond, and so on indefinitely, until, in order to stop somewhere, our reason posits a sort of all-inclusiveness, beyond which there is nothing. Philosophers give it different names: for instance, God, if they are interested in theology; or Being, if they do not want to overstep the strict boundaries of ontology. In this sense, we see ourselves as included within an objectively given reality of which we are only a part. Realism is such a view of the world: we ourselves are included *in* reality, and to know reality as it is, is the proper task of the human understanding.

But, Jaspers presently adds, there is another possible attitude, and not only possible but even unavoidable since Kant. All this objectively given being that includes me can also be considered as included in myself. It is included in the very understanding that knows it and posits it as an objectively given reality. From this second point of view, everything that is, is in me and by me. I now am appearing to myself as the all-inclusiveness in which and by which everything is. In other words, *I* am being (*Ich sein*); *I* am consciousness (*Bewusstsein*); *I* am the Spirit (*der Geist*). What is called Idealism is any such view of the world: reality is included in us, and the proper task of philosophy is to investigate human nature itself as the very *locus* of being.[16]

If we consider it in the light of the principles of Thomism, what should our own choice be? Thomism is a philosophy of being. Being itself is no genus; it transcends all genera. It is therefore certain, *a priori* so to speak, that we cannot find ourselves confronted with this alternative in the doctrine of Thomas Aquinas. We cannot have to choose between being and knowing; that is to say, between a world of things in which the knowing subject itself is included as one more particular thing, and a world of knowledge in which everything, including the knowing subject itself, is included as an object of cognition. Manifestly, in the doctrine of Thomas Aquinas, knowing itself must be conceived as a particular form, or case, of being.

This is so important to understand that, having to focus our attention on a small number of chosen points, we should feel justified in trying to realize the full meaning of at least this one. What is here at stake is nothing less than the sense in which the epithet "realism" can be correctly applied to the noetic of Thomas Aquinas.

In teaching philosophy, it is customary to present realism as an out-of-date position eliminated by modern idealism. Things are not that simple in philosophy. In metaphysics, at least, the latest piece of news is not necessarily the truest one. In the noetic of Thomas Aquinas, all rests upon the elementary experience that things can exist in two different ways: first, in themselves; second, in ourselves and for ourselves—that is, inasmuch as we are aware of their existence and cognizant of their natures. This is not something to be demonstrated; it is an irreducible fact that plays in the philosophy of Thomas Aquinas the part of a principle. And its recognition commands his whole doctrine of knowledge, which can be summed up in these few words: every cognition of an object other than ourselves is a real relationship between our own being and another being.[17] Far from imagining a world of things in themselves on the one side and a world of knowledge on the other side, Thomas Aquinas considers these two orders as always given, together and inseparably, within one single experience. For the thing known, to be known is to be in the knowing subject instead of only being in itself. For the knowing being, to know is to be another thing instead of merely being itself. There is no way to justify this primitive fact, not even by saying that knowing subjects have souls, or intellects. To limit ourselves to the case of man, we know that man has an intellect because he is able to know other beings, and not inversely; and we know that what we call man's intellect is immaterial because, in knowing another being, the intellect does not become this other being materially (in perceiving a tree, I do not become a tree); on the contrary, to know another being is to become it immaterially.

There is therefore a world for knowledge, but it is part and parcel of the universe of being. To know is to be after the manner of a knowing being; to be known is to be after the manner of a known being. Thus understood, knowledge is a class of natural happenings that take place in beings and between beings. To the question: "Why are there such beings as are able to know?" the answer is that, unless we consider the problem from the point of view of the final cause of creation in general, and of the creation of man in particular, we need not even ask the question. From the point of view of the possibility and nature of knowledge, we need to know only that, in fact, there are such beings as are able to become others by mode of cognition. And in saying "beings" I am not saying "minds," "spirits," "intellects," or "understandings"; I am saying "men," including both mind and body: men communicating with other bodies through their own bodies and becoming these other bodies, in an immaterial way, through their own powers of sense and of understanding.

This is to say that human knowledge is an animal function, or at least a biological one. Man lives, man moves, man acts, man knows, and for him to know is to exercise the highest function that a living being can possibly fulfill; but it belongs in the same general class as the other ones. If the knowing function is performed, under normal conditions, by a normally constituted knowing subject, then the cognition is true, just as a heart is sound if, being normally constituted, it functions under normal conditions. Error is just a pathological case of a natural function. Normal knowledge may well not be complete knowledge; indeed, it is never going to be complete knowledge; but normal knowledge is true from the very fact that it is knowledge. Truth is a straight case of normalcy in the mode of being that we call cognition.

It is certainly possible to think differently. Given any whole, it is always possible to decide that this whole can be reduced to one of its parts. Our present point is simply that the noetic of Thomas Aquinas insists, before anything else, on preserving the integrity of the whole, something that cannot be done in any philosophy that does not posit as its first principle the all-embracing notion of being. Starting from being, one can have knowledge; on the contrary, if one decides to start from the act of cognition of the knowing subject considered as an absolute point of departure, one will never get out of it. One will never succeed in attaining being.[18]

To conclude, let us look back at the whole field of inquiry that has been covered so far, and let us try to see it in the light of our initial conclusions. What we now are saying is that, in any kind of cognition, that which is intelligible necessarily precedes the intellection which our understanding has of it. This is what we were intimating in saying that knowledge is given in being, and *is* being. At the beginning of all the rest, as its origin and cause, there is a pure Act of Being, which we call God. Now, without doubt, God is supremely intelligible in Himself; being perfect, and being supremely immaterial, He is the summit of both intellection and intelligibility. God, Thomas Aquinas says, knows not only Himself but also all that which He has caused to be, is causing to be, will cause to be, or can cause to be if it pleased Him to do so. Yet, even in God, knowledge is not the deepest level of reality. The knowledge that God has of everything is ultimately His own self-knowledge.

Moreover, His own self-knowledge is identically His own Self, which itself is the pure Act of Being. Hence, even the divine ideas do not come first in reality. God Himself is not said to be because He knows; nor, for that matter, can He be said to know *because* He is; in God, to know is to be. In this sense, the realism of Aristotle has found its ultimate justification in the theology of Saint Thomas Aquinas. Aristotle had identified with Thought the innermost actuality of the Prime Being; in the doctrine of Thomas Aquinas, Thought itself is identified with Being.

Chapter 11. Man and will

There is a created universe, and man himself exists, because being is act and, by the same token, able to act. Hence, being supremely act, God is supremely apt to cause other acts of being. But these acts of being are likewise able to act and to produce other beings. Their efficiency is rooted in their own act of being (*esse*), but the manner of exercising this efficiency proper to every being is submitted to a certain rule, which is its very nature; that is to say, its form. The kind of operation performed by a certain being is determined by the kind of a being it is. Such is the meaning of the classic formula *operatio sequitur esse:* the operation of a being flows from its act of being, and then the nature of the operation performed is determined by the nature of the being that performs it.

Since it is proper to a cause to communicate itself under the form of an effect, all effects resemble their causes, not necessarily in that they reproduce their external features (although this is often the case), but at least in that something of the being of the cause has been transmitted to its effect. This entails two consequences. The first one is easy to understand. It is that being and its operational activities are two different moments of one and the same actuality. Speaking of life (*vivere*), which, in living beings, is their *esse*, Thomas Aquinas says that it is the "act of their soul, not their second act, which is operation, but their prime act": *non actus secundus, qui est operatio, sed actus primus.* Operation is therefore an act derived, through essence, from the first and fundamental one, which is to be.[1] The second consequence is that the operations of beings are, so to speak, directed to an end. This point deserves careful consideration.

All our previous reflections about causality have been dominated by the notions of the material cause, the formal cause, and, above all, the efficient cause. In saying that the operations of beings are directed to certain ends, we are introducing the notion of final cause, or of purposiveness. Far from being secondary in importance, the final cause has often been described by Thomas Aquinas as the first and foremost of all causes. And, indeed, it is in view of achieving a certain end that an efficient cause educes from matter the form of the thing or of the being to be produced. On the other hand, since for a being to act or to operate is to communicate something of itself to its effect, the end pursued by a being in its operations is largely determined by its nature and form. In this sense, the final cause is predetermined by the formal cause of the operating being. The end of understanding in its operation is to understand; the end of fire is to burn, and the same can be said of any kind of efficient cause. Causality is always about itself, either to communicate its own form, or else to find in something else what it needs in order to complete its own being.

The universe of Thomas Aquinas owes this characteristic to the notion of being conceived as act. Aristotle had already conceived the world as made up of active substances, each one of them giving or receiving some form of actuality, such as material qualities, motion under all its forms, and, finally, substantial being at the term of every process of generation. On this fundamental point, Thomism has truly fallen heir to the authentic Aristotelianism of Aristotle. This is even one of the chief reasons for Thomas' obstinate resistance to the more or less Platonized versions of the doctrine of the Philosopher in which the substances of this sublunary world are being acted upon by separate Intelligences rather than themselves acting and operating in their own right. But Thomas Aquinas has even protected the deepest inspiration of Aristotelianism against its own tendency to relapse into some sort of Platonism. The universal dynamism of substances taught by Aristotle became a universal dynamism of being (*habentia esse*) in the metaphysics of Thomas Aquinas. This innovation was inseparable from its Christian inspiration. Once more, itself a purely religious doctrine, Christianity changed the course of philosophical evolution.

The character proper to the Thomistic notion of the material world, including the intellectual substances (namely, human souls) that are substantially united to bodies is that, in it, the act of being of each substance is, by the same token, an act of "tending to": *esse est tendere*. Now, that to which a being is tending is, to that extent, its end. "Tendency," "inclination," "bent" are co-essential to Thomistic being. In other words, Thomas understood beings as always "bent upon" the pursuit of some end. To begin with, all beings are striving to preserve their own existence; they aim to be, and they instinctively shun all that which puts their being in jeopardy. For the same reason, they naturally tend toward all that which is susceptible of preserving, enlarging, and perfecting their being. Bodies move in order to obtain food and to continue to be; intellects likewise move, in their own way, in order to know and thus to be in a more perfect manner than they are. In short, to be, to operate, and to tend to certain ends are for every being one and the same thing.

These ends are not left to chance. There is a reason why a being tends to some of them rather than to others. This reason is a fact, an irreducible fact to be accepted as such; namely, the reciprocal complementarity of certain finite beings. Precisely because they are finite, all created beings are susceptible of receiving complementary additions. What they can become, and are not, they can find in, or receive from, only other beings that are in act what they themselves are only in potency. In simpler terms, every being is always seeking what it lacks and looking for it where it can be found. This relationship can be expressed in more or less technical terms, but common experience teaches us what it is. One may call it a relationship of potency to act: a being susceptible of being perfected by another one is in potency to it. No being is in potency to what it does not have the nature to receive or to acquire; nor is it in potency with respect to beings that are not acts in the very order in which it is itself in potency. Let us remember that, in concrete reality, there is no such thing as pure potency. Since act is being, pure potency would be non-being; hence, the relation of potency to act is always that of incomplete actuality to more complete actuality in the same line of being. The same relationship can be described in plain words as that which obtains between any being that is lacking anything and any other being from which what it lacks can be obtained. In the language of Thomas Aquinas, this same relationship is often called a *convenientia*, which means the aptitude of a being to actuate the potentiality of another one. There are between beings, one might say, relations of "fittingness" (or of unfittingness) in the very order of being.[2]

For a being thus to "fit" another being, as act fits what is in potency to it, is to be its "good."[3] There is no more realistic notion of the good than that which makes it consist in the fittingness of a being to the being of something else: *quod est conveniens alicui, est ei bonum.* Goodness is not a "value" superadded to being or attributed to it by the subject that desires it; goodness is being itself in its ontological relation to another being. Nor is goodness what looks like a good thing but is not; goodness is to be found in that which actually *is* fitting to the real being of another thing. Where there is only apparent fitting-ness, there is only an appearance of goodness. Incidentally, this is the reason why every agent acts for a good. For every agent acts according as it is act; now, since there must be fittingness in the end of its action, an agent:

> . . . *by acting tends to something similar to itself. Therefore it tends to an act. But an act has the nature of good, since evil is not found save in a potentiality lacking act. Therefore every action is for a good.*[4]

Such is the true justification for the well-known saying that Thomas Aquinas has borrowed from Aristotle: *the good is what all things desire.* What it says is true, but one should not understand it, as many feel tempted to do, as if it meant that good is such because all things desire it. In the realism common to Aristotle and Thomas Aquinas, good is not such because it is desired, but rather it is desired because it is good. If an action is itself desired as an end, it must be that the action is good. If the effect of the action is the end desired by the agent, then it must be that this effect itself is good.[5] In both cases, the object of the desire is good because it is a being befitting another being.

This desire of things for the good is coextensive with the order of acting and operating things; that is to say, with the totality of existing things. Hence the formula used by Aristotle in his definition of good: *quod omnia appetunt:* all things, or everything; that is to say, all that which is, taken singly and collectively. Now there are two general classes of operating beings; namely, those that act by nature and those whose operations are directed by intellectual knowledge. In both cases a desire proportioned to the operating being is found at the origin of its operations.

There is reason to affirm this proposition even concerning the non-knowing beings. Nature offers the spectacle of beings operating in certain determined ways and with a certain regularity. Now there are two ways to interpret natural causality: either things operate by chance, or else they are naturally ordered and disposed in view of producing determined effects. Chance cannot account for order. If they were act-ing in a haphazard way, the things of nature would hardly exhibit such a regularity in their operations. Even in the modern conception of the laws of nature, which interprets their regularity as expressing mere statistical averages, the problem still remains to know how it is that these average effects assume the form of regular structures operating in a regular way.

To this question, the answer is that, even in things that lack knowledge, there is an inner principle of operation in virtue of which things are inclined to act in a certain way, always the same and determined by their very nature. Thomas Aquinas conceives natures as determined but, at the same time, as endowed with a sort of spontaneity that inclines them to operate according to their own forms and, so to speak, for their own good:

All natural beings are inclined toward that which befits them, having in themselves a certain principle of inclination because of which their inclination is a natural one [i.e., and not a violent one, as would otherwise be the case]. *In this way, they are not simply led to their due ends but, rather, they themselves somehow proceed to them of their own accord* (ita ut quodammodo ipsa vadant, et non solum ducantur in fines debitos). *Violent operations alone are conducted, because they contribute nothing to the action of the mover, whereas natural operations proceed to their ends inasmuch as they co-operate with Him Who inclines and directs them through a principle innate in them.*[6]

Thomas could not reach the end of his explanation without revealing the ultimate reason why even non-knowing things so regularly proceed to appointed ends that they themselves do not know. The principle of their natural inclination directs them to the end to which it itself is being directed by their Creator. It is very important to understand that the God of Christian philosophy creates both natures and their inclinations without doing violence to their spontaneities. On the contrary, God causes and directs them to their ends as natural principles spontaneously operating and tending to these ends. Still, having no knowing power of their own, natures can act as though they know what they are doing, but this is true because their first principle has for them the knowledge they lack. The flying arrow does not know its goal, but it reaches its target because it has been directed to it by the archer. In the last analysis, even natures are operating under the guidance of an intellect.

What is the end of these operations? Since all natures are being inclined to their own ends by the Prime Mover, God, that to which each of them is being inclined must be what is willed and intended by God. But God has no other end than Himself, and because He Himself is the pure Act of Being, He is supremely good. More exactly, God is the Good Itself, which is His essence, which is in Him *Ipsum Esse*. To say, then, that all things operate with God as their end is tantamount to saying that all things operate in view of the good. Now, to operate in view of something is to tend to that thing, and to tend to something as to one's own end is to have an appetite for it. It is to desire it. The strength of this statement must not be overlooked. If natural beings were simply applied by God to their acts and to their ends, the word "desire" would not correctly describe the cause of their operations. On the contrary:

> . . . *since all things are ordained and directed by God to the good, in such a way that there is in each of them a principle whereby it itself is tending to the good, as if seeking its own good* (quasi petens suum bonum), *one must say that all things naturally* desire *the good.*[7]

The importance of the doctrine is such that a certain number of precisions are in order. First, in saying that "good" is that which all desire, Thomas does not mean to say that all good things are desired by all beings indiscriminately. As has been said, the good for a thing is that which befits its proper nature. The meaning of the formula is that whatever may be desired by any being is desired because it is good.[8] In short, "good" is the desirable (*appetibile*) as "true" is the knowable; or being is the desirable as good, as it is the knowable as true.

A second remark concerns the way non-knowing beings desire that which is good for them. This desire is nothing other than their very natures considered in their dynamic actuality and as ordered by the wisdom of God. In the often-quoted saying of Scripture that God has disposed everything *suaviter* (*Wisd. 8:1*), Thomas Aquinas reads the philosophical truth that, as has been said, God not only causes things to act in view of their good but, even more, by giving them an inner principle of operation and an inner tendency to good that is truly their own, God causes each and every one of them to tend to its God-appointed end, itself and of its own accord. *Sponte tendentia in bonum:* such is the concrete reality expressed by the formula: even non-knowing beings naturally desire good.[9]

A third consequence has become the source of endless discussions among theologians. And no wonder. Extremely simple if taken in exactly the meaning it has in the doctrine of Thomas Aquinas itself, the consequence becomes unintelligible as soon as the Thomistic meaning of a single one of its terms is inadvertently altered. It is that, "just as God, because He is the prime efficient cause, is acting in every agent, so also, because He is the ultimate end, God is being desired in every end." The reason for this conclusion is clear. Since even non-knowing beings are tending to good in virtue of an inner tendency caused in them by God, and since God is the Good Itself, every tending and desiring thing is tending to the ultimate end of God's action; namely, the absolute Good, God. This amounts to saying that, in fact, all beings naturally desire God. Far from finding anything untoward in this bold statement, Thomas once more is not aware of adding anything to Scripture, except its intellectual elucidation. For it is written that *universa propter semetipsum operatus est Dominus* (*Prov. 16:4*). If God has done everything in view of Himself, all operating creatures ultimately are operating in view of God. Now, as has been said, to tend to an end in virtue of an inner principle is to desire that end. The consequence necessarily follows: everything naturally desires the end in view of which it exists; but God has ordained all things to Himself as to their end; hence, all things naturally desire God.[10]

Such is the famous and much-discussed thesis of the "natural desire of God" in the doctrine of Thomas Aquinas. We are now in the best possible position to understand it, in the fullness of its meaning and without any danger of misconceiving it, precisely because it is now a question of the natural desire that even the physical, natural, and non-knowing substances have of God. Taken as such, the doctrine merely describes a fact, itself tied up with the very structure of a universe created by God. The creator has made everything in view of Himself, and everything is acting in view of God; and since nature consists of natural spontaneities, thus to act in view of God is to tend to God, to desire God. This conclusion should be neither carried beyond the limits of its validity nor unduly minimized.

The universe of Thomas Aquinas consists of dynamic, active, and spontaneously operating substances. To say that they are "desiring," however, is not to say that they are aware of their nature, of the object of their natural tendencies, or of the end of their operations. To some extent, as we shall see, some of them do know all this, precisely because these are intellectual substances; but even the substances that do not know these things are, in fact, acting as though they did know them. In fact, God knows for them the end appointed for them by His wisdom, so that, in the last analysis, they desire by His desire as they are by His being. This Thomas Aquinas tersely summarizes in saying that "all things naturally desire God implicitly, not, however, explicitly."[11] Thus to desire God *implicite*, although not *explicite*, is not, for such an operation, to *know* that it is tending to God, but rather to *be* a tending to God.

Within these precise limits, however, the doctrine is fully true. To tone it down for fear of substituting theology for philosophy is to forget that the philosophy of Thomas Aquinas is a Christian philosophy and that his universe, fully natural as it is, is nonetheless a religious universe. Everything in it is, subsists, and moves as an effect of God and in view of God.

The end of created beings cannot be to become so many gods. Between being in itself and caused being no confusion is possible. Nor can the end of the world as a whole be to know God such as He is in Himself. As will be seen later, this presupposes a free decision of God to elevate some of His creatures to a supernatural condition of which, left to themselves, they are incapable. Besides, not all creatures are able to know. Yet there is one way in which all creatures, even those that have no cognitive powers, can tend to God. However lowly situated on the scale of being, all creatures are the effects of God and as such resemble their cause; all things then tend to God by tending to be like unto God. This truth can be verified by direct observation. All things desire to be. What is commonly called the "instinct of self-preservation" is nothing else than this very love of life and of existence that resists whatever threatens its survival. Now all things have being in so far as they resemble HE WHO IS, whose effects they are. To love to be, then, is to desire to be like God. It is, for a creature, to desire to be by participation what God is by Himself. The most fundamental of all instincts thus bears witness to the fact that all that which is desires to be like its Cause. In this sense, merely to be is to tend to God.[12]

But creatures do not tend to resemble God only in that they are; they act and operate in view of increasing their resemblance to the divine goodness. What God is from the very fact that He is the pure Act of Being, His creatures have to acquire by likeness through a multiplicity of operations. The same initial notion of God that has dominated the whole Christian philosophy of Thomas Aquinas is here at work again. A thing is good inasmuch as it is perfect (and to be perfect is to be). Now, in God, all perfections are identical with His essence, which is His very act of being:

In God, to be, to live, to be wise, to be happy, and whatever else is seen to pertain to perfection and goodness are one and the same reality, as though the sum total of His goodness were God's very being. Again, the divine being is the substance of the existing God.[13]

The full force of these words is still better felt in their Latin original, for which there is no adequate English rendering: *quasi tota divina bonitas sit ipsum divinum esse, rursumque ipsum divinum esse est ipsius Dei existentis substantia.* Now, precisely, this reduction of all perfections to the very act of being is impossible in creatures, none of which is its own *esse: nulla substantia creata est suum esse.* Each creature has to acquire the goodness it can have, but is not, through certain actions and operations. This it does by way of motion, understood in its widest meaning as any kind of change. And indeed motion is the kind of act of which that which is in potency is capable. Hence, finite and composite beings progressively actualize themselves; that is, progressively perfect their being by means of their multiple powers and operations. Thomas says this in the simplest possible terms: "Creatures do not attain to the perfection of their goodness through their being (*esse*) alone, but through many things (*sed per plura*)."[14] Such is, in the last analysis, the reason for all the movements and changes observable in the universes. They make it possible for things to imitate their Cause, not only in their substantial being, but also in the perfections that are due to their respective essences.

Even the physical world of Thomas Aquinas is the scene of a universal ontological generosity. The purely metaphysical nature of this notion of natural causality is evident. Positive science is perfectly free to ascertain the laws of nature and even the nature of these laws without resorting to this sort of consideration. The ultimate origin and nature of physical causality is no apt subject of scientific investigation. For the very same reason, no consideration borrowed from the sciences of nature can threaten the validity of this metaphysical view of the world. Because they *are*, things tend to be like God inasmuch as He is, and they likewise tend to be like God inasmuch as He is a cause, for they too are causes of other things by their operations. Since being is good, to cause a being is to cause a good. It is therefore a good thing to be a cause, and to tend to cause other beings is to imitate the fecundity of the divine goodness: "Therefore things tend to a divine likeness by being causes of other things."[15]

It is necessary to know this doctrinal framework in order to understand correctly the nature of the human will. What we call "will" is but a particular case of this universal appetite by which all things, without exception, tend to imitate God to the very extent that they are. Non-knowing beings, such as minerals or plants, operate and are causes in determinate ways, according to their very natures. Animals occupy a higher degree in the scale of causes. Endowed with sense knowledge and even with an instinct that imitates intellectual knowledge, they already can exercise a certain choice within a variety of possible movements. As compared with the *natural appetite* of inanimate things, the *sensitive appetite* of animals represents a higher degree of perfection. Still, the inclination of the animal to its end is not in the power of the animal; it is determined externally by the object of sense perception, just as the natural inclination of the inanimate thing is determined by its nature. Confronted with an object of pleasure or of fear, animals cannot master their inclinations. In the words of John Damascene, *non agunt sed magis aguntur:* they do not act, they are rather being acted upon.

The reason for this inferiority is that the sensitive appetite of animals, like sense knowledge itself, is bound up with bodily organs. Man himself is submitted to these two kinds of determinations. As a body, man is like any other physical body: *e.g.*, a man falls like a stone; as an animal, man perceives external objects and is moved by a sensitive appetite very much like the other animals. Hunger and fear are quite familiar to him, and so also are pleasure and pain, love and hatred, anger, and all the other expressions of organic emotions and passions. But man differs from the other animals in that he has an intellect. This knowing power belongs to the soul *qua* spiritual substance endowed with an act of being of its own and, thereby, independent of its body. Instead of being restricted to a certain class of objects, as sense powers acting through sense organs naturally are, the human intellect owes to its immateriality the ability to know all that which is. It does not know everything and, in what it knows, the intellect does not know everything equally well; still, since of itself it is unrestricted by any material condition, it is able to become, by mode of knowledge, any conceivable object.

This is the meaning of the well-known formula: *intellectus est quodammodo omnia.* The intellect is in a way everything, because all that which has being can, more or less perfectly, be conceived by it. Another way of saying the same thing is the no less well-known saying that "common being" is the object of the human intellect. The words *ens commune* do not signify any actually existing common being. Only particular beings have actual existence. "Common being" signifies "being in general"; it is a general and abstract notion without existence outside the mind. *Ens commune* is a notion that refers to all that which is, so much so that it can be considered the object of metaphysics, the science of being *qua* being.[16]

Since the nature of appetite follows that of the form, the appetite of an intellectual and rational substance must be an *appetitus rationalis*. As such, this rational appetite or will has the same object as the intellect; namely, being. The only difference is that, whereas the object of the intellect is being known as being, the object of the will is being desired as good. Hence the statement common in Thomas Aquinas that just as the intellect has for its object universal being, the will has for its object universal good: "The object of the will, which is the human appetite, is the good in general (*universale bonum*), just as the object of the intellect is the true in general (*universale verum*)." This universality of the object of will is the very foundation of the freedom of choice. Instead of being determined to particular objects, as are natural appetite and animal appetite, the human form of appetite, which is the will, is offered by the intellect a choice of objects as wide as the whole compass of being itself.[17] Since all that which is, is good, and since all that which is, is knowable, all that which is either is, or at least can become, an object of the human will.

This description of the will and its object is correct, yet it is liable to become misleading because of the ambiguity latent in the notion "common good." In a sense, the difficulty is similar to that which attends the definition of the object of metaphysics: *being qua being*. In their first and obvious meaning, these words point out being in general or the abstract notion of being and its properties. On second thought, however, one cannot fail to see that, thus understood, the object of metaphysics is an abstraction, an *ens rationis*, without existence outside the intellect. This is to turn metaphysics into a sort of logic. In order to avoid such a consequence, metaphysicians often add to this first meaning of the expression another and quite different one, according to which it signifies that reality that truly deserves the title of being; namely, the separate substances, and God. In like manner, after saying that the object of the will is universal good, Thomas himself soon realized that goodness in general has no actual existence. Now the object of the human appetite, or will, must needs be something actual. Consequently, the notion of universal good, or of good in general, often merges into that of a good so universal in its comprehension that it includes the totality of goodness taken in its infinite perfection. In this second sense[18] the universal or common good is God, and this takes us back to our first conclusion: the natural object of the human will is God.

There is no opposition between the two interpretations of the doctrine. On the contrary, if the object of the human appetite, or will, is the good in general, it must needs include the good in itself; namely, God. On the other hand, precisely because the will pursues God in each and every good it desires, one can say of it that the will is tending to God "implicitly," not "explicitly." It has been shown that all natural beings desire to be like God and that the end of their many activities is to imitate God both as being and as cause. Now, men are beings of nature, like all the rest of creation. The will is the human form of appetite, so much so that Thomas often calls it the "human appetite." As such, the will itself is part and parcel of nature. It is a nature; namely, the natural appetite of man. It is evident that, as such, the will acts and operates like any other nature. All that which has been said of the desire of God implicit in all natures should be applicable to the will. Nor should one hesitate in following Thomas on this point, provided only that the doctrine of Thomas himself is restated in the very spirit from which it proceeds. Thomas usually proceeds in the following way. First, he strictly defines the limits within which a certain proposition is true, and then, within these limits, he affirms it unreservedly and without any attenuation.

Such is the case with the problem of the proper end of the human will. In the *Summa Contra Gentiles*, Thomas first situates the problem in its most universal context and, by the same token, gives to its answer its definite meaning:

> *Now, seeing that all creatures, even those that are devoid of reason, are directed to God as their last end, and that they all reach this end in so far as they have some share in a likeness to Him, the intellectual creature attains Him in a special way; namely, through its proper operation, by understanding Him. Consequently, this must be the end of the intellectual creature; namely, to understand God.*[19]

Those among the theologians who are frightened by the famous Thomistic doctrine on "the natural desire to see God" should realize that, were it not for this desire, man would be a unique exception in the universe. He would be the only species of beings, living or otherwise, not intending to be united to God, as closely as is possible for its nature, which, in man's case, is that of a knowing being:

For, as we have shown above, God is the end of each thing, and hence, as far as it is possible to it, each thing intends to be united to God as its last end. Now a thing is more closely united to God by reaching in a way to the very substance of God; which happens when it knows something of the divine substance, rather than when it reaches to a divine likeness. Therefore, the intellectual substance tends to the knowledge of God as its last end.[20]

The import of the doctrine is as striking as it is clear. For an "intellectual substance" (*i.e.*, the human soul) the way to reach God is the way of intellectual knowledge, since the operation proper to a thing is its end. Now, "understanding is the proper operation of the intellectual substance, and consequently is its end." Moreover, that which is most perfect in this operation is its "last" end. But intellectual operations derive their perfection from that of their objects, so that the understanding of the most perfect intelligible object, God, is the most perfect of all conceivable intellectual operations. Hence, Thomas concludes, "to know God by an act of understanding is the last end of every intellectual substance."[21]

This, Thomas has explicitly noted, is a more intimate relationship to God than simply to be and, generally, to operate. By being itself and operating, every being is an image of God, but it keeps within the bounds of its own nature. By knowing God (however imperfectly this may be), an intellectual creature becomes a participant, by mode of knowledge, in the infinite actuality of its object. It is often said that the intellect is somehow everything (*est quodammodo omnia*). Its manner of being everything is to become its objects by knowing them. This universal truth does not cease to be true when the known object is God. Instead of simply being itself and an image of God, the intellectual substance shares in the being of God inasmuch as it forms in itself a certain knowledge of God. Naturally, the actual being of the knowing substance in no way becomes the actual being of God. The divine being is completely separated from all the rest by the absolute purity of its act, and this marks the limits within which the truth to be stated must strictly be kept. But within these limits it must be unreservedly upheld: by knowing something of the divine substance, man "is more closely united to God" than by merely being himself and, to that extent, an image of God. The beatific vision and its mere possibility are not here in question. Such perspectives, open to man only by divine revelation, completely exceed the boundaries of natural knowledge and of philosophical speculation. The only point at stake is that, even for pagan philosophers such as Plato and Aristotle, who never suspected the possibility of the beatific vision—this Christian grace of graces—to know something of the divine substance was to be more closely united to God "by reaching in a way the very substance of God" than in any other way possible to them. To be sure, such natural knowledge of God is sorely inadequate to its object; still, by it, man *vicinius . . . conjungitur . . . Deo, per hoc quod ad ipsam substantiam ejus aliquo modo pertingit . . . quam dum consequitur ejus aliquam similitudinem.* In short, "the human intellect attains to God as its own end by understanding Him," and this is true of whatever knowledge of God we may have, for "however little be the knowledge of God to which the intellect is able to attain, this will be the intellect's last end, rather than a perfect knowledge of lower intelligibles."[22]

Such being the will as a nature, and such being its object, it is easy to know what the ultimate end of man actually is. It can be nothing else than to know God. The supreme felicity of man is to know God as perfectly as He can be known by such a creature as man. The will plays a necessary part in the acquisition of this felicity. First, as has just been said, the will desires it and, by its desire, sets the intellect on its way to such knowledge. In a well-ordered Christian life, intellectual life is entirely dedicated, directly or indirectly, to the task of acquiring, through the knowledge of His creatures, an always less imperfect knowledge of God.

Considered from this point of view, it is true to say that the doctrine of Thomas Aquinas is thoroughly intellectualistic in its inspiration. There are two reservations, however. For though it is by his intellect that man ultimately somehow reaches the very substance of God, man's intellect would yet never reach its end if it were not moved by man's desire. Man seeks God, loves God, and adheres to God by his will. So the ultimate felicity of man is to reach its ultimate end, and since this end is to know God, the ultimate felicity of man consists in an act of knowledge; namely, in knowing God. The delectation attending this act is not the very substance of man's felicity. Having attained the supreme object of its desire, Good, the will rejoices in it, but the beatitude or felicity of man consists essentially in an act of the intellect, prepared and attended by an act of the will.[23]

Another useful precision concerns the value of the intellectual knowledge actually accessible to man. There is a view of Saint Thomas, popular enough among his adversaries, which represents him as a sort of proud intellectualist. Nothing is further from the truth. Assuredly, Thomas Aquinas sets nothing above knowledge, except being and, in being, *esse*, but this does not mean that for him human knowledge succeeds easily and completely in grasping its object. Thomas' is a very modest brand of intellectualism, as indeed could be expected, for if a finite intellect sets God Himself as the ultimate object of its knowledge, it cannot help falling short of its goal.

The most striking expression of Thomas' intellectual modesty probably is the introductory chapter of Book IV of the *Summa Contra Gentiles*. In it, the Master announces his intention of proceeding to the more recondite part of theology which deals with the mysteries of faith. Quoting from *Job* (*26:14*), Thomas says: *Ecce, haec ex parte dicta sunt viarum ejus, et cum vix parvam stillam sermonum ejus audiverimus, quis poterit tonitruum magnitudinis ejus intueri?* (*Lo, these things are said in part, of his ways: and seeing we have heard scarce a little drop of his word, who shall be able to behold the thunder of his greatness?*) The thunder of God's greatness precisely symbolizes the truth about God that is knowable for us only as revealed by God, and even then not as understood, but as believed, pending the time when, in another life and with God's grace, it will be seen. As to the "ways" of God, they are His very creatures, with their natures, operations, and order, whose study progressively takes us less far from the knowledge of God naturally accessible to man. For the perfect good of man is to know God, and his Creator did not want to leave him unable to reach his end. Therefore, since the way down and the way up are one and the same, man can start from the lowest of creatures and progressively ascend, as by degrees, up to the prime cause of all. These are the ways, but, Thomas observes, because of the debility of our intellects, even the ways are not perfectly knowable to us: *nec ipsas vias perfecte cognoscere possumus;* and if even the ways are but imperfectly known to us, how could we attain through them to the very origin of the ways? The human appetite carries man's intellect along on the path to God, but even the path is obscure; only grace enables man to reach his goal.

As a nature, the will tends to that which befits it. One might better say that, through his will, man tends to that which befits his own nature and can perfect his own being. Will is being longing for being more; that is, for being still more that which it is. Just as one should not say that intellect knows, but rather that man knows through his intellect, so also the will does not will; man wills through his will. In the operations of free choice (*liberum arbitrium*) man chooses by his will among the various goods offered to him by his sense perception and his intellectual knowledge. Through his will, man tentatively experiences a sort of complacency in each one of these possible choices. And, indeed, since each and every one of them is a particular good, the will finds its pleasure in assaying each as a possible object of final choice. This complacency of the will, either provisory or final, in objects that befit the willing being, is called love.

Of its nature, love is inseparable from appetite. Everywhere there is appetite, there is a form of love proportioned to it. Inanimate things do not know and do not feel, but since they are operating in virtue of an innate principle of operation created, preserved, moved, and directed in them by God, even natural appetite is acting as a sort of *natural love*. Each and every natural being is moved by an unconscious, yet real, inclination to that which is, so to speak, "connatural" (that is, co-natural) to it. The sovereign good, which is God, is the cause of the goodness of all things good. By the same token, it is for all particular ends the cause that they are ends, since everything that is an end is so inasmuch as it is good; consequently, God is the supreme end of all appetite in the world. Even natural appetite is love; in fact, it is, in all natural things, a natural love of God. This, in the words of Dante, is "the Love that moves the sun and the other stars."[24]

Higher than these merely undergone desires and loves are those of the *sensitive appetite*. This is "sensitive love" (*amor sensitivus*), which is the "complacency" of the sensitive powers in their respective objects, such as is observable in brutes, and also in men, at least to the extent that men sometimes allow themselves to be carried away by their sense impressions, uncontrolled by reason.

Higher than sensitive love is "intellectual love," or "rational love," which attends intellectual, or rational, appetite and is proper to man. This form of appetite and love differs from the preceding ones in that its object is the good as known by intellect and reason, and it itself is undetermined in its choice. Stones have no choice; left to themselves, they fall. Animals enjoy a much higher degree of spontaneity, in that they consciously tend toward their objects, but if they perceive an object as befitting their own nature they cannot not love it and actively desire it. In man, even the sensitive appetite is partly regulated by reason, and the intellectual appetite itself, being entirely dependent on rational knowledge, is as free as the judgment of reason itself is. This does not mean "universally free." Let us not forget that even will is a nature: it is, as a nature, the appetite of the good known by reason. If, therefore, it found itself confronted by rational knowledge with an absolutely good object, the human will could not possibly not desire it. Thus, it would be both entirely determined and yet entirely free. It even would be supremely free since it would find itself in the full possession of the proper object of its natural desire. It is in this sense that the Blessed find beatitude in the permanent enjoyment of what is, in virtue of their own nature, the supreme end of their intellect and of their will. In this life, however, confronted as it is with a multiplicity of partial goods, the intellectual love of man enjoys the kind of freedom proper to free choice. Man freely chooses the objects of his love following the judgments of his intellect on their comparative goodness and the consecutive movements of his will.

Love has only one object. Whether it be a question of what our will loves inasmuch as it is itself a nature, or of what it loves in consequence of the free judgments of reason, its object is always apprehended as good. To be apprehended is to be apprehended by the intellect, and this is the ultimate foundation of the absolute superiority of intellect over will in the doctrine of Thomas Aquinas. But the part played by the will in this quest of the sovereign good is nonetheless a necessary one; moreover, there are particular reasons, owing to the present condition of man, which invite us to recognize that, in some respects, will takes precedence over intellect; that is, in fine, love over understanding.

Let us reconsider the definition of love: a modification of the appetite whereby it delights in a certain appetible. The relation of love to its object is directed to the object itself. It is a relationship of being to being; Thomas Aquinas never tires of restating the fact: the lover delights in the object of his love; the appetible causes the lover to adapt himself to it; and this mutual fittingness is the very *complacentia* we call love: *amor . . . nihil est aliud quam complacentia appetibilis;* for the same reason, lover and loved can properly be said to be "inherent in" one another, so that just as the loved is in the lover, so also the lover is in the loved. In fine, the passion of love has for its effect the achieving of the intimate union of two beings, for the lover is related to the object of his love as to himself—or at least as to something that is part of himself: *amans se habet ad id quod amat sicut ad seipsum, vel aliquid sui.*[25]

The object of these remarks is to stress the characteristic, proper to love in comparison with knowledge, of addressing itself to being, not inasmuch as it is knowable and known, but in itself, inasmuch as it is a good and a being. Certainly the will could not love an unknown object, and it therefore presupposes the intellect and knowledge, but knowledge applies itself to being as true, and truth chiefly resides in the intellect. It is founded in the thing, and even, as has been said, in the very *esse* of the thing. Even so, knowledge directly applies to being as apprehended by the intellect, whereas love directly applies to its object as it is in itself. In Thomas' own words, knowledge belongs to the intellect, but love is in *vi appetitiva, quae respicit rem secundum quod in se est.* Hence this consequence, that something is required for the perfection of knowledge that is not required for the perfection of love. One does not *know* something at first sight, except in a very superficial way. True cognition requires a series of intellectual operations analyzing, distinguishing, and recomposing its object. One does not know something well from having just conceived a global notion of it. On the contrary, love at first sight can be, and often is, true and complete love:

> *It is enough for the perfection of love that the thing be loved such as it is apprehended in itself, and this is the reason it happens that something is loved more than it is known, because that something can be perfectly loved even though it is not perfectly known.*[26]

Examples to substantiate this conclusion are easy to find. Thus did young Dante first love Beatrice. But Thomas Aquinas looks for supporting facts in another direction. He could have thought of Tristan, but what occurs to his mind is the phenomenon, no less striking in its own order, of the loves we have all felt for some techniques, disciplines, or sciences we did not know and which, precisely for this reason, we set out to learn. This truth, Thomas says:

> *. . . is particularly evident in the case of sciences* (maxime patet in scientiis), *which some love for the summary knowledge they have of them; for instance, because they know that rhetoric is a science whereby one is able to persuade; and for this they love rhetoric.*

But the case Thomas particularly has in mind is the one he mentions next in a few words: "and the same must be said of loving God."[27]

Similiter est dicendum circa amorem Dei. These last words should be weighed carefully. Nothing can be loved unless it is known, but some objects can be loved better than they are known. This is a purely philosophical conclusion, but what is here at stake is nothing less than the very possibility of the virtue of charity. For charity is love. More particularly, it is the peculiar form of love we call friendship, which consists in both loving and being loved, but more in loving than in being loved. Now, in loving God, man finds himself in a privileged position with respect to the knowledge he has of the same object. In this life, God is known in a mediated way only. We know God by His effects; that is, as being their cause, or as excelling them, or even as being none of them. This latter mode of knowledge properly is the "cloud of unknowing" described by some mystics; in more simple terms, it is the way of negation familiar to the readers of Dionysius. To be sure, God is knowable in Himself and for Himself, just as He is lovable in Himself and for Himself, being both the prime truth and the prime good; but because our knowledge begins with sense, God is for us the farthest removed of all knowable objects. On the contrary, the act of appetite, under all its forms, is an inclination of the appetite to the thing itself. I may know nothing of rhetoric except, roughly speaking, what it is about, but this is enough for me to desire it such as it is. In the same way, man knows very little of God except that, by and large, God is Being Itself and the Good Itself, but this is enough for man to love God precisely as the sovereign Good and the Prime Being deserve to be loved. And why? Because the motion of appetite tends to things such as they are in themselves, whereas the act of the knowing power is according to the condition of the knowing subject. We know God only as man can know Him, but we can love God as God is in Himself.[28]

The full meaning of the negative theology of Dionysius, as interpreted by Thomas Aquinas, appears only when it is thus completed by his doctrine of the will and his "affective" theology, or theology of love. Those who complain that the "agnosticism of representation" professed by Thomas Aquinas keeps them too far away from God are simply forgetting, not only that negative theology presupposes all the affirmative theology of which the human understanding is capable, but also that Thomas invites them to love wholly the God they cannot wholly know. Especially in this life, the love of God (*dilectio*) is something greater than the knowledge of God, precisely because where the knowledge of God comes to an end—that is, in the very object we know through other things—there love can begin at once: *ubi desinit cognitio . . . ibi statim dilectio incipere potest.*[29]

The ontological structure of the universe thus receives its completion from love. By the same token, the Christian view of the world receives the fullness of its meaning. Metaphysics is here assuming the form of a philosophical meditation leading to a religious contemplation. The levels of speculation remain formally distinct, but there is between them a continuity of order that ensures their unity. Starting from material objects, human reason progressively ascends to higher and higher objects, and although it knows less and less as it gains altitude, it nevertheless feels certain that what little it knows about these lofty objects is worth more than its most perfect knowledge of lower things. At the summit of its inquiry, human reason has to give up. In the words of Dante, "to the high fantasy here power fails,"[30] but where knowledge fails, love can still advance. And so it does. After leading the mind from creature to creature up to their Creator, love begins to flow down again from creature to creature, following the same way in which things first originated from it as from their source. So while knowledge, beginning from creatures, tends to God, love on the contrary begins with God as from the ultimate end and derives from Him to creatures. This, Thomas says, takes place after the manner of a sort of circulation (*per modum cujusdam circulationis*): owing to the complementarity of these two movements of knowledge and love, but always under the impulse of love, the Christian world of Thomas Aquinas is a universal circulation of love, from Being to Being, through beings.

Chapter 12. Man and society

The fundamental notions of Christian metaphysics provide the necessary foundations for moral, social, and political philosophy. These branches of philosophical speculation require a special treatment, and each of them has its own proximate principles. As such, they constitute distinct objects of study, but the elements of Christian philosophy are the same for the whole body of philosophical knowledge. The proper object of the following considerations will be to show how the problems related to man living in society depend for their answers on the philosophy of being developed by Saint Thomas Aquinas.

The remark has its importance. Those who profess the philosophy of Thomas Aquinas are sometimes invited to leave aside metaphysical generalities good only for contemplative minds and to turn their attention to the discussion of contemporary ethical and social problems in the light of the principles of Thomas Aquinas. This request is, indeed, entirely justified, for Thomas Aquinas himself always taught that the object of practical reason is to advise, direct, and prescribe in the practical order, which is always concerned with particular problems. When it comes to such problems, one is fully justified in asking for a lecture course made up of really practical lectures dealing with really practical problems. This can and must be done, but two conditions are, however, required. The one is that the philosopher discussing such practical problems should be fully acquainted with the nature of their data. The philosophy of law cannot be usefully discussed (when it comes to practical problems) except by competent lawyers or, at least, by philosophers having first submitted themselves to a serious legal training. The remark likewise applies to the discussion of problems in economics and politics. Nothing is more dangerous in such matters than a metaphysician who considers himself qualified to solve all particular problems because he knows the first principles of human knowledge. Metaphysical knowledge is necessarily required for all knowledge, but no particular knowledge can be deduced from it unless the metaphysician first consents to inform himself of all the pertinent facts.

On the other hand, it is a serious mistake to imagine that, because they are practical and even urgent, such problems are the first ones to be dealt with by philosophers. In a sense, even practically minded men would profit by a careful study of the speculative problems discussed by philosophers. Thomas Aquinas has left us certain principles applicable to the solution of social and political problems, but he himself has derived these fundamental notions from the principles of his own philosophy and theology. This is the reason that Pope Leo XIII placed at the very beginning of his encyclicals dealing with social and political matters his own encyclical *Aeterni Patris* "On the Restoration of Christian Philosophy in Schools." No Christian philosophy? Then no Christian ethics, no Christian sociology, no Christian economics, no Christian politics. And let no school, no college, no university, Christian or not, imagine that any short cut here will save any time. Even the urgency of the problems is no excuse. Such problems have always been urgent, and they always will be. Time is short indeed, but the shorter the time, the more important it is not to waste any of it in attempting what cannot be done. In the present case, however, there is no problem, for all our preceding inquiry has introduced us to the metaphysical principles that dominate the Thomistic notion of a well-ordered society.

Man has so far been considered as if he were a solitary rational animal pursuing in his own particular ways his own particular ends. For reasons of order, it was necessary to do so, but the notion of a solitary rational animal is absurd, since solitary life is hardly possible for a rational being. In point of fact, a solitary animal could not be fully rational.

Of his own essence, man is a rational animal that needs social life in order fully to develop his rationality. Some animals can live a quasi-solitary life without being deprived of the perfections to which they are entitled in virtue of their natures. Not being intelligent, they have nothing to learn from others, nothing to teach them, apart from the proper use of their bodily organs which, most of the time, they know by instinct and can, at the utmost, demonstrate by example. Man is endowed with an intellect that enables him to gather a large amount of knowledge, speculative and practical, but he cannot actualize the whole potency of his possible intellect without being helped by other men who, in turn, are likewise helped by him. If every man had to reinvent by himself the totality of human learning, how far would he go? Unless we share in the science of our own times, unless we inherit the wisdom accumulated by our forefathers, the knowledge we shall be able to acquire by ourselves will amount to very little. In the widest sense of the word "teaching," taken as including any transmission and communication of learning, each and every one of us needs to be taught, in order that, in turn, he himself may teach what he has learned with, if possible, some little improvement.

There is no real difference, then, between saying that man is a rational animal and saying that he is a social animal. In creating man endowed with intellectual knowledge, God has created human societies. Nor are there any other societies than human ones. The so-called "animal societies" are specifically different from human cities. Because they remember and can transmit memories, human groups enjoy a certain continuity in time and, by the same token, exhibit a certain historical continuity very different from the merely biological continuity proper to animal species. For these reasons society demands to be taken into account in a general view of the principles of a Christian philosophy conceived in the spirit of Saint Thomas Aquinas. Like the physical universe itself, human societies are the work of God, and human laws express the particular aspect assumed by the order of nature when the nature in question is that of an intelligent being.

We know that God has created all things by His power and wisdom. We also know that God keeps in existence and governs, not only the world in a general manner, but each and every single creature, and even each and every particular act and movement of each single creature. God's presence to all things by His essence accounts for the fact that He causes the totality of beings and directs them according to their respective natures, the purely natural ones according to their necessity, the intellectual ones according to their liberty. We also know that God has created everything according to His own Wisdom, which is Himself, the ultimate end of all. This Wisdom is given different names according to its different aspects. It is the Divine Word; it is Jesus Christ; it is the divine Art, or the divine Idea. From the particular point of view of the present problem—that is to say, considered as directing creatures toward their divinely appointed end—the Wisdom of God is called the "divine law."

The divine law is God Himself as creating natures such as they are and act in accordance with their respective essences. As such, the divine law is the source of every other law and, in the first place, of the laws of nature, collectively called "natural law." It could not be otherwise since, from the fact that a creature simply operates according to its own essence, or nature, it is, in fact, fulfilling the plan foreseen by the divine Wisdom. This is true of minerals, of plants, and of brutes, and it is true of men considered as merely natural beings; that is to say, apart from the fact that they are rational animals and intellectual substances. Natural law is one particular case of the divine law.

It is noteworthy that, in explaining this general proposition, Thomas Aquinas himself spontaneously resorts to examples borrowed from the social order. In his doctrine it is as legitimate to explain nature by comparing it with human society as it is to explain the nature of human societies by comparing it with that of the physical universe. In both cases there is a lawgiver at the head of the whole structure, a unique source of order, of power, and of authority, whose natural generosity and love prompt Him to care for His creatures and communicate Himself, following a scale of lower and lower degrees, down to the humblest among His subjects.

The metaphysical principle from which this notion of the social order is ultimately deduced has already been defined in accounting for the hierarchical structure of the world. To the question: whether the inequality of things is from God, Thomas answers in the affirmative, because the very diversity of natures presupposes their inequality:

> *Formal distinction always requires inequality, because, as the Philosopher says, the forms of things are like numbers in which species vary by the addition or subtraction of unity. Hence, in natural things, species seem to be arranged in a hierarchy . . . Therefore, just as the divine wisdom is the cause of the distinction of things for the sake of the perfection of the universe, so is it the cause of their inequality. For the universe would not be perfect if only one grade of goodness were found in things.*

An immediate corollary of this principle is that, in nature, just as there is a hierarchy of essences, there is a hierarchy of causes. This is not merely a matter of fittingness; since being is act, and since every being operates inasmuch as it is act, the order of natural operations necessarily follows the order of the natures. Consequently, the very inequality constituted by the divine wisdom in created things demands (*exigit*) that one creature should act upon another one.[1] More precisely, it demands that more perfect creatures should act upon less perfect ones.

To the question: how does Thomas Aquinas conceive societies? the best answer is: look at his conception of the world of nature. The universe is a structure of higher and lower beings, wherein the more perfect beings must act upon the less perfect ones. By thus acting upon them, the higher beings make the lower ones become similar to their causes (since causality is rooted in being and effects therefore resemble their causes); in this way, lower beings are naturally ordered to the higher ones as to their own ends. Taken collectively, all beings are thus guided toward Him Who is both the prime efficient cause of the world and its last end.[2] In the same way, a rightly constituted society should be a hierarchy of beings, made up of superior and inferior men, the superior men acting upon the inferior ones, and all of them proceeding to their ultimate end, which is their assimilation to God. All the particular conclusions of Thomas Aquinas in matters of social and political philosophy ultimately hang on these principles.

The problems related to society cannot be separated from those that are related to the physical world, because to do so would imply that the creator of man is not the same as that of nature, or else, that in creating nature, and man in nature, God did not intend that the two events should be correlated.

The unity of his approach to these two kinds of problems is easily perceived in the answer given by Thomas to the question: "Whether every law is derived from the eternal law?" On this point, nothing else will do except his own words:

> *I answer that, as was stated above,* law *denotes a kind of plan directing acts toward an end. Now wherever there are movers ordained to one another, the power of the second mover must needs be derived from the power of the first mover, since the second mover does not move except in so far as it is moved by the first. Therefore, we observe the same in all those who govern; namely, that the plan of the government is derived by secondary governors from the Governor-in-Chief. Thus the plan of what is to be done in a State flows from the king's command to his inferior administrators; and again in things of art the plan of whatever is to be done by art flows from the chief craftsman to the under-craftsmen who work with their hands. Since, then, the eternal law is the plan of government in the Chief Governor, all the plans of government in the inferior governors are all the other laws which are in addition to the eternal law. Therefore, all laws, in so far as they partake of right reason, are derived from the eternal law.[3]*

The physical world of Thomas Aquinas is here interpreted as if it were a body politic under the governance of one single sovereign, and in fact this is exactly what the world is in a Christian philosophy. Of course this notion must not be understood as a "scientific" view of the physical world. Modern physics has nothing to do with this sort of problem. Taking the world of natures such as it is, positive science (when it wisely keeps within its own limits) contents itself with investigating its laws. Conversely, the metaphysician is not qualified to say what these laws actually are; physics and biology are matters of observation and calculation, not of philosophical deduction. On the contrary, metaphysics is competent to ask questions that far exceed the boundaries of science, and one of these questions is that of the ultimate reason why the universe at large seems to be endowed with a hierarchical structure and, generally speaking, seems to obey a sort of master plan. As soon as, even at the level of pure science, questions are asked about the "general direction" followed by evolution, the metaphysical problem arises. Thomas Aquinas has answered it by analogy with what is observable in human societies, which themselves are part and parcel of nature; but, in giving such an answer, Thomas had in mind as much the clarification of the nature of human societies by comparing them with that of the physical world as the clarification of the nature of the physical world by comparing it with the structure of human societies. God is a Supreme Lawgiver, but all inferior lawgivers are co-operating with God in extending to human societies the legal structure of the created universe. In this view of the world, human laws are derived from the eternal law, so much so that, because it is not derived from the eternal law, an unjust law is *not* a law. Inasmuch as they are not derived from the eternal law, so-called unjust laws really are not laws at all. Strictly speaking, there are no such things as unjust laws. To issue such prescriptions and to attempt to enforce them is to rule, not by law, but by violence. We are not bound in conscience to obey such orders, or, if we are, the reason is not that such orders are laws.

We are not duty-bound to obey prescriptions edicted by the State that are not laws; but an important distinction must be introduced on this point. We are not obliged in conscience to consider as laws orders that are not laws; that is, if we do obey them, the reason is not that they are laws, which, as has been said, they are not, but because there are many instances when we are duty-bound to obey such commands for another reason; that is, as though they were laws worthy of the name. This additional consideration strangely complicates the problem and is the source of many misunderstandings in discussing the notion of society according to Thomas Aquinas. What is a law, and is an "unjust law" truly a law? This is one problem. It is a distinct problem, for every law can be obeyed in two different ways: either out of unconditional obedience to its sacredness as law, or else, despite the fact that it is known not to be a law, for some other reason we shall have to define. In the first case, law is being obeyed because it is a law; in the second case, it is a question of knowing if the established political power of the State should be obeyed, even when its orders do not exhibit the true character of laws. On this second point, the answer of Thomas Aquinas is clear: there is at least one aspect under which even an unjust law still looks enough like a law: it is the authority in virtue of which the lawgiver prescribes it. When he who exercises political power misuses his authority, we are not obliged to consider his orders as just, nor can we attribute to his prescriptions the character and the sanctity of laws; but political power as such is entitled to respect. Hence the conclusion of Thomas Aquinas: "even an unjust law, in so far as it retains some appearance of law by being framed by one who is in power, is derived from the eternal law; for all power is from the Lord God, according to *Romans, 13:1*."[4]

These two questions—namely, the legality of laws and the right of political power to obedience—must therefore be carefully distinguished. Obviously, they should not be separated in practice. How can one obey a law without asking oneself the question: "Is this truly a law?" Still, the two problems must be distinguished, be it only because the first one is a problem for the lawgiver (for instance, is prohibition truly a law?), while the second one is a problem for the citizen (given that prohibition is being enforced as a law, am I in conscience bound to observe it?). An unjust law is no law; still, it often must be obeyed because there is no practical difference, from the point of view of the example given, between refusing to obey a law and refusing to obey what pretends to be a law and perhaps is not.

Thomas himself never presented this doctrine as an innovation. On the contrary, he often introduced it in his writings as the authentic doctrine of Saint Augustine, who in turn followed the teaching of Scripture. When Thomas wishes to confirm the view that all just laws are derived from the divine and eternal law, he quotes *Proverbs, 8:15: By me kings reign, and lawgivers decree just things.* When he feels the need to reaffirm that God is the source of all political authority, Thomas quotes the *Epistle of Saint Paul to the Romans, 13:1–2: Let every soul be subject to higher powers. For there is no power but from God: and those that are ordained of God. Therefore, he that resisteth the power resisteth the ordinance of God. And they that resist purchase to themselves damnation.*

These are rather strong words. They are the more remarkable as, at least in this passage, Saint Paul speaks without reservation. In reading them, one should not forget that, at the time they were written, the State was a thoroughly pagan State, violently persecuting the Christians in hatred of Christ. Like Socrates, Saint Peter and Saint Paul knew they were being unjustly put to death, in virtue of an alleged law that really was no law, but there was no rebellion in their hearts. The two of them, and along with them the other martyrs, freely chose to endure the punishment meted out to them by the head of the State whose power they were accepting, at least to this extent and in this way, as permitted by the power of God. Why, some will ask, should a Christian not go the whole way and, for instance, abjure his religion in order to comply with the orders issued by the political authorities? Simply because, by obeying such pseudo-laws, the Christian would act as though he considered them true laws. Hence the only thing he still can do is to resist such laws and pay the price. There is even a strict obligation to disobey such laws (which are not laws) when they happen directly to contradict the law of God. For it is written: *We ought to obey God rather than men (Acts, 5:29).*

It is not to be expected that even the doctrine of Thomas Aquinas will give us ready-made formulas universally applicable to all particular cases in such matters. Ethics and politics are about particular problems. The philosopher and theologian can lay down only universally applicable principles; it is up to the virtue of prudence to apply them to each particular situation. No two concrete particular cases are ever identically the same, but all such problems should be solved in the light of the first principle of practical reason; namely, to will good and to shun evil. As often as not, a lesser evil has to be accepted as a sort of good. In all cases, however, the two orders of problems must be carefully distinguished. To decree just laws—that is, true laws, and not pseudo-laws—is a problem for the lawgiver himself or, at least, for each and every citizen in so far as he himself happens to share in the legislative power of his own country. This is a very high responsibility indeed; the highest rewards as well as the most severe punishments are attached by God to the good or bad fulfillment of this legislative function. But to submit to law, good or bad, is the business of each and every citizen inasmuch as, owing allegiance to a government, he calls himself a "subject." To the extent that we are, indeed, subjected to its authority, political power is entitled to our unconditional respect. We must look at it as at a participation in the divine power that has created the world and rules it as its Lord.

The better to understand this notion, let us consider "power" taken in itself. As Thomas Aquinas understands it, the word "power" primarily points out less the notion of strength than that of a certain order of superiority and inferiority. To have power is to dominate; it is to be higher than something else. Conversely, to be submitted to a certain power is, as the prefix *sub* indicates, to be situated under (*sub*), or below, that which has power over us. We have already quoted, with Thomas Aquinas, the words of Saint Paul (*Rom. 13:2*): *he that resisteth the power resisteth the ordinance of God.* Taking the word "ordinance" in the fullness of its meaning (to order), Thomas sees in it the proof that, of its very essence, power is a matter of order. In the passage of the *Summa Theologiae* from which we are now quoting, Thomas is dealing with the names of three angelic "orders"; namely, Dominations, Powers, and Principalities; and he shows that, according to Saint Paul, but still more explicitly according to Dionysius the Areopagite, "the name *power* signifies a kind of ordination both as regards the reception of divine things, and as regards the divine actions performed by superiors towards inferiors, by leading them upwards."[5]

This last remark adds one more important feature to the Thomistic doctrine of order. In the context from which these words are borrowed, they apply primarily to the celestial hierarchy (the angelic orders), but they likewise apply to the ecclesiastical hierarchy and, in fine, to the political hierarchy. Every relationship of order is essentially elevating, bringing up, raising the inferior term to the level of the superior one. This uplifting function is essential to the notion of order and, by the same token, to that of power. Whatever his name, the Emperor, the King, the Prince, the President, or the Prime Minister is, in fact, exercising a hierarchical function whose ultimate justification is that it leads to their ultimate end, God, all the subjects entrusted to his care. Because it is order, an ordaining of men by God and in view of God, power is in itself entitled to our respect. When crushed under any kind of arbitrary injustice, Christians call it an injustice, but they see it as an "act of God."

As has been said, this general principle does not lead Thomas Aquinas to set up any particular type of constitution or to recommend any particular policy. Politicians, jurists, and economists are in charge of organizing political societies suitable to the particular circumstances of place and time obtaining at a certain historical moment. Neither meta-physicians nor theologians are qualified to assume such responsibilities. Not, at least, as metaphysicians or theologians. On the other hand, Thomas Aquinas rightly feels qualified to lay down, in the light of the divine Wisdom, the necessary laws that every society must observe in whatever place and at whatever time, if it hopes successfully to fulfill its mission. All such problems are particular cases of the general law according to which the fecundity of Being communicates itself follow-ing a hierarchical order of perfections. A well-ordered society simply provides a scale of proportionable links for the universal circulation of being.

The intimate relationship of power to order has for its first effect the virtual elimination of any recourse to violence. Certain contem-porary Christian theologians advocate the absolute rejection of violence. If this is a mistake, it is a very noble one, and such an attitude should appeal to Christian souls more strongly than the opposite, and rather bellicose, view of religion. It does not seem that Thomas Aquinas him-self ever went to such length. He would not unreservedly subscribe to the absolute principle of non-violence advocated by some wise men from the East. There are cases when a little violence, if timely applied and with the necessary precautions, can bring about so much good that one could not well condemn it. Still, every time Thomas Aquinas asks himself a question of this sort, he regularly reminds us that, before using force in resisting evil, we should first wonder if resistance to evil by means of violence will not cause a still greater evil than the one to be avoided. A purely philosophical reason here deserves to be kept in mind: by definition, the violent is the reverse of the natural. Now, only natural means can cause natural effects, and only natural conditions can create sound normal situations. On this point, philosophy once more agrees with theology. And no wonder, since philosophy is chiefly about nature, and theology about God, but nature is the work of God, and since violence is opposed to nature, violence does not ordinarily fulfill the primary intention of God.

The rules to be observed by anyone who accepts violence are still more clear than those to be followed by anyone who uses it. One should resort to violence as seldom as possible, as moderately as possible, only in cases when its use is certain not to cause more harm than good and, above everything else, only in view of restoring the normal course of nature temporarily unsettled by evil. But in discussing cases when we have a choice between submitting to violence or resisting it, Thomas obviously favors an attitude of resignation and of submission. Not, however, an attitude of blind abdication before injustice. There is no case in which reason should abdicate its right and its power to discern true from false, good from evil. If a law is unjust toward God, we already know that our duty is to refuse to comply, and of course to be willing to pay the price for doing so. If the law is unjust only to us, then of course we should feel free to denounce its injustice, and even not to obey it, unless, Thomas adds, we decide to submit to violence,

> . . . *in order to avoid scandal and disturbance, for which cause a man should yield even his right, according to* Matthew, 5:40-41: And if a man will contend with thee in judgment and take away thy coat, let go thy cloak also unto him. And whosoever will force thee one mile, go with him other two.

A still more striking example is that of a man who, unjustly condemned to death, asks himself whether he should try to escape capital punishment. If he is justly condemned, Thomas says, it is a sin for such a man to try to escape the punishment he deserves. If, on the contrary, he has been unjustly sentenced, a man is justified in resisting injustice. His case is the same as if he were being attacked by gangsters, with this difference, however: that even an unjust ruler still is a ruler to whom obedience is due, because *all* power is from the Lord. Even an unjust punishment can be accepted if it is to avoid a scandal from which serious disturbances can possibly follow.[6] The death of Socrates, dying out of respect for the sanctity of law, is a well-known example of this refusal to oppose violence with violence. But we who are Christians know of an infinitely more noble one. It is the totally undeserved, unjust, and nevertheless most lovingly embraced death of our Lord Jesus Christ.

Violence should be avoided because it is against nature. Hence this second general rule to be observed by all societies: to accept nature as God has willed it to be. The will of God should be respected in nature as well as in His commandments, for in both cases it is the same God and the same will. Even apart from this religious reason, a very practical one forbids man to act in opposition to the will of God as expressed in the nature of things. It is that man cannot change nature any more than he can change the will of God.

God does not forbid man to act upon nature, to modify it within certain limits, and to make it serve his own ends. But, precisely, the only way to make use of nature is first to accept it as it is, then to learn to know it, and finally to channel its energies so as to make them useful in view of some desired effects. In order to modify nature usefully one must obey its own laws. But nature is modifiable only within certain limits. It is exceedingly dangerous to imagine that, unlike physical nature, human nature and human societies are free creations of man and, consequently, lie entirely within man's power. The punishment for this kind of error is terrible. Every society that disregards the fundamental laws of human nature and the order established by God brings about its own destruction. The teaching of Thomas Aquinas on this point was remarkably developed by Pope Leo XIII. Sorely disturbed at the sight of so many European revolutions, all of them causing untold destruction and losses in human lives and property, without resulting in any progress that could not have been obtained without resorting to violence, Leo XIII forcefully stressed the truth that even societies are facts of nature, to the extent, at least, that they consist of men; and human nature cannot be changed at will. Any society disregarding these facts is headed for its own ruin.

Concerning the proper constitution of the State, the relationship of the notions of power and order remain of paramount importance. In seeking to achieve a satisfactory communication and distribution of power, the prince or the head of the State, whatever his title, must strive to imitate the Prime Cause of the world. To be to the nation in a position similar to that of God with respect to the world, such is, in a nutshell, the ideal program that every prince should have ambitions to fulfill.

All causality derives from the Prime Cause to creatures, but this does not mean that there is in the universe no other causality than that of God. On the contrary, all that which exists participates in the causal efficacy of the Prime Cause in the same proportion as it participates in the actuality of being. The political society described by Thomas Aquinas would not be in keeping with the structure of the created universe if it consisted of only one single man concentrating within himself the political power, the efficacy, and the authority of the whole nation. No man should attempt to do in a human society what God Himself does not want to do in the world. First, the Christian head of a State will never forget, while exercising his legitimate authority, that since he is in the nation what God is in the world, he must act as a father no less than as a ruler. This means that he must temper authority with love and rule his people in view, not of his own advantage or glory, but of the common good of all. Next, rather than keep authority in himself, the Christian ruler will aim to communicate some of it to all his subjects according to the capacities of each, and this, too, he does in view of the common good.

What Thomas considers the best-balanced political regime is described in a justly famous passage of the *Summa Theologiae*, I–II, q.105, a.1. Far from advocating any dictatorial form of government, Thomas stresses two points which today would be considered rather "democratic" in their inspiration. The first one, borrowed from Aristotle's *Politics*, is "that *all* should take some share in the government, for this form of constitution insures peace among the people, commends itself to all, and is most enduring."[7] The second point is that the best there is in the best forms of constitution should be included in the constitution of the well-balanced State.

The three main forms of constitution are *monarchy*, according to which power is concentrated in the hands of one single ruler; *aristocracy*, according to which political authority is in the hands of an elite; and *democracy*, according to which the government is directly exercised by the people. In the well-balanced State there is monarchy, because there is monarchy in the created world, which is governed by one Lord. There likewise should be in it a measure of aristocracy, so that although they do not totally control the State, the best are at least permitted to share in the government. This, of course, is to the best interest of all, for even in the created universe of spiritual and material substances, the lower ones are submitted to the influence of the higher ones. How could it be otherwise in a world in which creatures form a hierarchy of beings and, by the same token, of causes? But the rest of the people should also share actively in the government of the country, because no single creature is deprived of its own efficacy, but, on the contrary, all participate in the general fecundity displayed by the substances that constitute the universe. Hence the remarkable conclusion of Thomas Aquinas:

> *Accordingly, the best form of government is in a state or kingdom, wherein one is given the power to preside over all, while, under him, are others having governing powers. And yet a government of this kind is shared by all, both because all are eligible to govern, and because the rulers are chosen by all. For this is the best form of polity, being partly kingdom, since there is one at the head of all; partly aristocracy, in so far as a number of persons are in authority; partly*

democracy—i.e., *government by the people—in so far as the rulers can be chosen from the people, and the people have the right to choose their rulers.*

Where did Thomas Aquinas find this notion of the ideal State? According to himself, in Holy Scripture. Such was the form of government established by God for the Jewish people, and since this people was placed under the special care of God, its constitution must have been the best possible one; that is, at least, given what human nature is and its condition after original sin. A moment of reflection should suffice to make us realize that, in fact, this still is the constitution of the politically mature states in our own time. In England a Prime Minister, in America a President of the Republic, represent the monarchic element in the constitution. In the same countries, ministers, representatives of the people, and the elite in all domains constitute the part of aristocracy present in the constitution. As to the people, it is now governing itself almost in the same way that it used to do in the good old days of the prophet Samuel. In election years, the citizens are invited to choose unto themselves a king, and as soon as they have him, they begin to wonder who is going to be the next one. Now, precisely, according to Thomas Aquinas, this is what keeps the rank and file in peace. By letting them share, however modestly, in the government of the State, they have the impression that they, too, are kings.

The treatment of these social and economic problems does not require the introduction of any new *principles*. At the high level of Christian wisdom, the only possible thing to do is to lay down certain general rules that must be respected by every form, or pattern, of social and economic order. Among these rules, one is not very palatable to the taste of modern men. Still, it is a truth that everyone has to recognize, although few men would dare openly to profess it. Since the world of nature is a hierarchy, the fundamental relations between beings are relations of inequality. In a world in which quiddities differ like numbers, to be *other than* a certain being is to be *more or less than* that other being. Moreover, although all men are men equally, within the species *man* there are many individual degrees of perfection: physical inequalities in health and in strength, intellectual inequalities of all sorts, moral inequalities too; in short, countless differences in perfection affecting practically all the elements that enter the composition of human nature. Assuredly, there is no reason why societies should make the consequences of these inequalities harder to bear than they naturally are. On the contrary, all that it is possible to do in order to compensate for these natural differences should be done by the State with the co-operation of all men of good will; the only thing that Thomas Aquinas warns societies against is denying the fact that, among human beings, such natural inequalities, such differences in perfection, exist. Societies that try to organize themselves on the supposition that these natural in-equalities do not exist are courting disaster. The punishment in store for them is the very same as that which awaits all the societies that deny the order of nature; namely, their own destruction.

This is a point on which it will never be easy to clothe Thomas Aquinas in modern equalitarian garb. He certainly does not mince his words. In Book III, chapter 81, of the *Summa Contra Gentiles*, Thomas Aquinas undertakes to situate man in his place within the universe and also, while he is at it, to situate men with respect to one another. He first recalls the fact that there is a hierarchical order within each and every human being. In each individual man, the physiological functions serve the sensitive ones, the sensitive functions serve the rational ones, and the whole being is ruled by the intellect, king of this world in miniature (microcosm) we call man. Then Thomas goes on to say:

> *For the same reason, there is an order among men themselves. For those among them who excel by their intellect naturally dominate the others; as to those who do not shine by their intellect, but whose body is robust, they seem to be destined by nature to servitude. This is what Aristotle says in his* Politics.[8] *And Solomon agrees with him, since he says (Prov. 11:29):* the fool shall serve the wise. *And it is likewise written in* Exodus, 18:21-22: And provide out of all the people able men, such as fear God . . . who may judge the people at all times.

This sounds rather harsh to modern ears, but the only question to ask about it is: is this true? The question is not whether this is how it should be, but is this how things actually are? Asked in more literary terms, the problem reduces itself to this: by and large, are the odds on Caliban, or are they on Prospero? If we consider modern societies, we hear a lot about political equality, social equality, and economic equality, but where does it exist? Is there a single civilized society whose structure is not a hierarchy? The only really new development since the time of Thomas Aquinas is that, in the more advanced types of "democratic" societies, where technocracy is taking the lead in guiding economic revolution, it is becoming more and more true to say that, whatever the name of the regime, the best assets for anybody to have are first health and next brains.

These remarks are not intended as a justification of Thomas Aquinas. The only duty of a historian is to make the meaning of his doctrine as clear as possible; but, precisely, this cannot be done without removing some of its traditional misinterpretations. One of these consists in imagining that Thomas is *advocating* inequality. Thomas simply says that, in fact, there *is* inequality in nature and that, as far as we can see, it is there to stay. For the same reason, we should not imagine Thomas as defending the establishment and protection of social inequalities founded on mere social conventions. Since these conventions exist, they deserve to be respected, but we can feel sure that, if they serve no useful purpose, these conventions will finally eliminate themselves. For instance, it is only in countries where the King has little executive power that his designation can be left to the hazards of heredity. In the social or economic order, the situation is the same. It is harder to keep money than to make it. It is a great privilege to inherit a fortune, but a silly man will waste it, just as, if he has no sense, a man who has inherited a robust constitution is likely to spoil it by all sorts of excesses. It is practically impossible to preserve accumulated and undeserved privileges beyond the time when a more intelligent man will find a way to convert them to his own profit. In short, nature is desperately aristocratic. In the long run, the odds are always on the more intelligent. And one can trust Thomas Aquinas to find even this truth in Scripture (*Prov. 17:2*): *A wise servant shall rule over foolish sons.*

In the last analysis, this conception of the political and social order confirms the philosophical thesis, so often restated by Thomas Aquinas, of the primacy of intellect in the nature of man as well as in the nature of things. In the order of being, the existential act comes first; in the order of quiddities, what comes first is the intellect, along with intellectual knowledge. The highest of all perfections is to be. The highest conceivable mode of being is to know. If one tries to define the social doctrines of Thomas Aquinas in their very essence, one will not be too far from the mark in describing society as the organization of an aristocracy of nature which, in the last analysis, is an aristocracy of the intellect, in view of the common good. Thomas does not say that the philosophers or the scientists should be kings; being himself a philosopher, he knows full well that the last thing philosophers want is to be kings. Nor would any true scientist exchange his laboratory for a kingdom. But if, finding himself in trouble, the king sets up a brains trust and consults experts, these experts will really do the ruling. And this again is written in the book of *Proverbs* (*24:5*): *A wise man is strong: and a knowing man, stout and valiant.*

Some will ask if we are not free to do as we please and to organize societies according to the desires of our own hearts. Most certainly we are! And we are doing this all the time, but we pay the price for it. And the price is always the same: to act in disregard of the demands of nature is, for a society, to be headed for self-destruction. We can decide that, of two traveling companions, the stronger will lead the way while the more intelligent will carry the bag. We can decide that, in the body politic, the rank and file will prescribe the course of affairs while the more intelligent will execute the orders of the crowd. We can pretend that, in modern business and industry, the unionized employees and workers are really creating the economic goods that are being consumed by parasitical scientists, engineers, and industrialists. Thomas Aquinas already knew this state of mind. His only remark on this point was that, when they obtain, such situations are against nature; so, because they are self-destroying, they cannot last. Such political regimes, Thomas admits, do not totally pervert nature, because the government of fools is weak unless it applies to wiser men for expert advice.[9] Unless it thus corrects itself, such a regime will not last. *Ecclesiastes* says (*10:5–8*): *There is an evil that I have seen under the sun,* and it came about, *as it were by an error, proceeding from the face of the prince: A fool set in high dignity, and the rich sitting beneath. I have seen servants upon horses: and princes walking on the ground as servants.* Then comes the conclusion: *He that diggeth a pit shall fall into it.*

From these general remarks flow the counsels which the popes, in their encyclicals, have so often given to men who did not want to listen. The whole teaching of *Rerum Novarum* can be summed up in four points: 1, men are socially and economically unequal because they are naturally unequal; 2, this inequality is a fact of nature, and it must be recognized as such because, in the last analysis, the order of nature follows from the will of God; 3, wealth is power, and those who own lawfully acquired wealth should not experience any guilty feeling in using the economic superiority that is theirs; still, they must always use it (even apart from the supernatural virtues, such as charity) in the same way that God wields His own power; that is, in view of the common good of all; 4, as to those who do not own economic power, or who own very little of it, they are welcome to improve their position by all means short of violence, and they should finally accept inequality in economic conditions as part of the whole scheme of nature intended and created by God.

This is not to teach workers a dumb resignation to their lot. Thomas Aquinas has no objection to anyone doing his utmost to improve his own economic condition. Still, there are such things as "conditions" and, in this case, it is particularly evident that, to the extent that they are different, economic conditions are unequal and differ like numbers. Thomas simply advises us to accept inequality as a law for man because it is first a universal law for things. The wisest thing to do is, for those who are at the top to live up to their moral obligations, and for those who find themselves at the bottom of the political and economic hierarchy not to make their situation even worse than it is by allowing envy, jealousy, and hatred to corrupt their souls. No man can add one inch to his own stature. To resent the fact that some are taller than we are will not alter the situation; let us therefore accept the order of nature in its essentials, not simply because this is the way things actually are, but because nature is order and the order of nature is divine in its origin: *quae a Deo sunt, ordinata sunt: there is no power but from God: and those that are ordained of God (Rom. 13:1).*

The doctrine of Saint Thomas exhibits a remarkable unity. It owes this unity to the constant presence of a small number of principles whose fecundity it is impossible not to admire. But other doctrines, bequeathed to us by other great philosophers, exhibit a similar inner coherency which, taken alone, is not a sufficient mark of truth. The doctrine of Thomas Aquinas has this superiority over the others: that its principles are, in a sense, the same as those of apparently different, and sometimes opposed, philosophies—with this difference only: that in Thomism these principles are taken in the fullness of their meaning. This accounts for the privilege of Thomism to be open to all truth and to provide a place even for truths that its author could not explicitly foresee. All that is true in any other philosophy can be justified by the principles of Thomas Aquinas, and there is no other philosophy that it is possible to profess without having to ignore, or to reject, some conclusions that are true in the light of these principles. Speaking in a more familiar way, one can be a Thomist without losing the truth of any other philosophy, whereas one cannot subscribe to any other philosophy without losing some of the truth available to the disciple of Thomas Aquinas.

It is therefore of capital importance to concentrate on the meditation and ceaseless consideration of the principles. All these principles are such with respect to a special aspect of reality or to a special class of beings. Each and every one of the parts of philosophy has its own principles, such as the notions of change and cause in physics, or those of man and of intellectual substance in anthropology, but all these specialized principles consist of the definition of a certain quiddity, or essence, operating according to the nature of its specific form and in view of its specific end. One proposition at least is true of all these real essences: they are all "beings," and besides being that which they are in virtue of their forms, they are all beings in virtue of their own acts of being, the *esse* that is the hallmark of genuinely Thomistic beings.

This is the central notion offered to our reflection by Thomas Aquinas, and it is for us the only gateway to the proper understanding of his philosophy. But the only beings given in sense experience are not pure acts of being. Determined as they are by various essences, owing to which they are placed in definite species, empirically given beings seem to be ordered according to a scale of increasing and decreasing perfection. The place occupied by each species on this scale is the higher in proportion to its immateriality; that is to say, to the actuality of its being. For matter is potency and intellectuality is act, since intellectuality and knowledge are being unrestricted by materiality. Ascending this scale of beings, from material forms determined to their own being only, we go through the relative immateriality of life, then of sense knowledge, up to the first intellectual creature, which is man. Owing to his intellect, man is the scene of a vast expansion of being, because, while other beings are only the particular beings they are, man is, as it were, all things because he is able to know them by his intellect.

This unique situation of man entitles him to a special care on the part of the Prime Cause. Higher than himself, man can infer the existence of still more perfect beings, the spiritual substances: first, pure intellects unhampered by matter but still limited by their respective essences; next, HE WHO IS, the pure unlimited act of being and the prime cause of all the rest. Causing all, preserving all, God is directing all to the appointed end, which is Himself. But His care of beings is proportioned to their order in the scale of beings, for all the parts are in view of the perfection of the whole, not the whole in view of its parts. Intellectual substances have a greater affinity for the whole since, in a sense, they themselves are the whole as being able to know the whole and to be it by understanding it. It is therefore natural that God should take care of the non-knowing beings in view of the knowing beings, and of the knowing beings in view of themselves. The gifts they receive from the divine providence are not given to them to procure the good of other beings, but that of their own being, whose end is to resemble God.[10]

To see the general structure of Thomism is, at the same time, to realize the twofold nature of its vocation. It is a philosophy inasmuch as everything in it hangs on the truth of a first metaphysical principle. On the other hand, what offers itself as the supreme result of a purely philosophical reflection on the principles can just as easily be interpreted as the conclusion of a meditation on the meaning of Scripture, the truth gratuitously revealed by God to man in view of man's salvation. Hence the title of Christian Philosophy *par excellence* given to this unique doctrine by the popes and the unique place assigned to it in the teaching of the Christian schools.

But just as stones themselves desire their natural places by a desire inborn in them, so too, and much more so, the human intellect cannot be put in possession of its object by some exterior agent that takes it there. There is for us no knowledge except our own knowledge, no truth except self-acquired truth. To acquire it is a life-long undertaking, which does not really end with this life. But the endeavor is a rewarding one, rich in deeper and deeper joys, and its felicitous termination is certain under the guidance of the Common Doctor of the Church.

NOTES TO THE TEXT

PART I. REVELATION AND THE CHRISTIAN TEACHER
Chapter 1. The teacher of Christian truth

1. As a first general introduction to Saint Thomas Aquinas, see G. K. Chesterton, *Saint Thomas Aquinas: The Dumb Ox*, with an Appreciation by Anton C. Pegis (New York: Doubleday Image Books, 1955). Doctrinal introduction: E. Gilson, *The Christian Philosophy of St. Thomas Aquinas*, translated by L. K. Shook, C.S.B., with *The Catalogue of St. Thomas' Works* by I. T. Eschmann, O.P. (New York: Random House, 1956). Bibliographical introduction: Paul Wyser, O.P., *Thomas von Aquin*, in the collection *Bibliographische Einführungen in das Studium der Philosophie*, 13/14 (Bern: A. Francke A G-Verlag, 1950).

2. M.-D. Chenu, "Les 'philosophes' dans la philosophie chrétienne médiévale," in *Revue des sciences philosophiques et théologiques*, 26 (1937) 27–40; E. Gilson, "Les Philosophantes," in *Archives d'histoire doctrinale et littéraire du moyen âge*, 19 (1952) 135–140 (Boethius, pp. 137–138).

3. This did not prevent medieval masters from recognizing the superiority of some theologians in the field of philosophy. For instance, Siger of Brabant has called Albert the Great and Thomas Aquinas *praecipui viri in philosophia* (E. Gilson, *History of Christian Philosophy in the Middle Ages*, New York: Random House, 1955, p. 397): They were theologians "eminent in the field of philosophy."

4. This often-made remark entails two consequences. First, the understanding of the Christian philosophy of St. Thomas Aquinas requires in advance at least an elementary knowledge of the authentic doctrine of Aristotle. Second, it should never be taken for granted that the meaning of a certain notion (being, substance, cause, etc.) is the same in the two doctrines. Aristotelianism and Thomism are two distinct philosophies.

5. Thomas Aquinas was well aware of this relationship between Augustine and the Platonic tradition. See *Summa Theologiae* I, q.84, a.5, Answer: "Consequently whenever Augustine, who was imbued with the doctrines of the Platonists, found in their teaching anything consistent with faith, he adopted it, and those things which he found contrary to faith he amended."

6. An interesting example of this state of mind is a quotation from the moderate Averroist, Agostino Nifo, *In Met.*, Bk. vii, disp. 13, as found in Cornelio Fabro art. "Tommaso d'Aquino" in *Enciclopedia Cattolica*, vol. XII, col. 266 (Florence: Tipografia "L'Impronta," 1954). The text of Nifo runs as follows: *Expositor Thomas raro aut nunquam dissentit a doctrina peripatetica, fuit enim totus peripateticus et omni studio peripateticus, et nunquam aliud voluit nisi quod peripatetici.* ("Expositor Thomas seldom or never disagrees with the teaching of the Peripatetics, for he was wholly a Peripatetic, indeed a Peripatetic in every field of study, and he never wanted anything other than what was wanted by the Peripatetics.") Nifo's text was quoted again by Louis B. Geiger, O.P., "Saint Thomas et la métaphysique d'Aristote" in *Aristote et saint Thomas d'Aquin* (Journées d'études internationales, Publications universitaires de Louvain, n.d., pp. 175–220). This excellent historian added: "A beautiful eulogy, indeed, of which it is difficult not to acknowledge that it is essentially correct." But what exactly did Nifo say? *Expositor* Thomas is not the author of the *Summa Theologiae;* he is the author of the commentaries on Aristotle, in which it is literally true to say that he seldom or never disagrees with the teaching of Aristotle. Now this is precisely the reason one cannot expound the philosophy of Saint Thomas out of his commentaries on Aristotle alone. As Aristotle's *expositor*, Thomas is a polytheist, there are no divine Ideas, the world has not been created *ex nihilo*, there is no divine providence in respect of singulars, there is no efficient causality as distinct from moving causality, the world is necessarily eternal, everything in it is either an eternal separate substance or a perishable compound of matter and form, there is no personal immortality of the soul. This is not to deny, or to minimize, the wide and deep indebtedness of Thomas Aquinas to Aristotle. We would prefer to say, speaking of philosophy *reduplicative ut sic*—that is, as the best that natural reason can say about God and the world—that he himself knew of no better philosophy than that of Aristotle, but as a theologian he had to elaborate a philosophy of his own; to wit, the philosophical demonstration of the part of revelation that deals with truth accessible to natural reason. This philosophy, which, according to Thomas himself, is part of his theology, appeals to no revealed knowledge; it is purely rational in both principles and method, and still, it is irreducible to the philosophy of Aristotle if only for the reason that the first principle of human knowledge, being, is not understood by Thomas and Aristotle in the same way.

7. *ST*, II-II, q.188, a.5.

8. *ST*, II-II, q.180, a.3.

9. *SCG*, I, c.1, ※2.

10. *SCG*, I, c.4, ※3.

11. *ST* II-II, q.188, a.5, ad 3. Incidentally, this exactly describes the place attributed to philosophy in theology by Thomas Aquinas. Unless we suppose he betrayed his religious vocation, as he himself understood it, the Saint cannot have done what a "philosopher" would naturally do; that is, study Aristotle for the sake of Aristotle and philosophy for the sake of philosophy only. As to the "continuity of development" owing to which Thomism followed from the philosophy of Aristotle by a sort of "natural unfolding," it should be noted that two elements of discontinuity at least have played a part in this story. First, the Incarnation of Christ and the preaching of the Gospel to the Western world; next, the birth of a man wholly dedicated to the task of turning "sacred doctrine" into an organized body of knowledge after the pattern of Greek *episteme*. There always is continuity at the level of nature, for indeed all that which happens to nature is bound to be natural, but the cause of a natural event can be supernatural. It is somewhat distressing that the same men who preach that grace can make a man a morally better man refuse to admit that revelation can make a philosophy a better philosophy. Even at the level of metaphysics, there has been the same continuity between the two doctrines as there is between the condition of the world before, and after, the Incarnation of our Lord Jesus Christ.

12. *SCG*, I, c.2, ⌗2.

Chapter 2. Sacred doctrine

1. M.-D. Chenu, O.P., "La théologie comme science au XIIe siècle" (*Études de philosophie médiévale*, XLV, Paris: Librairie Philosophique J. Vrin, 1957); "La théologie comme science au XIIIe siècle" (*Bibliothèque thomiste*, XXXIII, 3rd ed., Paris: Librairie Philosophique J. Vrin, 1957). Related to an earlier stage of the conversation, but still important: J. Fr. Bonnefoy, O.F.M., "La nature de la théologie selon saint Thomas d'Aquin" in *Ephemerides Theologicae Lovanienses*, 14 (1937) 421–446, 600–631; 15 (1938) 491–516. These articles have been published separately; the reprint contains, over and above the preceding articles, an answer to the essays of R. Gagnebet, O.P., "La nature de la théologie spéculative" in *Revue thomiste*, 44 (1938) 1–39, 213–255, 645–674. Also: G. F. Van Ackeren, S.J., *Sacra Doctrina. The Subject of the First Question of the Summa Theologiae of St. Thomas Aquinas* (Rome: Catholic Book Agency, 1952). Extensive bibliography, pp. 123–128. A general survey of the European part of the discussion is found in A. Hayen, S.J., "La théologie aux XIIe, XIIIe et XXe siècles" in *Nouvelle revue théologique* (Museum Lessianum-Section théologique) 80 (1957) 1009–1028; 81 (1958) 113–132.

Let us note that, in the doctrine of Aristotle, the problem could not arise because, according to him, what we call metaphysics really was theology

itself. This should be the title of the work we now call his *Metaphysics:*
"Evidently, then, there are three kinds of theoretical sciences—physics,
mathematics, theology" (*Metaph.*, K, 6, 1064 b1–3). Theology includes
the science of being qua being because the science of the cause includes
(by unity of consecution) that of its effects. Now being qua being is
God's first and most universal effect. Since the theology of the Philosopher was a science, and the noblest of all, Thomas Aquinas undertook to
show that the theology of the Christians could likewise be called a
science, with, of course, the adaptations made necessary by the fact that,
in his own sacred theology, the first principles were held to be true by
faith in the word of God, itself a partial communication to man of the
science whereby God knows Himself, and which is His very being.

2. *ST*, I, q.1, a.1; Aristotle, *Metaph.*, V, 1, 1026 a19.

3. Thomas Aquinas is extremely free in his use of words, provided, however,
there is at least one reason justifying a certain use of a certain word. By
and large, the central meaning of *sacra doctrina* is: a teaching sacred in
its origin, which is God. *Sacra scriptura* essentially means: the whole body
of revealed truth as contained in the canonical writings. *Theologia* is the
science whose subject matter is God, either as knowable to natural reason
(natural theology, the crowning piece of metaphysics) or else as known
in the light of the divine revelation (and, as such, sharing in the nature
of *sacra doctrina*). All the difficulties arise for the reader from the fact
that the "theology that belongs to sacred doctrine" (*ST*, I, q.1, a.1, ad 2)
is, for this very reason, often called *sacra doctrina*. And it is *sacra doctrina*
inasmuch as it borrows its principles from the divine revelation. Moreover, since revelation is contained in Scripture, there is no difference
between sacred doctrine and Scripture: *Sacra Scriptura, seu doctrina*
(*ST*, I, q.1, a.2, ad 2). But this does not mean that sacred theology is
identical with Scripture and with revelation. It belongs in the order of
sacred doctrine inasmuch as it receives its principles from Scripture and
works in its light. In this sense, all sacred theology, including scholastic
theology, is essentially "biblical." Consequently, whatever is revealed
truth in a theology is sacred doctrine in the primary sense of the expression; whatever, in a theology, *necessarily* follows from revealed truth
also is sacred doctrine in the strict sense of the words; but all that the
theologian borrows from philosophy and the sciences, or adds of his own
in order to clear up the meaning of revealed truth and to facilitate its
entry into human minds, belongs to his own theology as such. No particular theology, then, is of itself an object of faith whose knowledge and
acceptance are required for salvation. The receivability of any particular
theology, the degree of its fidelity to the teaching of *sacra scriptura*, its
title to being considered part of *sacra doctrina*, these are questions to be
asked, and answered, by the authority of the Church alone.

4. On the position proper to Cajetan in his commentary on the *Summa Theologiae* and the reasons for its rejection (that is, if one professes to follow Thomas Aquinas), see E. Gilson, "Note sur le *Revelabile* selon Cajetan" in *Mediaeval Studies*, 15 (1953) 202–203. On the position of Bañes on the question, same article, p. 205, note 19. — On the following problem (how many men could know philosophical truth), one of the main sources of Thomas was Moses Maimonides, *Guide for the Perplexed*, Bk. I, ch. 33 (ed. Friedländer, pp. 366–370). See P. Synave, O.P., "La révélation des vérités naturelles d'après saint Thomas d'Aquin" in *Mélanges Mandonnet*, vol. I, pp. 327–370. Synave concludes that the personal contribution of Thomas Aquinas was to add to Maimonides' clauses, *pauci* and *post multum tempus*, this third one: *cum admixtione multorum errorum*, introduced for the first time in *ST*, I, q.1, a.1. With keen insight, J. B. Gonet, O.P., availed himself of this opportunity to reintroduce the patristic argument *per errores philosophorum*, which Thomas is here echoing: see his *Clypeus Theologiae Thomisticae*, Disputatio prooemialis, art. 10 (Antwerp, 1744, vol. I, p. 23).

5. *SCG*, I, c.4.

6. *ST*, I, q.1, a.1.

7. *ST*, II-II, q.2, a.4.

8. *ST*, II-II, q.1, a.8, ad 1.

9. *ST*, I, q.2, a.2, ad 1.

10. *ST*, II-II, q.1, a.5, ad 3.

11. *ST*, II-II, q.1, a.7.

12. On the "theological" part of philosophy according to Aristotle, see *Metaphysics*, E, 1, 1026 a19 and K, 7, 1064 b3. An important source of Thomism on this point is Augustine, *De Civitate Dei*, Bk. VIII, ch.1 and 6. — For a perfect formula of Thomas' own position, see *Expositio Super Librum Boethii de Trinitate*, V, 4:

Sic ergo theologia sive scientia divina est duplex. Una, in qua considerantur res divinae, non tanquam subjectum scientiae, sed tanquam principia subjecti [metaphysics considers God as cause of being], *et talis est theologia quam philosophi prosequuntur, quae alio nomine metaphysica dicitur. Alia vero, quae*

Theology or divine science, therefore, is thus twofold. There is one, in which divine things are considered not as the subject of the science, but as the cause of the subject; and such is the theology with which philosophers are occupied, which by another name is called metaphysics. The other considers divine

ipsas res divinas considerat propter seipsas, ut subjectum scientiae [sacred doctrine has for its subject God, not as cause, but as God] *et haec est theologia quae in Sacra Scriptura traditur.*	things in their own right as the subject of the science, and this is the theology that is taught in Sacred Scripture.

Note in this passage the equivalence of *theologia* and *sacra scriptura.*

13. *ST*, I, q.1, a.1, ad 2.

14. *ST*, II-II, q.1, a.5.

15. Two causes of misunderstanding should be avoided. First, one must remember that Thomas puts the problem with regard to mankind in general. Even if it were superfluous to offer to a certain man for belief a truth that he is able to know, it would still remain useful for mankind as a whole (*ST*, II-II, q.2, a.4, ad 1). Second, as a theologian, Thomas is chiefly interested in the theological knowledge of God, the only one that can lead man to salvation, and there is no such knowledge without faith. The object of faith is the Prime Truth, assented to because it is revealed by God. All that we believe is either God or something somehow related to God (*ST*, II-II, q.1, a.1). Hence, directly or indirectly, *objectum fidei est quodammodo veritas prima.* Among the truths included under the Prime Truth, and therefore in the object of faith, some can be investigated by natural reason. One of these is the existence of God. Thomas himself has raised the objection:

That which pertains even to non-believers cannot be placed among the acts of faith. But to believe that God exists pertains even to non-believers. Therefore, it must not be placed among the acts of faith. The answer: *To believe God does not pertain to the non-believers in the way it should in order to be counted an act of faith. For they do not believe that God exists under the conditions determined by faith. And therefore they do not truly believe God.* (*ST*, II-II, q.2, a.2, obj. 3 and ad 3).

This Thomas confirms by an appeal to the Philosopher himself (*Metaph.* IX, lect. 11, no. 1907): when it comes to knowing simple things, the only possible defect in cognition is not to attain them totally (*ST*, II-II, q.2, a.2, ad 3). Consequently (our own conclusion), the assent of the philosopher to the existence of God and the assent of the faithful to the existence of God not only do not take place under the same formal light, but they do not even have exactly the same object, because while the God of faith is also the Prime Mover, the Prime Mover is not the God of faith. We can therefore know the existence of the Prime Mover (which all call God) and still believe in the God of faith, for such belief is the only way to salvation: *Credere oportet accedentem ad Deum quia est, et quod inquirentibus se remunerator est (Heb. 11:6).*

The distinction is well marked by the fact that, while the common as well as the philosophic knowledge of the existence of God are "pre-ambles" to the knowledge of God by faith, the act of faith in God's existence grasps the very being of God and, along with it, the totality of the articles of faith as implicitly contained in it.

16. *ST*, II-II, q.1, a.5.

17. *ST*, II-II, q.1, a.5, ad 2.

18. *ST*, I, q.1, a.2.

19. *De Trinitate*, XIV, 1 (*PL* 42, col. 1037).

20. That is to say, of a science higher than themselves. In other words, there is no other science interposited between arithmetic and the natural light of reason.

21. This text (*ST*, I, q.1, a.2) has given rise to the notion of theology as a science "sub-alternated" to the science of God, since it borrows from it its own principles. Cajetan considers that *theologia secundum se est vere scientia simpliciter subalternata (ad loc.)*. Bañes does not agree: *Sic nostra theologia non est proprie subalternata, sed solum se habet ut imperfectum et perfectum intra eandem speciem* (ad loc., I, 22). Thomas himself has spoken of a *quasi* subalternation only: *Est ergo theologia scientia quasi subalternata divinae scientiae a qua accipit principia sua* (*In Sent.*, Prologus, q.1, art.3). In the *Summa Theologiae* (so far as we have been able to ascertain), Thomas did not even make use of the formula. It is found again, however, and without the *quasi*, in the questions *EBT*, q.II, a.2, ad 5. — In fact, even when Thomas does not write it, the *quasi* is necessarily implied. In a true subalternation, the inferior science sees in the same light as the higher science from which it receives its principles; but theology sees truth in the faith of the theologian in the word of God, not in the light of the divine science itself, which is one with God, and is the very *esse* of God. Between our theology and the divine science, there is a relationship of imperfect to perfect, of effect to cause and, consequently, of order, but there is discontinuity in the very essence of intelligible light. This is probably the reason Thomas Aquinas has, at least once, spoken of a *quasi* subalternation, and, in other cases, has omitted all reference to subalternation. As is so often the case, the commentators have attributed to what was a simple comparison an importance out of proportion with its actual place in Thomas' doctrine.

22. See, below, note 33.

23. *ST*, I, q.1, a.2, obj. 3.

24. *ST*, I, q.1, a.3.

25. *ST*, I, q.1, a.2, ad 2.

26. Aristotle, *Post. Anal.*, I, c.28, 87 a38.

27. *ST*, I, q.1, a.3, ad 1.

28. *ST*, I, q.1, a.3, obj. 2.

29. On this somewhat neglected power of the soul, see Bernard J. Muller-Thym, "The Common Sense, Perfection of the Order of Pure Sensibility," in *The Thomist*, 2 (1940) 315–343, especially pp. 332–342. The unifying function of common sense is excellently marked, pp. 335–336, and this is probably the property of this internal sense that prompted Thomas to compare its relation to external senses with the relation of theology to philosophic doctrines. "It is necessary that there be a sense which apprehends in the manner of one that which in the external senses is many" (p. 333). One could not easily find a more fitting description of the part that the theology of Thomas Aquinas is constantly playing with regard to the various philosophies (and even theologies) whose conclusions it assimilates by unifying them in the higher light of the word of God.

    Thus in man himself it is manifest that the common sense which is higher than the proper sense, although it is but one power, knows everything apprehended by the five outward senses, and some other things which no outer sense knows; for example, the difference between white and sweet (*ST*, I, q.57, a.2).

    It is strictly true that, as a theologian, Thomas is most anxious to show that he knows everything known by the philosophers, plus some other things (even in philosophy) which, so far, no philosophy has ever known. It is of the essence of a higher power that it "regards a more universal formality in its object than the lower power" (*ST*, I, q.77, a.3, ad 4). Thus does theology act with respect to philosophical disciplines. In this it resembles the way separate substances (angels) know all singulars through intellect alone (no senses); on this occasion, Thomas once more quotes the case of common sense (*SCG*, II, c.100, ※3).

30. See, for this discussion on the common sense, Saint Thomas' Commentary on the *De Anima* of Aristotle: III, lect. III, nos. 599, 602, 605, 610; lect. XII, no. 773.

31. *ST*, I, q.1, a.3, ad 2.

32. *ST*, q.1, a.3, ad 2. It is essential to remember and to take as literal truth this description of sacred doctrine as a stamp of the divine science in the human mind. Otherwise, the main reason Thomas has to exalt theology above all other sciences is being overlooked:

> *Fourth, this consideration endows men with a certain likeness to God's perfection. For it was shown in Book One that, by knowing Himself, God beholds all other things in Himself. Since, then, the Christian faith teaches man principally about God, and* makes him know creatures by the light of the divine revelation, there arises in man a certain likeness of God's wisdom. *So it is said:* But we all beholding the glory of the Lord with open face, are transformed into the same image (*II Cor. 3:18*) (*SCG*, II, c.2, #5).

33. *ST*, I, q.1, a.4.

34. *ST*, I, q.1, a.5.

35. *ST*, I, q.1, a.5, ad 2.

36. It is often objected to Thomas Aquinas that his position finally turns philosophy into theology, and so destroys it. He would concede that the theologian turns philosophy into theology by making it subservient to theology, but he would add that, far from harming philosophy, this amounts to a sort of transfiguration for philosophy. Some theologians had reproached him with mixing the water of philosophy with the wine of Scripture (*Isa. 1:22*). Thomas first answers that a metaphor cannot prove anything. Then he observes that, in a mixture, the two component elements are both altered and the result is a third substance, different from these elements. In theology, on the contrary, there is no mixture. What happens is that philosophy simply passes under the authority of theology. To make philosophy serve faith is not to mix water with wine, but rather to change water to wine:

> *Et tamen potest dici quod quando alterum duorum transit in dominium alterius, non reputatur mixtio, sed quando utrumque a sua natura alteratur. Unde illi, qui utuntur philosophiciis documentis in sacra doctrina redigendo in obsequium fidei, non miscent aquam vino, sed aquam convertunt in vinum* (*EBT*, q.2, a.3, ad 5).

> And yet it can be said that, when one of two things comes under the authority of the other, the result is not considered a mixture; this happens only when both are changed from their natures. Hence, those who use philosophical teachings in sacred doctrine by bringing them under the authority of faith are not mixing water with wine, but converting water into wine.

Some editions read "in naturam" instead of "in dominium," but the meaning remains the same in both cases. The example being the miracle of

Christ at Cana, where He changed water into wine, Thomas certainly means to say that the theologian likewise changes philosophy into theology by making it subservient to faith. But just as grace does not suppress nature by making it subservient to its own ends, so also theology can assimilate philosophy without corrupting it. If, in a real sense, philosophy did not preserve some of its essential characteristics, how could it serve theology? Our language is borrowed from nature; no comparison can correctly express a relation between two terms, one of which belongs in the supernatural order.

37. *ST*, I, q.1, a.6.

38. *ST*, I, q.1, a.6, ad 2.

39. *ST*, I, q.1, a.7.

40. *ST*, I, q.1, aa.6 and 2.

41. *ST*, I, q.1, a.8, ad 2.

42. In *SCG*, II, c.4, ※4, Thomas explains:

> . . . *any things concerning creatures that are considered in common by the philosopher and the believer are conveyed through different principles in each case. For the philosopher takes his argument from the proper causes of things; the believer, from the first cause—for such reasons as that a thing has been handed down in this manner by God, or that this conduces to God's glory, or that God's power is infinite.*

After this, Thomas goes on to say:

> *Hence, again, the two kinds of teaching do not follow the same order. For in the teaching of philosophy, which considers creatures in themselves and leads us from them to the knowledge of God, the first consideration is about creatures; the last, of God. But in the teaching of faith, which considers creatures only in their relation to God, the consideration of God comes first, that of creatures afterward. And thus the doctrine of faith is more perfect, as being more like the knowledge possessed by God, Who, in knowing Himself, immediately knows other things.*

Cf. *De Potentia*, q.1, a.4: *Eodem modo* . . . – Practically speaking, this means that the problem of the existence of God, for instance, will be treated by Thomas Aquinas using the method of philosophy, but at its theological place.

1. *ST*, I, q.2, a.1, obj. 1 — St. John Damascene, *De Fide Orthodoxa*, I, c.1, 3 (*PG* 94, coll. 789, 793).

2. *SCG*, I, c.11, ⚹1.

3. R. Descartes, *Meditations on First Philosophy*, Med. III.

4. *ST*, I, q.2, a.1, ad 1.

5. *ST*, I, q.2, a.1, ad 1.

6. *ST*, I, q.2, a.2.

7. As quoted in E. Gilson, *God and Philosophy* (New Haven: Yale University Press, 1941), p. 32.

8. *ST*, I, q.2, a.2, ad 1. *Cf*, *ST*, II-II, q.2, a.10, ad 2.

9. *ST*, I, q.2, a.2, ad 1. *Cf*, *ST*, II-II, q.2, a.4. The doctrine taught by this article is sometimes overlooked because it deals with faith in its concrete condition rather than with its abstract notion. Its import is that "it is necessary to believe the things that can be proved by natural reason." Three arguments justify this conclusion: that which is known by faith is known sooner, more generally and more certainly. For instance, the existence of God can be believed by a child, but it can be known only in metaphysics, the last science a man is called on to study.

10. *SCG*, I, c.4, ⚹3.

11. D. Bañes, *Scholastica Commentaria in Primam Partem Summae Theologiae S. Thomae Aquinatis*, I, q.2, a.2, ad 1; ed. Luis Urbano, Madrid, 1934, p. 110.

12. D. Bañes *loc. cit*. The light of faith and the light of reason both bear upon the same truth, the existence of God, but they do not attain it in the same way (under the same formal reason). The light of faith fortifies the supernatural certitude of our assent to it; the light of reason makes us see it as a sort of scientific evidence. This distinction eliminates the frequent objection that, in resorting to reasoning in matters of faith, scholastic theology substitutes the shaky certitude of reason for the unshakable certitude of the word of God. When reason offers its conclusions as preambulary to the supernatural knowledge of faith, it does

not offer them as being, in any sense, so many *foundations* of faith; such conclusions merely are a sort of material antecedent of faith.

13. Ancient sources of the five ways: R. Arnou, S.J., *De Quinque Viis Sancti Thomae ad Demonstrandam Dei Existentiam apud Antiquos Graecos et arabes et Judaeos Praeformatis vel Adumbratis* (Rome: Pontificia Universitas Gregoriana, 1932). — Selected texts: J. A. Baisnée, S.S., "St. Thomas Aquinas' Proofs of the Existence of God Presented in their Chronological Order" (*Philosophical Studies in Honor of . . . Ignatius Smith, O.P.*, Westminster, Md.: Newman Press, 1952), pp. 29–64.

The number of the five ways has nothing necessary about it. Their very choice could have been different without the authentic meaning of the doctrine being altered. See A. R. Motte, O.P., "A propos des cinq voies" in *Revue des sciences philosophiques et théologiques* 27 (1938) 577–582. In the *SCG*, I, c.13, ☒ 1, Thomas himself introduces the four ways expounded in I, 13 as "the arguments by which both philosophers and Catholic teachers have proved that God exists." He does not even claim the arguments as his own; not, at least, as being of his own invention. — The quotations from the *SCG* will be borrowed from *On the Truth of Catholic Faith: Summa Contra Gentiles*, Book One, newly translated, with an Introduction and Notes, by Anton C. Pegis (New York: Doubleday Image Books, 1955).

14. Unless otherwise indicated, we are quoting the English translation by A. C. Pegis, *Introduction to Saint Thomas Aquinas* (New York: Random House, 1948). See also, by the same author, *The Basic Writings of St. Thomas Aquinas* (2 vols., New York: Random House, 1945).

15. *ST*, I, q.2, a.3. On the various meanings of *potency*, or *potentiality*, in Aristotle, see his *Metaphysics*, V, 12, and IX, 1. In its present context, *potentiality* points out, in being, that in virtue of which it can be "passively changed by another thing, or by itself *qua* other" (*The Basic Works of Aristotle*, edited and with an Introduction, by Richard McKeon, New York: Random House, 1941, p. 620). The marble is in potency to the statue, etc.

16. The ties of the first way with the cosmography of the times are clearly seen in the simple version of it given in the *Compendium of Theology*, I, c.3:

We observe that all things that move are moved by other things, the lower by the higher. The elements are moved by heavenly bodies, and among the elements themselves, the stronger moves the weaker; and even among the heavenly bodies, the lower are set in motion by the higher. This process cannot be traced back into infinity. For everything that is moved by another is a sort of instrument of the first mover. Therefore, if a first mover is lacking, all things that move will be instruments. But even the unlearned perceive how ridiculous it is to suppose that instruments are moved, unless they are set in motion by some principal agent. This would be like fancying that, when a chest or a bed is being built, the saw or the hatchet performs its functions without the carpenter. Accordingly there must be a first mover that is above all the rest; and this being we call God.

(Translated by Cyril Vollert, S.J., St. Louis: B. Herder Book Co., 1947, p. 9.) As presented here, this proof forcibly suggests that Thomas Aquinas was interpreting the efficacy of the Prime Mover as that of an efficient cause. Not so in the *Summa Theologiae*, although, from his own point of view, Thomas Aquinas himself must have felt free to choose between the two interpretations.

17. The scientific crudity of the formulation of the proof by Maimonides is striking in this respect. One cannot help seeing that he is arguing from a finite universe, circular in shape, made up of a small number of concentric spheres and kept in motion by the perpetual influence of an astronomical body circling around the universe. Having ascended to this *Primum Mobile*, Maimonides demonstrates, by a proper dialectical argument, that even this ultimate astronomical body must have a cause of its movement; this is the Prime Immobile Mover. See Moses Maimonides, *Guide for the Perplexed*, Bk. II, ch. 1 (pp. 149–151).

18. *SCG*, I, c.13 ⚡⚡3, 28, and 33–34.

19. A curious argument, in *SCG*, I, c.13, ⚡18, sounds so purely dialectical that its presence causes some surprise:

Again, if two things are accidentally joined in some being, and one of them is found without the other, it is probable that the other can be found without it. . . . Therefore, if mover and thing moved are accidentally joined in some being, and the thing moved be found without the mover in some being, it is probable that the mover is found without that which is moved.

This is simply borrowed from the commentary of Averroes on the *Metaphysics* of Aristotle. Averroes gives the argument as used by Alexander of Aphrodisias: *Dixit Alexander . . . (In Metaph.,* lib. XII, Summa secunda, cap.i; ed. Juntas, Venice, 1574; vol. VIII, foll. 317v–318r). Thomas Aquinas may have inserted this argument in the long demonstration of *SCG*, I, c.13, precisely because this time no particular system of the world was involved.

20. Dominic Bañes still was of the opinion that to doubt the possibility of a rational demonstration of the existence of God that was sufficiently certain to make it for us a duty to worship Him, was a heresy. All theo-

logians would subscribe to this conclusion. But Bañes adds that "if somebody says that [the existence of God] cannot be demonstrated following the method of Aristotle, this is not an error in the faith, but in physics, or in metaphysics, and it is temerarious in the faith" (*Commentaria in ST*, I, q.2, a.2; p. 109). There is no reason to follow Aristotle, except in those of his doctrines that are true, and Thomas Aquinas himself would not have us adopt another attitude on this point. — Cf:

The question, then, is not one of revising the philosophical proofs, but rather of inquiring into the physical foundations from which they flow . . . There is no reason to be fearful of surprises. Not even science itself aims to go outside that world which today, as yesterday, presents itself through these "five modes of being" whence the philosophical demonstration of the existence of God proceeds and draws its force (Pope Pius XII, "Modern Science and the Existence of God" in *The Church and Modern Science*, New York: The America Press, 1951, p. 32).

21. The distinction between being and becoming was inherited by Aristotle from Plato. See Plato, *Timæus*, 87 b. Cf. E. Gilson, *Being and Some Philosophers* (Toronto: Pontifical Institute of Mediaeval Studies, 1949), p. 14.

22. See, above, note 20.

23. For Averroes' view, see, below, note 47.

24. This accounts for the fact that a true Thomist finds it difficult to admit that Thomas himself really intended to present the first way as self-sufficient and really distinct from the second one. See Bañes, *op. cit.*, p. 114: "And because the Prime Mover must be the Prime Efficient (otherwise the Prime Mover would be moved by the Prime Efficient), for this reason Thomas demonstrates that there must be one Prime Efficient." But if this be true, why not directly argue from the efficient cause of movement? The intention of Saint Thomas seems rather to have been to prove that there is a God, first in a universe of moving causes, and then in a universe of efficient causes.

25. See the text, above, in note 16.

26. In the physical world of Aristotle, there is no efficient cause properly so called; what we call efficient cause was to him a moving cause; that is, the origin of motion. Under circumstances tied up with the notion of creation, some Moslem theologians distinguished between the moving cause (cause of motion) and the efficient cause (cause of being). On Avicenna as a witness to this event, see E. Gilson, *History of Christian Philosophy in the Middle Ages*, p. 211. With Thomas Aquinas, the expres-

sions "moving cause," "agent cause," and "efficient cause" are generally equivalent. The problem will be examined for its own sake in dealing with the Christian notion of causality.

27. *ST*, I, q.2, a.3.

28. For a discussion of causality, to which this point leads, see A. Michotte, *La perception de la causalité* (Publications Universitaires de Louvain, 2nd ed., 1954). This work provides the scientific demonstration that causality is given in sense perception. It even shows *how* this experience takes place. See particularly ch. XVII, "L'origine de la notion de causalité," p. 251–262, where Hume's notion of causality is discussed in the light of experimental facts.

29. See, below, note 34.

30. This care on the part of Thomas Aquinas to avoid getting unnecessarily entangled in the astronomy of Aristotle may have been due in part to the example given by Moses Maimonides. Extremely well versed in the various systems of the world, Maimonides considers that of Aristotle full of difficulties, and he formulates them with force: *Guide for the Perplexed*, II, 24, pp. 196–199.

31. The doctrine that the number of the intermediate causes is irrelevant, since, whatever their number, they count only as one, is fully developed in Avicenna, *Metaphysics*, VIII, 1. The origin of the notion is, of course, Aristotle, *Physics*, VIII, 5, 256a; but its formulation by Avicenna (himself following "Eliph junior") is present behind the language of Thomas Aquinas. One cannot help thinking that the *Liber de Causis* has been influential in helping to formulate the doctrine.

32. In the scheme preferred by Avicenna, every such argumentation can be reduced to three terms: the prime efficient cause, which causes and is not caused; the intermediate cause, which is both causing and being caused; the ultimate effect, which does not cause and is solely caused.

33. The second way is not borrowed from Aristotle, nor from Averroes. Neither one of these two philosophers ever carried his investigation beyond the order of the moving cause. True enough, Thomas Aquinas has referred to Aristotle for a proof taken from efficient causality (*SCG*, I, c.13, ※33), but the corresponding passage in Aristotle (*Metaph.*, Ia, 2, 994 a1) makes no mention of efficient causality. Avicenna has undertaken to prove that there must be a prime cause in every one of the four divisions of causes (which was the position of Aristotle in the text that has just been quoted); only, in his own argumentation, the moving cause

is replaced by an agent or efficient cause (*Metaph.*, VIII, 1). Now, from the very moment existence itself is at stake, it is true that only three terms are included in the argumentation. With respect to existence, all the non-necessary beings are equal. Hence the remark made by Avicenna that even if the intermediate causes were infinite in number, they still would count as only one, because, in Avicenna's own words, what is at stake is not the size of the collection of effects under consideration, but the existence of a prime cause on which the existence of the whole collection hangs (*quidquid est de illa collectione, causatum est ejus a quo pendet esse totius collectionis: Metaph.*, VIII, 1, A).

34. This position is safe against the various criticisms of the notion of efficient causality made by Malebranche, Hume, and their many successors. The criticism of Hume is directed against the illusion that we can form a mental representation of the sort of energy whereby the efficient cause brings about the being of its effect. Hume also denied that the relationship of efficient cause to effect can be conceived as a purely analytical one; that is, as a consequence of the principle of contradiction alone. The proper answer to Hume is that efficient causality is a relationship experienced in sense perception and intellectually explicated in the abstract notions of cause and effect as well as in the intelligible laws that preside over their relations in general. As to the way these laws themselves are formulated, it must be said that they obey strictly the exigencies of the first principle of all judgments; namely, the principle of contradiction. But this does not mean that effects follow analytically from their causes in the same way as consequences follow from principles. An abstract principle is not an efficient cause. Everything happens in conformity with the requirements of the first principle of knowledge (*i.e.*, being and the principle of contradiction), but from the first principle of knowledge alone, nothing follows in reality. The error of Kant was not that for him causality was synthetic knowledge but rather that causality was an *a priori* synthetic judgment. It is, precisely, an *a posteriori* synthetic judgment whose terms are synthetically united in the sense experience of efficient causality. Let us not forget that sense experience has its own evidence, and that, in their own way, sensations themselves are principles.

35. *ST*, I, q.2, a.3.

36. Avicenna's proofs of the existence of God (*Metaph.*, VIII, 1 and 3) essentially consist in establishing that there is a prime cause in each one of the four divisions of causes. In the last analysis, this leaves only two prime principles, prime matter (material cause) and God (efficient, formal, and final cause). After submitting the material cause to the creative power of the prime efficient cause, Duns Scotus will use a similar method in his own demonstrations of the existence of God. There is in Avicenna no explicit demonstration of the existence of God taken im-

mediately from the possible and the necessary, but he has posited necessity as the characteristic of the Prime Principle. In his *Metaph.*, VIII, 4, where he shows that *omne habens quidditatem causatum est*, Avicenna has provided the material for such an argument. A first elaborating of the proof is found in Dominic Gundisalvi, *De Processu Mundi*, ed. G. Bülow, pp. 6–8. Thomas Aquinas gave to the argument its strictest conceivable formulation. Still, it derives its strength from the deep notion of being from which it follows rather than from the logical faultlessness of its formulation.

37. *ST*, I, q.2, a.3. — Aristotle, *Metaph.*, Ia, 1, 993 b30; b25.

38. This is a remarkable example of the free handling of a metaphysical proof of God's existence by Thomas Aquinas. This very same proof that is here related to Augustine, and rightly so, is also found in the *SCG*, I, c.13, ⌗34, where it is introduced as an argument "gathered from the words of Aristotle." The argument really is Augustinian in both origin and substance; only, since Thomas is addressing the gentiles, he wants to dress up the argument of Augustine in Aristotelian garb. This Thomas does by combining two texts of Aristotle which fit the thought of Augustine rather loosely:

In Metaphysics II (Ia, 2, 993 b30) *Aristotle shows that what is most true is also most a being* [because, being eternal, the heavenly bodies and their Movers are eternally true and eternally causing all derivative truths as well as all derivative beings]. *But in* Metaphysics IV (IV, 4, 1008 b37) *he shows the existence of something supremely true from the observed fact that of two things one is more false than the other, which means that one is more true than the other. This comparison is based on the nearness to that which is absolutely and supremely true. From these Aristotelian texts we may further infer that there is something that is supremely being. This we call God.*

Note that the text of *Metaphysics* IV, 4, does not speak of something supremely true (such as God), but of an absolutely correct truth (if there are four things, to say so is absolutely true; he who says these things are five is nearer to truth than he who says they are one thousand). As modified in *SCG*, this proof is another version of the fourth way of the *Summa Theologiae*. Nothing shows better the fluid nature of the formulation of the proofs, although their unity of structure remains unbroken.

39. *De Potentia*, q.3, a.5.

40. *Ibid.*

41. *ST*, I, q.2, a.3.

42. *SCG*, I, c.13, ※35.

43. *De Fide Orthodoxa*, I, c.3; *PG*, 94, col. 796CD.

44. *ST*, I, q.2, a.3.

45. *SCG*, I, c.13, ※1.

46. Cajetan has well seen that the way of motion leads only to a prime mover, unmoved in itself, but movable by accident. Bañes answers that, in order to meet the objection, we must take into account *any kind* of motion, not only physical, but also spiritual, metaphysical, or moral, prompted by the desire of some higher end (*Scholastica Commentaria*, p. 115). This, of course, entails the consequence that the "first way" ceases to be exclusively physical. Because he himself still interprets the five ways from the point of view of philosophy as such (which is not coextensive with that of rational certitude), Bañes reaches the conclusion that

> since the demonstrations introduced by Saint Thomas are, some of them physical, others metaphysical, and one of them, at least, ethical (namely, the last one, by the governance of the world, which can be fitted to moral conduct), they are not equally evident (non sunt aequaliter evidentes) (*op. cit.*, p. 114).

There is nothing, in the text of Thomas Aquinas, to justify this restriction. Thomas would admit that the first way is "more manifest," because motion itself is supremely manifest, but nothing indicates that he considered the first way more "evident" than the second or the third one. A simpler explanation might well be that, from the point of view of the theologian, all valid ways to God are equally valid. But of course there is little hope of convincing most of the readers of Thomas Aquinas that his approach to philosophical problems was a theological one; and to persuade them that, furthermore, his theological approach to philosophy has enabled him to perfect it is a desperate undertaking.

47. Here is the relevant passage of Averroes, which Thomas Aquinas certainly knew:

> *Et ideo impossibile est declarare aliquid abstractum esse* [that an immaterial being exists] *nisi ex motu, et omnes aliae viae quae reputantur esse ducentes ad primum motorem esse* [to the conclusion that there is a Prime Mover] *aequal-*

Hence it is impossible to prove that something immaterial exists except by means of motion, and all the other ways that are thought to lead to the existence of a Prime Mover are equally inadequate; moreover, were they true, they would have

iter sunt insufficientes, et, si essent been set forth in First Philosophy.
verae, essent numeratae in Prima For it is impossible to demonstrate
Philosophia. Prima enim principia first principles.
impossibile est ut demonstrentur
(Averroes, *In Metaph.*, XII, comm.
5; ed. Juntas, 1574, fol. 293rC).

After recalling that Alexander should not be followed on this point, Averroes turns to Avicenna, who nevertheless seems to have followed Alexander. Thomas Aquinas could not possibly have been unaware of this important controversy, but we do not remember him saying anything about it. The reason may be that he himself was considering the problem from the point of view of theology, in which case ways taken from physics and metaphysics become compossible. This, however, is our own interpretation of the fact. In itself, the fact is independent of it.

The position of Avicenna is not less easy to recognize. Its main features are as follows. To demonstrate the existence of God in physics is impossible; only metaphysics can achieve this demonstration (Avicenna, *De Philosophia Prima sive de Scientia Divina*, in *Opera Omnia*, Venice, 1508; Tr.I, cap.I, C). — Physics can investigate the prime cause of being in motion *qua* in motion; metaphysics investigates "the prime cause from which all caused being flows, inasmuch as it is caused being, not being in motion . . ." (I, 2 E). God is therefore investigated as *causa agens;* now, the physicists understand by these words the cause of motion only, whereas the theologians understand them as meaning "the principle of existence, and its Giver; that is, the creator of the world" (VI, 1 A).

It is easy to see, on this crucial point, how far Thomas stands from Aristotle and Averroes and how near he stands to Avicenna's metaphysical position.

48. One will note the absence of the principle of causality (*principium causalitatis*) from the formulation of the five ways by Thomas Aquinas himself. To him, causality was a fact given in sense experience and, in itself, as evident as change or motion. Moreover, according to him, all principles are reducible to the first principle, which in the order of judgment is the principle of contradiction. Now, taken in itself, there is nothing contradictory in the proposition: there is a being that neither moves nor is being moved. Such, in fact, would be the case if God had freely decided not to create the world. In short, the notion of causality is not necessarily tied up with that of being. Descartes proved the existence of God on the strength of the "principle of causality," but he saw quite clearly that, if he uses causality as a principle in proving the existence of God, one cannot drop this principle after reaching one's conclusion. The only resource left then is to do as Descartes did; namely, affirm that God is, somehow, cause of Himself. Thomas Aquinas would

not subscribe to this conclusion, but the problem did not even arise in his own doctrine. For him, causality was not a first principle of the intellect, since it was not a property of being *qua* being:

> *Now, to be caused by another does not appertain to a being inasmuch as it is being; otherwise, every being would be caused by another, so that we should have to proceed to infinity in causes—an impossibility, as was shown in Book I of this work* [SCG, I, c.13]. *Therefore, that being which is subsisting must be uncaused* (SCG, II, c.52, ※5).

49. If each one of the five ways is considered in isolation from the rest, their interpretation is often difficult. How can the first way conclude to anything like what the Christians call "God" if the prime mover of the conclusion is not the efficient cause of motion? But if, on the contrary, the five ways are considered as forming a whole, what difference is there between the first way and the second one? Again, if God is the necessary being, cause of existence for all merely possible beings, what difference is there between the third way and the second one? The import of the question can be seen from the penetrating article of P. Gény, "Les preuves thomistes de l'existence de Dieu" (*Revue de Philosophie*, 24 (1931) 578–586). Full of dialectical scruples, P. Gény maintains that the formulation of the third way in *ST*, I, q.2, a.3, is less satisfactory than it is in *SCG*, I, c.15, ※5. Now, what Thomas sets about to prove in the latter passage is not that there is a God, but rather that if one has proved the existence of God as that of a necessary being, then by the same token this necessary being is also eternal. If P. Gény were right, then the proof of the existence of God is less satisfactory in the *ST*, where Thomas attempted to prove it, than in *SCG*, I, c.15, ※5, where Thomas intended to prove something else. Incidentally, there has been a great deal of discussion on the point of knowing if this third way is "Aristotelian" and in what sense it is. The fourth way, from the degrees of being, is a battlefield. Some interpreters consider it the best of all the five demonstrations, while others find it hard to reconcile its obviously Platonic inspiration with the so-called Aristotelianism of Thomas Aquinas. As to the fifth way, we have seen even Bañes hesitating to place it on the same level as the preceding ones. This intellectual disorder suggests that another point of view should be adopted with respect to the Thomistic ways to God. See *The Christian Philosophy of Saint Thomas Aquinas*, p. 452, note 41.

50. See *The Christian Philosophy of Saint Thomas Aquinas*, p. 453, note 49.

51. *SCG*, I, c.13, ※35. — Saint John Damascene, *De Fide Orthodoxa*, I, 3 (*PG*, 94, 796 CD).

Chapter 4. Metaphysical approaches to the knowledge of God

1. Among the passages that can be quoted as contributing to the discussion of this problem, the following are particularly important: *De Ente et Essentia*, ch. IV; *ST*, I, q.44, a.2; *De Potentia*, q.3, a.5; *In Joannis Evangelium* (Prooemium).

2. For instance, among the ways to God, there is a particularly manifest one (*prima et manifestior via*), the first way, taken from motion. It is most manifest because everybody *sees* motion, or *feels* it. In his *Exposition on the Gospel of Saint John* (Prooemium), written between 1269 and 1272—that is to say, very late in his life—Thomas Aquinas is commenting upon the "contemplation" of Saint John. His intention is not to demonstrate the existence of God, but to show how understanding can come by some knowledge of God's nature. Thomas recalls the four manners (*modi*) by which the "ancient philosophers" have succeeded in knowing God. Some of them have done so by considering the governance of the world by God, and this is a most efficacious way (*et haec est via efficacissima*). And indeed, the immediate conclusion of the first way limits itself to the *existence* of a Prime Mover, but the consideration of purposiveness opens much wider immediate possibilities to the philosopher's meditation about the *nature* of God. The biblical glorification of God in His works well illustrates the infinite wealth of this theme of meditation.

3. *ST*, I, q.44, a.2.

4. *Metaph.*, I, 3, 983 a25–26.

5. *De Potentia*, q.3, a.5.

6. In the mind of Thomas Aquinas, the name of Plato immediately evokes the notion of participation, which occupies a central place in Thomism itself. Only, in the doctrine of Plato, participation is ultimately understood in terms of formal causality, whereas in Thomas Aquinas participation ultimately refers to efficient causality. This transposition has enabled Thomas Aquinas to assimilate the Augustinian notion of truth. There is no Augustinian proof of the existence of God by way of truth in Thomas Aquinas, but there is room in Thomism for a thoroughly Augustinian contemplation of God. See *Exposition on the Gospel of Saint John* (Prooemium):

Some arrived at the knowledge of God from the incomprehensibility of Truth. Every truth that our intellect can grasp is finite, for according to Augustine, all that which is known is rendered finite by the comprehension of the knower. Now, if it has been rendered finite, it has been determined and particularized. Consequently, the prime and supreme truth, which is above all understanding, must be incomprehensible and infinite, and this is God.

7. Leibniz, *Correspondance avec Arnauld*, lettre XX (ed. Georges le Roy, Paris: Librairie Philosophique J. Vrin, 1957, pp. 164–165): ". . . I consider an axiom this self-identical proposition, diversified by stress only: that *that which is not truly* one *being is not truly* a being *either*" (p. 165).

8. *De Potentia*, q.3, a.6.

9. *ST*, I, q.2, a.3: *Quarta via;* q.44, a.1; *De Potentia*, q.3, a.5: *Secunda ratio.* — Aristotle, *Metaph.*, Ia, 1, 993 b25.

10. *ST*, I, q.44, a.1; Saint Augustine, *De Civitate Dei*, VII, c.4 (*PL*, 41, col. 231).

11. *ST*, I, q.44, a.1.

12. Avicenna, *Metaphysics*, VIII, c.7, and IX, c.6.

13. The true nature of this metaphysical (and theological) consideration of the notion of God conceived as His own pure act of being is clearly seen from the place it occupies in the prologue of the *Exposition on the Gospel of Saint John*. Commenting upon the "contemplation" of Saint John, Thomas summarizes the whole matter in these terse lines:

Since, then, all the things that are participate in existence (esse), *and are beings by participation, there must needs be, at the summit of all things, something that is existence itself by His own essence* (aliquid . . . quod sit ipsum esse per suam essentiam), *so that His essence is His existence* (idest quod sua essentia sit suum esse); *and this is God, Who is the most sufficient, the most worthy and the most perfect cause of the whole being, from whom all that which is participates in being.*

Once more, the common scheme is visible: participation, causality, Cause. But one should not understand such passages (for instance, the magnificent development of *On Being and Essence*, IV, tr. A. Maurer, pp. 46–47) as demonstrations of the existence of God. Actual existence is evidently given in sense experience, but the very act of being (*ipsum esse*) is not perceptible to sense as motion and being are. In fact, its reality has very often been either overlooked or denied by philosophers, even among the Scholastics. After demonstrating that there is a God, it still remains to go a long way before reaching this supreme metaphysical notion: a being whose very essence is *to be*. The critics who denounce the defects of this argumentation considered as a proof of the existence of God simply are denouncing their own misinterpretation of it.

Chapter 5. The essence of God

1. *EBT*, q.I, aa.1–2, ed. B. Decker, pp. 56–68.

2. *EBT*, q.I, a.1, p. 60.

3. *EBT*, *ibid.*, p. 61: *ST*, I, q.105, a.5.

4. *EBT*, q.I, a.2, p. 65.

5. Pseudo-Dionysius, *De Divinis Nominibus*, VII, 4; see *In Librum de Divinis Nominibus*, *loc. cit.*, ed. C. Pera, nos. 727–733.

6. *EBT*, q.I, a.2, ed. B. Decker, pp. 66–67:

Tertio in hoc quod magis ac magis cognoscitur [Deus], *elongatus ab omnibus his quae in effectibus apparent. Unde dicit Dionysius in libro De Divinis Nominibus quod cognoscitur ex omnium causa et excessu et ablatione. In hoc autem profectu cognitionis maxime juvatur mens humana, cum lumen ejus naturale nova illustratione confortatur; sicut est lumen fidei et doni sapientiae et intellectus, per quod mens in contemplatione supra se elevari dicitur, in quantum cognoscit Deum esse supra omne id quod naturaliter comprehendit. Sed quia ad ejus essentiam videndam penetrare non sufficit, dicitur in se ipsam quodammodo ab excellenti lumine reflecti, et hoc est quod dicitur Gen.* 32:30 *super illud "Vidi dominum facie ad faciem," in* Glossa Gregorii: *"Visus animae, cum in Deum intenditur, immensitatis coruscatione reverberatur."*

Third, in that God is known more and more as removed from the things that are found in His effects. Hence Dionysius says, in the book *The Divine Names*, that the cause of all things is known both by excess and by remotion. In this progress in knowledge, the human mind is especially aided when its natural light is strengthened by a new illumination: for example, the light of faith, and the gifts of wisdom and understanding, through which illumination the mind is said to be raised in contemplation above itself in so far as it knows God to be above everything that it naturally grasps. But because the mind does not have the power to reach the vision of the divine essence, it is said to be in a manner thrown back upon itself by the excelling light. And this is what we read in the *Gloss* of Gregory on *Genesis 32:30* ("I have seen God face to face"): "When the gaze of the soul is directed toward God, it is beaten back by the dazzling light of His immensity."

7. *EBT*, q.I, a.2, ad 1, p. 67.

8. *SCG*, I, c.14, ⸭⸭2 and 3.

9. St. Augustine, *De Doctrina Christiana*, I, c.32, no. 35 (PL, 34, col. 32); *De Civitate Dei*, V, c.2, no. 3 (PL, 42, col. 912). Cf. *Sermo* VII, 3, 4 (PL, 38, col. 61).

10. *SCG* I, 22, ⸭10. This does not make it improper to apply the word *substantia* to God. There is a level of reflection on which it is true to say (with Augustine; see the preceding note) that God is substance. And, indeed, "substance" does not signify any difference superadded to "being"; it only points out a certain way of being, namely, that of such beings as are able to have an act of *esse* of their own. In *De Veritate*, q.1, a.2, Thomas still resorts to the older formula: the name of substance signifies: *per se ens.*

11. *SCG*, I, c.21, ⸭⸭7, 9, 10.

12. *ST*, I, q.3, a.2.

13. *ST*, I, q.3, a.3.

14. *ST*, I, q.3, a.4.

15. *Ibid.*

16. *Ibid.*

17. *ST*, I, q.3, a.6.

18. *ST*, I, q.3, a.5.

19. *ST*, I, q.3, a.6.

20. *ST*, I, q.3, a.7.

21. *ST*, I, q.3, a.8.

22. *ST*, I, q.4, a.1, ad 3.

23. *ST*, I, q.4, a.2; q.3, a.4. For Dionysius, cited in the next sentence, see *De Divinis Nominibus*, V, 1 (PG, 3, col. 816B).

24. *ST*, I, q.13, a.11. See *De Potentia* q.3, a.16, ad 3; q.9, a.3.

25. *De Potentia*, q.4, a.1.

26. Aristotle, *Post. Anal.*, II, c.7, 92 b10.

27. Aristotle, *Prior. Anal.*, II, c.7, 92 b14–17.

28. *De Ente et Essentia*, IV, ed. A. Maurer, pp. 45–46; V, p. 51. For Avicenna, see references in A. Maurer, p. 50, note 1.

29. Judgment posits *esse* as separated from essence although, in finite beings, it cannot subsist apart.

30. *SCG*, I, c.22, ⚘2; c.42, ⚘⚘8, 10; c.18, ⚘3.

31. This position immediately justifies the consequence that God is included in no genus. For all that which is in a genus has an essence distinct from its act of being:

Aliquid enim est, sicut Deus, cujus essentia est ipsum suum esse; et ideo inveniuntur aliqui philosophi dicentes quod Deus non habet quidditatem vel essentiam quia essentia sua non est aliud quam esse suum. Et ex hoc sequitur quod ipse non sit in genere: quia omne quod est in genere oportet quod habeat quidditatem praeter esse suum; cum quidditas aut natura generis aut speciei non distinguatur secundum rationem naturae in illis quorum est genus vel species; sed esse est in diversis diversimode (De Ente et Essentia, V).

There is a being, namely God, whose essence is His very act of being. That is why there are some philosophers who say that God does not have an essence, since His essence is not something other than His act of being. From this it follows that God is not in a genus, because everything in a genus must have its quiddity by addition to its act of being. For the quiddity or nature in a genus or a species is not distinguished according to the notion of the nature in those things that belong to a genus or a species; whereas the act of being is found diversely in diverse things.

Dicendum quod Deus non sit in genere . . . Primo quidem, quia nihil ponitur in genere secundum esse suum, sed ratione quidditatis suae; quod ex hoc patet quia esse uniuscujusque est ei proprium, et distinctum ab esse cujuslibet alterius rei; sed ratio substantiae potest esse communis: propter hoc etiam Philosophus dicit quod ens non est genus.

We must reply that God is not in a genus. . . First, because nothing is located in a genus according to its act of being, but by reason of its quiddity. This is apparent from the fact that the act of being belonging to each thing is its own and distinct from the act of being belonging to any other thing. But the notion of substance can be something com-

Deus autem est ipsum suum esse: unde non potest esse in genere (De Potentia, q.7, a.3).

mon; which is why the Philosopher himself says that being is not a genus. But God is His own act of being and therefore cannot be in a genus.

32. *Ens commune* has two meanings, not unrelated, yet distinct. First, it signifies the notion of being in general, being as predicable of all that which is. Thomas lists it among the most universal principles—namely, *ens et ea quae consequuntur ens, ut unum et multa, potentia et actus;* in short, being as a universal along with the transcendentals. In a second sense, it signifies all that which is, has been, or ever can be; in other words, all beings collectively considered in their totality; for instance: *Potentia autem intellectiva angeli se extendit ad intelligendum omnia: quia objectum intellectus est ens vel verum commune* (*ST*, I, q.55, a.1). In this second sense Thomas can also speak of *esse commune,* under the influence of the Latinized Dionysius, but this must be understood in the same sense as *ens commune.* These expressions do not at all signify an *ens* or an *esse* that would be common to all beings. Only the abstract notion of being contains all beings, but it has no reality of its own. Real "common being" has no reality apart from particular beings, actual or possible. — See *In Dionysii de Divinis Nominibus,* V, lect. 2, no. 660:

"Ipsum esse commune est in primo Ente, quod est Deus . . ." and again (*ibid*):

Omnia existentia continentur sub ipso esse communi, non autem Deus, sed magis esse commune continetur sub ejus virtute, quia virtus divina plus extenditur quam esse creature.

All existing things are contained under common being, but not God; rather, common being is contained under His power, because the divine power extends beyond created being.

33. *De Potentia,* q.7, a.2.

34. *De Potentia,* q.1, a.2:

Unde patet quod Deus est infinitus: quod sic videri potest. Esse enim hominis terminatum est ad hominis speciem, quia est receptum in natura speciei humanae; et simile est de esse equi, vel cujuslibet creaturae. Esse autem Dei, cum non sit in aliquo receptum, sed sit esse purum, non limitatur ad aliquem modum perfectionis essendi, sed totum esse in se habet; et sic, sicut esse in

It is thus evident that God is infinite, as can be seen from the following. The act of being belonging to man is limited to man's species, because it is received in the nature of the human species; and the same is the case with the act of being belonging to a horse or to any other creature. But since God's being is not received in anything, but is the pure act of being, it is not limited

universali acceptum ad infinita se potest extendere, ita divinum esse infinitum est; et ex hoc patet quod virtus vel potentia sua activa est infinita.

to some mode of perfection in being, but contains within itself the whole act of being. And thus, just as "act of being" taken universally can extend to an infinity of things, so too is the divine act of being infinite. From this it is clear that His virtue, or active power, is infinite.

1. *ST*, I, q.13, a.5; *De Potentia*, q.7, a.7.

2. *SCG*, III, c.54, ⚜13. Another way to express the same truth is clearly formulated in the two last paragraphs of *SCG*, I, c.32. God is by essence all that which He is; other beings are that which they are only by participation; consequently nothing can be said of God and finite beings univocally. This argument rests upon the assumption that *per se* being is the cause of participated being.

3. *SCG*, I, c.29, ⚜6.

4. *SCG*, I, c.35.

5. *SCG*, I, c.30, ⚜2.

6. *ST*, I, q.13, a.2.

7. On this question, which Thomas Aquinas has discussed several times (*ST*, I, q.13, a.5; *SCG*, I, cc.32–34; *De Veritate*, q.2, a.2; *Compendium Theologiae*, c.27), nothing can be clearer, nor more forcibly formulated, than the discussion of the position of Moses Maimonides in *De Potentia*, q.7, a.7. For the quotation, see *De Pot.*, q.7, a.5.

8. *SCG*, I, c.32, ⚜7.

9. *SCG*, I, c.33, ⚜⚜1–2.

10. *SCG*, I, c.34, ⚜⚜5–6.

11. *In Librum Dionysii de Divinis Nominibus*, VII, lect. 4, nos. 728–732. In other words, our true judgments concerning God are true of His substance, and the names we give to God in consequence of these judgments signify His very substance, except that they fail to represent Him: ("praedicantur de Deo substantialiter, sed deficiunt a repraesentatione ipsius," *ST*, I, q.13, a.2).

12. *ST*, I, q.13, a.11.

13. The name *Deus* (God) is interpreted by Thomas (following Saint Ambrose, *De Fide*, I, 1; PL 16, col. 553) as naming a nature. It points out the nature of God as known to us from one of His operations; namely, the providence He exercises over all (*ST*, I, q.13, a.8). Hence:

> *. . . this name HE WHO IS is the name of God more properly than this name* God, *both as regards its source, namely, being, and as regards the mode of signification* [completely indeterminate] *and of consignification* [it signifies being in the present].

On the other hand, the very indetermination of HE IS prevents it from naming any nature. Consequently, as a name of nature, God is more appropriate. But there is a still more appropriate one: "the name Tetragrammaton [Yahweh] imposed to signify the substance itself of God, incommunicable and, if one may so speak, singular" (*ST*, I, q.13, a.11, ad 1). Cf. Maimonides, *Guide*, I, 61, where it is shown that, appropriately enough, we do not know how to pronounce this name of God's individual nature.

14. "Nec hoc debet movere, quod in Deo idem est essentia et esse, ut prima ratio proponebat. Nam hoc intelligitur de esse quo Deus in seipso subsistit, quod nobis quale sit ignotum est, sicut ejus essentia" (*SCG*, I, c.12, ℀7). This is why we say of God that He is *ipsum esse:* "quod enim per essentiam suam est, si vis locutionis attendamus, magis debet dici quod est ipsum esse, quam sit id quod est" (*De Potentia*, q.7, a.2, ad 8). But, like His essence, or substance, His *esse* is unknown: "est idem esse Dei quod est substantia: et sicut ejus substantia est ignota, ita et esse" (*De Potentia, ibid.*, ad 1).

15. *ST*, I, q.12, a.12, ad 1. Of God's "whatness" we know only that He is the cause of all beings, surpassing them all in perfection.

16. *ST*, I, q.3, a.4, ad 2.

17. *ST*, I, q.13, a.10, ad 5.

18. *De Potentia*, q.7, a.2, ad 1.

19. On the transcendental notion of "oneness," see the very remarkable book of Ludger Oeing-Hanhoff, *Ens et Unum convertuntur. Stellung und Gehalt des Grundsatzes in der Philosophie des hl. Thomas von Aquin* (*Beiträge zur Geschichte der Philosophie und Theologie des Mittelalters* [XXXVII, 3], Münster Westfalen, 1953).

The word "transcendentals" stands for the Latin word *transcendentia*. Thomas Aquinas applies this name to certain notions that define properties of being *qua* being. Since being as such transcends all genera, these notions likewise transcend all genera and categories. In other words, like being itself, they are predicable of that which is, inasmuch as it is. Hence their name of "transcendentals." For instance, "thing" (*res*) is such a transcendental. The three transcendentals Thomas Aquinas is chiefly interested in are the "one," the "true," and the "good." We shall examine them in this same order, which Thomas considers their essential one: *Unde istorum nominum transcendentium talis est ordo, si secundum se considerentur, quod post ens est unum, deinde verum, deinde, post verum, bonum* (*De Veritate*, q.21, a.3). Thomas Aquinas himself has not followed this order in his own writings for reasons tied up with the nature of the problems at stake. He was not considering them *secundum se*, but rather with respect to God. In the *Summa Theologiae* the order is: the good (I, q.5), the one (I, q.11), the true (I, q.16). In the *Summa Contra Gentiles*, the order is the same: the good (I, c.37), the one (I, c.42), the true (I, c.60). The reason probably is that even the theologian speaks of God in terms borrowed from his knowledge of creatures; now, as beings created and perfected by God, creatures are first perfected by goodness (since, inasmuch as they are, they are good); then, for those who are able to know, comes the perfection of truth: *cognitio autem est posterior quam esse; unde et in hac consideratione ex parte perfectibilium bonum praecedit verum* (*De Veritate*, q.21, a.3).

The source of the doctrine is Aristotle: "It makes no difference whether that which is be referred to being or to unity. For even if they are not the same but different, at least they are convertible; for that which is one is also somehow being, and that which is being is one" (*Metaph.*, K, 3, 1061 a15–18).

20. *ST*, I, q.11, a.1.

21. *Ibid.*

22. *In Metaph.*, IV, lect. 2, no. 560:

Unum enim quod cum ente convertitur, ipsum ens designat, superaddens indivisionis rationem, quae, cum sit negatio vel privatio, non ponit aliquam naturam enti additam. Et sic in nullo differt ab ente secundum rem, sed solum ratione. Nam negatio vel privatio non est ens naturae, sed rationis, ut dictum est.

The "one" that is convertible with "being" designates "being" itself, adding to it the notion of indivision, which, as a negation or privation, does not posit any nature added to being. And, thus, it is in no way different from being in reality, but only in notion. For negation or privation is not a being in nature, but a being of reason, as has been said.

Ibid., 1974:

Ens et unum sunt idem subjecto, differunt tantum sola ratione.

"Being" and "one" are the same in subject, and differ only in notion.

Ibid., 553:

Patet autem ex praedicta ratione, non solum quod sunt unum re, sed quod differunt ratione. Nam si non

From the preceding argument it is clear not only that they are one in reality, but also that they differ in

different ratione, essent penitus synonyma; et sic nugatio esset cum dicitur, ens homo et unus homo. Sciendum est enim quod hoc nomen homo *imponitur a quidditate, sive a natura hominis; et hoc nomen* res *imponitur a quidditate tantum; hoc vero nomen* ens *imponitur ab actu essendi; et hoc nomen* unum, *ab ordine vel indivisione. Est enim unum ens indivisum. Idem autem est quod habet essentiam et quidditatem per illam essentiam, et quod est indivisum. Unde ista tria, res, ens, unum, significant omnino idem, sed secundum rationes diversas.*

notion. For if they did not differ in notion they would be synonyms, so that to say "a being man" and "one man" would be pointless. We must observe that the name "man" is taken from the quiddity or nature of man, while the name "thing" is taken from the quiddity alone; but the name "being" is taken from the act of being, and the name "one" is taken from order or from division, since "one" is "undivided being". Now, it is one and the same reality that has an essence, and that is undivided. Hence, these three names, "thing", "being", "one", signify absolutely the same thing, but they do so according to diverse notions.

23. *De Potentia*, q.9, a.7.

24. *Quaestiones Quodlibetales*, quodl. X, q.1, a.1.

25. *De Pot.*, q.9, a.7, ad 5.

26. This should be kept in mind in interpreting the passages where, starting from one, Thomas says that a thing is being inasmuch as it is one: *unumquodque inquantum est unum, in tantum est ens, unde ens et unum convertuntur* (*Quaestiones Quodlibetales*, quodl. VI, a.1). One only posits being inasmuch as itself is undivided being. This is seen in the same text from the fact that the unity of the being at stake (*i.e.*, the divine essence) is founded on the principle: *Est autem unumquodque ens per suam formam, unde et unumquodque per suam formam habet unitatem.* — In *De Anima*, a.11, discussing the question whether, in man, the rational soul, the sensitive, and the vegetative are one substance, Thomas answers in the affirmative, because otherwise man would consist of three distinct substances, which is impossible, because *ex diversis actu existentibus non fit aliquid unum per se.* Hence the conclusion: *Et ita etiam non erit homo ens simpliciter, quia unumquodque in tantum est ens, in quantum est unum.* Here again the argument means: if there were three substances in man, man would not be a *being*, because he would not be *one* being. — In *Metaph.*, III, lect. 12, no. 493.

27. *SCG*, I, c.42, ※ 17.

28. *Ibid.*, ※ 18.

29. *ST*, I, q.11, a.3.

30. *ST*, I, q.11, a.4.

31. Aristotle, *Metaph.*, VI, 4, 1027 b25–34.

32. *In Metaph.*, VI, lect. 4, no. 1241. This did not prevent Aristotle from teaching that "the disposition of things is the same in being and in truth." Thomas has often quoted this principle (e.g., *ST*, I, q.16, a.3, s.c.)

33. *Ibid.*

34. *ST*, I, q.16, a.1.

35. *Post. Anal.*, I, c.2, 72 a29.

36. *ST*, I, q.16, a.1. See *De Veritate*, q.1, a.3: ". . . thirdly [things are called true] inasmuch as they conform to the divine intellect . . ."

37. *ST*, I, q.16, a.1.

38. *Ibid.* This is the reason that truth resides properly in judgment rather than in the simple apprehension of essences; only judgment is concerned with the actual existence of its objects: *ST*, I, q.16, a.2.

39. *ST*, I, q.16, a.3. (See *De Anima*, III, 8, 431 b21.)

40. *Ibid.*, ad 1. The difference between Aristotle and Thomas Aquinas on this point ultimately rests on the fact that, in Aristotle, there is no doctrine of the divine ideas and no notion of a creation of finite beings after the pattern of such models in the intellect of God.

41. *Ibid.*, ad 3.

42. *ST*, I, q.16, a.4.

43. *ST*, I, q.16, a.4, ad 2. — A very difficult but highly rewarding study would be a comparison of the two problematics followed by Thomas Aquinas on the same questions in the *Summa Contra Gentiles* and in the *Summa Theologiae*. Such a study would throw a vivid light on the nature of theology as Thomas himself understood it. In the *SCG*, Thomas shows that God is truth by four arguments all related to the already-established conclusion that God is His own *esse*; but, in fact, the conclusion had already been reached as early as I, c.45: "That God's act of understanding is His essence." From that moment on, Thomas does not let us forget

that this is the point: "God's understanding is His being (*esse*)" (*SCG*, I, c.45, ⁂7); "Intelligere Dei est suum esse" (*SCG*, I c.46, ⁂6); ". . . cum esse suum sit suum intelligere" (*SCG*, I, c.47, ⁂5). On the other hand, Thomas can go out of his way to answer a question in a manner appropriate to certain minds or to certain kinds of philosophers. The extraordinary Aristotelian synthesis contained in *SCG*, I, c.13, obviously implies that the readers to be persuaded are, first and foremost, minds with an Aristotelian formation. The same remark applies to *SCG*, I, c.44, ⁂27, where, at the price of a complicated demonstration, perfectly superfluous so far as he himself was concerned, Thomas demonstrated that "making the supposition that the first mover moves himself, as the philosophers intended, we must say that God is intelligent".

44. *ST*, I, q.16, a.5.

45. *ST*, I, q.16, a.6, ad 2.

46. Many Thomists assure us that the "philosophy" of Thomas Aquinas is contained in his commentaries on Aristotle. A lacuna in their system is that, whereas the *Metaphysics* and its commentary provide adequate information concerning the relationship of "being" and the "one," they say practically nothing of the "good" as convertible with being. The Manichean dualism that was then a very active threat to the Christian faith invited the theologians to maintain the identity of the good and being and thus to eliminate the duality of good and evil considered as first principles of reality. Thomas Aquinas has followed this example. He has even written a treatise *On Goodness in General* and inserted it as near to the beginning of the *ST* as possible (I, q.5). It is a purely philosophical treatment of the nature of the good in its relationship to being. The impossibility of finding anything like it in Aristotle accounts for the fact that Siger of Brabant, an Averroist, has simply borrowed the substance of this question and inserted it in his own questions on the *Physics* of Aristotle. Not finding it in Aristotle himself (and for good philosophical reasons), Siger took it where it could be found. The true cause of Siger's interest in this problem can be seen from what he himself says in introducing the subject:

Quaeritur si primum sit causa mali, utrum scilicet vitia et peccata in moribus et natura sunt ex ordine providentiae divinae. Sed quia non cognoscitur si Deus est causa mali, nisi cognoscatur malum, et malum ·non cognoscitur nisi per bonum, ideo de bono est sermocinandum

It is asked whether the first principle is a cause of evil, that is to say, whether vice and sins in morals and in nature belong to the order of the divine Providence. But since we do not know whether God is the cause of evil unless evil itself is known, and since evil is known only

breviter. Circa quod quaero, utrum   through good, we shall therefore
bonum sit res differens ab ente.   deal briefly with the good. On this
point I ask whether the good is a
reality different from being.

(Albert Zimmermann, *Die Quaestionen des Siger von Brabant zur Physik des Aristoteles,* Inaug.-Diss., University of Cologne, 1956.)

47. *Nicomachean Ethics,* I, 1, 1094 a3; *SCG,* I, c.37, ✠4. — Thomas has two reasons to stress the significance of the saying *id quod omnes appetunt.* First, as will be seen, it invites us to look for the cause of the desirableness of the good; next, and this is the point of the present remark, it points out the very important character of the good, to be a "final cause." This aspect of the problem almost completely dominates the discussion of the nature of the good in *De Veritate,* q.21, a.2. Even there, however, the desirableness of the good is founded on the natural desire which, in things as yet imperfectly actualized, prompts them to acquire the being they lack: *quae enim nondum esse participant, in esse quodam naturali appetitu tendunt.* Hence, *ipsum igitur esse habet rationem boni (ibid.).*

48. *ST,* I, q.5, a.1. — After making sure of the fundamental meaning of the notion of the good, it will prove useful to read the answer to the first objection in this article. The point is that, because of the distinction of reason between the two notions, they are not predicated of a thing in exactly the same sense. Both of them point out the same thing, but being signifies it as being actually, and not only potentially; while goodness signifies this same actuality as perfection and, consequently, as desirable:

Nam cum ens dicat aliquid proprie esse actu, actus autem proprie ordinem habet ad potentiam, secundum hoc simpliciter aliquid dicitur ens, secundum quod primo discernitur ab eo quod est in potentia tantum . . . Sed bonum dicit rationem perfecti, quod est appetibile; et per consequens dicit rationem ultimi. Unde id quod est ultimo perfectum dicitur bonum simpliciter.

For since "being" says that in a proper sense something exists in act, and act is properly ordered to potency, a thing is said to be a being absolutely according as it is first distinguished from that which is only in potency . . . But "good" expresses the nature of something perfect, which is appetible, and consequently the nature of something ultimate. Hence, that which is in an ultimate sense perfect is said to be good absolutely.

49. *ST,* I, q.5, a.2.

50. *ST,* I, q.5, a.3.

51. *ST,* I, q.5, a.2, ad 1. See *Liber de Causis,* Prop.4, and Dionysius, *De*

Divinis Nominibus, IV, 1 (PG 3, col. 693B). — On the universal causality of the good in Dionysius as interpreted by Thomas Aquinas, see *In Librum De Divinis Nominibus*, IV, lect. 3, ed. C. Pera, nos. 306, 308, 312.

52. *ST*, I, q.5, a.4.

53. *De Natura Boni*, c.3 (PL 34, col. 299).

54. *ST*, I, q.5, a.6 — Aristotle, *Metaph.*, VIII, 3, 1043 b34.

55. *ST*, I, q.5, a.6 and ad 1. — Saint Ambrose, *De Officiis*, I, c.9 (PL 16, col. 35).

56. *De Div. Nom.*, IV, 4 (PG 3, col. 700A). In St. Thomas' Commentary on this work, see ch. IV, lect. 3.

57. *ST*, I, q.6, a.3.

58. *ST*, I, q.6, a.4. See Aristotle, *Metaph.*, II, 4, 996 b26.

59. *SCG*, I, c.38, ※2.

60. On the notion of the "beautiful" in Saint Thomas, see the remarkable study of Umberto Eco, *Il problema estetico in San Tommaso* (Torino: Edizioni di "Filosofia", 1956). — The only problem we are dealing with is the metaphysical problem of the nature of the beautiful considered as one of the convertible properties of being. The problem of art, for instance, is entirely distinct from this one. For the metaphysician, the problem of beauty is to know what it is; for the artist, the problem of beauty is to produce it. — *ST*, I, q.5, a.4, ad 1. See Dionysius, *De Div. Nom.*, IV, 7; PG 3, col. 701C. On the Dionysian notion of the good, see the Commentary of Saint Thomas *In Librum De Divinis Nominibus*, IV, lect. 5.

61. *ST*, I, q.5, a.4, ad 1.

62. *ST*, I-II, q.27, a.1, ad 3. See Dionysius, *De Div. Nom.*, IV, 10 (PG 3, col. 708A).

63. *ST*, I, q.39, a.8. See Saint Hilary, *De Trinitate*, II; (PL 10, col. 51); Pseudo-Dionysius, *De Divinis Nominibus*, IV, 5 (PG 3, col. 701A); in the Commentary of Saint Thomas, *In Dionysii de Div. Nom.*, IV, lect. 5, nos. 340, 346 and 349.

Chapter 7. Being and creation

1. See, above, ch. V, p. 103.

2. *Avicennae Metaphysices Compendium,* translated into Latin by Nematal-lah Carame (Rome: Pont. Institutum Orientalium Studiorum, 1926), p. 126.

3. *ST,* I, q.3, a.4; q.7, a.1; q.14, a.1. — Aristotle, *De Anima,* III, 8, 413 b21.

4. *ST,* I, q.19, aa.1 and 3. *SCG,* I, cc.80–83. — For a technically developed justification of the doctrine, see *De Veritate,* q.23, a.4.

5. *ST,* I, q.19, a.2. — Saint Augustine, *Liber 83 Quaestionum,* q.46 (PL 40, col. 30).

6. *ST,* I, q.10, a.2, ad 1. This, of course, is true only of God. Even angels (since they are finite and composed of essence and being) are not their own understanding and their own will: *ST,* I, q.54, a.2.

7. *ST,* I, q.19, a.5. This implies that the will of God always has a reason (since it is God's own being, which is itself God's own knowing), but it has no cause: *SCG,* I, cc.86, 87. Hence the compossibility of divine providence and of God's absolute liberty: *SCG,* III, c.97.

8. *ST,* I, q.25, aa.4 and 6, ad 3. In a.6 the reply to the third objection ex-presses the point of view of Thomas on this question with perfect lucidity:

   Given the things that actually exist, the universe cannot be better, for the order which God has established in things, and in which the good of the universe consists, most befits things. For if any one thing were bet-tered, the proportion of order would be destroyed; just as if one string were stretched more than it ought to be, the melody of the harp would be destroyed. Yet God could make other things, or add something to the present creation; and then there would be another and a better universe.

   (Trans. A. C. Pegis, in *Basic Writings,* vol. I, p. 209.)

9. This unity of the act of being in every actually existing thing, nature, or substance is such an absolute principle in the doctrine of Thomas Aquinas that it applies even in God. "All being (*esse*) in the divinity is essential [*i.e.,* is that of the essence], nor does the person exist except by the being of the essence" (*De Potentia,* q.2, a.6). Essence; *i.e., esse.*

10. The notion of God as pure *esse* permits us to show the non-impossibility of the generation, by the Father, of a second person, the Son, whose essence is the same as that of the Father. In the order of natural beings, the form or nature of the father subsists in a matter; consequently, it has to be received in a matter by the son; for this reason, in the beings of nature, the essence of the son is other than that of the father. Not so in God. The divine nature is subsisting in itself, not in a matter; if it communicates itself, it will be received, not in a matter, but such as it is in itself; the communicated essence will therefore be one and the same in the Father and in the Son. — The theologian can advance one step further into the darkness of the mystery. For since the essence of God is, in fact, His own being (*esse*), it does not receive existence through the subjects (*supposita*) in which it is. The divine essence, therefore, is the very same being (*esse*) in that which communicates it (the Father) and that to which it is communicated (the Son); it is numerically one and the same in both (*De Potentia*, q.2, a.2). This theological doctrine is inseparable from the Thomistic notion of God conceived as a pure act of being, which is a philosophical notion. The mystery remains entire, only, using philosophy as an instrument, it achieves its accurate formulation.

11. *ST*, I, q.27, a.4.

12. This philosophical notion enables the theologian to give to a classical question its correct answer. The question is whether, in the Trinity, the power of begetting signifies the divine essence or a divine person (the Father). The answer is that of course the power of begetting points out the Father, but that it *principally* points out the essence. And indeed:

   . . . the individual form in things created constitutes the person begetting, but it is not that by which the begetter begets, or otherwise Socrates would beget Socrates. Hence neither can paternity be understood as that by which the Father begets, but rather as constituting the person of the begetter, for otherwise the Father would beget the Father. But that by which the Father begets is the divine nature, in which the Son is like to Him . . . And therefore the power of begetting signifies the divine nature directly, but the relation (i.e., paternity) indirectly (ST, I, q.41, a.5).

   Cf. *De Potentia*, q.2, a.2.

13. *ST*, I, q.45, a.6.

14. See D. Bañes, *Scholastica Commentaria*, pp. 154–158. The position of Bañes is that secondary causes can produce beings, *minus* their very acts of being.

15. At any rate, the very being of the secondary efficient cause, as well as its operating power, are themselves creatures of God; consequently, they cannot produce effects from nothing:

Primus autem effectus est ipsum esse, quod omnibus aliis effectibus praesupponitur et ipsum non prae-supponit aliquem alium effectum; et ideo oportet quod dare esse inquantum hujusmodi sit effectus primae causae solius secundum propriam virtutem; et quaecumque alia causa dat esse, hoc habet inquantum est in ea virtus et operatio primae causae, et non per propriam virtutem (De Pot., q.3, a.4).	The first effect is the act of being itself, which is presupposed by all other effects and which itself does not presuppose any other effect. Therefore, to give the act of being considered as such is the effect of the first cause alone according to its proper power; and whatever other cause gives the act of being does so in so far as there is in it the power and the operation of the first cause; it does not do so through its own power.

16. *ST*, I, q.45, a.1; *SCG*, II, c.16.

17. *De Potentia*, q.3, a.1:

Et ideo agens naturale non producit simpliciter ens, sed ens praeexistens et determinatum ad hoc vel ad aliud, ut puta ad speciem ignis, vel ad al-bedinem, vel ad aliquid hujusmodi. Et propter hoc agens naturale agit movendo; et ideo requirit materiam, quae sit subjectum mutationis vel motus, et propter hoc non potest aliquid ex nihilo facere. Ipse autem Deus e contrario est totaliter actus, et in comparatione sui quia est actus purus non habens potentiam per-mixtam, et in comparatione rerum quae sunt in actu, quia in eo est om-nium entium origo; unde per suam actionem producit totum ens sub-sistens, nullo praesupposito, utpote qui est totius esse principium, et secundum se totum. Et propter hoc ex nihilo aliquid facere potest; et haec ejus actio vocatur creatio. Cf. *SCG*, II, c.17.	Therefore, a natural agent does not produce what is a being absolutely, it produces a pre-existent being determined in this or that respect, for example, a being that belongs to the species fire, or to whiteness, or to something similar. And this is why a natural agent acts by moving and therefore must make use of matter, which is the subject of change or motion; and this is why it cannot make anything from nothing. But, on the contrary, God Himself is totally act, and this both with reference to Himself, since He is act without any admixed potency, and with reference to the things that actually exist, since the source of all things is to be found in Him. Hence, through His action God produces the whole of subsistent being, without anything presupposed to His action, since He is the cause of all being (*esse*) and this according to the whole of Himself. This is why He can make something from nothing. This action of His, moreover, is called creation.

18. *ST*, I, q.45, a.4. *De Potentia*, q.3, a.1, 12: "Proprie autem creatur res subsistens, quaecumque sit."

19. *Liber de Causis*, Prop.4: "Prima rerum creatarum est esse."

20. *ST*, I, q.8, a.1. *Cf.* I, q.4, a.1, ad 3, and I, q.7, a.1. — The connection between this notion and the notions of creation, causality, and the intimate presence of God in things is clearly stated in an early text of Saint Thomas:

Respondeo dicendum quod Deus essentialiter in omnibus rebus est, non tamen ita quod rebus commisceatur, quasi pars alicujus rei. Ad cujus evidentiam oportet tria praenotare. Primo . . . Secundum est quod esse cujuslibet rei et cujuslibet partis ejus est immediate a Deo, eo quod non ponimus, secundum fidem, aliquem creare nisi Deum. Creare autem est dare esse. Tertium est quod illud quod est causa esse non potest cessare ab operatione qua esse datur, quin ipsa res etiam esse cesset. Sicut enim dicit Avicenna (lib. I Sufficientiae, cap. XI), haec est differentia inter agens divinum et agens naturale, quod agens naturale est tantum causa motus, et agens divinum est causa esse. Unde, juxta ipsum, qualibet causa efficiente remota, removetur effectus suus; et ideo, remoto aedificatore, non tollitur esse domus, cujus causa est gravitas lapidum quae manet, sed fieri domus cujus causa erat; et similiter, remota causa essendi, tollitur esse . . . Ex quibus omnibus aperte colligitur quod Deus est unicuique intimus, sicut esse proprium rei est intimum ipsi rei, quae nec incipere nec durare posset, nisi per operationem Dei, per quam suo operi conjungitur ut in eo sit.

(*In I Sent.*, d.38, q.1, a.1; ed. P. Mandonnet, pp. 857–858.)

In reply we must say that God is essentially present in all things, not however in such a way that He is mixed with them as a part of anything. To understand this point we must begin by noting three things . . . First . . . The second is that the act of being of each thing, and of each of its parts, comes immediately from God, since according to faith we posit that only God creates. *Now to create is to give the act of being.* The third point is that the cause of the act of being cannot cease from the operation by which that act is given without the consequence that the thing itself ceases to be. For, as Avicenna says, the difference between the divine agent and a natural agent is this, that the natural agent is the cause only of motion whereas the divine agent is the cause of the act of being. Hence, according to Avicenna, suppress any given efficient cause and its effect is suppressed. Hence, when you suppress a builder, the act of being of a house is not removed since its cause is the weight of the stones, which weight still remains; what is removed is the coming to be of the house whose cause the builder was. And in the same way, remove the cause of being and the act of being is removed . . . From all these ideas we may clearly gather that God is intimately present to each thing, in the same way as the act of being proper to each thing is intimately present to it; for the thing cannot begin to be or endure without the action of God, through which God is joined to what He does so as to be present in it.

— On the place of Avicenna in the history of the notion of efficient causality, see ch. VIII, pp. 186–188.

21. *ST*, I, q.105, a.5.

22. *ST*, I, q.8, a.1. The corollaries following from the notion of the immediate presence of God to things and in things can be found in the articles devoted by the *Summa Theologiae* to "the special effects of the divine government" (*ST*, I, q.104). The more important ones will be examined in the following chapter, but it will prove useful for the reader to consult at once q.105: "The movement of God in creatures." God can move the matter immediately to the form; God can move bodies immediately: "intellectual operation is performed by the intellect in which it exists as by a secondary cause, but it proceeds from God as from its first cause" (*ST*, I, q.105, a.3, ad 1); God moves the created will, not as forcing it, but because He "gives the will its own natural inclination" (*ST*, I, q.105, a.4, ad 1). In short, "God works in every agent" (I, q.105, a.5). This last article is the one whose conclusion has just been the matter of our reflections: "and because in all things God Himself is properly the cause of the universal being which is innermost in all things, it follows that God works intimately in all things."

23. *ST*, I, q.8, a.3 and ad 1.

24. Hence the constant opposition of Thomas Aquinas to "those who deprive the things of nature of their own actions" (*SCG*, III, c. 69). All forms of occasionalism are thereby excluded from true Christian philosophy. The reason is that one cannot deprive a creature of its own efficacy without depriving it of its own being (*esse*), from which naturally flow all its operations. — Historical background of the doctrine: *ST*, I, q.115, a.1, and *De Potentia*, q.3, a.7.

25. Leo XIII, Encyclical Letter *Aeterni Patris;* any edition; for instance, in E. Gilson (ed.). *The Church Speaks to the Modern World*, Doubleday Image Book (Garden City, N.Y.: Doubleday and Company, Inc., 1954), p. 38.

Chapter 8. Being and causality

1. In view of the modern controversies concerning physical causality, it should be noted that Thomas Aquinas does not seem to think that there can be causality where there is no necessity. Even granting the statistical nature of physical laws (and physicists are those who know if it should be granted), the particular causal actions which the laws summarize still should be conceived as so many necessary consecutions of effects from causes. Two notions should be distinguished: causality and previsibility. Where there is causality, there is necessity, but there is not necessarily previsibility. A cause can be a free cause, or its particular action can be due to chance; its effect is therefore not previsible; nevertheless, *if* the cause does act, its effect follows from it with necessity; otherwise it is not a cause. Inversely, the global result of a large number of particular causal actions can be previsible; it then assumes the form of a natural law; as such, it expresses the statistical (average) result of many relations of causality, each of which is (or can be) at one and the same time both imprevisible in some aspects of its effect and necessarily determined in producing it. A great deal of confusion arises, in contemporary discussions concerning the nature of physical laws, from the fact that the notion of causality is conceived as inseparable from that of previsibility. — See *ST*, I-II q.75, a.1, obj. 2; *De Malo*, q.3, a.3, ad 3.

2. We are here contrasting the authentic Augustinian notion of "seminal reasons" with the Thomistic conception of efficient causality. According to Augustine, each and every future effect is already hidden in its causes as a child is present in the mother's womb (*De Trinitate*, III, c.9; PL 42, 878). Thomas Aquinas identifies these latent seeds (among other meanings) with the Aristotelian elements. And, indeed, since everything is made up of some combination of these elements, it can be said that all things were created in them as in their universal causes from the very beginning of the world (*ST*, I, q.115, a.2.). Thomas Aquinas is here saving the authority of Saint Augustine much more than he is really adopting this doctrine. It should be noted, however, that Thomas has always considered unlikely what looks to us as the obvious interpretation of the doctrine of Augustine on this point.

3. Avicenna, *Metaphysics*, Tr. VI, ch. 1. See *History of Christian Philosophy*, pp. 210–211.

4. L. Gardet, *La pensée religeuse d'Avicenne* (Ibn Sina) (Paris: Librairie Philosophique J. Vrin, 1951).

5. There is a material proof that Thomas Aquinas carefully read Avicenna on causality. In his own commentary *In Metaphysicam Aristotelis*, lib.V,

lect. 2, nos. 766–770, Thomas has developed the notion that "according to Avicenna, the efficient cause is fourfold in kind; namely: *perficiens, disponens, adjuvans,* and *consilians";* there is the same division in the commentary *In Octo Libros Physicorum Aristotelis,* lib.II, lect. 5, no. 180: *perficiens, praeparans, adjuvans et consilians.* In neither passage does Thomas Aquinas mention the all-important problem raised by Avicenna concerning the religious origin of the notion of *causa agens,* or, in the language of Algazel's translator, of *causa efficiens.*

6. Saint Augustine, *De Diversis Quaestionibus 83,* q.28 (PL 40, col. 18); Saint Thomas, *ST,* I, q.45, a.5.

7. The assimilation of the two notions of *causa movens* and *causa efficiens* is completed in the *Commentary* on *Metaphysics,* V, lect. 2, no. 765:

Tertio modo dicitur causa unde primum est principium permutationis et quietis; et haec est causa movens, vel efficiens . . . Et universaliter omne faciens est causa facti per hunc modum, et permutans permutati.

In a third sense a thing is said to be a cause as being the first source of change and rest. This is the moving cause, or the efficient cause . . . And, in general, every maker is in this sense the cause of the thing made, and every transformer of the thing transformed.

And, again, no. 770:

Ad hoc autem genus causae [i.e. causae efficientis] *reducitur quicquid facit aliquid quocumquemodo esse, non solum secundum esse substantiale, sed secundum accidentale; quod contingit in omni motu. Et ideo non solum dicit* [Aristoteles] *quod faciens sit causa facti, sed etiam mutans mutati.*

To this class of cause is reduced whatever makes something to be in any manner, and this not only according to a substantial mode of being but also according to an accidental one. This takes place in all motion. That is why Aristotle says not only that a maker is the cause of the thing made, but also that a changer is the cause of the thing changed.

In the last lines, note the words *faciens causa facti,* translating the words of Aristotle: *to poioun tou poioumenou (Metaph.,* V, 2, 1013 a31–32). The class of the *to poioun*—that is, of "the making"—is for him a particular case of causality by mode of transmutation, itself of the same nature as causality by mode of motion. The influence of the notion of creation has led Christian philosophers to conceive the moving cause as an efficient cause, whereas in Aristotle's philosophy the efficient (making) cause was rather conceived after the manner of a moving cause.

8. *De Potentia,* q.7, a.2.

9. *In Met.*, V, lect. 1, no. 751.

10. *De Veritate*, q.27, a.7; *De Potentia*, q.7, a.5.

11. *SCG*, II, c.6, ※4; c.21, ※9; c.22, ※3.

12. *SCG*, I, c.25, ※10.

13. Aristotle, *Metaphysics*, VIII, 3, 1043 b32–1044 a11 (quoted from the translation by W. D. Ross, in *Basic Writings*, vol. I, p. 816). See Thomas Aquinas, *De Anima*, a.9.

14. The doctrine of Dionysius should not be hardened into an opposition between the Plotinian notion of God as the One-and-Good and the Christian notion of God as Being. An essentially Christian doctrine, the theology of the *Divine Names* does not separate God as "being" from God as "one" or "good." This enabled Thomas Aquinas to assimilate the doctrine of Dionysius to his own theology of HE WHO IS, although even in Thomas Aquinas, their distinction remains perceptible. See *In Librum Dionysii de Divinis Nominibus*, V, lect. 1; ed. C. Pera, no. 629.

15. *ST*, I-II, q.49, a.2; *SCG*, I, c.50, ※ 7. *In Librum Dionysii de Divinis Nominibus*, ed. cit., no. 775, where an Augustinian source is quoted.

16. *SCG*, III, c.83.

17. *ST*, II-II, q.104, a.1: *and therefore just as, following the natural order itself established by God, the lower among natural things are subject to the motion of the higher, so too in human affairs according to the order of natural and divine law those who are subjects are obliged to obey their superiors.*

18. *SCG*, III, c.19, ※5.

19. *SCG*, III, c.21.

20. *SCG*, II, c.38.

21. *ST*, I, q.104, a.4.

22. *ST*, I, q.65, a.1, ad 1.

23. This position is made possible, in the philosophy of Avicenna, by his doctrine of the radical indifference of essences with respect to existence or non-existence. For this reason, the existential status of an essence (neces-

sary, possible, etc.) never belongs to it in virtue of itself, but only in virtue of its cause. The case of God is different precisely because "God has no essence." All the existential determinations of essences come to them from without.

24. *De Potentia,* q.5, a.3.

25. *Ibid.* See *ST,* I, q.104, a.4.

26. *SCG,* II, c.30.

1. See E. Gilson, *Introduction à l'étude de saint Augustin*, pp. 53–56.

2. Thomas has denied, against Nemesius (whom he mistook for Gregory of Nyssa), that Aristotle had conceived the human soul as a material form similar to other material forms. Gregory (Nemesius), he says, has arbitrarily construed the doctrine of Aristotle in this sense (*imposuit Aristoteli quod posuit animam non per se subsistentem esse: De Spirit. Creat.*, a.2). Cf. *SCG*, II, c.79, ✗ 14:

   > It is clear from the texts of Aristotle that, while he maintains that the soul is a form, he does not say it is non-subsistent and therefore corruptible —an interpretation which Gregory of Nyssa attributes to him. For Aristotle excludes the intellective form from the generality of other forms, in saying that it remains after the body *and* is a certain substance.

   The problem, precisely, was to know if the intellective form *is* a separate substance, or, on the contrary, the substantial form of a body.

3. A. C. Pegis, *St. Thomas and the Problem of the Soul in the Thirteenth Century* (Toronto: Institute of Mediaeval Studies, 1934) pp. 77–120.

4. See the Disputed Question *De Spiritualibus Creaturis*, a.2, which shows the position of the problem with the clearness of a blueprint. Thomas asks whether a spiritual substance can be united with a body, and the *Sed Contra* answers, yes, the thing is bound to be possible, because on the one hand Dionysius says in his *Divine Names* that the soul is an intellectual substance having an everlasting life (IV, 2; PG, 3, col. 696c), while, on the other, Aristotle defines the soul as the form of the body (*De Anima*, II, 1, 412 a19–21); consequently, the human soul must be both a substance and a form. The fourth objection was that the soul must be united to the body by its very essence, not as a form, because otherwise, not being essential, their union would be accidental. The answer is that:

   > . . . it is according to its essence that the soul is the form of the body, and not according to something superadded. Nevertheless, inasmuch as it is attained by the body, it is form (in quantum attingitur a corpore, est forma), whereas, inasmuch as it exceeds the proportion of the body, it is called spirit, or spiritual substance (*De Spirit. Creat.*, a.2. ad 4).

   As will be seen, far from representing any concession to another doctrine, this exactly formulates the position proper to Thomas Aquinas: the soul can be both a substance and the form of a body, because it is *qua* spiritual substance that it is form: *anima secundum suam essentiam est forma corporis.*

5. E. Gilson, *Introduction à l'étude de saint Augustin*, pp. 254–258.

6. *In I Sent.*, d.8, q.5, a.2 (ed. P. Mandonnet, pp. 229–230):

Si autem inveniamus aliquam quid-ditatem quae non sit composita ex materia et forma, illa quidditas aut est esse suum aut non. Si illa quid-ditas sit esse suum, sic erit essentia ipsius Dei, quae est suum esse, et erit omnino simplex. Si vero non sit ipsum esse, oportet quod habeat esse acquisitum ab alio, sicut est om-nis quidditas creata . . . Unde an-gelus vel anima potest dici quidditas vel natura vel forma simplex, in-quantum eorum quidditas non com-ponitur ex diversis; sed tamen advenit ibi compositio quidditatis et esse.

If we should find some quiddity that is not composed of matter and form, this quiddity is its own act of being or it is not. If it is, it will be the essence of God Himself, which is its own act of being, and it will be absolutely simple. But if it is not its own act of being it must acquire that act from another, and such is every created quiddity . . . Hence, an angel or a soul can be called a simple quiddity or nature or form, in so far as their quiddity is not composed of diverse elements. Nevertheless, there is here present a composition of quiddity and the act of being.

De Anima, a.1, ad 6:

Ad sextum dicendum quod anima humana, cum sit subsistens, com-posita est ex potentia et actu. Nam ipsa substantia animae non est suum esse, sed comparatur ad ipsum ut potentia ad actum. Nec tamen sequitur quod anima non possit esse forma corporis; quia etiam in aliis formis id quod est ut forma et actus in comparatione ad unum est ut potentia in comparatione ad aliud; sicut diaphanum formaliter advenit aeri, quod tamen est potentia re-spectu luminis.

To the sixth objection we must re-ply that since the human soul is sub-sistent, it is composed of potency and act. For the substance itself of the soul is not its own act of being, but is related to it as potency to act. Nor does it follow from this that the soul cannot be the form of the body, since, even among other forms, that which is form and act in relation to one thing is as potency in relation to another; as the diapha-nous is formally present to air but yet is in potency with respect to light.

See (*De Spirit. Creat.*, a.1, end of the Answer.)

ST, I, q.75, a.5, ad 4 (*Basic Writings*, vol. I, p. 691):

But in intellectual substances, there is composition of actuality and poten-tiality, not, indeed, of matter and form, but of form and participated being. Therefore some [Boethius] say that they are composed of that whereby they are and that which they are, for being (esse) itself is that by which a thing is.

7. *In I Sent.*, ibid.

8. *De Anima*, a.1, ad 1:

Non tamen sequitur quod corpus ei [animae] accidentaliter uniatur, quia illud idem esse quod est animae communicat corpori, ut sit unum esse totius compositi.	Nevertheless, it does not follow that the body is joined to the soul accidentally, since the very same act of being that belongs to the soul is communicated by it to the body, so that the whole composite has one act of being.

Note in a.9, the transition from *actus primus* to *actus secundus* and operation:

Sed quia eadem forma quae dat esse materiae est etiam operationis principium, eo quod unumquodque agit secundum quod est actu, necesse est quod anima, sicut et quaelibet alia forma, sit etiam operationis principium.	However, since it is the same form that gives the act of being to matter and is likewise the principle of operation, for the reason that each thing acts according as it is in act, it is necessary that the soul, like any other form, be also the principle of operation.

Whereupon the principle of the hierarchical order of causes presently follows:

Sed considerandum est quod secundum gradum formarum in perfectione essendi est etiam gradus earum in virtute operandi, cum operatio sit existentis in actu. Et ideo quanto aliqua forma est maioris perfectionis in dando esse, tanto etiam est maioris perfectionis in operando (op. cit., a.9).	But we must consider that according to the gradation of forms in the perfection of being there is also among them a gradation in the power of operation, since operation belongs to that which exists in act. And therefore, the more perfect a form is in giving the act of being, the more perfect it is in operation.

This unity of *esse* for the whole substance is expressed with particular force in a passage of the *De Spirit. Creat.*, a.2:

Ad tertium dicendum quod anima habet esse subsistens, in quantum esse suum non dependet a corpore, utpote supra materiam corporalem elevatum. Et tamen ad hujus esse communionem recipit corpus, ut sic sit unum esse animae et corporis, quod est esse hominis. Si autem secundum aliud esse uniretur sibi corpus, sequeretur quod esset unio accidentalis.	To the third objection we must say that the soul has a subsistent act of being in so far as its act of being does not depend upon the body since it is raised above corporeal matter. Nevertheless, the soul receives the body into communion in this act of being, so that there is one act of being for soul and body, which is the act of being of man. But if the body were joined to the soul according to another act of being it would follow that the union would be accidental.

9. Cf. *In Librum de Causis*, II, lect. 8; *SCG*, II, c.68.

10. *SCG*, II, c.79, ※2.

11. E. Gilson, *Jean Duns Scot. Introduction à ses positions fondamentales*, p. 468.

12. Here is one of the more curious among these theological consequences. Having to describe the miraculous preservation of the species of bread and wine after the consecration, Thomas Aquinas, with remarkable intrepidity, turns to his own notion of substantial being. He says that, before the consecration, the accidents of the two substances, bread and wine, have no *esse* of their own; as is normal, they then have no other *esse* than that of their substance; their *esse est inesse*. After the consecration it is not so; the accidents of bread and wine should lose their existence in losing the substance in which alone they have being (*esse*); in fact, since we still see them and touch them, they still continue to exist. The only way to describe this miracle is to say that, after the consecration, the eucharistic accidents receive from God an act of being of their own. Thomas Aquinas resolutely enters this amazing way. According to him, a eucharistic accident is composed of its essence (the sensible quality it is) and its own act of being. Hence the formula, speaking of such accidents: *sunt composita ex esse et id quod est*, "just," Thomas intrepidly adds, "as it has been said in the case of angels" (*ST*, III, q.77, a.1, ad 4). We now therefore have these miraculous beings, separate accidents! "This," Scotus says, "I do not understand" (*sed istud non capio*). To him, every entity (*essentia*) has its own *esse*; now accidents are entities, so that they too must have their own *esse* (E. Gilson, *Jean Duns Scot*, p. 206, note 1). To him, as to Thomas Aquinas, the subsistence of the accidents is miraculous, but the miracle consists in their being preserved apart from their substance, not in their being given by God acts of being specially created to this end. *Omnis essentia est actus*, Scotus says; yes, Thomas would answer, but only one essence is an *actus essendi*, the essence of God.

13. E. Gilson, *Jean Duns Scot*, p. 487.

14. *SCG*, II, c.59, ※※1–6.

15. *SCG*, II, c.70, ※1. Thus to reverse authorities was a dialectical move often used in medieval disputations. Such a move was very different from what we call a historical demonstration.

16. It must be noted that there is no necessity to subscribe to the conclusions of Averroes even if one does not agree with Thomas Aquinas. Nothing proves that the Averroistic interpretation of Aristotle is historically cor-

rect. Pomponatius was of the opinion that both Averroes and Thomas Aquinas were wrong in saying that Aristotle had considered the human intellect immortal (Petrus Pomponatius, *Tractatus de Immortalitate Animae*, c.IV, ed. G. Mora, Bologna: Nanni & Flammenghi, 1954, p. 66), but he also considered the Averroistic doctrine of the unity of the human intellect not only as *falsissima, verum inintelligibilis, et monstruosa et ab Aristotele prorsus aliena, immo existimo quod tanta fatuitas nunquam fuerit nedum credita, verum excogitata (op. cit.*, ch. IV, p. 48). Pomponatius has nothing to add to the refutation of this position by Thomas Aquinas, who so completely destroyed it that the supporters of Averroes were left without an answer. *Totum enim impugnat* [Thomas], *dissipat et annihilat, nullumque Averroistis refugium relictum est, nisi convicia et maledicta in divinum et sanctissimum virum (ibid.*). It was therefore possible to maintain against Averroes that Aristotle did not teach the unity of the human intellect, and to maintain against Thomas Aquinas that Aristotle never taught the immortality of the intellective souls of men.

17. The arguments used by Thomas Aquinas to prove that "according to the words of Aristotle the intellect must be said to be united to the body as its form" (*SCG*, II, c.70) hardly keep faith with their promise, at least in so far as our own notion of an Aristotelian statement is concerned. In order to justify the title of this chapter, Thomas should have quoted a passage of Aristotle saying that the intellect is united to the body as its form. Instead, Thomas first demonstrates that "the heavens are composed of an intellectual soul and a body" (*SCG*, II, c.70, ✗3) and then that "the intellect, by its substance, is united to the heavenly body as its form" (*ibid.*, ✗5); in fine, Thomas argues that:

. . . *the human body is the noblest of all lower bodies, and by its equable temperament most closely resembles the heavens, which are completely devoid of contrariety; so that in Aristotle's judgment the intellectual substance is united to the human body not by any phantasms, but as its form* (ibid., ✗6).

This kind of argument amounts to acknowledging that the statement under discussion is not to be found anywhere in the writings of Aristotle. The texts of the *De Anima* (II, 3, 414 b19 and 415 a9) quoted by Thomas Aquinas in this chapter do not say that men, and the other beings in which "there is intellect and the power of understanding," are united to this intellect and power as to their forms. And this is what had to be demonstrated.

18. *Dictionnaire de théologie catholique*, vol. VIII (1925), coll. 2681–2683.

19. Mansi, *Amplissima Collectio*, vol. XXXII, col. 843, as quoted by M. H. Laurent, O.P., in his Introduction to Cajetan, *De Anima*, ed. J. Coquelle, pp. xxxviii–xxxix.

20. Quoted by M. H. Laurent, *loc. cit.*, p. xxxv.

21. On the controversy conducted by the Dominican Chrysostom of Casale (Javelli) in his own *Quaestiones in tres libros de anima Aristotelis*, as well as by Spina in his *Propugnaculum*, consult the remarkable Introduction of M. H. Laurent, O.P., to the already-quoted Coquelle edition of Cajetan's *De Anima*. Harvey of Nedellec (Hervaeus Natalis), also a Minister General of the Dominican Order (1318), the man who promoted the canonization of Thomas Aquinas and fought many a fight for his doctrine, saw nothing wrong with denying the real composition of essence and existence in finite beings. The unavoidable consequence was that, two centuries before Cajetan, Harvey declared the immortality of the human soul impossible to prove.

22. What Thomas' doctrine of the immortality of the soul represents in the mind of some of his present-day disciples can be seen from an article by J. Y. Jolif, O.P., "Affirmation rationnelle de l'immortalité de l'âme chez saint Thomas," in *Lumière et vie*, 4 (1955), 59–78.

Chapter 10. *Man and knowledge*

1. John Locke, *An Essay Concerning Human Understanding*, Book III, ch. 1, 1–3 (why man was fitted by God to articulate sounds), Bk. II, ch. 11, 9–10 (abstraction puts a perfect distinction between men and brutes).

2. *De Veritate*, q.15, a.1: *Perfectio autem spiritualis . . .*

3. *ST*, I, q.75, a.7, ad 3.

4. *ST*, I, q.76, a.1.

5. *Ibid.*, and ad 4.

6. *Ibid.*, ad 5. — The same doctrine is found in *SCG*, II, c.68, ✗ 3, and in the already-quoted perfect text: *De Spiritualibus Creaturis*, a.2, ad 3. — On the relation between the notion of *esse* and this problem, *De Anima*, a.9.

7. *ST*, I, a.55, a.2. See I, q.89, a.1.

8. *ST*, I, a.79, a.8. See *De Veritate*, q.15, a.1.

9. *ST*, I, q.1, a.7: *De Anima*, a.13; *In Aristotelis Libros de Anima*, II, lect. 6 and 7.

10. Intellectual knowledge is not properly *caused* in us by sensible things. It

is caused by the sense powers to the extent that these cause in us the phantasms without which there is no intellectual knowledge;

. . . but since the phantasms cannot of themselves immute the possible intellect, but require to be made actually intelligible by the agent intellect, it cannot be said that sensible knowledge is the total and perfect cause of intellectual knowledge, but rather is in a way the matter of the cause (*ST*, I, q.84, a.6; see *Quodlibetum* VIII, q.2, a.1).

Still, the intellect cannot understand without turning to the phantasms, first and always. Even when using already acquired knowledge, we must turn to the imagination in order actually to understand it. For the same reason, teachers resort to examples in order to help students understand abstract truth. But the general principle from which this conclusion can be deduced is that, in all knowing subjects, the proper object of a power of knowledge is proportioned to the nature of this power. Because animal souls are material forms, their proper object is the material form perceived by sense with all the individuating characteristics resulting from its materiality. Because angels are separate substances, the proper object of their intellect has to be an intelligible substance separate from matter: "Whereas the proper object of the human intellect, which is united to a body, is the quiddity or nature existing in corporeal matter." This brings us back to the conclusion that, "for the intellect to understand actually its proper object, it must of necessity turn to phantasms in order to perceive the universal nature existing in the individual" (*ST*, I, q.84, a.7). These are texts, not only to read, but to meditate upon, until the cardinal notion of *objectum proprium* is clear in the mind. See also *De Veritate*, q.10, a.6.

11. *In Boethium de Hebdomadibus*, cap. II (in *Opuscula Omnia*, ed. P. Mandonnet, vol. I, pp. 173–174). — See John Locke, *Essay*, II, 8, 1, particularly:

. . . each abstract idea being distinct, so that of any two the one can never be the other, the mind will, by its intuitive knowledge, perceive their difference; and therefore in propositions no two whole ideas can ever be affirmed one of another. For how near of kin soever they may seem to be, and how certain soever it is that man is an animal, or rational, or white, yet every one, at first hearing, perceives the falsehood of these propositions: "Humanity is animality," or "rationality," or "whiteness"; and this is as evident as the most allowed maxims.

12. *In I Sent.*, d.19, q.5, a.1.

13. *In I Sent.*, d.19, q.5, a.1, ad 7 (ed. P. Mandonnet, vol. I, p. 97). In his *Commentary* on the *Metaphysics* (VI, lect. 4, no. 1232), Thomas notes the distinction of the two operations of the intellect, but, perhaps because

he is here interpreting Aristotle, who never mentioned any act of being (*esse*), the commentary does not appropriate the apprehension of essence to the *indivisibilium intelligentia* nor the apprehension of existence to judgment. On the contrary, in his commentary on the *De Trinitate* of Boethius (q.V, a.3) Thomas again affirms that *prima quidem operatio respicit ipsam naturam rei . . . secunda operatio respicit ipsum esse rei.* Thomas maintained this important position to the end of his life.

14. *SCG*, I, c.14, ※ 2.

15. *In I Sent.*, d.3, q.1, a.1, ad 4. — As has been expressly noted (above, p. 140), the negative theology of Thomas Aquinas presupposes a positive, or affirmative, theology without which the "way of negation" itself would not be conceivable. Neither one of the two "ways" should be neglected, but there is no doubt that, in the doctrine of Thomas Aquinas, the way of negation has the last word. The ultimate reason for this is that, in God, everything is the very act of being (*De Veritate*, q.2, a.11). In this question Thomas establishes that the names of creatures are predicated of God neither purely univocally nor purely equivocally. The two aspects of the question, and their exact balance, are perfectly expressed in the definition of the Fourth Lateran Council, Decretal 3, *Damnamus ergo . . .* : "However great a similarity one can assign between the Creator and His creature, one should mark between them an even greater dissimilarity."

16. K. Jaspers, *Vernunft und Existenz. Fünf Vorlesungen* (Bremen: Jos. Storm Verlag, 1949), ch. II, pp. 34–41.

17. On this point Thomas Aquinas simply fell heir to the natural realism of the Greeks, especially that of Aristotle. The decisive passage on which to meditate is found in *Metaphysics*, IV, 6, 1011 a3–14 (in the Commentary of Thomas Aquinas, IV, lect. 15, nos. 708–710). The position common to Aristotle and Thomas is that, since everyone clearly knows whether he is asleep or awake, well or sick, and so on, it is silly to ask for a demonstrative justification of a cognition of which we are sure. Those who do so do not content themselves with knowing, they also want to prove to themselves that they do know. This, Aristotle says, is to look for a demonstration of that of which there is no demonstration.

18. An illusion to be avoided is that the problems related to the conditions under which human knowledge is possible are today considered as either scientifically settled or philosophically out of date. It is not so. Einstein credited Kant with having established that it is senseless to posit an external world devoid of all intelligibility. But how is it that the world is intelligible? "The eternally incomprehensible about the world," Einstein has said, "is its comprehensibility": *Man kann sagen: das ewig*

Unbegreifliche an der Welt ist ihre Begreiflichkeit . . . ("Physik und Realitat" in *Zeitschrift für freie deutsche Forschung*, Paris, 1938, pp. 6–7). Similar remarks are found in Erwin Schrödinger's essay, "What Is Life?" Speaking of the hereditary transmission of certain types permanent for centuries, Schrödinger observes:

That is a marvel than which only one is greater; one that, if intimately connected with it, yet lies on a different plane. I mean the fact that we, whose total being is based on a marvelous interplay of this very kind, yet possess the power of acquiring considerable knowledge about it. I think it possible that this knowledge may advance to little short of a complete understanding.

(Erwin Schrödinger, *What Is Life? & Other Scientific Essays.* New York: Doubleday Anchor Books, 1956, p. 32.) In other words, it is a matter for wonder whether science can account for its own possibility. And, indeed, only philosophy can ask the question with any chance of finding a valid answer.

Chapter 11. Man and will

1. This view has been opposed by Yves Simon, in his excellent book *Ontologie du connaître* (Paris: Desclée de Brouwer, 1934), pp. 76–77. To our interpretation, the author says, we can oppose this categorical text: *essentia est actus primus, operatio actus secundus* (*De Anima*, a.6, ad 2). The formula quoted by Yves Simon is simply not to be found in this text. Thomas even says there the very reverse; to wit, that *ipsum esse est actus ultimus*, which means, the *ultimate* act in the sense of *supreme*, above which there is no other.

2. See, for instance, *De Veritate*, q.22, a.1, at the beginning of the Answer, where Thomas speaks of the *convenientia* of effects with their causes; also, of *hujusmodi convenientiae et utilitates.* In the same Answer: *omnia naturalia in ea quae eis conveniunt sunt inclinata.* Since resemblance (*similitudo*) is "similarity in form" (*convenientia in forma*), the same relationship can be described as a resemblance in nature (*similitudo secundum esse naturae*—ad 3). Again: *unumquodque appetit bonum naturaliter sibi conveniens* (ad 4). Strictly speaking, all that which is, is good; being and goodness are the same thing, but not every being is the good of every other being.

3. *SCG*, III, c.3, ⁂⁂1–2.

4. *SCG*, III, c.3, ⁂6. The doctrine of evil is but a corollary of the doctrine of the good. With great insistence, because of the survival of Manichaeism in the doctrines of the Albigenses (affirming that, along with goodness,

evil is a positive principle in reality), Thomas establishes that since goodness is being, evil is only non-being. The arguments whereby some
maintain that "evil is a nature or a thing" are set forth and answered
in *SCG*, III, c.8 and c.9. Since evil is non-being, absolute evil is impossible;
absolute being and absolute good are possible, absolute non-being and
absolute evil are nothing. So the cause of evil always is some good (otherwise it would have no cause: *SCG*, III, c.10). For the same reason, the
subject of evil must be a good (because non-being cannot be the subject
of anything: *SCG*, III, c.11). This realism of the good justifies the metaphysical optimism that befits a Christian conception of the universe seen
as the effect of the pure Act of Being and an analogical participation in
it. One must read, on this point, the enlightening chapter of *SCG*, III,
c.12, *That evil does not entirely destroy good*. Evil always has a cause
(*SCG*, III, c.13), but this is always an accidental cause (*SCG*, III, c.14);
namely, instead of good, a semblance of good. The reduction of this
problem to the fundamental notion of being (*habens esse*) is effected by
Thomas himself in a few perfect lines:

Each thing has being (esse) *according to its essence. Now, in so far as it
has being* (esse), *it has a share of good; for if good is what all desire, being
itself must be called a good, since all things desire being* [lit., desire to be:
cum omnia esse appetant]. *Therefore a thing is good in so far as it has
an essence. But good and evil are opposed to each other. Therefore
nothing is evil in so far as it has an essence. Therefore no essence is evil*
(SCG, III, c.7, ✕3).

5. *SCG*, III, c.16, ✕1. See Aristotle, *Nic. Eth.*, I, 1094 a2.

6. *De Veritate*, q.22, a.1.

7. *Ibid.*

8. *ST*, I, q.6, a.2, ad 2.

9. *De Verit.*, q.22, a.1.

10. *De Verit.*, q.22, a.2.

11. *Ibid.*

12. *SCG*, III, c.19.

13. *SCG*, III, c.20, ✕2.

14. *Ibid.*, ✕7. See Aristotle, *Physics.*, III, 1, 201 a28.

15. *SCG*, III, c.21, ✕4.

16. The principle of this answer is posited in *SCG*, I, c.26, ※5:

Quod est commune multis non est aliquid praeter multa nisi sola ratione: sicut animal *non est aliud praeter Socratem et Platonem et alia animalia nisi intellectu . . . Multo igitur minus et ipsum esse commune est aliquid praeter omnes res existentes nisi in intellectu solum.*	What is common to many things is not something outside the many except in notion alone, as *animal* is not something outside Socrates and Plato and the other animals except in notion . . . Much less, therefore, is common being itself something outside existing things except in notion alone.

Incidentally, this is one reason God cannot be *esse commune*, for He does not exist only in the intellect, but also *in rerum natura:* in reality.

17. *ST*, I-II, q.5, a.8:

   . . . *all things in their own way are inclined by appetite toward good, but in different ways. Some are inclined to good by their natural disposition, without knowledge, as plants and inanimate bodies. Such inclination toward good is called* natural appetite. *Others, again, are inclined toward good, but with some knowledge. Not that they know the very nature of goodness; they rather apprehend some particular good, as is the case with the sense, which knows the sweet, the white, and so on. The inclination that follows this apprehension is called* sensitive appetite. *Other things, again, have an inclination toward good, but with a knowledge whereby they perceive the nature of goodness. This belongs to the intellect. Things so inclined are most perfectly inclined toward what is good; not, indeed, as if they were guided only by another toward the good, like things devoid of knowledge, nor as if they were guided only toward some particular good, as things that have only sensitive knowledge, but as inclined toward the universal good itself. Such inclination is* termed will.

   Note the expression: *inclinata in ipsum universale bonum.*

18. The shift in meaning is perceptible in the very text quoted above, *ST*, I-II, q.5, a.8. After saying that the object of the will is universal good, Thomas presently adds: "from which it appears that nothing can quiet the will of man, except the universal good (*universale bonum*), which is not to be found in anything created, but only in God, because every creature has a participated goodness."

19. *SCG*, III, c.25, ※1.

20. *SCG*, III, c.25, ※2; c.17.

21. *SCG*, III, c.25, ※3.

22. *SCG*, III, c.25, ※ ※ 2, 5, 6.

23. *SCG*, III, c.26.

24. A short and complete explanation of the nature of love is found in
ST, I-II, q.26, a.2. Strictly speaking, love is understood, in a quite realistic
way, as a passion. A passion is an alteration undergone by a subject. The
special passion called "love" consists in a sort of "coaptatio"; that is, in a
determination of the structure of a certain being, by which the agent
causes it to be adapted to itself (the patient is being coadapted to the
agent). In simpler terms, this means that, in such cases, the agent causes
itself to be felt or known by the patient as "good." This condition of
befittingness, precisely, is the "complacency" of the desiring subject in a
certain object. The initial immutation of desire by the desirable, which is
this very complacency, is love: *Prima ergo immutatio appetitus ab appeti-
bili vocatur amor, qui nihil est aliud quam complacentia appetibilis* (*ST*,
I-II, q.26, a.2). From love (*i.e.*, this very complacency) a movement of
the subject to the loved object naturally follows. In the qualitative
physics of Aristotle, heaviness is caused in a stone by the "connaturality"
there is between it and its natural place. In Newtonian language, it is
"attracted" to it. The point to understand here is that "heaviness itself,"
which is the origin of the motion of the stone to its natural place (*i.e.*,
down), is that which can be called "natural love": *et ipsa gravitas, quae
est principium motus ad locum connaturalem . . . potest quodammodo
dici amor naturalis* (*ST*, I-II, q.26, a.2). The complete description of the
situation is as follows: 1. an immutation of appetite by the desirable (this
immutation is called *love*, and it consists in the complacency of appetite
in the appetible); 2. following from this complacency, a movement
toward the object (this movement is called *desire*); 3. finally, if it be
not frustrated, desire rests in the possession of the desired object: this
rest, or repose, in the object of love is *joy* (*gaudium*) (*ST, loc. cit.*).
See *SCG*, III, c.17, ※ ※ 2–3; Dante, *Paradiso*, 33, 145.

25. *ST*, I-II, q.26, a.2 and ad 2; q.28, a.2.

26. *ST*, I-II, q.27, a.2, ad 2.

27. *Ibid.*

28. *ST*, II-II, q.27, aa.1–2.

29. *ST*, II-II, q.27, a.4, ad 1. The word *dilectio* is defined in *ST*, I-II, q.26, a.3.
Four words, Thomas says, are in some way related to one and the same
thing: *amor* (love), *dilectio* (dilection), *charitas* (charity), and *amicitia*
(friendship). The word *dilection* signifies the same thing as love, with,
over and above this fundamental meaning, the connotation of a choice

preceding love properly so called (*addit enim dilectio supra amorem electionem praecedentem, ut ipsum nomen sonat*). For this reason, only the human appetite (will) is capable of dilection, because it is the only form of appetite that presupposes intellectual knowledge and, thereby, leaves open the possibility of a choice (*election:* to elect, to choose).

30. Dante, *Paradiso*, 33, 142.

Chapter 12.   Man and society

1. *ST*, I, q.47, aa.2 and 3. See Aristotle, *Metaph.*, VII, 3, 1043 b34.

2. *SCG*, III, cc17–18.

3. *ST*, I-II, q.93, a.3.

4. *ST*, I-II, q.93, a.3, ad 2.

5. *ST*, I, q.108, a.5, ad 3.

6. *ST*, I-II, q.96, a.4; II-II, q.69, a.4.

7. Aristotle, *Politics*, II, 6, 1270 b17.

8. Aristotle, *Politics*, I, 2, 1254 b15.

9. *SCG*, III, c.81, ⚌6.

10. *SCG*, III, c.112.

BIBLIOGRAPHY

The present Bibliography includes the principal sources used in the writing of the text, as well as the books and articles which have been referred to in the Notes.

A. PRINCIPAL SOURCES

1. Saint Thomas Aquinas

   A. OPERA OMNIA: Parma, 1862–1870, 25 volumes; Paris: Vivès, 1870–1871, in 34 vols., by Fretté et Maré; Leonine Edition: Rome, 1882– , 16 volumes to date.

   B. INDIVIDUAL EDITIONS:
      I. *De Ente et Essentia*, ed. M.-D. Roland-Gosselin, O.P. Paris: Librairie Philosophique J. Vrin, 1926.
      II. *De Spiritualibus Creaturis*, ed. Leo Keller, S.J. Rome: Universitas Pontificia Gregoriana, 1946.
      III. *Expositio Super Librum Boethii De Trinitate*, ed. Bruno Decker. Leiden: E. J. Brill, 1955. Questions Five and Six have also been edited by Paul Wyser, O.P. Fribourg: Société Philosophique, 1948.
      IV. *Summa Contra Gentiles.* Rome: Apud Sedem Commissionis Leoninae, 1934.
      V. *Summa Theologiae.* 5 vols. Ottawa: Institut Albert-le-Grand, 1941 ff.
      VI. *Super Librum de Causis Expositio*, ed. H. D. Saffrey. Fribourg: Société Philosophique, 1954.

   C. CONVENIENT REPRINTINGS:
      I. *Opuscula Omnia*, ed. P. Mandonnet, O.P., 5 vols. Paris: P. Lethielleux, 1927.
      II. *Opuscula Omnia*, vol. I, *Opuscula Philosophica*, ed. Joannes Perrier, O.P. Paris: P. Lethielleux, 1949.
      III. *Opuscula Philosophica*, ed. R. M. Spiazzi, O.P. Rome-Turin: Marietti Editori, 1954.
      IV. *Scriptum Super Sententiis*, ed. P. Mandonnet and M. F. Moss. Paris: P. Lethielleux 1929–1947 (4 vols. to date).
      V. *Quaestiones Disputatae*, ed. R. M. Spiazzi. 2 vols. Rome-Turin: Marietti Editori, 1949.
      VI. *Quaestiones Quodlibetales*, ed. R. M. Spiazzi. Rome-Turin: Marietti Editori, 1949.

VII. *In Librum Dionysii de Divinis Nominibus,* ed. C. Pera, O.P. Rome-Turin: Marietti Editori, 1950.

VIII. *In Aristotelis Libros Peri Hermeneias et Posteriorum Analyticorum Expositio,* ed. R. M. Spiazzi, O.P. Rome-Turin: Marietti Editori, 1955.

IX. *In Ar. Librum De Anima Commentarium,* ed. A. Pirotta (ed. tertia). Rome-Turin: Marietti Editori, 1948.

X. *In Octo Libros Physicorum Ar. Expositio,* ed. M. Maggiolo, O.P. Rome-Turin: Marietti Editori, 1954.

XI. *In XII Libros Metaphysicorum Ar. Commentaria,* ed. R. Spiazzi. Rome-Turin: Marietti Editori, 1950.

XII. *In X Libros Ethicorum Ar. ad Nicomachum Expositio,* ed. R. Spiazzi, O.P. Rome-Turin: Marietti Editori, 1949.

D. ENGLISH TRANSLATIONS:

I. *On Being and Essence,* by Armand Maurer, C.S.B. Toronto: Pontifical Institute of Mediaeval Studies, 1949.

II. *The Compendium of Theology,* by Cyril Vollert, S.J. St. Louis: B. Herder Book Co., 1947.

III. *Basic Writings of Saint Thomas Aquinas,* by Anton C. Pegis. 2 vols. New York: Random House, 1944.

IV. *Introduction to Saint Thomas Aquinas,* by Anton C. Pegis. New York: Random House, 1948.

V. *On the Truth of the Catholic Faith (Summa Contra Gentiles),* by Anton C. Pegis (I), James Anderson (II), Vernon J. Bourke (III), Charles J. O'Neil (IV). 5 vols. Garden City: Hanover House, 1954–1956.

2. Aristotle, *Opera,* ed. J. Becker. 5 vols. Berlin: G. Reimer, 1831. *The Works of Aristotle,* translated in English, ed. W. D. Ross. 11 vols. Oxford: Clarendon Press, 1928–1931. *The Basic Works of Aristotle,* ed. Richard McKeon. New York: Random House, 1941.

3. Ambrose, Saint, *Opera Omnia.* PL, vols. 14–17.

4. Augustine, Saint, *Opera Omnia.* PL, vols. 32–47.

5. Averroes, *Aristotelis Stagiritae Libri Omnes . . . cum Averrois Cordubensis Variis in Eosdem Commentariis.* Venetiis apud Juntas, 1574, 10 vols. The *Commentary* on the *Metaphysics* is in vol. VIII.

6. Avicenna, *Opera in lucem redacta ac . . . emendata.* Venetiis, 1508.

7. Bañes, Dominic, O.P., *Scholastica Commentaria in Primam Partem Summae Theologiae S. Thomae Aquinatis,* ed. Luis Urbano. Madrid, 1934.

8. Boethius, *Opera Omnia,* PL, vols. 63–64.

9. Descartes, René, *Oeuvres,* ed. C. Adam et P. Tannery. 13 vols. Paris, 1891–1912.
Oeuvres et lettres, ed. André Bridoux (Bibliothèque de la Pléiade). Paris: Librairie Gallimard, 1952.

The Philosophical Works of Descartes, translated by E. S. Haldane and G. R. T. Ross. 2 vols. Cambridge, 1911–1912, with paperback reprintings.

10. De Vio, Thomas, Cardinal Cajetan, *Commentaria in De Anima Aristotelis,* ed. J. Coquelle. Vol. I. Rome: Institutum Angelicum, 1938. There is a substantial Introduction on Cajetan's commentary on the *De Anima* by M.-H. Laurent, O.P., pp.VI–LII.

11. Dionysius the Pseudo-Areopagite, *Opera Omnia,* PG, vols. 3–4.

12. Hilary of Poitiers, Saint, *De Trinitate,* PL, vol.10, coll.25–472.

13. John Damascene, Saint, *Expositio Accurata Fidei Orthodoxae.* PG, vol. 94, coll. 789–1228.

14. *Liber de Causis,* ed. R. Steele. Oxford: Clarendon Press, 1935.

15. Locke, John, *Essay on Human Understanding,* ed. A. C. Frazer. 2 vols. Oxford: Clarendon Press, 1894.

16. Maimonides, Moses, *Guide for the Perplexed,* translated by M. Friedländer. 2nd ed. London: G. Routledge, 1936.

17. Nemesius (Pseudo-Gregory of Nyssa), *De Natura Hominis.* Greek text and Latin translation, PG, 40, coll. 503–818. The Latin translation by Burgundio of Pisa has been edited by C. Burkhard (Vienna: Karl Ludwig Gymnasium, 1891–1902).

18. Pomponatius, Petrus, *Tractatus de Immortalitate Animae,* ed. Gianfranco Mora. Bologna: Nanni & Fiammenghi-Editori, 1954.

19. Siger of Brabant. See A. Zimmermann under Part B of this Bibliography.

B. MODERN STUDIES

1. Arnou, René, S.J., *De Quinque Viis Sancti Thomae ad Demonstrandum Dei Existentiam apud Antiquos Graecos et Arabes et Judaeos Praeformatis vel Adumbratis.* Rome: Pontificia Universitas Gregoriana, 1932.

2. Baisnée, Jules A., S.S., "St. Thomas Aquinas' Proofs of the Existence of God Presented in their Chronological Order" in *Philosophical Studies in Honor of . . . Ignatius Smith, O.P.* Westminster, Md.: Newman Press, 1952.

3. Bonnefoy, J., Fr., O.F.M., "La nature de la théologie selon saint Thomas d'Aquin" in *Ephemerides Theologicae Lovanienses,* 14 (1937) 421–446; 600–631; 15 (1938) 491–516.

4. Chenu, M.-D., O.P., "La théologie comme science au XIIIᵉ siècle" in *Études de philosophie médiévale,* XLV; *Bibliothèque thomiste,* XXXIII. Paris: Librairie Philosophique J. Vrin, 1957.
"Les 'philosophes' dans la philosophie chrétienne médiévale" in *Revue des sciences philosophiques et théologiques* 26 (1937) 27–40.

5. Eco, Umberto, *Il problema estetico in San Tommaso.* Turin: Edizioni di "Filosofia," 1956.

6. Einstein, Albert, "Physik and Realität" in *Zeitschrift für freie deutsche Forschung.* Paris, 1938.

7. Fabro, Cornelio, "Tommaso d'Aquino, santo" in *Enciclopedia Cattolica,* Florence: Tipografia "L'Impronta." XII, 1954, 252–297.

8. Gagnebet, R., O.P., "La nature de la théologie spéculative" in *Revue thomiste*, 44 (1938) 1–39, 213–255, 645–674.

9. Gardet, Louis, *La pensée religieuse d'Avicenne* (Ibn Sina). Paris: Librairie Philosophique J. Vrin, 1951.

10. Geiger, Louis B., O.P., "Saint Thomas et la métaphysique d'Aristote" in *Aristote et saint Thomas d'Aquin*, Journées d'études internationales. Publications universitaires de Louvain.

11. Gény, Paul, S.J., "Les preuves thomistes de l'existence de Dieu" in *Revue de Philosophie* 24 (1931) 578–586.

12. Gilson, Etienne, *Being and Some Philosophers*. Toronto: Pontifical Institute of Mediaeval Studies, 1949.

13. —*The Christian Philosophy of Saint Thomas Aquinas*, with A Catalogue of St. Thomas' Works by I. T. Eschmann, O.P., translated by L. K. Shook, C.S.B. New York: Random House, 1956.

14. —*God and Philosophy*. New Haven: Yale University Press, 1941.

15. —*History of Christian Philosophy in the Middle Ages*. New York: Random House, 1955.

16. —*Introduction à l'étude de saint Augustin*. Paris: Librairie Philosophique J. Vrin, 1929, etc.

17. —*Jean Duns Scot. Introduction à ses positions fondamentales*. Paris: Librairie Philosophique J. Vrin, 1952.

18. —"Note sur le *Revelabile* selon Cajetan" in *Mediaeval Studies* 15 (1953) 199–206.

19. —"Les Philosophantes" in *Archives d'histoire doctrinale et littéraire du moyen âge* 19 (1952) 135–140.

20. —*The Unity of Philosophical Experience*. New York: Charles Scribner's Sons, 1937.

21. Hayen, André, S.J., "La théologie aux XIIe, XIIIe et XXe siècles" in *Nouvelle revue théologique* (Museum Lessianum—Section théologique) 80 (1957) 1009–1028; 81 (1958) 113–132.

22. Jaspers, Karl, *Vernunft und Existenz. Fünf Vorlesungen*. Bremen: Jos. Storm Verlag, 1949.

23. Jolif, J. Y., O.P., "Affirmation rationelle de l'immortalité de l'âme chez saint Thomas" in *Lumière et vie*, 4 (1955) 59–78.

24. Laurent, M.-H., O.P., see Cajetan.

25. Michotte, A., *La perception de la causalité*. Louvain: Publications Universitaires de Louvain, 2nd ed., 1954.

26. Motte, A. R., O.P., "A propos des cinq voies" in *Revue des sciences philosophiques et théologiques* 27 (1938) 577–582.

27. Muller-Thym, Bernard J., "The Common Sense, Perfection of the Order of Pure Sensibility" in *The Thomist* 2 (1940) 315–343.

28. Oeing-Hanhoff, Ludger, *Ens et Unum convertuntur. Stellung und Gehalt des Grundsatzes in der Philosophie des hl. Thomas von Aquin*. Beiträge zur Geschichte der Philosophie und Theologie des Mittelalters, Münster Westfalen, 1953.

29. Pegis, Anton C., *Saint Thomas and the Problem of the Soul in the Thirteenth Century*. Toronto: Institute of Mediaeval Studies, 1934.
30. Schrödinger, Erwin, *What is Life? & Other Scientific Essays*. New York: Doubleday Anchor Books, 1956.
31. Simon, Yves, *Ontologie du connaître*. Paris: Desclée de Brouwer, 1934.
32. Synave, P., O.P., "La révélation des vérités naturelles d'après saint Thomas d'Aquin" in *Mélanges Mandonnet*, vol. I, pp. 327–370. Paris: Librairie Philosophique J. Vrin, 1930.
33. Van Ackeren, G. F., S.J., *Sacra Doctrina. The Subject of the First Question of the Summa Theologiae of Saint Thomas Aquinas*. Rome: Catholic Book Agency, 1952.
34. Wyser, Paul, O.P., "Thomas von Aquin" in collection: *Bibliographische Einführungen in das Studium der Philosophie*, 13/14. Bern: A. Francke A. G. Verlag, 1950.
35. Zimmermann, Albert, *Die Quaestionen des Siger von Brabant zur Physik des Aristoteles*. Inaug. Diss., University of Cologne, 1956.

C. ABBREVIATIONS

1. PL   J. P. Migne, *Patrologiae Cursus Completus, Series Latina*, 221 volumes, Paris, 1844–1864, with later reprintings.
2. PG   J. P. Migne, *Patrologiae Cursus Completus, Series Graeca*, 162 volumes, Paris, 1857–1866, with later reprintings.
3. ST   *Summa Theologiae*
4. SCG *Summa Contra Gentiles*
5. EBT *Expositio Super Boethii de Trinitate*

INDEX OF PROPER NAMES

SUBJECT INDEX

Abstraction
——abstractions as mutually exclusive, 230
——and its order, 226-7
——as an immaterial operation, 207
——as consisting in the intellectual assimilation of the form, 207, 226
——as the mode in which we conceive things, 229

Act of being
——act of *esse*, 123; other than the essence or quiddity, 127; except in God who is His own act of being, 135
——and potency, 206
——as a distinct object of understanding, 131; an object of the intellect, not of sense perception, 57
——as more intimate to a substance than the essence by which its *esse* is determined, 182
——as the actuality of every thing, 154
——as the proper effect of God and innermost in every being, 177, 178, 179-80
——finite acts of being and creation, 188, 190
——God as supremely act because He is Being, 172; and the supreme perfection, 123
——that, absolutely speaking, being is act, 115
——that only what is in act can bring something from potency to act, 60, 62
——that whatever is is act inasmuch as it is, 115

Analogy
——as a sharing in being, 12
——as a non-generic resemblance, 124
——the basis of man's knowledge of God, 139
——the meaning of analogical knowledge, 140

Angels
——as called spiritual substances, 204
——as composed of potency and act, 205, 210; of essence and *esse*, 206; not of matter and form, 210
——as different from man, 224
——as immaterial and incorruptible, 211
——as not needing abstraction and sensation, 226
——as not needing to reason from principles to conclusions, 226-7
——as separate substances, 205, 208
——as simple forms or natures, 206

Anthropology, 203, 209

Appetite, 255, 256, 259

Articles of faith
——as constituting, with their consequences, single complex objects of belief, 52
——as headings containing the unseen about God, 52
——as likened to first principles in philosophy, 26, 52
——as principles of sacred doctrine, 38-9

Beatitude
——and grace, 255
——and the will, 254
——as the end of the intellectual creature, 252, 253, 254, 255, 258

Beauty
——an object of knowledge, 161
——as a certain but distinct good, 160
——God as Beauty, 163
——has the character of a formal not a final cause, 160
——its constituents, 162
——related to form as known, 160
——related to knowledge as the good is related to the desire of the will, 162

Being
——act and potency add nothing to being, 62